Search Find and Kill

SEARCH FIND AND KILL

Coastal Command's U-boat Successes

Norman L.R. Franks

Aston Publications

Published in 1990 by Aston Publications Limited
Bourne End House, Harvest Hill
Bourne End, Bucks, SL8 5JJ

ISBN 0 946627 55 X

Designed by Chris Hand

Sole distributors to the UK
book trade,
Springfield Books Limited
Norman Road
Denby Dale
Huddersfield, West Yorkshire, HD8 8TH

Sole distributors for the USA,
Motorbooks International
Osceola, Wisconsin 54020
United States

Printed in England by the Amadeus Press Ltd., Huddersfield

Acknowledgements

In compiling this reference book of U-boats sunk by Coastal Command, I was privileged to gain the help of a number of former members of that Command who were closely involved in the anti-submarine war. From them I was able to glean first-hand accounts of attacks they were involved with, which has added colour to many of the stories contained herein.

I am sincerely grateful to them:

Squadron Leader J.B. Stark, DFC
58 Squadron – Halifax
Flight Lieutenant E.L. Hartley, DFC
58 Squadron – Halifax
Flight Lieutenant A.R. Burns   58 Squadron – Halifax
Group Captain P.R. Casement, DSO, DFC★
61 Squadron – Lancaster
Flying Officer S. Norris   86 Squadron – Liberator
Flight Lieutenant R. Fallon   120 Squadron – Liberator
and 547 Squadron – Liberator
Squadron Leader G.L. Hatherly
120 Squadron – Liberator
Flight Lieutenant J. Luker   120 Squadron – Liberator
Wing Commander B.E. Peck, DFC
120 Squadron – Liberator
Flying Officer N.R. Tingey, RNZAF
120 Squadron – Liberator
Flying Officer B.W. Turnbull, DFC, JP, RNZAF
120 Squadron – Liberator
Flight Sergeant D.A. Radburn
172 Squadron – Wellington
The late Group Captain P.H. Stembridge, DFC, AFC
172 Squadron – Wellington
Air Vice Marshal R.G. Knott, DSO, DFC
179 Squadron – Wellington
Flight Lieutenant L.H. Baveystock, DSO,DFC★, DFM
201 Squadron – Sunderland
Flight Lieutenant B.W. Landers
201 Squadron – Sunderland
Captain I.F.B. Walters, DFC★
201 Squadron – Sunderland
Squadron Leader H.R. Sheardown, RCAF
202 Squadron – Catalina
Flight Lieutenant A.D. Beaty, DFC★
206 Squadron – Fortress
Flying Officer J.J.V. Glazebrook, DFC
206 Squadron – Fortress
Flying Officer F.J. Appleton   210 Squadron – Catalina
Flight Lieutenant W.R. Travell, DFC
220 Squadron – Fortress
Flight Lieutenant E. Cheek, AFC, DFM
224 Squadron – Liberator
Wing Commander P.J. Cundy, DSO, DFC,AFC, TD
224 Squadron – Liberator

Air Vice Marshal J.C.T. Downey, CB, DFC,AFC
224 Squadron – Liberator
Wing Commander M.A. Ensor, DSO★, DFC★,AFC
224 Squadron – Liberator
and 500 Squadron – Hudson
Flight Lieutenant H.W. Thomson, RNZAF
233 Squadron – Hudson
Group Captain S.G. Nunn, OBE, DFC, AE
248 Squadron – Beaufighter
Squadron Leader A.A. Bishop, DFC, RCAF
423 Squadron – Sunderland
J. Barrow   461 Squadron – Sunderland
Flight Lieutenant D. Musson
461 Squadron – Sunderland
Flight Lieutenant J.A. Paine, DFM
500 Squadron – Hudson
Flight Lieutenant A.A. Bruneaux, DFC, RCAF
547 Squadron – Liberator
C.V. Brignall   612 Squadron – Wellington
J.M. Dally   612 Squadron – Wellington
Flight Lieutenant N. Earnshaw
612 Squadron – Wellington
and 248 Squadron – Mosquito
Flight Lieutenant I.D. Gunn
612 Squadron – Wellington
Flight Lieutenant T.F.P. Frizell, DFC
4 OTU – Sunderland
Captain H.J. Baker, USN   VP63 Squadron – Catalina
Lt Commander M.B. Cummins, USN
VP63 Squadron – Catalina
Commander V.A.T. Lingle, USN
VP63 Squadron – Catalina
Commander R.C. Spears, USN
VP63 Squadron – Catalina
Commander T.R. Woolley, USN
VP63 Squadron – Catalina
Flying Officer C.V.T. Campbell
RAF Armament Specialist
Wing Commander J. Staff-Brett   Station Signals Officer

I should also like to express my sincere thanks to the following, all of whom have given freely their help and assistance: Admiral Curtis Hutchings, USN, former CO of VP63, R.W. 'Bob' Coppeck of the Naval Historical Branch, MoD – a mine of rational information. Air Historical Branch, MoD. Bernard F. Cavalcante, Head of Operational Archives, Dept of the [US] Navy. Eddie Cheek, AFC, DFM, who has been engaged in his own U-boat research. John Evans, fellow writer and historian. Mrs Jean Parker. As always to my great friend, author and confidant, Chaz Bowyer, who is always willing to help.

And of course, to Heather.

Contents

Glossary

A/S (bombs)	– Anti Submarine/Anti Submarine bombs
ASV	– Air to Surface Vessel (radar)
Cobra, etc.	– Code words (snake names) for convoy patrol patterns
D/C	– Depth Charge
E/V	– Escort Vessels, Naval ships
HI	– High Intensity (flares)
M/V	– Merchant Vessels (ships)
MAD	– Magnetic Anomaly Detector
Musketry	– Biscay patrol area (also Percussion, Derange, etc.)
PLE	– Prudent Limit of Endurance
S/E	– Special Equipment (code for airborne radar)
SNO	– Senior Naval Officer (convoy commander)
U/T	– Under Training (aircrew)
VGO	– Vickers Gas Operated (drum-fed machine gun)
VLR	– Very Long Range (aircraft. eg, Liberator, Halifax)

Convoy Code Letters

OB	– Liverpool to Halifax, Nova Scotia
ON	– Great Britain to Halifax
HX	– Halifax to Great Britain
SC	– Great Britain to USA
OG	– Great Britain to Gibraltar
HG	– Gibraltar to Great Britain
KM	– Great Britain to Gibraltar Introduced after 26 October, 1942.
MK	– Gibraltar to Great Britain Introduced after 26 October, 1942.
OS	– Great Britain to West Africa
SL	– West Africa to Great Britain (slow)
SLS	– West Africa to Great Britain (fast)
JW	– Great Britain to Russia
PQ	– Great Britain to Russia
QP	– Russia to Great Britain

Navigational Position

To ascertain a position of a ship or U-Boat at sea, the navigational map reference is usually shown as follows. For a position in the Bay of Biscay, for instance, it would be written 46 degrees, 33 minutes N (north), by 11 degrees, 12 minutes W (west). For ease of reference in this book, the same position would be shown as 4633/1112.

INTRODUCTION

Who sank the U-boats credited to Royal Air Force Coastal Command crews? Even today it is not clear in some cases. Soon after the end of World War II, and after captured German U-boat records could be examined by the Allies, it was possible to attempt to match up Allied claims of U-boats sunk with the actual losses sustained. In many cases, who sank who was clear cut, but not in every case.

During the war it was very difficult to assess accurately when a U-boat had been 'killed'. If survivors were picked up, seen in the water, or if a U-boat had actually been seen to break up by the attacking aircraft crew, there was no doubt at all. But where an aircraft had attacked a U-boat and it just disappeared from sight, there could be no sure way of knowing if that submarine had been destroyed, merely damaged, or been totally untouched. The best that could be done in these circumstances was to make an intelligent assessment on the evidence of the attacking crew, photographs of the attack (if taken) and perhaps later evidence from Royal Naval vessels or even from German radio intercepts. On some occasions, returning damaged U-boats were reported through the French resistance workers. Yet many British and American crews were able to claim, in good faith, an excellent attack, with either depth charges or bombs, see what was thought to be oil and debris, and be certain that their attack had sunk their victim. On the other hand, other Air Force crews made attacks which they felt did not inflict any damage, but in truth sent the U-boat to a watery grave, leaving no visible sign of its loss.

When the flying and submarine records were compared, a reasonable list of who sank who was made and published. Over the intervening years, some of these assessments have been changed. It is a very complex business. In those early days, if a U-boat last radioed its base on, say 9 May, and an aircraft claimed a U-boat sunk on 9 May in roughly the same position as the U-boat had been, then it was assessed that that aircraft made the kill. However, it might not have been lost until 11 May,

merely not radioing in on the 10th, and lost before its next planned transmission. And it could have been lost to many causes; it could have hit a mine, hit the ocean floor, collided with hidden debris, or through a major technical problem. Thus, in some assessments, two and two made three!

Even when the 'who sank who' list, was made, the published version only stated that U-XYZ was sunk by aircraft A/999 Squadron. But who was flying aircraft letter 'A' of No. 999 Squadron? And not just the pilot, but who was in his crew? It was a team effort, after all. It was the desire to know and record in more detail the 'who sank who' which began this study and research to list as much as possible about the flying men of RAF Coastal Command who had achieved the U-boat kills. While so doing, later research was noted, mainly by the Naval Historical Branch, and in some cases reassessments have been made. There are still some cases under review, and while the lists in this book are pretty accurate, especially where there is absolutely no doubt about who sank who, it is not claimed to be 100% – and probably never will be. Even the reassessments are based on the best possible evidence, but where doubt exists, doubts will remain in some cases. And an airman who made an attack, saw oil and debris, perhaps even a body or two, will never be convinced that he and his crew did not make a kill. And he may be right! Nevertheless, it might well be explained that the boat was only damaged, had some planking ripped from its deck and the U-boat captain was forced to leave a man or two in the conning tower in order to save his command. There are any number of stories of unfortunate sailors being left 'top-side', being not quick enough to get down a hatch, or lingering too long at a gun, gallantly defending his vessel.

However, the lists in this book represent the best of the evidence, in a form for easy reference, for any would-be aviation, naval/submarine historian, or anyone merely interested in the anti-U-boat war. It lists, wherever possible, the full crew of the aircraft and their crew position when known, the aircraft serial number (when known), as well as letter, the position of the attack and a brief narrative of what occurred. A list in this form has never been published before. As readers will see, there were a few men who had a number of successful attacks, and some crewmen were involved in two or even three successes, but with other pilots. There is also a brief mention of the U-boats, their types, captains, and some notes on their number of cruises and ships sunk.

One might question the term 'damaged' as far as a U-boat was concerned. There were undoubtedly any number of U-boats damaged by aircraft attack that are not listed here. Mostly, the damage sustained was not serious, and was overcome and repaired at sea. Where, however, it was serious enough to either force the U-boat to return to base, or, if it was on its way home anyway, compel it to undergo extensive repairs once it limped into harbour, then it has been listed. This is because it was understood during the war that any U-boat forced to abort its war patrol, and/or be kept in dock for a long period of repair, was the second best thing to a certain kill. At least that boat was out of action, unable to sink Allied ships, kill, drown or maim Allied seamen and stop the supply of vital war materials, etc. Some U-boats, while undamaged, had to return to port because of casualties to crew members. This too was a 'victory', for the boat was out of the war, for whatever reason or whatever period.

RAF Coastal Command was as ill-prepared for war as its sister commands, Bomber and Fighter, when war began. Its aircraft were few, and the Command was at least third on the list of any priorities. It didn't even have a suitable weapon to attack, let alone sink, a U-boat, and virtually no way of finding a U-boat, other than by luck of a sighting, provided, of course, that the U-boat was sailing on the surface. This might beg the question to the layman as to why an 'Unterseeboot' should be on the surface in any event. This is not a book of tactics, but to answer this question, the facts are that submarines at this stage of development had to surface from time to time to re-charge their batteries and refresh their air supply. It could also travel faster on the sea rather than it could beneath it. Later in the war the advent of the 'schnorkel' overcame the former problem, although it added another. The schnorkel tube caused a wave or 'feather' of water that could be seen in certain conditions, and often showed a hint of smoke discharge.

When the war began, the anti-U-boat weapon was the anti-submarine bomb but it soon became obvious that, to destroy a U-boat, something better

was needed. Direct hits with a bomb on a diving U-boat were more luck than judgement, and once the boat was under the waves, bombs became even less effective. The Royal Navy had the depth charge, which had changed little since World War I, but in the spring of 1940, trials were carried out to see if an aircraft could drop depth charges. These trials proved successful, provided the aircraft was not flying too fast or too high. Thus the standard Naval Mark VII depth charge became the 'new' weapon for Coastal Command aircraft. Later the Mk VIII depth charge was produced which replaced the Command's 100 lb and 250 lb anti-submarine bombs. If dropped close to the U-boat's hull, it should cause a sufficient concussion to fracture, damage or crush the hull of the boat. It was understood that the lethal range was 20 feet. Anti-submarine aircraft crews were trained to attack at low altitude, generally averaging 50 feet, and dropped a stick of depth charges (D/Cs) in such a way as to straddle the target. In this way at least one or two D/Cs would hopefully fall within lethal range. As U-boats could crash-dive and be under the water within 25 seconds, a sighting and then an attack needed to be accomplished quickly and efficiently, doing in perhaps seconds what they had been training for do for months. Many RAF crews spent whole tours without even seeing a single U-boat.

Torpex-filled depth charges (which looked very like an oil drum) became the standard weapon of Coastal Command's anti-submarine war, but there were other weapons that were developed as the war progressed. Those mentioned in the following attack narratives were, in the main, the Mk 24 mine, the rocket, the 600 A/S bomb, and Retro-bombs (used with Magnetic Anomaly Detection (MAD)). (Torpex was an improved explosive material containing TNT and powdered aluminium.)

The Mk 24 mine, code name 'Fido', was in fact a torpedo, reference to a 'mine' being made in order to keep the weapon a secret. It was developed in the USA from the autumn of 1941 and began to be used in 1943. It weighed 680 lb, was 19 in. in diameter, 84 in. in length, carried 9216 lb of Torpex and had a range of 4000 yards, running at 12 knots for 10 minutes. It was propelled by a battery-powered electric motor and had to be dropped from 250 feet when the aircraft was flying at 125 knots. It homed in on its undersea target by crystal hydrophones which were placed around the body, steering itself towards the cavitation from moving propeller blades. RAF crews carrying them had, at one time, to actually sign a note on the Bible that under no circumstances would they ever mention or discuss this weapon with anyone. RAF and American aircraft dropped 488 of them and scored a number of successes. Use was a little restricted as they couldn't be dropped near friendly ships, eg convoys. They were generally dropped against U-boats that had just dived or were schnorkelling.

The torpedo was a 3 in. rocket projectile (R/P) as used by Typhoon ground attack aircraft, and was fitted to and used by Beaufighter and Mosquito aircraft against shipping and U-boats from the mid-war years and also by some Coastal Command Liberators. The MAD was also developed by the US, whereby a submarine could be detected under water by its magnetic field, while its crew had no idea it had been detected. However, its detection came just as the aircraft was almost directly over the unseen sub, with no chance of dropping any weaponry on it. Thus the 'Retro-bomb' was developed, a 35 lb impact-fused bomb with a solid fuel rocket fitted to the tail. Once a submarine was detected below, the button was pressed and the rocket propelled the Retro-bombs backwards from launching rails under the aircraft's wings. When the rockets ceased burning, the bombs came to a stop and thus fell into the sea and on to the target. They exploded on contact – either with the undersea object, or the sea bed! They were fitted to American Catalina aircraft, 12 under each wing, and fired off in three salvos of eight within 1½ seconds. As the undersea target could be anything other than a sub, this in turn helped the sonobuoy to be developed.

Sonobuoys consisted of a small floating radio transmitter, from which a hydrophone was suspended on a line. This picked up any underwater sounds and passed them through the transmitter to the circling aircraft's special receiver. These could detect U-boats and depending upon which pattern of sonobuoy picked it up, its location could be discovered. It could also hear a U-boat breaking up following a successful attack. These were used later in the war by other aircraft in order to help U-boat detection.

Colin Campbell was an armament and torpedo officer with the RAF, and in 1940 was posted to Coastal Command, serving at Detling, then Castle Archdale and then in Iceland. Later he went to HQCC and was then put in charge of Specialist Armament Officers courses at the Empire Air Armament School, RAF Manby, in 1943. Although not aircrew, he was lucky enough to fly with Terry Bulloch when the latter was experimenting with rockets on Liberators, and to be aboard when Bulloch attacked and sunk U-514 on 8 July, 1943. Of Coastal Command armaments, Colin explains: 'When I arrived on Coastal Command the anti-submarine weapon was the 100 lb, 250 lb or 500 lb Mk IV A/S bomb. This had a short delay tail fusing system. When the first Catalinas arrived at Castle

Archdale we fitted 450 lb depth charges with the ordinary naval depth pistol, a large, unwieldy brass device which could be set safe, or to explode at a water pressure of 50, 100 or 150 feet. The charge was filled with Amotol and enclosed in a large nose or tail fairing. Soon the 250 lb aircraft D/C arrived to be used with the same type pistol. By the time I arrived in Iceland we were using a Minol and then a Torpex filling, with much, much more shattering force than the other two. But for its presence in the 250 lb D/C, we could never have begun at long last to sink U-boats.

'The pistol was rapidly improved to have a firing depth of 25 feet and was fitted with an arming wire so that it was safe until armed and released from the aircraft. We were well into 1942 by this time and another serious fault had to be remedied. It was realized from the standard pictures brought back from the power operated F24 camera mounted vertical against a mirror and triggered by the pilot that the simple 250 lb cylinder often bounced along the wave tops before sinking. Until concave-nosed D/Cs were available we were supplied with and fitted a concave spoiler to the nose of the charge and a special tail unit that would partly break off and act as a rudder, throwing the D/C quickly sideways. Command tactical instructions required the D/Cs to be dropped together in a stick with 100-foot spacing between each pair and the attack to be at an acute angle to the sub's course.

'The lethal range was thought to be about 25 feet. Ideally it was best to attack as the U-boat commenced its dive. Of course, by 1943 the U-boat command realized that the aircraft was a bigger menace than the warship and they began to augment the AA armament. [To defend against sudden air attack, or when the submarine captain decided to stay on the surface and fight it out. N.F.] Two twin 20mm and a power-operated 20mm Vierling gun on the bandstand was common by the end of that year. Meantime, at Command, the desperate need to provide VLR aircraft had meant that all surplus gear had to be removed, including mid-upper turrets, front turrets or guns, and only the rear turret was left in some Liberators, Halifaxes and Fortresses. When losses from U-boat fire began to rise my colleagues were scouring the country for additional .303 or .5 guns.

'When I arrived at HQCC, I found I was in charge of problems concerning the supply, fitting and use of the 3 in. R/P, developed from a rather daft AA rocket that equipped the "Z" batteries round our big cities during the latter days of the Blitz. The Beaufighter strike wings used this with a converted 6 in. naval shell as the warhead and the A/S units concerned used the 3 in. AP head. It was discovered in trials that if the rocket was released at an angle of about 30 degrees and 300–400 yards from the target, then the R/P would travel some 70 yards under water before curving upwards and emerging again, the impact having caused the red hot tube to bend. The R/P unit took four R/Ps mounted with saddles on rails and one unit each side, eight rockets in all. The angle of the rails could be varied to obtain a spaced salvo.

'This was sighted with the standard reflector sight in front of the pilot, who would try to aim at the waterline between bow and tower. A camera gun was synchronized to observe the fall of shot. It called for experienced flying, but was without doubt the best weapon up to this point against the surfaced or diving U-boat – as subsequent attacks proved.

'Already, the American Mk 24 acoustic torpedo was available in the greatest secrecy and was about to make an even bigger impact on the U-boat war. Also, to counter the U-boats that stayed up to fight and formed groups to do so, a 600 lb anti-submarine bomb had been developed. Together with these weapons, the older and short burning flame float had been replaced by the much longer burning marine marker and a later variant of this had a time delay device, allowing hours to pass before it ignited.

'The actual attack position could be marked with accuracy so that the aircraft could hang about and decide if the attack had been successful or so that back-up aircraft could locate the position during "swamp" procedures. Thus when the aircraft had a target, to activate the weapons and complete the electric circuit to the bomb firing switch, the bomb master switch was put to "ON", the bomb switches were put to "ON" for each position, the bomb fuse switches were put to "FUSED", the distributor was checked (Mickey Mouse) for ground speed and bomb spacing (it was normally preset – cocked) and the bomb bay doors were opened; this would be done by the pilot, second pilot or the engineer, and the first lot by the navigator if he was nearest the panel. The pilot would order these operations, and in the case of R/Ps, he selected and switched on the sight and the camera gun. And there was still found to be a snag – the bomb bay doors could creep back slightly against the hydraulic pressure and break the circuit. The Flight Engineer would have to dart down the catwalk and jam them open with a screwdriver. All this, perhaps in the face of a wall of 20mm flak, with tracer and self-detonating HE – and often in darkness!'

Having briefly mentioned the armament, the other problem was finding the target U-boat. At first it was really a case of flying a patrol and hoping to spot one sailing on the surface. When in known danger areas the U-boat would obviously sail under the surface, but in the early war years, all boats had to resurface to recharge their batteries and to air the vessel. Early radar was of little help to Coastal Command crews, but as ASV radar was developed so a target boat, or a conning tower or even just a periscope, could be picked up. Later still, centimetric radar improved things still further. These developments are really a story in themselves and books such as Alfred Price's *Aircraft versus Submarines* give a full account of the anti-submarine war from the radar point of view.

As for Coastal Command itself, it initially had just three Operational Groups, 15, 16 and 18, plus a training Group, 17. At the outbreak of WWII, 15 Group had its Headquarters at Plymouth, worked closely with Naval Command and was mainly responsible for convoy escort and anti-submarine patrols in the Western Approaches. After the fall of France, Royal Navy C in C Western Approaches moved to Liverpool and 15 Group was also transferred to continue its association. 15 Group made its HQ at Stranraer, and its main flying bases were Limavady, Aldergrove, Lough Erne, Eglington, Nutts Corner and Ballykelly – all in Northern Ireland – plus Benbecula and Tiree in the Western Isles of Scotland. The Group covered the Western and North Western Approaches from the Atlantic.

No. 16 Group was formed before the war with its HQ at Gillingham in Kent. Its main bases were Bircham Newton, Thorney Island and Detling. Although not directly an anti-submarine Group, its aircraft were involved with U-boats in the last days of the war.

When the war began, 18 Group HQ was divided into a temporary Operations Room at RN Air Station, Donibristle while the admin. section was at Pitreavie. Here it also had a permanent underground ops room built. Its main bases were at Leuchars, Dyce, Invergordon, Wick, Oban, Helensburgh, Abbotsinch and Montrose, but only Leuchars, Wick and Helensburgh remained as part of the Group throughout the war. As the war progressed, Greenock and Tain came under Group control and in late 1944, Milltown, Dallachy, Banff and Fraserburgh were added to counter anti-U-Boat sorties from Norway and Germany following the loss of Biscay ports. It also had bases in the Shetlands – at Sumburgh and Sullom Voe.

When 15 Group moved to the north-west, its old bases at Mount Batten, Pembroke Dock and St Eval were taken over by 19 Group, which was formed at that time. The new Group took over the old HQ building and controlled all Coastal Command stations situated in South Wales and south-west

England, operating mainly over the Biscay area and later the Channel area following the invasion of France. This Group scored the most U-boat successes, but it did cover the area of greatest U-boat activity, for German submarines had to exit and re-enter their French bases across the Bay of Biscay. Even boats sailing from German or captured Norwegian ports would end their first patrols in one of the French bases.

In addition to UK-based Groups, Coastal Command set up a Headquarters at Gibraltar a week after war began, covering the southern areas of the Bay of Biscay, the western coast of Spain, and of course, the important Straits of Gibraltar. This latter area was important to the Germans, as any U-boats ordered to operate in the Mediterranean had first to pass through the heavily guarded and patrolled Straits – and many failed to do so.

Coastal Command also spread its area of coverage to Iceland, in an attempt to give aircraft the range to reduce the important Atlantic Gap – the area out of range of land-based aircraft from the UK or Canada, and later the USA. It began to operate in late 1940 and by 1942 its aircraft were giving cover to Atlantic convoys and giving the U-boats a major problem in the convoy battles.

In late 1943, after British-Portuguese negoti-ations, Coastal Command put aircraft on the Azores (247 Group). Operations began in October with the arrival of two Fortress squadrons supported by two Leigh Light detachments from Gibraltar.

The Group's fortunes changed as the war changed. As it was not envisaged that France would fall, Coastal Command's plans covered a war in the North Sea or around the north of Scotland, then out into the northern Atlantic. As France did fall, the U-boat arm took over bases along the western coast of France in order to fight the Battle of the Atlantic. This was covered by the newly formed 19 Group. The U-boats' main problem was that they had to cross the vulnerable waters of the Bay of Biscay in order to reach these French ports. Thus they were constantly harried from both the UK and Gibraltar in and on the approaches to the Bay area. After the invasion of France, 19 Group's successes declined after the successes in the Channel, and 18 Group in the north-east began to encounter more and more U-boats, as they operated from Norway and Germany in the last year of the war.

A whole variety of aircraft were used by Coastal Command in its anti-submarine war, both land and sea planes. Early operations were flown by Ansons, Hudsons, Wellingtons and Whitleys, then Hampdens, Sunderland flying boats and Catalina flying boats. Other commands, especially Bomber Command, took heavy demands on new four-engined aircraft but gradually Coastal received Halifaxes, Liberators and Fortresses – all four-engined aircraft with good range and bomb loads. As the Command grew, Beaufighters and Mosquito squadrons were not only used for anti-shipping and fighter patrols, but as anti-submarine aircraft.

The records that now follow are the successful attacks on German and Italian submarines by aircraft under Coastal Command control during WW2. The list does not include U-boats sunk by other commands, the Fleet Air Arm or the American Navy and USAAF or Royal Canadian Air Force. Where RCAF, US Navy or US Army Air Force squadrons are covered, is when squadrons from these units came, from time to time, under the control of RAF Coastal Command HQ in England.

15 Group

30 January, 1940

U-55, a type VIIB submarine, commanded by Kapitänleutnant Werner Heidel, sunk.

Sunderland 'Y' N9025, 228 Squadron, on patrol 1205–1735 hrs.

FO E.J.Brooks	Pilot
PO T.A. Trotter	2nd pilot
Sgt Baxter	Nav
LAC Davies	Fitter II
LAC D. Evans	Fitter AE
LAC Jones	Rigger
AC1 Broomhead	WOP/EL/M
AC2 Davies	WOP
AC2 Price	Mech U/T

At 1130 hrs Flight Lieutenant Brooks was called to the Operations Room at Pembroke Dock and instructed to search for and attack a submarine reported in position 4820/0704. Setting course for the Scillies he arrived at the position briefed at 1320, where he was given the latest position of the boat – 4837/0746. Shortly after 1400 hrs Brooks sighted the escort vessel, the sloop HMS *Fowey* and the French destroyer 'X.32' in the vicinity of a torpedoed ship and picking up survivors. After making contact he then flew north to a second pair of destroyers. Half an hour later, up sun of the position but under a bank of cloud, the U-boat was seen on the surface with a number of men visible on her decks. Making a hurried attack with just one bomb from 700 feet, it fell about 20 feet from the boat. Brooks flew round as more men were seen to appear and then the U-boat opened fire, returned by Sergeant Baxter at the mid-ships gun. It seemed clear the boat was unable to submerge and Brooks called up the naval ships, who were only 5 miles away. He flew to the destroyers and flashed a signal 'U-boat – follow me', then returned to the sub. LAC Jones spotted the boat and then saw a bright crimson flash from the boat's stern. HMS *Fowey* then approached, the U-boat having disappeared, but the sloop found and then picked up 11 German survivors as other ships arrived.

U-55, on her first patrol, had sunk four ships before becoming the first U-boat sunk with the help of a Coastal Command aircraft in WWII. Earlier on this day she had torpedoed the British tanker *Vaclita* but the convoy escort ships had depth charged and damaged her. She had later to surface and, being unable to dive, was found by 228 Squadron's Sunderland and bombed and strafed, and when surface vessels began to close in, the boat was scuttled. The kill was officially credited to the destroyer *Whitshed*, the sloop *Fowey* and Y/228 Squadron, escorting convoy OA 80 G.

1 July, 1940

U-26, a type IA submarine, commanded by Kapitänleutnant Heinz Scheringer, sunk.

Sunderland 'H' P9603, 10 RAAF Squadron, on patrol 0200–1100 hrs.

F/L W.N. Gibson	Captain
PO H.G. Havyatt	1st pilot
Sgt H. O'Conner	Observer
Cpl J. Grubb	1 WOP
LAC K. Phillips	2 WOP
Cpl J. Burnham	1 Fitter
LAC W. Vout	2 Fitter
LAC A. deWynne	Rigger
LAC A. Couldrey	AG

On convoy patrol, at 0557 hours the SS *Zarian* was seen to be hit by a torpedo. She began to list to port and was down by the stern. Fifteen minutes later the Sunderland crew spotted the U-boat and dived immediately, releasing four bombs when the sub had gone down to periscope depth. It surfaced again almost at once and a further four bombs were dropped close to it. The crew were then seen to be jumping into the water and then the boat sank stern first. Forty-one survivors (the total complement) were later picked up by HMS *Rochester*, one of the convoy escorts.

U-26 had sunk eight ships during its six patrols since the beginning of the war. The first patrol began just before war was declared, on 29 August, 1939. On 1 July, 1940, after attacking the convoy, she had been depth charged by the corvette HMS *Gladiolus* and damaged. Forced to try to escape on the surface, she was found and attacked by Gibson. With *Rochester* fast approaching the German commander had ordered the boat scuttled.

Gibson received the DFC and was promoted to squadron leader. He rose to Air Commodore and later in the war saw service in the South Pacific with the RAAF, becoming a CBE.

16 August, 1940

U-51, a type VIIB submarine, commanded by Kapitänleutnant D. Knorr, damaged.

Sunderland 'H' P9624, 210 Squadron, on patrol 0624–1849 hrs.

FO E.R. Baker	Pilot
PO J.G. Bowie	2nd pilot
Sgt Keill	
LAC Bowen	Front gnr
and crew.	

Flying over a small five-ship convoy (OA 198), the aircraft was asked to carry out a search for a Norwegian ship about 20 miles astern, but found nothing. Later the SNO informed the aircraft that the *Empire Merchant* had been torpedoed in position 5521/1340 and told them to search for a U-boat. Some five hours later, Pilot Officer Bowie spotted the deck and conning tower of a U-boat and a D/C was dropped 20 feet ahead of the conning tower and the boat was blown to the surface. A second D/C seemed to blow the boat out of the water, and it heeled over before going down sideways. It was then bombed with four A/S bombs and a gush of oil came to the surface followed by air bubbles. The SNO was informed and a destroyer was sent to the position but found nothing.

However, U-51 had not sunk but had been damaged. She only survived another four days, being attacked and sunk on 20 August by the British submarine HMS *Cachalot*. In her four patrols she had sunk eight ships.

Flying Officer Ernest Reginald Baker later received the DFC.

10 February, 1941

U-93, a type VIIC submarine, commanded by Kapitänleutnant Klaus Korth, damaged.

Whitley 'T' P5050, 502 Squadron, on patrol 1110–2030 hrs.

FO J.A. Walker	Pilot
2/Lt P.G.F. Dumas	2nd pilot
PO B. Jones	Nav
Sgt G. Miller	WOP
Sgt P. Millington	AG

While escorting convoy WS 6, sighted a U-boat at 1647 hrs in position 5630/1438, on the surface.

Approached down-sun, but at 2 miles the boat began to submerge. Two D/Cs dropped and after seeing an upheaval in the water, the boat reappeared. White smoke came from the sub and it then fired on the aircraft, hitting its front turret. Obviously disabled, the boat headed away on a zigzag course, then 10 minutes later submerged stern first.

It was U-93's second war cruise, having left Lorient on 11 January. It had to put back on 13 February. It was sunk on its sixth patrol, which began on 23 December, 1941, from St Nazaire under the command of KvtLt Horst Elfe, who had been in U-99 under Otto Kretschmer. HMS *Hesperus* claimed the boat while escorting convoy SL 97G on 15 January, 1944, and picked up its commander and other survivors.

16 August, 1942

U-89, a type VIIC submarine, commanded by Kapitänleutnant Dietrich Lohmann, damaged.

Liberator 'F' AM917, 120 Squadron, on patrol 1110–0233 hrs.

SL T.M. Bulloch, DFC	Pilot
FO R. Goodfellow (NZ)	2nd pilot
Sgt B.W. Turnbull (NZ)	3rd pilot
FO M.B. Neville (NZ)	Nav
Sgt R.J. McColl	Eng
Sgt G. Clayton	WOP/AG
Sgt J.S. Scoular	WOP/AG
F/Sgt J.C.B. Harrison	WOP/AG
Sgt G.W. Turner	WOP/AG

On convoy escort, met the ships at 4650/2110 – 33 M/Vs, three sloops and two corvettes. An hour and a half after meeting the convoy, at 1935 hrs, sighted a U-boat and attacked with six D/Cs, which fell across its bows as the boat was submerging. Wreckage was later seen, but this was apparently only some planking blown off the deck.

U-89 was damaged and had to end its second cruise, which began on 2 June from Brest. It had sailed to the American seaboard and was making its way back when attacked. It survived until its fifth cruise, which began on 25 April, 1943, for she was sunk near convoy HX 237 by HM ships and a Fleet Air Arm Swordfish of 811 Squadron from the escort carrier *Biter*.

This was the first success for Terry Bulloch, who was to become the most successful U-boat hunter in the RAF. Bryan Turnbull was under training on Liberators, having flown a tour on Hudsons. He was to be involved in two damaging attacks with Bulloch, then, as an aircraft captain, was to sink one and damage two more U-boats.

18 August, 1942

U-653, a type VIIC submarine, commanded by Kapitänleutnant Gerhard Fieler, damaged.

Liberator 'F' AM917, 120 Squadron, on patrol 1202–2359 hrs.

SL T.M. Bulloch DFC	Pilot
FO R. Goodfellow (NZ)	2nd pilot
Sgt B.W. Turnbull (NZ)	3rd pilot
FO M.B. Neville (NZ)	Nav
Sgt R.J. McColl	Eng
F/Sgt S.C. Harrison	WOP/AG
Sgt G. Clayton	WOP/AG
Sgt G.W. Turner	WOP/AG
Sgt J.S. Scoular	WOP/AG

Airborne from Predannack as escort to convoy SL 118. At 1846 hrs sighted a U-boat and attacked with six D/Cs, while five men could be seen in the conning tower. D/Cs straddled and then aircraft attacked with cannon and machine-gun fire. Climbing, it then dropped two A/S bombs (which Bulloch had had put aboard largely as an experiment). Now without any way of finishing off the sub, he could only watch as it slowly submerged. Bad weather over southern England cut short the patrol and Bulloch had to return home.

U-653 was badly damaged and had to abort this her fourth patrol under her new commander. She arrived back at Brest on the 31 August and was in the repair yards for three months. Her first three cruises had been under the command of Ltn Kandler. U-653 went on to make nine patrols, but was lost on 15 March, 1944, sunk by HM ships and a Swordfish of 825 FAA Squadron.

15 September, 1942

U-261, a type VIIC submarine, commanded by Kapitänleutnant Hans Lange, sunk.

Whitley VII 'Q' BD426, 58 Squadron.

Sgt B.F. Snell	Pilot

(Records are missing for September 1942, but in August, Sergeant Snell's crews consisted of PO Ramsey, PO May, FS Murray, Sgt Bickley, Sgt K.E. Ladds, Sgt K. Brodie and Sgt Matthews, some of whom would have been with him on this date.)

Visibility was 20 miles despite occasional showers over a rough sea. At 1500 hrs, a surfaced U-boat was sighted 7 miles away in position 5949/0928. Approaching through cloud, Snell dropped three D/Cs from 20 feet, one hitting the bridge, and the rear gunner reported a straddle. When the explosions subsided, the bows of the U-boat were sticking out of the water and the Whitley came in again for another attack. The remaining D/Cs were dropped around the boat, which then slid under the water. Debris, wood and an oil drum were left on the surface, in the centre of a large oil patch.

U-261 had begun her first patrol from Kiel on 8 September and went down north-west of the Butt of Lewis.

Sergeant Basil Furness Snell had joined the squadron in September 1941, when it was part of Bomber Command. He received the DFM in December 1942 and was tour expired in January 1943. If Sgt K.E. Ladds was with him on this patrol, he was later to be involved in the sinking of U-221 on 11 September, 1943 – with very different results! (see 19 Group).

27 October, 1942

U-627, a type VIIC submarine, commanded by Kapitänleutnant Robert Kindelbacher, sunk.

Fortress 'F' FL457, 206 Squadron, on patrol 0630–1540 hrs.

PO R.L. Cowey	Sgt S.G. Clements
Sgt G.A. Earl	Sgt J.H. Morris
FO G.B. Windeler	Sgt L. Hollinshead
FO J. Duns	Sgt R. Fabian

Flying cover to convoy SC 105, sighted a surfaced U-boat at 1125 hrs and attacked with seven D/Cs which fell 25 feet ahead of the swirl as the boat crash dived. The straddle appeared to go across the estimated track of the sub. Afterwards a patch of light iridescent oil, 100 yards long, appeared, but little else.

Despite little evidence of a kill, U-627 had gone straight to the bottom. She was on her first war patrol, having left Kristiansund for the North Atlantic on 15 October. The attack took place south of Iceland, position 5914/2249.

Pilot Officer Cowey was to achieve another kill six months later, in April 1943.

15 January, 1943

U-337, a type VIIC submarine, commanded by Oberleutnant Kurt Ruhwiedel, sunk.

Fortress IIA 'G' FL452, 206 Squadron, on patrol 0733–2015 hrs.

PO L.G. Clark	Pilot
Sgt P.F. Dyer	2nd pilot
F/Sgt J.D. Ackerman	Nav
Sgt G.J. Jones	
Sgt W.E. Pollard	
F/Sgt A. Garnham	
Sgt F.W. Allison	

On a sweep for convoy ON 160, flying at 2000 feet over a calm sea, a surfaced submarine was sighted 5–6 miles on the port bow in position 5740/2710, at around 1440 hrs. Attacking from 80 feet, Clark dropped seven Mk VIII D/Cs while the target was still on the surface. Three D/Cs failed to fall, but the others straddled the boat. After the attack the boat was still visible for 3–4 minutes, during which time the rear gunner fired 300 rounds. The U-boat gradually slipped backwards with its bows at a steep angle, then went down leaving bubbles and foam for up to 6 minutes. Clark flew from the scene at 1455 hrs.

The attack was assessed as only inflicting minor damage, but U-337 had been destroyed. She had been on her first voyage, leaving Kristiansund on Christmas Eve for the North Atlantic.

Pilot Officer Les Clark was to achieve other successes in March and June 1943.

3 February, 1943

U-265, a type VIIC submarine, commanded by Oberleutnant Leonhard Aufhammer, sunk.

Fortress II 'N' FL456, 220 Squadron, on patrol 0548–1720 hrs.

PO K. Ramsden	Pilot
Sgt L. Richards	2nd pilot
PO H. Tasche	Nav
Sgt F.L. Fitzgibbons	
Sgt A. Crane	
F/Sgt T. Brodie	
Sgt W. Keen	

On a covering sweep to convoy HX 224, flying

through occasional showers, a U-boat was sighted on the surface at 4 miles, through a gap in the clouds, in position 5635/2249 at 1106 hrs. The Fortress was at 3000 feet, 29 miles from the convoy. Gaining a position with the sun behind him, Ramsden made an approach to drop seven Mk XI D/Cs from 50 feet while the boat was still visible. Aircraft turned to port, circling to fly back over the spot and something which looked like diesel oil could be seen, but this did not remain for very long. Nothing more was seen, nor when the aircraft flew back an hour later.

The attack was assessed as not very conclusive, which was true, but U-265, on her first cruise, was sunk. She had sailed from Kristiansund on 21 January.

7 February, 1943

U-624, a type VIIC submarine, commanded by Kapitänleutnant Ulrich Graf von Soden-Fraunhofen, sunk.

Fortress II 'J' FL459, 220 Squadron, on patrol 1230–2308 hrs.

PO G. Roberson	Pilot
PO P.H. Grove	2nd pilot
Sgt L. Deighton	3rd pilot
F/Sgt T. Britton	Nav
F/Sgt J.S. Sutton	
Sgt H. Pratt	
Sgt R. Thacker	
Sgt A. Torkington	
F/Sgt H. White	

Protection sweep to convoy SC 118, which was sighted at 1740 hrs through frequent showers, although visibility was 20 miles in clear weather. When 55 miles from the convoy, a U-boat was seen some 9 miles off, on the surface, in position 5542/2617. Roberson climbed into cloud and approached, finally breaking cloud three-quarters of a mile from the sub. An attack was made through a rain squall at 1807 hrs, with full surprise, to drop seven D/Cs from 50 feet while the conning tower was still half out of the water. The bomb aimer and the rear gunner saw the boat right beneath them and the D/Cs straddle, with Nos. 4 and 5 falling either side of the hull. After the plumes fell back, a long, rounded object, 12 feet long, rose out of the water about 5 feet. Black oil welled up, and later, lighter-coloured oil. Pieces of yellowish-coloured and other bits of wood could also be seen floating on the waves.

U-624, on her second cruise, having left St Nazaire on 7 January, went down SE of Greenland.

She had sunk six Allied ships. The assessment of the attack was generous in that it 'seems to indicate a kill.'

9 February, 1943

U-614, a type VIIC submarine, commanded by Kapitänleutnant Wolfgang Strater, damaged

Fortress 'L' FL195, 206 Squadron, on patrol 0655–1720 hrs.

SL R.C. Patrick, DFC	F/Sgt L.R. Swain
FL W. Michelson	Sgt W.T. Gilmore
FL T.F. Kennan	Sgt W.M. Easton
F/Sgt J.G. Edwards	Sgt E.J. Thomas

Flying in support of convoy SC 118, on a parallel track sweep. At 1030 hrs, destroyer '33' with corvette 'K.05' in tow was seen in position 5617/2039. The destroyer signalled, asking to be guarded all day while towing and the aircraft began a square search to a radius of 31 miles. At 1242 hrs a U-boat was sighted 5–6 miles ahead in position 5612/2059 and a stick of six D/Cs straddled it forward of the conning tower. The boat seemed to be lifted bodily out of the water, then slewed round to starboard and lost all forward speed. As the Fortress circled the boat sank straight down with an uprush of bubbles.

U-614 was badly damaged in this attack. She had been at sea for exactly one month, having sailed from Kristiansund. It put into St Nazaire on 26 February. She went down on her third patrol in July 1943, sunk by 172 Squadron (see 19 Group).

21 February, 1943

U-623, a type VIIC submarine, commanded by Oberleutnant Hermann Schroeder, sunk.

Liberator III 'T' FK223, 120 Squadron, on patrol 0929–0333 hrs.

SL D.J. Isted. DFC	Pilot
FO R.A. Crumpton	2nd pilot
WO W.E. Ferris	Nav
Sgt H. Richardson	Eng
F/Sgt R.T. Bedford	WOP/AG
Sgt A. Allwood	WOP/AG
F/Sgt R. Timoney	WOP/AG
FL M.P. Thompson	Passenger – Gunnery Officer

Flying from Aldergrove, to fly escort to ON 166, duly met the 46 M/Vs and six E/Vs and patrolled on SNO's orders. Over a calm sea, a U-boat was sighted at 9 miles in position 4808/2937, 15 miles from the convoy. Isted climbed into cloud, breaking out at 4–5 miles from the sub, only to sight a second U-boat 2–3 miles to port. Isted continued with his planned attack on the first boat, dived to 50 feet and released six D/Cs. As he did so, the second boat began to dive. The whole stick exploded opposite the conning tower, and six men could be seen in the tower but the sub had made no move to dive. As Isted circled the boat was seen to go down but slowly, and some 45 seconds later the gun platform was still visible. The boat seemed to have difficulty in diving and as Isted flew over, his rear gunner fired 150 rounds at it. Some seconds later the boat finally went below the waves and the SNO, having been informed, sent a destroyer and a corvette to investigate. They only found two large oil patches near the burning Marine Marker.

Assessed as possibly damaged, U-623 had been destroyed. She was on her second patrol, having sailed from St Nazaire on 2 February. Her loss was reported by U-91 – the other boat – whose commander had witnessed the attack.

Desmond Isted had damaged U-465 earlier this month flying from Iceland.

7 March, 1943

U-633, a type VIIC submarine, commanded by Oberleutnant Bernhard Muller, sunk.

Fortress II 'J' FL459, 220 Squadron, on patrol 0313–1636 (1831) hrs.

FO W. Knowles	Pilot
Sgt J. Burnett	2nd pilot
Sgt R. Gurnham	Nav
F/Sgt P. Sim	
F/Sgt J. Gallagher	
Sgt L. Morgan	
Sgt A. Crane	
Sgt J. Paterson	

Escort to convoy SC 121, flying at 2500 feet, sighted the track of a U-boat at 5 miles in position 5714/2630, at 0928 hrs. Bill Knowles turned to port and dived, dropping seven D/Cs from 80 feet, 12 seconds after the boat had submerged. They straddled and the stern of the sub was seen to rise from the water as they exploded. Diesel oil became plainly visible 45 seconds later and darker oil two minutes afterwards, but that was all.

U-623 was another boat that did not survive its first patrol. It had sailed from Kristiansund on 20 February and went down south-west of Iceland.

Bill Knowles landed at St Angelo, refuelled and then returned to Aldergrove. Less than two weeks later he was to score again. For Fortress FL459, U-633 had been her second sub kill in a month, having accounted for U-624 on 7 February, exactly one month before. She would make a total of four kills, with two more from the Azores.

19 March, 1943

U-666, a type VIIC submarine, commanded by Oberleutnant Ernst Wilberg, damaged.

Fortress II 'M' FK203, 220 Squadron, on patrol 0532–1638 hrs.

FO W. Knowles	Pilot
Sgt J. Burnett	2nd pilot
Sgt R. Gurnham	Nav
F/Sgt P. Sim	
F/Sgt J. Gallagher	
Sgt L. Morgan	
Sgt A. Crane	
Sgt J. Paterson	

Met convoy SC 122 at 0956 hrs, and was ordered to fly a 'Cobra 20' patrol, at 1005 hrs. Just 9 minutes later they sighted a U-boat from 5000 feet in position 5355/2351, which had earlier been spotted astern of the ships. As the boat made a sharp turn and dived, the Fortress attacked and dropped four D/Cs, which exploded ahead of the swirl. Diesel oil gushed to the surface and the U-boat surfaced 50 seconds later with decks awash and with no forward movement. The Fortress was too close to make an immediate attack so circled and then came in again, as the boat submerged, dropping three D/Cs along its track. Flowing oil increased and after 10 minutes a patch 200 yards in diameter had formed. At 1157 hrs, Bill Knowles was over the sinking M/V *Luckenbach* and guided escort vessels to rescue the crew, who were in four lifeboats and two rafts.

U-666, on its first patrol, was damaged. It had sailed from Kristiansund on 25 February, and limped into St Nazaire on 10 April. On the second patrol this boat shot down 'N' of 58 Squadron and on the fourth sortie was damaged again, this time by surface D/Cs. She was finally sunk on 10 February, 1944, by ships and a Swordfish aircraft of 842 FAA Squadron from the escort carrier *Fencer*.

With this crew's second success also came Sergeant Crane's third, for he had been part of the crew which sank U-265 on 3 February. William Knowles received the DFC.

19 March, 1943

U-384, a type VIIC submarine, commanded by Oberleutnant Hans-Achim von Rosenberg-Gruszazynski, sunk.

Fortress 'B' FK208, on patrol 0418–1614 hrs.

PO L.G. Clark	Pilot
Sgt P.F. Dyer	2nd pilot
F/Sgt J.D. Ackerman	Nav
F/Sgt F.W. Allison	
Sgt W.E. Pollard	
F/Sgt W.E. Garnham	
F/Sgt F.G. Jones	
Sgt D.A. Kempson	

Reached convoy HX 229 at 0905 hrs, comprising 24 M/Vs and four E/Vs, and began to fly a patrol around it, 30 miles out. Searching under a rain squall astern, they found a U-boat in position 5418/2615, at 0924. Clark attacked and made a good straddle with his D/Cs, and after the explosions a heavy black substance was seen floating on the water. A report was passed to the SNO and the oil patch was still visible some hours later.

U-384 had been on her second patrol, sailing from La Pallice on 6 March for the North Atlantic. After the war she was assessed to have been sunk by 201 Squadron on 20 March, but indications are that that attack was upon U-631, which was not sunk.

25 March, 1943

U-469, a type VIIC submarine, commanded by Oberleutnant Emil Claussen, sunk.

Fortress 'L' FK195, 206 Squadron, on patrol 0444–1630 hrs.

F/L W. Roxburgh	F/Sgt E.H. Nelson
Sgt L.R. Meech	F/Sgt D. Eley
F/Sgt J. Griffith	Sgt J.K. Churchill
Sgt R.E. Thomas	

Flying a creeping line ahead search for convoy RU

67, at 0959 hrs, a U-boat was observed 4–5 miles off the starboard bow. An attack sent six D/Cs down from 200 feet while aircraft was in a steepish dive. Three D/Cs fell on either side of the boat, which afterwards appeared to be listing slightly to port. The stern then came up in a rolling motion at a steep angle. It hung in this position as the Fortress came in again to drop the rest of the D/Cs from 50 feet. The boat seemed to be sinking as this attack was carried out and at 1040, oil had accumulated on the surface in a patch 1000 x 600 yards with debris scattered about.

U-469 was on her first patrol, having sailed from Kiel on 16 March. She went down south-east of Iceland in position 6212/1640.

William Roxburgh later received the DFC.

27 March, 1943

U-169, a type IXC/40 submarine, commanded by Oberleutnant Hermann Bauer, sunk.

Fortress 'L' FK195, 206 Squadron, on patrol 0450–1608 hrs.

FO A.C.I. Samuel	Pilot
PO L.G. Healey	2nd pilot
PO J.W. James	
PO C.J. Goodyear	
F/Sgt R.C. Hopkins	
F/Sgt A.S. Bunney	
F/Sgt E.G. Butler	
Sgt C. Cutler	

A creeping line ahead search was begun at 0746 hrs and at 1130 hrs a U-boat was seen in position 6054/1525. It was 3 miles on the starboard bow and clearly seen by the second pilot. Diving from 2000 feet, it met flak from the boat, gun flashes and tracer aimed in their direction. D/Cs were dropped which fell close amidships and the rear gunner saw the sub heel right over to starboard then submerge. As the aircraft circled the boat reappeared with bows at an acute angle. More D/Cs fell in a second attack and the rear gunner also opened up as they went over. Then men were seen scrambling about on the conning tower as the boat began to sink, going down almost vertically – or as the pilot later remarked – 'Like a dose of Eno's'.*

U-169 was on her first patrol, sailing from Kristiansund on 18 March.

(*) Liver salts.

6 April, 1943

U-632, a type VIIC submarine, commanded by Kapitänleutnant Hans Karpf, sunk.

Liberator III 'R' FL930, 86 Squadron, on patrol 1047–0230 hrs.

F/L C.W. Burcher	Pilot
Sgt J. Lloyd	2nd pilot
F/Sgt A.D. Paine	Nav
FO S.C. Cox DFM	Eng
Sgt J. Pheasey	1 WOP/AG
Sgt J.E. Parrott	2 WOP/AG
Sgt R. Crump	3 WOP/AG

Carrying out patrols ordered by the SNO to convoy HX 231, sighted a U-boat at one mile in position 5802/2842, 18 miles from the convoy. ASV was in use but did not pick up the boat. Burcher lost height and approached down the sub's track. No flak was experienced despite seeing men on the deck and conning tower most of whom scrambled down the hatch before the attack. This came from 50 feet, but only one of four D/Cs released, the one falling 60 feet to port. As the Lib passed over, the boat turned and began to dive. In a second attack, four D/Cs went down on to the diving sub, the stern still visible, again from 50 feet. A straddle was obtained about 180 feet ahead of the swirl. Aircraft circled and saw a patch of oil and a black object which may have been a man left on the deck. The attacks were made at 1917 hrs and the aircraft returned to report to the convoy at 1940 hrs, then resumed patrol. At 2146 they sighted another U-boat and attacked with the remaining D/Cs, but again only a patch of oil was seen.

Assessed as no damage due to insufficient evidence, U-632 nevertheless failed to return and was credited to Cyril Burcher and his crew. It was on its second patrol, having left Brest on 15 March. During its career it had sunk four ships.

24 April, 1943

U-710, a type VIIC submarine, commanded by Oberleutnant Dietrich von Carlowitz, sunk

Fortress 'D' FL451, 206 Squadron, on patrol 1410–2013 hrs.

FO R.L. Cowey	Sgt L. Hollinshead
Sgt A.P. Gamlin	Sgt J.H. Morris

F/Sgt N.H. Wright   Sgt R.Fabian
Sgt S.B. Crump   Sgt C.C. Rogers
PO D.E. Bryan

Flying from Benbecula, on a parallel track sweep for convoy ONS 5, a U-boat was seen at periscope depth at 1725 hrs in position 6130/2010, 8 miles ahead. Cowey attacked and a gun aft of the conning tower opened fire, six men being seen. Six D/Cs straddled at right angles, the explosions seeming to lift the boat out of the water. Aircraft circled and made a second attack and, afterwards, 25 survivors were seen swimming amongst debris and wreckage. At the end of the patrol the aircraft landed at Reykjavik.

U-710, on her first cruise, sailed from Kristiansund on 15 April for the Atlantic.

For Robert Leonard Cowey, this was his second sub kill and Hollinshead, Morris and Fabian had been involved in both. Cowey's DFC was Gazetted on 1 June, 1943.

4 May, 1943

U-109, a type IXB submarine, commanded by Oberleutnant Joachim Schramm, sunk.

Liberator 'P' FL955, 86 Squadron, on patrol 1247–0525 hrs.

PO J.C. Green	Pilot
Sgt J. McNab	2nd pilot
PO W.F. Emery	Nav
F/Sgt J. Pringle	Eng
Sgt J. Caffrey	WOP/AG
Sgt A. Adamson	WOP/AG
Sgt L.W. Taylor	WOP/AG
FO J.H. Lyall	Passenger

Flying towards convoy HX236, north-east of the Azores, sighted and attacked a U-boat in position 4710/2257 at 1835 hrs. Four D/Cs straddled the sub, two on each side just forward of the conning tower. As the plumes subsided, wreckage consisting of bright-coloured planks and two white cylinders amid a huge oil patch could be seen. The SNO was informed by R/T and aircraft returned to its patrol, informing a sloop of the location of the wreckage. The convoy was met at 2215 hrs, and the RAF crew received congratulations from the SNO.

U-109 was on her ninth war patrol, having left Lorient on the 28 April. A successful U-boat, she had sunk 13 ships, including five off West Africa in the summer of 1942 under Kapitänleutnant

Bleichrodt. Her first patrol in May 1941 did not start off her career well when her first CO was relieved of his command.

12 May, 1943

U-456, a type VIIC submarine, commanded by Kapitänleutnant Max Martin Teichert, damaged, then sunk.

Liberator 'B' FK229, 86 Squadron, on patrol 0344–2200 hrs.

F/L J. Wright	Pilot
Sgt W.C.H. Sheppard	2nd pilot
FO H.N. Webb	Nav
F/Sgt W.J. Knill	Eng
F/Sgt M. Cullen	WOP/AG
F/Sgt E. Whitworth	WOP/AG
Sgt J.T. Alexander	WOP/AG
Sgt A.R. Craine	WOP/AG

Airborne from Aldergrove in showery weather to escort convoy HX237, sighted and attacked a U-boat at 1313 hrs in position 4640/2620. A Mk 24 mine was used (acoustic homing torpedo) in the attack which caused damage to the boat, which surfaced. It was apparent that the sub was unable to dive. The SNO was informed and a destroyer was subsequently directed on to it.

Early the next day, U-456 was located by:

Sunderland 'G' W6006, 423 RCAF Squadron, on patrol 2343–1424 hrs.

F/L J. Musgrave	Sgt A.L.D. Welch
FO N.V. Martin	Sgt E.J. Carden
F/L R.W. Thompson	Sgt J. Vaughen
F/Sgt L.J. Sullivan	Sgt C.A. Maul
F/Sgt A. Hayden	

The convoy was met at 0800 hrs – 43 M/Vs and 8 E/Vs. Half an hour later a fully surfaced U-boat was seen in position 4845/2215, 10 miles from the convoy. Taking advantage of cloud cover the boat was taken by surprise but it opened fire when one mile away. As the boat was obviously going to fight it out on the surface, the SNO was advised and a corvette was contacted. The Sunderland continued to exchange gunfire with the sub and the aircraft was hit by a cannon shell. When the corvette arrived and began to shell the U-boat, it began to submerge and then a Swordfish aircraft too arrived. The Sunderland then made an attack, dropping two D/Cs from 50 feet, both seen to explode 30 seconds after the boat had gone down. The corvette then began to drop depth charges and the Swordfish dropped smoke floats. Fifteen minutes later the Sunderland returned to the convoy, as the corvette and a frigate continued the attack.

U-456, already damaged on the 12th, was finally sunk on the 13th, shared between the Sunderland, the frigate *Lagon* and the Canadian corvette *Drumheller*. She sank in position 4837/2239. She had earlier been part of the Arctic Flotilla, in 1942, her first patrol into the Atlantic coming in early 1943. Her second and last Atlantic patrol began from Brest on 24 April. She had sunk five ships.

Both John Wright and John Musgrave were to achieve other successes and both were decorated.

14 May, 1943

U-266, a type VIIC submarine, commanded by Kapitänleutnant Ralf von Jessen, sunk.

Liberator 'B' FK229, 86 Squadron, on patrol 0949–0217 hrs.

PO B.F. Gaston RAAF	Pilot
Sgt P.H. Thomas	2nd pilot
F/Sgt D.H. Hardie	Nav
F/Sgt G.B.H. Miller	Eng
F/Sgt L.P.V.J. Ricks	WOP/AG
Sgt M. Manley	WOP/AG
Sgt J.F. McLeod	WOP/AG
Sgt R.M. Daniel	WOP/AG

As escort to convoy SC 129, at 1633 hrs, sighted and attacked a U-boat in position 4745/2657, dropping an acoustic homing torpedo. At 1711 hrs sighted another U-boat nearby but no attack was made as the boat crash-dived and the swirl was lost, while manoeuvring for position. Half an hour later the aircraft reached the convoy and informed the SNO of the attack.

Although not very conclusive as an attack, U-266 failed to return and was credited to Gaston and his crew. She was on her second patrol, having left St Nazaire on 14 April. She had sunk four ships.

Gaston received the DFC. Liberator FK229 had damaged U-456 two days earlier when flown by John Wright.

29 May, 1943

U-552, a type VIIC submarine, commanded by Kapitänleutnant Erich Topp, damaged.

Liberator 'S' FL984, 59 Squadron, on patrol 1232–0436 hrs.

FO H.A.L. Moran RAAF	Pilot
PO H.R. Aldcroft	2nd pilot
FO R.D. Stevenson	Nav
Sgt L. Hadfield	
Sgt J. Moorby	
Sgt K. Regan	
PO L. Stalker	

At 1730 hrs in position 4850/1405, sighted and attacked a U-boat with four D/Cs while the conning tower was still visible. The bows broke surface at an angle of 45 degrees and the U-boat slowly surfaced. A second attack from the beam sent four more D/Cs down. Men appeared on deck and opened fire, which was returned. After 50 minutes the U-boat, which had been steering an erratic course, submerged. With its D/Cs all used, the aircraft could do nothing except join the convoy and patrol, which it did for nearly 4 hours.

U-552 had had a lucky escape, on this her 12th patrol. She had sailed from Brest on 4 April and limped back to St Nazaire on 13 June. Her first patrol had been carried out in early 1941 and in all she survived 14 patrols and sank 31 Allied ships, including seven off the US coast on her eighth patrol in March and April 1942. After her last patrol she became a training boat in Bergen. Erich Topp received the Knight's Cross and Oak Leaves.

31 May, 1943

U-440, a type VIIC submarine, commanded by Oberleutnant Werner Schwaff, sunk.

Sunderland 'R' DD835, 201 Squadron, on patrol 1034–0731 hrs.

F/L D.M. Gall	Pilot
FO S.C. Roberts	2nd pilot
F/Sgt D.M. Briden	
Sgt T. Lansdale	
FO J.C. Hamer	
Sgt E. Thompson	
Sgt W.G. Turner	
Sgt T.G. Grosvenor	

F/Sgt D.M. Burden
Sgt W. McKonkey
SL N.L. Smith   Passenger
PO H. Martin   Passenger

Douglas Gall, who until this day had flown 732 hours in the squadron's Sunderlands and was beginning to think there were no U-boats to be sighted, remembers: 'It came as a tremendous surprise to us when the submarine was sighted visually in the distance and we headed straight towards it, making our best speed, which was something in the region of 150 knots – downhill! We were going downhill, as we wanted to get to our depth charge height of 50 feet as quickly as possible. I'm afraid I didn't even think about refinements such as coming out of the sun. I just wanted to get there before he dived, because that's what he was going to do – any second.

'We all expected him to dive and when he did not I asked my navigator to check whether we were near one of the "free lanes" for our own submarines. I was pretty sure we were not, but I had to be absolutely certain.

'As we approached, I still had this haunting fear that it might be one of ours, and when he began to flash at us, I had the navigator check the recognition letter of the Day. I don't recall what it was, but it was certainly not an "H" or "S", which was what he was flashing.

'It was my Scottish rear gunner who eventually put my mind at rest by calling on the intercom, "He's no' flashin' skipper; he's firin'!"

'We were fortunate that day to have the squadron gunnery officer as a "guest" crew member, PO Martin. Luckily, too, he was manning the front turret at the time, using the "pea-shooter", as we called the one forward firing Browning. And he used it to great effect, as witnessed by the dead bodies I saw in the conning tower as we passed over.

'We dropped our stick of four D/Cs from about 50 feet above the water. The dropping in these days was done visually by the pilot and I must admit that I missed by yards! But it was to be my lucky day, for the U-boat captain decided to turn at the last minute. I was amazed at the speed with which he turned through 90 degrees, but delighted to see that he made the turn the "wrong way" right into the middle of the stick.

'As we turned, we saw a shimmering explosion over the surface of the sea, the bows came out of the water to a vertical position and then slid slowly down. There was much jubilation and cheering on board "R" of 201, but even in the excitement then, I couldn't help feeling, as I have felt so often since, the poor devils!'

U-440 went down at 1715 hrs, in position 4538/1304. She was on her fifth war patrol, sailing from St Nazaire on 26 May. She had sunk two ships since her first cruise in September 1942.

Douglas Gall received the DFC. He had been with the squadron since October 1941. He was later to command 88 Squadron (Sunderlands) after the war with the rank of Wing Commander.

6 June, 1943.

U-450, a type VIIC submarine, commanded by Oberleutnant Kurt Boehme, damaged.

Fortress 'A' FL458, 220 Squadron, on patrol 0420–1615 hrs.

SL H. Warren	Pilot
FO E. Lidstrom	2nd pilot
F/Sgt C.F. Wyndels	Nav
F/Sgt G. Best	
F/Sgt A. Boyce	
F/Sgt J. Catherall	
FO A. Owens	
Sgt J. Bitcon	

Flying on a search for a missing Sunderland. At 1057 hrs, a fully surfaced U-boat was sighted in position 6212/1528. Attacked with three D/Cs and U-boat turned sharply just before the drop and the D/Cs fell off track, but No. 1 fell close to the starboard side. Five crewmen seen in the conning tower but no flak experienced. Another run was made to drop the last D/C, but this failed to release. The sub submerged slightly but then resurfaced with the men still in the tower, the bows seeming to be much higher than the stern. Then the boat slowly went down by the stern. Returning later to the scene, an oil patch could be seen. The Fortress was diverted to land at Reykjavik.

U-450 was on her first patrol, having left Kristiansund on 25 May. Badly damaged she made Brest on 22 June. She did not sail again until mid-October, when she went to the Med. She was eventually sunk on 10 March 1944, south-west of Anzio by HM destroyers.

11 June, 1943

U-417, a type VIIC submarine, commanded by Oberleutnant Wolfgang Schreiner, sunk.

Fortress 'R' FA704, 206 Squadron, on patrol 0710 hrs.

WC R.B. Thomson	Pilot
F/Sgt A.F. Chisnall	2nd pilot
FO J.F. Clarke	Nav
FO J.L. Humphries	1 WOP
Sgt R. Owens	
Sgt R.A. Senior	
Sgt F. Sweetlove	
F/L A.R.D. Barrett	Station Arm't Officer, RAF Benbecula

Aircraft reached patrol area at 0910 and at 1110 hrs, in position 6400/1045 Thomson sighted a U-boat from 1500 feet, 7 miles away. The boat began to make short, sharp turns to port and starboard and also opened fire. As the Fortress closed in it was hit through the nose, cockpit, mainplanes, bomb bays and rear turret. Despite the damage, Thomson carried out his attack and dropped four D/Cs from 50–60 feet which straddled. When next seen, the bows were up, then the sub slipped below the water stern first, leaving 20 to 30 men in the water, many covered with oil. As the aircraft turned back the No. 2 engine, which had been vibrating badly, stopped, and No. 1 engine too began to give trouble. Being unable to maintain height, Thomson was forced to ditch, the Fortress sinking in 90 seconds. The port dinghy inflated and all the crew got in, but the supplies were lost. They were in the dinghy for three days until rescued shortly after midday on the 14th by a 190 Squadron Catalina ('L' FP102, SL J.A. Holmes, DFC). An earlier attempt by a USN Catalina had ended in failure when the flying boat crashed. The RAF Catalina was well over weight and 140 gallons of petrol had to be drained off before they could take off from the water.

U-417, had been on its first patrol, having sailed from Kristiansund just eight days before it was sunk, in position 6320/1030, north-west of the Faeroes.

Wing Commander Thomson, who had earlier been a flight commander on 179 Squadron, was to receive the DSO and DFC for his work with Coastal Command. He later became an Air Vice Marshal CB. Flight Lieutenant A.R.D. Barrett had seen action in France in 1940 with a Battle squadron.

17 June, 1943

U-338, a type VIIC submarine, commanded by Kapitänleutnant Manfred Kinzel, damaged.

Fortress 'F' FL457, 206 Squadron, on patrol 1536–2336 hrs.

FO L.G. Clark DFC	Pilot
PO G. Niven	2nd pilot
PO J.D. Ackerman	Nav
WO A. Garnham	
F/Sgt G.J. Jones	
Sgt W.E. Pollard	
F/Sgt F.W. Allison	
Sgt K. Jarvis	

Flying on a Musketry patrol from St Eval, the front lookout, Sergeant Pollard, sighted a fully surfaced U-boat, at about 7 miles. Due to a problem with the intercom he was unable to attract the attention of the pilot, but the navigator yelled back. U-boat at once began evasive action in order to direct aft gun at aircraft. It then opened fire, but only one small piece of shrapnel hit the starboard wing. After a dive, Clark reduced speed to 200 mph and at 1925 hrs, six D/Cs were released, 4 from the outside racks, operated by the navigator. After a climbing turn a second attack was made, but the U-boat had crash-dived and only the stern was visible. Five D/Cs went down and after the explosions at least two of the crew saw the boat partially surface, but nothing else was seen.

U-338 was damaged in this attack in position 4342/0937 and forced to return to St Nazaire. She had sailed from Bordeaux on her second cruise only two days earlier. On her first patrol in February/March 1943, she had shot down aircraft 'B' of 502 Squadron, which had attacked her. On her 3rd patrol, which did not begin until September, she was sunk on the 20th by a Liberator of 120 Squadron (see Iceland).

This was Clark's third successful attack, resulting in two sunk and one damaged U-boats, and Ackerman, Allison, Garnham, Jones and Pollard had been part of his crew on each occasion.

23 June, 1943

U-650, a type VIIC submarine, commanded by Oberleutnant Rudolf Zorn, damaged.

Liberator 'K' FK231, 86 Squadron, on patrol 0630–0001 hrs.

F/L J. Wright DFC	Pilot
Sgt W.C.H. Sheppard	2nd pilot
FO H.N. Webb	Nav
F/Sgt W.J. Knill	Eng
F/Sgt E. Whitworth	WOP/AG
Sgt J.T. Alexander	WOP/AG
Sgt A.R. Craine	WOP/AG

Airborne from Aldergrove. In good weather, flying cover to convoys WS 31 and KMF 17, they sighted three U-boats on the surface, at 1154 hrs, and although attacked, they dived. Meeting the convoy at 1323 hrs, they carried out a Cobra and an Adder patrol, remaining with the ships for 4 hours. At 1839 hrs, again three U-boats were seen, in a vic formation. The port U-boat dived while the other two opened fire. Aircraft circled for a position and other two boats began to go down. Wright made an attack on the leading sub, dropping a 600 lb bomb. A large explosion was seen but otherwise no results.

U-650 was sailing from Kristiansund to St Nazaire on her first patrol when damaged in this attack. She was out of action until December, when she twice tried to sail, but on each occasion had to return after two days at sea. Her second patrol was not begun until 1 January, 1944. After six patrols she failed to return from her seventh, in January 1945, due to unknown causes in the Channel.

27 June, 1943

U-518, a type IXC/40 submarine, commanded by Oberleutnant Hans Offermann, damaged.

Sunderland 'P' W6005, 201 Squadron, on patrol 0532–2138 hrs.

FO B.E.H. Layne RNZAF	Pilot
FO L.W.H. Stevens	Sgt J. Williams
Sgt M. Glicker	Sgt B. Campbell
F/Sgt J. Sweet	Sgt K.W. Smithies
F/Sgt C. Churm	Sgt J. Greenwood
Sgt D. Ball	Sgt J. Watkins

While on a Seaslug II patrol, sighted a U-boat at

5 miles at 1235 hrs and attacked with two D/Cs from 75 feet as it was going down. It was down 3 or 4 minutes, but then resurfaced and Layne attacked again, with the boat fully surfaced, guns manned and firing back. Fire was returned by front and rear gunners and the Lib wasn't hit. Layne made several attacks from astern, but each time the sub turned into the attack, bringing a concentration of fire on the aircraft. Brian Layne stayed in position until 1352 and began homing other aircraft, but then the boat went down and contact was lost.

U-518 was on her third patrol, sailing from Lorient on 24 June, having to return seriously damaged on 2 July. On its homeward journey it was attacked again by 10 RAAF Squadron on 30 June (F/L H.W. Skinner). Its first patrol had occurred in late 1942, landing an agent in the Gulf of St Lawrence on 9 November. Later she became part of Group 'Seawolf' and on her eighth patrol was sunk on 22 April, 1945, by two US destroyers, off the Azores. She had sunk 11 ships.

4 August, 1943

U-489, a type XIV tanker submarine, commanded by Oberleutnant Adalbert Schmandt, sunk.

Sunderland 'G' DD859, 423 RCAF Squadron, on patrol 0455 hrs.

FO A.A. Bishop	Pilot
FO D.M. Wettlaufer	2nd pilot
PO H. Parliament	Nav
FO A.E. Mountford	WOP/AG
F/Sgt J.A.V. Richardson RAF	WOP
F/Sgt J.B. Horsburgh RAF	WOP
F/Sgt J.S. Kelly	AG
Sgt P. McDonnell RAF	Eng
Sgt H. Gossop RAF	Eng
Sgt F. Hadcroft RAF	WOP
Sgt H.E. Finn	OP/AG

At 0910 hrs a U-boat was sighted on the surface from 4000 feet, 4–5 miles away, which immediately commenced weaving as aircraft dived to 600 feet. Al Bishop remembers: 'As we circled the submarine we soon saw that the only advantage we might have in an attack was to approach down-sun. We proceeded with such an attack as we descended to sea level. As we approached the sub, they started shooting with what appeared to be cannons with exploding shells, and machine-guns. I took evasive action by undulating the aircraft. As I levelled out at 50 feet for the final attack, the shells started to hit us. Two of my crew in the front of the Sunderland returned fire. I was successful in tracking over the sub and dropped a six D/C stick, which straddled it.

'After the attack the crew advised me that there was a fierce fire in the galley and bomb-bay areas with flames coming upstairs. I discovered that the starboard engines were running at full power and there was very little aileron control. This was apparently caused by a shell which had burst under my seat, severing the exactor controls. I had to throttle back and shut off the starboard engines and use the rudders to maintain what little control I had. I decided to attempt a landing and advised the crew. All this happened in a few seconds.

'In trying to land we bounced and I had trouble controlling the aircraft. As we hit the water again, the left wing dropped a little. The left float caught in the water and we cartwheeled into the sea. I recall putting my right arm in front of my face and the next thing I knew I was under water, rising to the surface.

'I came up slightly to the rear of the port wing. What was left of the aircraft was on fire and also fire on the water around it. I swam through an open space and as I swam I heard Sergeant Finn say, "Skipper, can you give me a hand?" I swam towards him to discover that he had no Mae West and was obviously badly hurt. He did not struggle, probably because of his injuries, and his extensive swimming experience. I grabbed hold of him with my right arm but could not see any of the others, but a short while later I saw the U-boat, stern down, not too far away. Its crew was getting on to their rafts, and as the boat sank there was a big explosion. The crew made no attempt to come over and help us.

'For the next 50 minutes I don't recall anything. Sergeant Finn was on my right arm, which had been bruised in the crash and was getting sore and stiff. I attempted to change to the left arm but every little move caused him to scream with pain. Next I recall looking around and seeing the RN destroyers. Apparently they were patrolling in the same area and an alert look-out had seen the Sunderland dive down, then saw black smoke from the crash. They launched life-boats and picked us up.

'Once aboard we were taken into the wardroom and with the warmth we started to shiver violently. Before I could bed down I was called on deck to identify Sergeant Hadcroft's body and to witness his burial at sea.'

They had been picked up by the destroyers HMS *Castleton* and *Orwell*, but only six of the Sunderland crew had survived. They were taken to Iceland, where Bishop and Mountford flew back to Ireland in a Liberator, on the 13th. Al Bishop was operating again by 2 October.

The original destination of U-489, according to the survivors, had been Japan, but after 10 days she was ordered to patrol off Madagascar. She had sailed from Kristiansund on 22 July. All the crew escaped, but the Engineering Officer died as a result of the explosion which occurred as he was leaving. Survivors included three Luftwaffe men, rescued by U-489 after their Blohm & Voss aircraft had been shot down by a Beaufighter of 404 RCAF Squadron, off Aarlsund, Norway. The sub crew consisted of six officers, eight chief/petty officers and 40 men – 54 in all. The sub went down in position 6111/1438 west of the Faeroes. She had been attacked and slightly damaged by aircraft 'J' of 269 Squadron on the previous day. The forward battery hatch had been ruptured and had leaked water. After a difficult passage through the Rosengarten the batteries were completely exhausted and she had to surface on the 4th. She was unable to dive until they had been recharged. It was then she was caught by 423 Squadron.

Bishop received an immediate DFC for his actions. Those of his crew who did not survive were, Parliament, Gossop, McDonnell, Hadcroft and Horsburgh. Bishop completed his tour of ops in March 1944, when he returned to Canada, ending the war as a squadron leader.

8 October, 1943

U-419, a type VIIC submarine, commanded by Oberleutnant Dietrich Giersberg, sunk.

Liberator 'R' FL930, 86 Squadron, on patrol 0150–1737 hrs.

F/L J. Wright DFC	Pilot
F/Sgt W.H. Sheppard	2nd pilot
FO H.N. Webb	Nav
F/Sgt W.J. Knill	Eng
WO E. Whitworth	WOP/AG
F/Sgt J.T. Alexander	WOP/AG
WO A.R. Craine	WOP/AG
F/Sgt J.J. Roy	WOP/AG
F/Sgt M.J. Cullen	WOP/AG

At 0807 hrs, while it was still dark, convoy SC 143 was reached and the Liberator was asked to carry out a Cobra 12 patrol. Not long afterwards a surfaced U-boat was seen in position 5631/2656, but it quickly began to dive. Of the four D/Cs dropped, two straddled the track and the subsequent explosions enveloped the diving swirl. Nothing was seen so the SNO instructed the Liberator to resume its patrol.

An hour later Wright returned to the scene of the attack, and at 0954 hrs sighted the same U-boat, but this time it did not submerge. The last two D/Cs were dropped, which fell alongside the boat's hull. There was a violent explosion with a white flash and a dirty cloud of smoke. As the scene cleared, 30 feet of the bows were seen sticking vertically out of the water, and when it had sunk, some 15 men were seen in the water, amongst debris and an oil patch. After the Liberator had returned to the convoy, it was requested to fly a Mamba patrol and another U-boat was seen and attacked with machine-gun fire. They then homed in aircraft 'Z' of 86 Squadron (FO Burcher), which attacked (see next entry). At 1312 hrs 'R' left for base, having been on patrol around the convoy for five hours.

U-419 was on her first patrol, sailing from Bergen on 13 September. The CO, Oberleutnant Giersberg, was the only survivor of the 49 crew, and was picked up by one of the convoy's escort ships.

John Wright became a squadron leader in November and received a bar to his DFC. This was his first confirmed kill, having previously damaged two U-boats.

8 October, 1943

U-643, a type VIIC submarine, commanded by Kapitänleutnant Hans Speidel, sunk.

Liberator 'Z' FL954, 86 Squadron, on patrol 0158–1822 hrs.

FO C.W. Burcher, DFC	Pilot
F/Sgt J. Lloyd	2nd pilot
PO S. Tuckett	
F/Sgt A.D. Paine	Nav
FO S.C. Cox, DFC, DFM	Eng
Sgt J. Pheasey	WOP/AG
Sgt J.E. Parrott	WOP/AG
Sgt R.C. Crump	WOP/AG
Sgt F. Newchurch	

Liberator 'T' FK223 120 Squadron, on patrol 0829–0005 hrs.

FO D.C.L. Webber, DFC	Pilot
WO J. Luker	2nd pilot
FO H.L. Matthews	Nav
F/Sgt J.G. Jeans	Eng
WO H. Lea	WOP/AG
F/Sgt J. Bradley	WOP/AG
F/Sgt A.J. Allan	WOP/AG

Burcher had met convoy SC 143 at 0809 hrs and been requested to fly an Adder patrol. At 1120 hrs he intercepted a sighting report from Wright's aircraft (see previous entry), who homed him in, finding the U-boat at 1137 hrs, in position 5600/2710. It began to submerge as Burcher approached and four D/Cs were released which straddled the track of the boat but only some oil and scum were left on the surface. An hour later he returned to the spot and found 'T' of 120 Squadron, attacking a surfaced U-boat. Burcher then made an attack, 2 D/Cs falling close to the sub's hull. Another attack was then made by T/120, followed by several machine-gun attacks by both aircraft. Meantime, other aircraft had arrived in the attack area – G/120 (WO Bryan Turnbull) and L/86 (F/L E.A. Bland). (Turnbull made an attack on another sub with one 600 lb mine, then dropped 3 x 250 lb D/Cs ahead of the swirl as it crash dived. This was U-762 (see Iceland), which was damaged.) U-643's crew could now be seen congregating in the conning tower. They began to inflate dinghies and put on life jackets. John Luker, the second pilot in T/120, recalls: 'We took off from Meeks Field, Iceland. We normally flew at cloud base or 5000 feet, whichever was the lower. On this day we were at cloud base flying on auto-pilot with both pilots on the alert for anything. At 56.18N, 26.30W, the radar operator reported a contact dead ahead at 10 miles; both pilots saw the U-boat almost simultaneously. Denis Webber immediately pulled into the cloud in an endeavour to conceal our approach, but when we came out we were too high and could not get lower than about 300 feet – too high for D/C dropping. We came round a second time at about 50 feet and the U-boat fired everything at us. I can still see the bursts of heavier flak above us and tracer streaming underneath us! Fortunately we were not hit, thanks no doubt to Denis's evasive action before straightening up for the final run-in. We dropped a stick of four D/Cs (operated by our navigator, Bert Matthews, using a low-level bomb sight) and, of course, our front and rear gunners gave everything they had.

'We came hard around to drop another stick (this time from 30 feet) and as we passed over the U-boat, I remember observing from the pilot's blister in the window that all the U-boat's gunners and guns seemed to have disappeared. This time, Bert's stick of four was a perfect straddle, with the U-boat right in the middle of the subsequent explosions. The U-boat stopped dead on the surface and we were amazed to see the crew tumble out of the conning tower, wearing life jackets and carrying dinghies. Though no white flag appeared, we ceased firing as the crew were obviously set to abandon ship. Burcher of 86 Squadron must have been at PLE because we were left to home in destroyers to pick up survivors and, hopefully, to secure a live U-boat. The weather began to close in and we dropped smoke floats to make sure we didn't lose her. I remember seeing the U-boat's crew shaking their fists at us, but what they didn't appreciate was that we were securing their rescue, for they would not last long in the water in those sea conditions.

'Without warning, the U-boat disappeared, leaving the crew in the sea. We thought they had scuttled, but I later read that the captain said she just blew up. It has been recorded that we fired at them in the water, but I can categorically deny any such suggestion. The Navy arrived to pick up survivors, including the captain, and then we reached PLE and had to turn for home. We never saw the convoy! As the weather was duff in Iceland, we were diverted to Ballykelly, and landed after a flight of 15 hours 50 minutes.'

Webber had continued to circle as Bland arrived. Bland saw Turnbull make an attack on a diving sub and then saw T/120 Squadron, which was calling up one of the convoy's escorts. Bland could see the Germans about to abandon ship and the boat was down at the bows. The SNO forbade any further attacks, so Bland circled, taking pictures. At 1445 hrs, there was a violent explosion seen by Bland's and Webber's crews. After this, 15–20 survivors could be seen in the water, and were picked up later upon the arrival of HMS *Orwell*.

U-643 had been on her first cruise, having left Bergen on 14 September to become part of the Rossbach Group in the attack on SC 143. She went down in position 5614/2655, south-west of Iceland. Twenty-one men were rescued, so some 30 others perished.

This was Cyril Burcher's second sub kill. Flight Lieutenant Stephen Charles Cox had only recently received his DFC to add to his DFM. Denis Webber received an immediate DFC, and some weeks later Herbert Matthews and James Jeans received the DFC and DFM respectively.

8 October, 1943

U-610, a type VIIC submarine, commanded by Kapitänleutnant Baron Walter von Freyberg-Eisenberg-Allmendirzen, sunk.

Sunderland 'J' DD863, 423 RCAF Squadron, on patrol 1027–0248 hrs.

FO A.H. Russell   Pilot

FO A. Menaul
WC A.F.F. Frizzle
FO H. Forrest
Sgt W. Alexander, RAF
Sgt R.G. Locke

Sgt W.J. Lancaster
Sgt D.T. Bromhead, RAF
WO F.R. Haar
Sgt D.C. Douglas, RAF
Sgt A.R. Caterham

In the continuing battles around convoy SC 143, Russell and his crew, which included the squadron commander, Wing Commander Frizzle, met the ships at 1734 hrs. They were ordered to patrol astern of the convoy and coming out of some low cloud 2 hours later, sighted the wake of a fully surfaced U-boat, just 100 yards on the port bow. The rear gunner fired as they flew over and the sub replied with a heavy gun as well as machine-gun fire. The Wing Commander had been in the pilot's seat, but immediately handed over to Russell, and then he stood between the two pilots for a grandstand view of the subsequent attack. Russell banked round and attacked from 100 feet, in the first attack position obtainable. Only three of the four D/Cs selected released, but Nos. 2 and 3 straddled the conning tower. The boat was lifted out of the water and it disappeared. Coming round again, nothing could be seen except 15 live sailors in the water amidst much debris and oil.

U-610 was on her fifth patrol, having sailed from St Nazaire on 12 September. She had sunk six ships, including the Polish destroyer ORP *Orkan* on this very day.

Flying Officer Russell was awarded the DFC. On 5 December, he was injured in a crash when nine out of 16 people aboard a Sunderland crashed into Knocklayd Mountain near Ballykelly. Of his crew, Sergeants Bromhead and Douglas were killed, Flying Officer Forrest and Sergeant Alexander were injured.

16 October, 1943

U-964, a type VIIC submarine, commanded by Oberleutnant Emmo Hummerjohnn, sunk.

Liberator 'Y' FK241, 86 Squadron, on patrol 0854–0209 hrs.

FO G.D. Gamble, DFC, BEM	Pilot
Sgt H.E. Miskiman	2nd pilot
FO D. Sivyer	Nav
WO A. Mercer	Eng
WO J. Kenyon	WOP/AG
F/Sgt R.J. Leach	WOP/AG
Sgt E.P. Williams	WOP/AG
Sgt J.R.J. Hole	WOP/AG

Met convoy ON 206 at 1505 hrs and 2½ hours later, when flying towards convoy ONS 20, a U-boat was sighted in position 5727/2817. An attack was made with three D/Cs, but the results were unobserved. Because of intense flak, a second attack was postponed as Gamble tried to contact the SNO in order to home in an escort vessel. However, this proved unsuccessful, so at 1910 hrs, as the light was beginning to fade, another attack was mounted. One of the three remaining D/Cs fell near the hull of the sub and within minutes the bows were seen to be low in the water and puffs of black smoke were coming from each side of the after-deck. The boat slowly slid under the waves, leaving 35 survivors in dinghies and in the sea. As the aircraft started for home, contact was made with ONS 20, informing the SNO of the attack position.

U-964 was sunk on her first patrol, which began from Bergen. Later five survivors of the crew were picked up by U-231.

George Gamble had won the BEM for rescuing the crew of a crashed aircraft in Ireland. He had flown Hudsons with 220 Squadron, and as a Warrant Officer received the DFC in March 1943.

16 October, 1943

U-470, a type VIIC submarine, commanded by Oberleutnant Gunther Grave, sunk.

Liberator 'E', 120 Squadron, on patrol 1515–2350 hrs.

F/L H.F. Kerrigan, RCAF	Pilot
Sgt M. Weiner	2nd pilot
F/L W.N. Kenyon	Nav
FO E. Stanley	2 Nav
Sgt T.W. Chapman	WOM
WO J.T. Foy	WOP/AG
Sgt W. Hunt	WOP/AG
Sgt T. Levinsky	WOP/AG
Sgt J.J. Grassam	WOP/AG

Liberator 'Z', 120 Squadron, on patrol 0908–0058 hrs.

F/L B.E. Peck	Pilot
FO E.N. Jennings	2nd pilot
FO J.W. Rickard, RCAF	Nav
Sgt E.P. Priddy	Eng
F/Sgt L.B. Sheldon	WOP/AG
Sgt J.G. Nugent RCAF	WOP/AG
Sgt N.R. McGrath RCAF	WOP/AG
Sgt J.H. Holland	WOM
Mr Clearwater	Passenger

Liberator 'C' FL973, 59 Squadron, on patrol 0937–0130 hrs.

PO W.G. Loney	Pilot
F/Sgt J.F. Clark, GM	F/Sgt K.J. Field
FO C.E. Goodwin	WO G.L. Parker
F/Sgt R.G.V. Coston	Sgt J.E. Dixon
Sgt W.R. Sills	

The two Libs of 120 Squadron were airborne from Reykjavik, 59 from RAF Ballykelly. Barry Peck had met convoy ON 206 at 1153 hrs and carried out the SNO's orders. Kerrigan met the convoy at 1741 hrs. Flying a Lizard patrol, Kerrigan sighted a U-boat at 1858 hrs in position 5820/2920 and attacked, experiencing heavy flak, a close explosion causing the beam window to be blown out, which hit the tail. Circling, the attack was resumed at 1912 hrs with four D/Cs and machine-gun fire, the No. 4 D/C landing very close to the boat's stern. As 'E' then circled, 'Z' made an attack. Barry Peck recalls:

'Shortly after our arrival over the convoy, we heard over the R/T that a Liberator had been hit by gunfire from a U-boat and was in trouble, then came the calm exchange of voices between the pilot and SNO – "I have to ditch." "Roger, ditch in the centre of the convoy, and I will arrange pick-up."

'It was a cloudy but clear day, with a trace of a swell on the sea. We were "sweeping" at 500 feet without sighting a submarine for some 6½ hours, when the RN commander instructed us to proceed outward from the convoy on a bearing and to a certain distance to investigate a contact. Warrant Officer Shilton, who was operating the radar, soon confirmed the contact, on to which we homed. Shortly after, we sighted U-470 on the surface heading for the convoy; we approached amidst a hail of flak, and fearing that it might soon dive, we laid a pattern of six D/Cs into its forward path. I believe this first attack, although delivered at too high an altitude, had clipped the submarine's stern and rendered the steering gear inoperative. In the event, in turning steeply to starboard to observe the result, amidst another hail of flak, it appeared to be floudering in the water.

'In the circumstances we had plenty of time to line up for the second attack, which was finally delivered astern of U-470. No flak this time, when we came in from 100 feet and Joe Rickard, an absolute "ace" on the Mark III bombsight, opened up with the .5 nose gun, scoring hits on the conning tower. On Joe's "Go!", we released 2 x 250 lb D/Cs which straddled the U-boat and we turned quickly and steeply to starboard in our excitement to view the result. It was blown clear out of the water, with daylight between hull and surface. The U-boat went down to the bottom of the Atlantic absolutely vertical, leaving 15–20 survivors in the sea.

'I asked the SNO to release an escort vessel to verify the kill and to pick up survivors and in the event HMS *Duncan* was homed to the area, but owing to the threat of considerable U-boat activity around this particular convoy, the ship's commander decided to sail through it at medium speed with grappling nets out. The U-boat commander, Gunther Grave, and the cook, who were the only survivors, managed to cling on to the nets and were hauled aboard *Duncan*. I did see another Liberator in the area, but I did not see any other attack. However, this is quite possible as it took some time to line up an aircraft of that size.'

In the event, the 59 Squadron Liberator arrived on the scene, directed also by the SNO, and attacked the sub under a moderate flak barrage, and straddled the boat with four D/Cs. This appears to have occurred as E/120 circled, for Kerrigan saw Peck's attack, then saw the third Lib arrive and attack, before Peck made his second attack. The boat was officially credited to the three Liberator crews. Barry Peck continues:

'Two interesting features emerge from this particular episode. U-470, built at Kiel, was the first submarine, so far as I am aware, that was covered with an outer lining of a rubber compound to counteract the effects of Asdic – this information was revealed to HMS *Duncan*'s captain by Oblt Grave; it does not seem to have been very effective.

'Second, Mr Clearwater, a technician seconded to the USAAF, was aboard our aircraft because his Company had just produced the "Sonar Buoy", which subsequently was to be of such importance in the U-boat war. This device, with its underwater trailing antennae, when dropped in a set pattern, together with a Receiver in the aircraft, provided a clear presentation of a submarine's track and speed underwater, from propeller vibrations. However, because U-470 was on the surface, we dropped a sonar buoy near the site after the sinking, but from the earphones we could hear it breaking up under sea with one violent explosion and many smaller ones.'

U-470 had indeed been on her first cruise, having left Bergen on 28 September for the North Atlantic, and went down south-west of Iceland.

Barry Peck later received the DFC, and retired from the RAF as a Wing Commander. This was Harold Kerrigan's first successful action, and he was later to damage U-737 in March 1944, with some of the above crew. He had previously been on an Air Sea Rescue squadron. For W.G. Loney and some of his crew, another success would come in January

1944, when they damaged U-621.

17 October, 1943

German U-boat damaged – probably U-470 (see previous entry).

Sunderland 'S' JM712, 422 RCAF Squadron, on patrol 0411 hrs.

F/L P.T. Sargent	Pilot
FO A.R.B. Bellis	2nd pilot
F/Sgt B. Campbell, RAF	3rd pilot
FO C.B. Steeves	Nav
WO J.H. Shand	WOP/AG
WO W.F. Beals	Gunnery Officer
WO J.D. Stafford	WOP/AG
F/Sgt J.Y. Rutherford, RAF	WOM
F/Sgt L.T. Needham, RAF	Eng
F/Sgt D. Mesney, RAF	FME
FL P.A.S. Woodwork, RAF	Group Gunnery Leader.

The Liberator Barry Peck had heard so calmly ditch into the sea on this morning was flown by Paul Sargent from Toronto. He had been on patrol to convoy ONS 20, having taken off from Castle Archdale. The Sunderland had obtained two radar blips while in a rain cloud and on coming out two wakes had been seen, then two U-boats seen dead ahead in position 5950/3000, at 1350 hrs. Sargent attacked one of them despite severe gun fire from the sub, but no hits were sustained in the first run, and Woodwork, manning a .5 gun, and Needham, firing the front VGO gun, seemed to clear the decks with their return fire. Three D/Cs fell from 50 feet, but undershot by 30 feet. Coming in again flying an undulating course at about 100 feet, the gunfire began again but this time the Sunderland was badly hit. The R/T was shot away and the front turret recuperator was smashed, Needham dying at his post. The automatic pilot was blown out of the aircraft, W/T destroyed, radar set damaged, control quadrant hit, throttle and pitch propexocters destroyed, wing dinghy blown out, mid-upper turret hit and the hull generally riddled. Chesley Steeves the Navigator was mortally wounded, but was able to give Sargent a course to the convoy before he died. Woodwork, the Group Gunnery Leader, was also killed at his gun. Sargent made his second attack, but one D/C failed to release. The others made a perfect straddle about 15 feet on either beam of the U-boat, after which it disappeared. The second U-boat remained on the surface and continually fired at the Sunderland when in range.

Sargent set course for the convoy and with the

radar repaired the convoy was met and a visual signal made to HMS *Drury*. He then circled the ship, telling the captain of his need to ditch which was carried out ahead of the escort vessel. Touching down on top of a swell then rising, on second contact the Sunderland buried its nose in and the hull disintegrated, the whole tail assembly coming off. There was no opportunity to use normal ditching procedure although ditching stations were assumed. The surviving crew members were in the sea for 15 minutes before being picked up, but the gallant pilot, who became entangled in the wreckage, went down with the aircraft, despite attempts to free him.

Flying Officer Bellis, who was at the galley gun during the attack, and Warrant Officer Beals were both awarded the DFC. In addition to the four who died, Flight Sergeants Rutherford and Mesney were both injured, the latter suffering a broken leg. Flight Sergeant Campbell had been in the second pilot's seat during the attack.

23 October, 1943

U-274, a type VIIC submarine, commanded by Kapitänleutnant Gunther J. Jordan, sunk.

Liberator 'Z', 224 Squadron, on patrol 0516–1823 hrs.

SL E.J. Wicht	Pilot
FO E. Allen	2nd pilot
FO R.W. King	Nav
F/Sgt G.T. Lenson	
WO G. Skidmore	
Sgt D.G. Yerby	
Sgt C. Owen	Eng
Sgt F.S. Prickett	

On passage from Ballykelly to convoy ON 207, equipped with rockets, aircraft was instructed to find Escort Group B7, who were patrolling 100 miles north-west of convoy, and to drop a radar transformer to one of the vessels. Homing in on radar, a contact was made dead ahead at 10 miles, which was not the convoy. Wicht immediately climbed into cloud, and when coming out, at 1800 feet, there ahead was a surfaced U-boat, 2 miles, in position 5714/2750. The sub appeared taken by surprise and there was no sign of activity on the bridge. Despite a difficult angle of approach, the Lib fired two rockets at 1000 yards 1000 feet, which went into the water 20 yards beyond the sub, the second pair at 800 yards 800 feet, while the remaining four were fired at 400 yards. The port two

of the salvo either struck the U-boat's stern or went below. Nothing further seen of the R/Ps and no evidence of damage. Aircraft flew over and fired into the boat, the sub's gunners finally firing back, and then Wicht circled 2 miles off and contacted the Escort Group. They were about 18 miles to the south and the SN0 made full steam for the area. During this time, as Wicht circled, the U-boat was sailing a zigzag course and made tight circles, keeping its stern to the Liberator, and flak began whenever it seemed as if the aircraft might make an attack run. It was gradually moving westwards, but at 1110 hrs it set off to the south west and shortly afterwards began to dive. Wicht at that moment was some 4 miles away, but quickly made an attack, dropping two D/Cs from 50 feet about a minute after the boat had gone down. Flame floats too were dropped and a watch kept until 1200 when HMS *Duncan* arrived. Later more ships arrived and the radar package was dropped to HMS *Sunflower*. Wicht, his original task completed, set course for the convoy leaving the Navy to continue the attack.

U-274 was credited to 120 Squadron, shared with the destroyers *Duncan* and *Vidette* of the Escort Group B7. The sub's first cruise, which began on 1 September, was aborted when it was damaged by ice on the 13th. Sailing again from Tronhiem on 13 October it was pure chance that put her in contact with the Liberator. In the official assessment of the action, it was doubted whether Wicht's attacks had caused any damage, but the sight of the D/C explosions had aided *Duncan* to find the location quickly, resulting in the boat's final destruction.

Squadron Leader Edgar Jacques 'Billy' Wicht was a Swiss national serving with the RAF, and he later received the DFC. In April 1944 he also received the DSO. Of his crew on this occasion, Allen, King and Owen had all been involved in earlier anti U-boat successes with 224 Squadron.

16 November, 1943

U-280, a type VIIC submarine, commanded by Oberleutnant Walter Hungershausen, sunk.

Liberator 'M' FL931, 86 Squadron, on patrol 0255–2012 hrs.

FO J.H. Bookless (Aust)	Pilot
PO H. Lewis	2nd pilot
PO C.C. Cooper (Aust)	Nav
Sgt R.F. Burchett	Eng
WO R.H. Carroll (Can)	AG
F/Sgt J. Hamilton	WOM/AG

Sgt B.I. Wade   WOP/AG
Sgt R.G. McDonald   WOP/AG

After meeting convoy HX 265 at 0906 hrs, started to fly a Cobra 40 patrol on SNO's instructions. At 1025 hrs a U-boat was sighted in position 4911/2732 and an immediate attack was carried out. On the run in WO Carroll, the Fire Controller in the front gun position, fired and scored hits on the conning tower. Flak from the sub was intense and accurate, one shell hitting the leading edge of the port wing and knocking out the outer engine. In the attack the D/Cs overshot, so the aircraft prepared for a second run. Three minutes later, during the run-in, the nose gunner again fired effectively, scoring hits and knocking out the boat's forward gunner. This time the D/Cs only made a slight overshoot and a few minutes later the sub was slightly submerged without any apparent forward movement. Aircraft circled the scene for over an hour but saw no apparent evidence of damage to the U-boat, and despite flying on three engines stayed with the convoy for another hour before returning to Ballykelly.

U-280, on its first war patrol, had left Kiel on 12 October for the North Atlantic, and went down north of the Azores, being credited to John Bookless and his crew.

13 January, 1944

U-621, a type VIIC submarine commanded by Kapitänleutnant Max Krushka, damaged.

Liberator 'A' FL990, 59 Squadron, on patrol 0355–2014 hrs.

FO W.G. Loney   Sgt J.E. Merger
FO C.E. Goodwin   WO J.F. Clark, GM
F/Sgt R.V.G. Costin   F/Sgt K.J. Field
Sgt W.H. Wilson   Sgt J.E. Dixon

A sweep was commenced in support of convoys SL 144 and MKS 35 at 0831 hrs, but it was not until 1500 hrs that a fully surfaced U-boat was spotted 8 miles away. Loney made an approach from out of the sun, but at 4 miles the boat opened fire and began to turn. D/Cs were dropped over the conning tower from 50 feet, the first of the six falling right alongside the hull. In a second attack, two D/Cs went down, falling half-way between the conning tower and the stern. This was followed by three machine-gun attacks by nose, beam and rear gunners. One German gunner was seen to fall and the rest of the crew went below. Two minutes later

the boat dived, stern up, but left no debris.

U-621 was on her sixth patrol, and had to return to Brest, damaged, from where she had sailed on the 6th. Her first patrol was in late September 1942 and in June 1943 she had been adapted as a flak boat after making four cruises. For this sixth cruise she had reverted to a normal flak armament. Later fitted with a schnorkel, she finally completed 10 patrols. In the English Channel at the time of the Normandy invasion she sank an LST. On her ninth patrol under a new CO – Stuckmann – she sank HMS *Prince Leopold*. On her final cruise she was sunk on 18 August, 1944, while *en route* to La Pallice, by Canadian destroyers of Escort Group 11. She had sunk a total of 12 ships.

10 February, 1944

U-545, a type IXC/40 submarine, commanded by Kapitänleutnant Gert Mannesmann, sunk.

Wellington 'O', 612 Squadron, on patrol 1621–0310 hrs.

PO M.H. Painter (Aust)   F/L W.T. Dulley (Aust)
Sgt G. Borlace   Sgt G. Seckington
PO J.W. McKay (Aust)   Sgt D.L. Smith
FO J. Staff-Brett Passenger (Station Signals Officer)

On a convoy support mission from Limavady, flying a creeping line ahead search, a radar contact was made at 2037 hrs at 8 miles. The weather had been very bad with low cloud and fog. Out of 25 flame floats dropped to measure drift, only five had been seen, causing the aircraft to be 8 miles north of its intended track – which was pure bad luck as far as the U-boat was concerned. In the attack area the weather had cleared, with good visibility and a calm sea. The boat was picked out in the moonlight at one mile and the D/Cs went down for a perfect straddle. The radar contact was lost two minutes later, but when flying back over the scene, debris of oval objects, each with small lights, were seen on the surface. Jack Staff-Brett, who retired from the RAF in 1968 as a Wing Commander, remembers: 'As Station Signals Officer responsible for briefing W/Ops, I thought it would be a good idea to demonstrate that I could actually do the job as well as tell them how to do it, so asked if I could fly on a U-boat patrol. It was originally planned that I should fly on the 9th, but the sortie was aborted before take-off when we burst a tyre whilst taxying.

'When we flew on the 10th, we made the attack whilst I was doing my stint on the radio so that I actually sent the 'Sub Attack' signal. Two other memories remain – firstly looking at the orange lights in the water, indicating that some of the sub crew had taken to the dinghies, thus confirming the sinking, and secondly, the loss of the gold presentation watch given to me by my firm when I joined the RAF in 1935. I had taken the watch off and hung it on the R1155 receiver so that I could read off the times more easily for the log entries. In the euphoria of the attack success, I forgot to take the watch with me when we landed, so perhaps it ended up in some obscure recess of 'O' 162.

'Of course, I was greeted with some envy in the mess since I had been engaged in a "sub kill" on my first operational sortie, whilst some members of the squadron were on their second tour and had not yet had a sighting!'

U-545 sailed from Kiel on her first sortie on 9 December, 1943, and had sunk one ship before this night. Badly damaged, the crew had quickly abandoned her, taking to dinghies and life rafts. The sub went down in position 5817/1322, west of the Butt of Lewis. The crew were lucky enough to be rescued by U-714 (on her 3rd cruise) and taken to St Nazaire on 25 February. Gert Mannesmann later commanded U-230 and U-2502, but was killed in an air raid on Hamburg in 1945.

Max Painter later received the DFC.

11 February, 1944

U-283, a type VIIC submarine, commanded by Oberleutnant Gunter Ney, sunk.

Wellington XII 'D' MP578, 407 RCAF Squadron, on patrol 2205–0825 hrs.

FO P.W. Heron	FO R.C. Hayes
FO J.O. Hornby	WO L.W. Tunney
FO C.J. Sullivan	F/Sgt J.G. McDonald

In the early hours of the 11th, a radar plot was picked up, dead ahead, 6 miles in position 6045/1250. Homed in and at 1–2 miles while, at 100 feet, the navigator in the nose, and then the second pilot, who was operating the Leigh Light, saw the submarine in the moonlight. At 0410 hrs the Light illuminated the sub, with decks awash. Heron went straight in from 60 feet and a stick of six D/Cs went down. As the plumes subsided, the rear gunner saw a dull red glow, just as the boat began to fire at the Wellington. Circling to starboard, Heron came back towards the flame float, the sub still on radar but not moving. Then the contact was lost as the sub

apparently went down. Nothing further seen although the aircraft circled for another hour.

U-283 had sailed from Kiel for her first patrol on 13 January. On the night of 10 February she had been attacked by aircraft 'N' of 612 Squadron, which she had shot down.

Flying Officer Heron later received the DFC.

10 March, 1944

U-625, a type VIIC submarine, commanded by Oberleutnant Siegfried Straub, sunk.

Sunderland 'U' EK591, 422 RCAF Squadron, on patrol 1125–2331 hrs.

WO W.F. Morton	Pilot
F/L S.W. Butler, RAF	(captain)
FO R.J. Simard	2nd pilot
WO F.J. Cauley	Nav
Sgt E.E. Higgins	Eng
FL A. Ormorod	2 Nav
PO J.E. Nespor	AG
F/Sgt C.L. Holland	WOM/AG
F/Sgt F.W. Gallagher	WOP/AG
F/Sgt W.E. Roberts	FMA/AG
Sgt J.F. Rushton	FME/AG

Flight Lieutenant Butler was screening this Canadian crew, who were flying their first mission, with Flight Lieutenant Ormorod checking the crew's navigation. Butler was in fact at the controls when at 1500 hrs, before reaching their assigned patrol area (to cover convoy SC 154), a U-boat was sighted by Butler, 6 miles off to port. They were flying at 1000 feet, Butler quickly dropping to 400 feet at one mile. The boat saw the Sunderland and began firing, but the shells mostly fell midway between the sub and aircraft. The sub was trying to keep its stern to the aircraft, and Butler was taking avoiding action from the gunfire. With the front gun also firing, Butler went down to 50 feet and it seemed that only one German gunner was still firing as they closed in. The Sunderland too was hit, one shell going into the hull on the port bow, below the water line. Six D/Cs went down to straddle the target, which then submerged. It resurfaced about 3 minutes later, moving at a slow speed and turning to the right. The flying boat circled for nearly 1½ hours, when the U-boat signalled visually to the aircraft – 'Fine Bombish!' and then the crew began to abandon the vessel in one large and numerous small dinghies. At 1740 hrs the U-boat sank by the stern.

U-625, in company with U-741, had shot down a

Wellington of 407 RCAF Squadron on the night of 10 March (PO E.M. O'Donnell in HF311, who had sunk U-669 on 7 September, 1943). She was not so fortunate when she met 422 Squadron just a few hours later. U-625 had made at least three patrols with the Arctic Flotilla in 1943 before going to the Atlantic station in October. On her first Atlantic cruise, she had lost her commander, Korvetten-leutnant Hans Benker and one seaman overboard after an attack by aircraft 'C' of 224 Squadron on 2 January, 1944. On that occasion, Liberator G/224 (PO J.E. Edwards) had found the U-boat, but flak from the boat had damaged the aircraft and wounded the WOP, forcing the captain to return home. Then Liberator C/224 (FO E. Allen) arrived, found the marker left by 'G' and later made radar contact with U-625. They attacked with eight D/Cs, causing the loss of the two men from the bridge.

Now on her second patrol, which began from Brest on 29 February, she had been sunk. Despite Butler and his crew seeing the Germans take to their dinghies, none of the 53 submariners survived. The sub went down in position 5235/2019, west of the mouth of the River Shannon.

Flight Lieutenant Sidney William Butler, who certainly showed this new crew 'how to do it', received the DFC.

25 May, 1944

U-990, a type VIIC submarine, commanded by Kapitänleutnant Hubert Nordheimer, sunk.

Liberator 'S' FL984, 59 Squadron, on patrol 1956–1155 hrs.

SL B.A. Sisson	Pilot
FO R.A. Williams	2nd pilot
PO W. Whittaker	Nav
FO H. Humphries	
F/L A.A. Fox	
WO W. McLoughlin	
F/Sgt N.W. Beames	
F/Sgt A.R. Playford	
Sgt J. Kelly	

In the early hours of the 25th, this aircraft followed a radar contact and found an armed auxiliary vessel which was engaged by the port beam gun and turret guns after the ship had opened fire. Evasive action was taken and then the patrol resumed. Flying on a creeping line ahead search, a surfaced U-boat was seen at 0623 hrs in position 6505/0728, escorted by a surface vessel. Sisson waited for an opportunity to attack under cover of an approaching rain squall, not wanting to risk the joint fire from sub and escort. When the squall came, he attacked, dropping 6 D/Cs across the U-boat (Nos. 7 and 8 did not release), the nearest exploding 10–15 yards short of the conning tower. Making a wide circle, the RAF crew could see a large oil patch by the sub and the escort vessel was closing in to it. Flak had been experienced from both vessels and the Lib had replied with nose and tail guns. At 0803 hrs, the sub was seen in the act of submerging, and Sisson flew over the swirl, but did not make an attack. Sisson had taken off from Ballykelly and landed back at Tain.

U-990 had made two patrols with the Arctic Flotilla in early 1944 and had sunk the destroyer *Mahratta*. When attacked by 59 Squadron, she was on passage to Narvik. She had sailed to Bergen on 8 April, then on 22 May left for Narvik. She rescued 21 of the crew of U-476, which had foundered after an attack by 'V' of 210 Squadron on 24 May (see 18 Group). Fifty-two of the joint survivors of these two boats were rescued by the German patrol boat VP5901.

27 May, 1944

U-292, a type VIIC submarine, commanded by Oberleutnant Werner Schmidt, sunk.

Liberator 'S' FL984, 59 Squadron, on patrol 1945–1200 hrs.

F/L V.E. Camacho	Sgt W. Derbyshire
FL J.R. Morrill	WO W. Wilkinson
FO R.S. Shewry	F/Sgt L.E. Proudfoot
Sgt L.M. Waltham	F/Sgt R.L. McLeary

From Ballykelly, carried out a search in area 6263/0102. At 0810 hrs a radar contact was obtained at 15 miles but lost at 3 miles. Aircraft broke cloud at 250 feet in position 6237/0057 and found a fully surfaced U-boat about 1½ miles away, which was attacked with six D/Cs. The rear gunner saw them explode about the sub and the starboard beam gunner saw a bright yellow explosion. This man then crossed to the port window as the aircraft turned, and saw the boat's bows out of the water at an angle of 20 degrees. Then the sub was seen stationary and submerging on an even keel, leaving a patch of oil. Gunfire had been exchanged during the attack and the Lib sustained some damage to a port engine. They landed at Tain.

This was U-292's first and last patrol, having sailed from Bergen on 24 May.

9 June, 1944

U-740, a type VIIC submarine, commanded by Kapitänleutnant Gunther Stark, sunk.

Liberator V 'F', 120 Squadron, on patrol 2255–1346 hrs.

F/L A.K. Sherwood	Pilot
O L. Mitchell	2nd pilot
Sgt C.H. Cheslin	Nav
F/Sgt A. Alexander (Aust)	2 Nav
Sgt E.G. Hunt	Eng
FO H.E. Kennedy (Aust)	WOP/AG
F/Sgt G.A. Henderson (Aust)	WOP/AG
WO R.M. Ritchie	WOP/AG
Sgt R.A. Ward	WOM

From Ballykelly on a Cork Air Patrol, sighted a wake at 0840 hrs in position 4909/0837, in the western approaches to the Channel. It was 5 to 6 miles off and submerging. Five seconds after the periscope disappeared, six D/Cs went down from 60 feet, falling 20 feet ahead of the swirl, and a large patch of dark oil appeared, followed by a lighter patch. One sonar buoy was released and motor sounds heard, also screeching and clanging noises. The motor noises ceased at 0902. A nearby Escort Group and HQ were informed and then the aircraft made for England, landing at St Eval.

U-740 had left Brest on 6 June for the Scillies and the Lizard, her second patrol. Her first had been between March and April, sailing from Bergen to Brest.

Flight Lieutenant Alfred Kenneth Sherwood later received the DFC.

22 March, 1945

U-296, a type VIIC submarine, commanded by Kapitänleutnant Karl Heinz Rasch, sunk.

Liberator VIII 'M', 120 Squadron, on patrol 1229–1636 hrs.

SL L.J. White	Pilot
FO F.J. Cornish	2nd pilot
FO G.H. Smith	Nav
FO G.A. Robertson	2 Nav
FO F.G.P. Payne	Eng
WO R. Tetley	WOP/AG
F/Sgt A.L. Meier	WOP/AG
WO J. Zakreski	WOP/AG
Sgt A. Newman	AG

Sgt D. Badcock	WOM
WO L.F. Broom	AG

Diverted to hunt for a U-boat sighted by 172 Squadron (FO Chambers). On arrival at the scene, dropped a basic sonar buoy pattern, at 1400 hrs, following which a definite contact was made and an attack with two acoustic torpedoes was carried out, and explosions heard. Aircraft then co-operated with escort vessels, which continued the search when the aircraft left at 1613 hrs.

The 172 Squadron Wellington had twice located a U-boat between 1000 and 1140 hrs, north-east of Malin Head and had dropped six D/Cs from 50 feet, straddling a swirl, before homing the Liberator.

U-296 was on her third patrol, having left Bergen for Northern Irish waters on 28 February. It failed to return and was credited to 120 Squadron.

In 1985, the Naval Historical Branch (MoD) felt that the U-boat 172 Squadron had located was U-1003, which escaped damage, but was lost the next day. The depth of water in the attack area was only 50 fathoms and the two explosions heard by 120 Squadron on their sonar buoy receiver might have been the two torpedoes hitting the bottom. The present assessment is that U-296 may have hit a mine, but is currently listed as lost to unknown causes in first half of March 1945.

29 April, 1945

U-1017, a type VIIC/41 submarine, commanded by Oberleutnant Werner Riecken, sunk.

Liberator VIII 'Q', 120 Squadron, on patrol 1152–0003 hrs.

FO H.J. Oliver	Pilot
F/Sgt A.A. McPhee	2nd pilot
Sgt R.H. Law	3rd pilot
F/L A.W.P. Leslie	Nav
Sgt E. Dent	Eng
WO A.J. Creane	WOP/AG
Sgt E.H. Keenan	WOM
Sgt L.J. Martin	WOP/AG
Sgt G. Renals	AG
Sgt J.T. Yates	AG

Patrolling off Malin Head a wake was sighted at 1312 hrs in position 5604/1106 by the second pilot, 3 miles away. At 2 miles schnorkel smoke could be seen and aircraft attacked with four D/Cs and a 'purple' HT also dropped. Whilst passing over the schnorkel, another wake and schnorkel seen 1½ miles further on, but it disappeared before an attack could be made. Loud and long-drawn-out explosions were heard on the HT after the D/C explosions ended. A complete sono buoy pattern was then laid and one explosion heard on the 'yellow', while other noises heard on the blue, orange and red. (Each buoy carried a different frequency. Purple was always dropped nearest to the suspected U-boat position, followed by the others in three large circles around that location.)

U-1017, on its second cruise, failed to return from its sortie to the Channel from Trondheim, which it left on 14 April.

FO H.J. 'Pop' Oliver had been second pilot to Bryan Turnbull before taking over his own crew, and had been involved in earlier attacks against U-boats.

30 April, 1945.

U-242, commanded by Kapitänleutnant Riedel, sunk.

Sunderland 'H' ML783, 201 Squadron, on patrol 0612–1817 hrs.

F/L K.H. Foster	Sgt L.A. Nicklin
Sgt R.J.L. Armstrong	Sgt D.G. Brown
F/Sgt G. Bellamy	Sgt E. Dobson
Sgt T.F. Cater	Sgt M.L. Mooney
Sgt W.G. Smyth	PO S.A. Smith
Sgt R. Amann	

At 0810 hrs smoke was seen on surface 4 miles away, and upon investigation, an attack was made on a schnorkel in position 5342/0455 (Irish Sea area) from 300 feet. The attack was not a success as the port bomb door would not open. A second attack was made from 200 feet, but the port rack did not run out and the D/Cs were not released. A 'purple' sono buoy pattern was laid, but only water noises could be heard. A square search was begun. At 1133 hrs, spray and schnorkel smoke again seen and Ken Foster made another attack, six D/Cs falling from 70 feet, but again no results. Again only water noises were heard from an orange pattern. While tuning in, noises were heard on the blue sono pattern, which was identified as a submarine and a radio could be heard. RN escort vessels then arrived and were given details of both attacks before the aircraft resumed patrol. News was later received that a bottom contact had been made and an attack resulted in diesel oil and debris, including bits of wood and some tins of German manufacture, had come to the surface.

U-242 had been assigned to patrol in the Irish Sea. She vanished without trace, and the Navy credited her destruction to HM ships, assisted by 201 Squadron. Earlier it had been thought that the U-boat sunk was U-325 (Oblt Erwin Dohrn), but its patrol area was to have been around Land's End and the Lizard. U-325 also vanished without trace.

16 Group

3 May, 1945

U-2524, a prefabricated submarine, commanded by Kapitänleutnant Ernst von Witzendorff, sunk.

Beaufighters of 236 Squadron

led by SL S.R. Hyland, AFC
FO C.F. Barnes   NV542 'W'

Beaufighters of 254 Squadron on patrol 1424–1930 hrs.

led by FL T.F. Leaver-Power
FL A. Musto   'A'

Thirteen Beaus of 236 in company with 17 from 254 Squadron, led by the Strike Wing Leader, Wing Commander E.P.W. Hutton, DFC, were out searching for enemy shipping, escorted by Mustang fighters of 65 and 118 Squadrons. At 1720 hrs a fully surfaced U-boat was sighted and attacked by five Beaus of 236 with rockets, and six of 254 with cannon. All crews reported the boat to be hit and later in flames before it exploded. Shortly afterwards some crews saw wreckage and survivors in the water. The Wing went on to attack other shipping in the general area.

U-2524 went down in position 5555/1045.

4 May, 1945

U-2503, commanded by Kapitänleutnant Karljung Wachter, sunk.

U-2338, commanded by Oberleutnant Karl E. Kaiser, sunk.

U-393, commanded by Oberleutnant Friedrich Herrle, sunk.

U-236, commanded by Oberleutnant Herbert Mumm, sunk.

Beaufighters of 236 and 254 Squadrons.

236 led by
SL S.R. Hyland AFC and
FO G.E. Barnes   NV542 'W'

254 led by
F/L T.F. Leaver-Power
F/L A. Musto   'A'

Leading the North Coates Wing, comprising 12 Beaus of 236 and 10 of 254 (with Mustang escort), Squadron Leader Hyland, acting as outrider, sighted three U-boats in shallow water at 1615 hrs. They were on the surface in position 5520/0950, making 10 knots. Nearby were two escort vessels. One Beau of 236 attacked the leading boat with cannon fire, which immediately crash dived. This was followed by three attacks by 254 aircraft on the second boat. This heralded an orgy of attacks by both squadrons, with cannon and rocket fire, obtaining numerous hits and near misses on the second two boats, as well as hits on the escort ships. Hyland saw the third sub explode and two large oil patches were left on the surface; one escort vessel was seen to be listing and later it sank, leaving rafts and survivors in the sea. Two Beaus were slightly damaged by gunfire, but all returned after clearing the area at 1700 hrs.

Although only three submarines were reported, there were in fact four. The two prefab U-boats were on their first patrols, attempting to escape to Norway, in company with the two type VIICs. Kaiser had previously commanded U-986 (1944), while Herrle had commanded U-307 between 1942 and 1944 and then U-312, 1944 and 1945. U-393 had sunk eight ships and her crew scuttled her after being severely damaged.

Squadron Leader Hyland received the DFC.

---

18 Group

25 October, 1940

U-46, a type VIIB submarine, commanded by Kapitänleutnant Englebert Endrass, damaged.

Three Hudsons of 233 Squadron, on patrol 0915–1337 hrs.

Hudson 'E' P5156

PO A.T. Maudsley DFM
PO E.L. Baudoux
and crew

Hudson 'K' T9365

PO Winnicott
PO Dimmock
and crew

Hudson T9284

PO Walsh
PO Vanderwater
and crew

Three Hudsons were on patrol off the Norwegian coast and had just started to turn for home when they sighted the U-boat. It was 1125 hrs and they had been flying only 10 miles off Stavanger. PO Baudoux was at the controls of 'E', Maudsley climbing into the nose to check the bombing gear. They released 10 x 100 lb bombs, which fell on both sides of the sub, as it in turn opened fire with cannon and machine guns. The Hudson was hit in the petrol tanks and elevator. 'K' then attacked, its bombs also straddling the target, and black smoke hid the stern of the boat. The third Hudson dived down, but its bombs failed to release, but the stern of the boat was seen to rise and then list to port after the first two attacks. As Baudoux pulled back on the stick nothing happened, as the elevator controls had gone. However, he managed to level out by using the trim tabs and gunning the engines. With no elevator and fuel leaking from both holed tanks the Hudson made for England escorted by the other two aircraft, but managed to land safely at base.

U-46 was on her seventh war patrol, heading for Kiel from St Nazaire, which she had left on 13 October. Damaged, she made port on the 29th. Her first cruise had begun in August 1939, and she was in the Atlantic by the time war began (Ltn Sohler). She went on to complete 11 patrols and sink 31 ships before becoming a training ship in August 1941. At the war's end she was scuttled in Wilhemshaven. Englebert Endrass took command of U-567 and in 1941 received the Knight's Cross, but was lost with his command on 21 December. 1941.

Arthur Terance Maudsley and Everett Baudoux were later awarded DFCs, and the latter, a Canadian, won the DSO in 1943 and rose to the rank of Wing Commander in the RCAF. Maudsley was an ex-Halton apprentice (1933) and became an air gunner with 142 and 37 Squadrons (1935–37), before becoming a pilot in 1937. He joined 233 Squadron in September 1938. He failed to return from an escort sortie from Gibraltar, in a Beaufighter (T9323), on 7 September, 1943.

23 September, 1942

U-253, a type VIIC submarine, commanded by Kapitänleutnant Adolf Friedrichs, sunk.

Catalina 'U' FP115, 210 Squadron, on patrol 2330–1755 hrs.

F/Sgt J.W. Semmens	PO G.R. Dowson
Sgt N.J. Langdon	Sgt A.E. Hayden
Sgt W. Marshall	Sgt F. Jenner
Sgt C.E. Wilde	Sgt A.J. Laney
Sgt A. Marshall	LAC R.S. Hayhurst

Flying from Sullum Voe as air cover to convoy PQ 14, they patrolled at 600 feet over a very rough sea, sighting a U-boat at ¾ of a mile in position 6819/1350. The Catalina attacked from 50 feet, releasing six Mk VIII D/Cs with Mk 13 star pistols, as the U-boat was going under. The stick straddled, with three explosions on either side of the boat's line of advance. The sub reappeared on its side and then sank below the surface. At the same time there was a mushroom of water, 20 feet in diameter, in the middle of which could be seen what looked like a length of metal piping, which was thrown 50 feet into the air. Several seconds later a violent upheaval of bubbles appeared and then the U-boat again came to the surface on her side. After 5 seconds one end of the boat rose clear of the sea, exposing a double row of square vent holes, hovered in this position for a few seconds and then turned completely over and sank almost vertically.

U-253 was on her first patrol, which began from Kiel on 12 September. She had sailed to the north of Iceland for action against the convoy. (There is now a suggestion that her loss came on the 25th, when she hit a mine north-west of Iceland.)

26 September, 1942

U-262, a type VIIC submarine, commanded by Kapitänleutnant Heinz Franke, damaged.

Hudson 'A', 48 Squadron on patrol 0839–1359 hrs.

PO E. Tammes	PO J.C. Hamer
Sgt J.T. Russell	Sgt L. Ackroyd

Hudson 'Z', 48 Squadron, on patrol 1230–1845 hrs.

PO R. Horney	Sgt T. Pearson
Sgt N.O. Morrow	Sgt J.M. Day

Both Hudsons were patrolling an area designated as 'Flora E', when at 1038 hrs, Tammes sighted a surfaced U-boat at 4 miles, north-east of the Faeroes. He dived to attack and dropped 4 x 250 lb D/Cs from 50 feet, while some 80 feet of the diving boat was still visible. The air gunner saw an explosive disturbance about 20 yards ahead of the conning tower before it went under. Large air bubbles were seen which lasted for half a minute. After circling for half an hour and then returning 20 minutes later, nothing could be seen.

Five hours later the U-boat was found again by Horney. He dived and dropped four D/Cs from 50 feet, 12 seconds after the boat had crash dived. They exploded about 30 yards ahead of the swirl. After circling and again returning to the spot, nothing else was seen.

However, U-262 had been damaged, ending her first patrol, which had only begun from Bergen two days earlier. She later went on to complete nine war cruises and sink eight ships. In 1945, Heinz Franke was in command of U-2502.

22 October, 1942

U-412, a type VIIC submarine, commanded by Kapitänleutnant Walter Jahrmarker, sunk.

Wellington 'B' HX776, 179 Squadron, on patrol 1928–0525 hrs.

F/Sgt A.D.S. Martin	Sgt C.H. Bramwell
Sgt E. Widdows	Sgt A. Stabler
Sgt Kirkwood	Sgt R.W. Tozer

Flying north of the Shetlands, commenced a creeping line ahead search at 2155 hrs and an hour later obtained a radar contact at 5 miles on the port beam, but this was immediately lost. Continuing patrol, a further contact was made at 0106 hrs, again at 5 miles. Dived to low level, homed in and at 1½ miles the Leigh Light was switched on. Two minutes after the initial contact, a U-boat was illuminated, on the surface. The aircraft immediately attacked, dropping four D/Cs from 150 feet, which exploded, two each side of the target. A patch of oil and air bubbles were seen but nothing further.

U-412, on her first patrol, went down in position 6355/0024. She had left Kiel just five days earlier.

F/Sgt Arthur Desmond Stanley Martin received the DFM in 1943.

26 March, 1943

U-339, a type VIIC submarine, commanded by Kapitänleutnant Georg Wilhelm Basse, damaged.

Catalina 'M' FP125, 190 Squadron, on patrol 0027–1319 hrs.

PO J. Fish	Sgt D.A. Barfield
FO H.B. Cookson	Sgt E.L. Jones
Sgt W.A. Hughes	Sgt B.F. Taylor
Sgt A.J. Balderson	Sgt T.J. Burke
Sgt L.E. Croucher	

Airborne from Sullum Voe to fly a special ice reconnaissance. At 0641 hrs, sighted a surfaced U-boat at ¾ of a mile from 350 feet and attacked. Four D/Cs were released from 50 feet in the face of gunfire from the boat, fragments of 20mm shells hitting the aircraft. Turning for a second attack, two more D/Cs went down. Circling, some of the Cat crew saw an explosion just aft of the conning tower, a water spout reaching some 70 feet into the air. The boat then submerged, leaving an oil slick. A second swirl was also seen, believed to have been a second U-boat. The patrol was resumed and at 1159 hrs another surfaced boat was seen but this quickly dived.

U-339, that had left Bergen on 22 March for her second patrol, was badly damaged and had to put into Trondheim on the 28th. She later went to Kiel for major repairs and was then relegated to a training ship. Georg Basse went on to command U-314 and was lost with her on 30 January, 1944.

30 April, 1943

U-227, a type VIIC submarine, commanded by Kapitänleutnant Jurgen Kuntze, sunk.

Hampden 'X' AN149, 455 RAAF Squadron, on patrol 0751–1359 hrs.

F/Sgt J.S. Freeth, RAAF	Pilot
Sgt A.J. Wheatcroft	Nav
Sgt R.T. Patterson (Can)	WOP/AG
Sgt H.R.J. Downing (Can)	WOP/AG

Flying over a rough sea, a U-boat was sighted at 1½ miles at 0955 hrs in position 6405/0640. It began firing at the aircraft as it dived to attack. Six D/Cs were released from 50 feet, three of which exploded on the starboard side, three astern. The stern of the boat rose 10 feet out of the water and then began to list to port. The Hampden made a second attack, dropping the last two D/Cs from 50 feet, both straddling the bows. After the attacks the bows of the sub were seen to rise steeply out of the water and then sink back and then the boat slithered under. Oil was observed and then some 30 men. Some life jackets and a dinghy could also be seen. The Hampden only sustained six bullet holes.

U-227 had left Kiel for her first war patrol on 24 April. She had earlier been damaged when she hit an RAF-laid mine in Danzig Bay on 9 September, 1942, while on her acceptance trials.

Flight Sergeant Freeth had previously been with 144 Squadron. He was killed in a flying accident on 24 May, 1943 – the day after his 23rd birthday.

17 May, 1943

U-229, a type VIIC submarine, commanded by Oberleutnant Robert Schetelig, damaged.

Catalina 'E' FP215, 190 Squadron, on patrol 1132–0908 hrs.

F/L F.J. Gosling
WO N.J. Langdon
(the rest of the crew possibly made up by: FO D.J. Kirk, F/Sgt W.M. Marshall, F/Sgt L.W. Mann, Sgt F. Jenner, Sgt T.E. Ervine, Sgt A. Marshall)

Flying from Castle Archdale, picked up an S/E contact at 1916 hrs while above cloud. Coming down, sighted a surfaced U-boat from 1500 feet at 1½ miles. On the first run the pilot could not pull out of a steep turn in time to make a good attack so only attacked with machine guns. Another run was better, but the boat was beginning to go down. Four D/Cs were dropped, falling on the starboard side, and the explosions brought part of the boat to the surface again before it finally went down, leaving oil and bubbles.

U-229 had left St Nazaire on 11 May and returned damaged to Bordeaux on 7 June – ending her second patrol. She did not sail again until 31 August, and was sunk on 22 September by HMS *Keppel* escorting convoy ONS 18, south-east of Greenland.

22 December, 1943

U-1062, a type VIIF torpedo transporter submarine, commanded by Oberleutnant Karl Albrecht, damaged.

Beaufighters of 144 and 404 Squadrons.

144 Squadron on patrol 0933–1322 hrs.

F/L R.A. Johnson PO M.C. Potts	'A' LZ182	
F/Sgt P.G. Smith Sgt F.S. Holly	'C' LZ158	
FO S.R. Cooke Sgt J.E. Beaman	'B' LZ126	
FO N.T. Lawrence Sgt D.H. Hogg	'T' LZ180	
FO R.S. Cheshire FO W.B. Naples	'N' LZ216	
WO W.A. Baughman FO K.E.B. Wilks	'R' LZ222	

404 Squadron on patrol 0932–1325 hrs.

PO K.S. Miller PO J. Young	'R' NE198
F/L R. Munro FO W.B. Conn	'H' LZ452
FO I. Gillespie PO J.E. Glendinning	'F' NE323

Four torpedo-carrying Beaus and two anti-flak Beaus of 144 Squadron, with three more anti-flak Beaus of 404 Squadron were on a Rover patrol at 50 feet over a rough sea. At 1132 hrs, in position 5759/0652, they sighted a destroyer and a U-boat in line astern. Beaufighter 'B' made an attack on the sub, dropping his torpedo from 800 yards but due to the heavy seas, no result was observed. 'B' also fired 200 rounds of 20mm cannon, hitting the conning tower. Flak was experienced from the destroyer, the sub and also from the shore guns.

Aircraft 'R'/144 also attacked with 'H' of 404 Squadron, with cannon, but 'H' was hit and dived straight into the sea. R/404, in company with F/404 and N/144, also dived into the attack, firing cannon from 700 yards. Shells seen striking the conning tower, and the aircraft turned to make a second run. More hits were scored, but F/404 was hit and also seen to plunge into the sea.

U-1062 was being used as a blockade runner, having left Kiel on 18 December. Badly damaged and with crew casualties, she put into Bergen on the 23rd. In the first half of 1944 she made three cargo trips, two to Penang and one to Norway, but was sunk on 30 September, 1944, by an American destroyer south-west of Cape Verde Island.

Miller and Young of 404 Squadron were later awarded DFCs.

25 February, 1944

U-601, a type VIIC submarine, commanded by Oberleutnant Otto Hansen, sunk.

Catalina 'M', 210 Squadron, on patrol 2355–1555 hrs.

SL F.J. French	Pilot
F/Sgt G.A. Stewart	2nd pilot
FO A.H. Jackson, RCAF	Nav
FO C.B. Schmuck, RCAF	2 Nav
PO H.L. McGuinty, RCAF	Eng
F/Sgt D.H. Dawson	FME
FO J. Farmer	1 WOP
WO F.W. Hammett	2 WOP
Sgt T. Toner	WOM/AG
Sgt D. Brown	Rigger

Flying to escort convoy JW 57, they failed to make contact. At 0920 hrs an S/E contact was made at 24 miles, when in position 7035/1133. Five minutes later the captain sighted a U-boat with decks awash at 4 miles, position 7026/1240. Cannon and machine gun fire met the Catalina from 1½ miles, but it proved inaccurate. The Catalina attacked from the boat's stern starboard quarter, with two D/Cs. As they circled, wreckage was seen and 8 to 10 survivors in the water. At 1030 hrs all contact was lost in a snow storm.

U-601 had made one patrol from Bergen in April 1943, putting into Narvik on 15 May, under KvtLt Grau.

Frank John French received the DFC.

24 April, 1944

U-672, a type VIIC submarine, commanded by Oberleutnant Ulf Lawaetz, damaged.

Sunderland 'A' DD862, 423 RCAF Squadron, on patrol 0708–1832 hrs.

F/L F.G. Fellows	Sgt E.G. Dyer
FO R.G. Scott	Sgt R. Guiver
FO H. Niblett	Sgt T.H. Edwards
FO H.M. Calvert	Sgt R. Oliver
WO J. Carslake	Sgt G. Stevenson
WO S. Cowan	

This U-boat was first spotted by Liberator 'M' of 120 Squadron at 0100 hrs on the morning of the 24th, in position 5144/1953. F/L L.T. Taylor had homed in, switching on the Leigh Light at one mile which picked out the sub. Taylor attacked from 150 feet with six D/Cs but without visible results.

The U-boat was sighted again at 1339 hrs, 16 miles dead ahead, in position 5040/1840, by the Sunderland crew. They closed in and the U-boat remained on the surface and began firing when the Sunderland was 5 miles off and down to 1800 feet. The U-boat was keeping its stern towards the aircraft and Fellows tried to keep the sun behind him as he came in at 50 feet, to let go six D/Cs, while his gunners raked the boat as they flew over. One D/C appeared to explode prematurely or on contact, the explosion damaging the Sunderland as it went over. The rear gunner was knocked out and his turret damaged. The aircraft's electrics were damaged and the rear-facing camera leads blown out. The whole airframe was twisted and the elevator control damaged. Fellows rightly decided to fly home, which he did successfully. The U-boat was seen to be lifted out of the water, but then it disappeared.

It was initially thought after the war that this attack had sunk U-311 (KvtLt Joachim Zander), but it is now understood to have been on U-672, which was extensively damaged.

U-672 was on her second patrol into the North Atlantic, having sailed from St Nazaire on 24 February. On her return journey she had laid Thetis buoys. Fitted with Schnorkel, she sailed on 28 June, 1944, but had to return with a defect before sailing again on 6 July. She was sunk on 19 July by the frigate *Balfour*, survivors, including Lawaetz, being rescued by Air Sea Rescue launch.

16 May, 1944

U-240, a type VIIC submarine, commanded by Oberleutnant Gunther Link, sunk.

Sunderland 'V' JM667, 330 Norwegian Squadron, on patrol 1327–1918 hrs.

S/Lt C.T. Johnsen	Pilot
S/Lt F. Meyer	2nd pilot
S/Lt F. Buck	3rd pilot
S/Lt E.S. Pedersen	Nav
QM N. Borresen	Eng
QM J.E. Johnsen	WOP/AG
QM K.I. Halvorsen	FME/AG
QM A.J. Johansen	FMAS/AG
QM L. Faberg	WOM
QM D.J. Brannvoll	AG
QM K. Naevdahl	WOP/AG

At 1720 hrs, in position 6310/0310, a surfaced U-boat was seen at 3 miles. In the first attack, none of the D/Cs released, but the front and rear gunners fired into the target. The aircraft was hit by flak in many places, but several of the German gunners were seen to be hit. During the second run the flak was not so heavy, but the Sunderland was still hit again and the front gunner, Alf Johansen, was killed and Kristian Halvorsen and Ferdinand Buck were both wounded. The first pilot was temporarily blinded by smoke caused when the cockpit was hit, plus flames from the front turret. He pressed home the attack, however, the released four D/Cs from 50 feet, three of which seemed to explode close to the sub's port side. The boat's bows rose up at a sharp angle, then went down, as the whole craft submerged stern first. With the Sunderland's two starboard engines having also been damaged the pilot had to leave the scene and return to base. At 1750 hrs one of the starboard engines cut and the aircraft vibrated violently. An SOS was sent and 1050 gallons of fuel were jettisoned. At 1805 hrs the SOS was cancelled as aircraft began to gain height. They landed back at Sullom Voe safely despite the damage and the hull having been shot up.

U-240 went on its first cruise in March 1944 and was in Kristiansund at the beginning of April. Joined the Arctic Flotilla on 11 May and moved to Bergen on the 13th. Sailed for Narvik on the 14th, meeting 330 Squadron two days later.

Fredrik Meyer later wrote a history of the Norwegian Air Force during World War II.

17 May, 1944

U-668, a type VIIC submarine, commanded by Kapitänleutnant Wolfgang von Eickstedt, damaged.

Catalina 'C' JV933, 333 Norwegian Squadron, on patrol 1142–0530 hrs.

S/Lt H.E. Hartmann	Pilot
Pty/O J.H. Frogner	2nd pilot
Pty/O F.C. Christiansen	Eng
Pty/O E.M. Marcussen	Obs (Nav)
Pty/O O.W. Hofsrud	WOP/AG
Pty/O L. Sjonnesen	WOP/AG
Pty/O H.N. Stein	WOM/AG
Pty/O O. K-Berg	FME/AG
Pty/O H. Lochting	FMA/AG

At 1840 hrs proceeded to search for a submarine reported by aircraft 'V' of 330 Squadron in position 6305/0310. Finally, after several search patterns, saw two U-boats at 2221 hrs and attacked. The Catalina was seriously damaged by flak, and the starboard blister gunner, Petty Officer Kyrre-Berg, was killed when a shell exploded between the navigator's and the engineer's compartments. In the attack the sub was thought also to be damaged and some of the crew saw an explosion in the conning tower ten minutes after the attack. The pilot, Harold Hartmann, returned to base, where he made a successful landing despite the damage to the aircraft.

U-668 joined the Arctic Flotilla on 11 May, 1944, and while moving to Bergen was damaged by 333 Squadron. It later began its first patrol from Narvik. It made other cruises under Captain Henning and was in Trondheim at the end of the war.

18 May, 1944

U-241, a type VIIC submarine, commanded by Oberleutnant Arno Werr, sunk.

Catalina 'S', 210 Squadron, on patrol 0643–1155 hrs.

FO B. Bastable	Pilot
F/Sgt C.L. Sheppard	2nd pilot
FO R.T. Martin	Nav
F/Sgt D. McAdam	Eng
WO R. Henderson	WOP/AG
F/Sgt F. Chadbourne	WOM/AG
F/Sgt J.B. Underwood	WOP
F/Sgt W. Stuart	FME/AG
WO D.L. Snedden	WOP
F/Sgt T.E. Southern	FMA/AG

At 0940 hrs in position 6333/0146, sighted from 200 feet, 5–8 miles, a fully surfaced U-boat and attacked. Achieved a good straddle with six D/Cs, the centre of the stick going right across the boat's mid-ships. Afterwards a large oil patch could be seen, 200 x 50 yards. In an exchange of gunfire during the run-in, the front gunner of the Catalina hit the conning tower with a good burst of fire. The pilot saw one sailor fall into the water. The port blister gunner too joined in, firing 100 rounds of .5 ammunition. As the aircraft began to circle, the U-boat began to sink stern first at an angle of some 30 degrees and many survivors were seen in the water. The Catalina had some slight damage to its tailplane.

U-241 had moved from Kiel to Kristiansund in April and was in Bergen by 2 May, sailing on its first cruise on the 13th. It went down north-west of Standtlander, Norway.

Flying Officer Bastable and Warrant Officer Henderson, who had manned the front gun, both received immediate DFCs.

21 May, 1944

U-995, a type VIIC/41 submarine, commanded by Kapitänleutnant Walter Kohntopp, damaged.

Sunderland III 'S', No. 4(C) OTU, on patrol 0550–1814 hrs.

PO E.T. King	Pilot
FO S. Pearce	Nav
WC A. Whittome	Passenger
(rest of crew not known)	

Flying at 2000 feet over a moderate to rough sea, with a heavy swell, the RAF crew saw a black object, which became a surfacing U-boat, distance 2–3 miles, in position 6355/0224. The time was 1248 hrs and an attack was made immediately, six D/Cs falling from 50 feet. The explosions completely enveloped the sub and it appeared to sink very fast on an even keel with no forward movement, leaving a greenish oil patch on the surface.

U-995 had left Bergen on 18 May and was damaged in this attack just three days later. It did not sail again until 4 July when it made its first Atlantic patrol from Narvik. It was to make at least five cruises and was in Trondheim at the end of the war.

No. 4 Coastal Operational Training Unit flew

operational sorties in support of normal Coastal operations, a trainee crew generally under the experienced eye of a former operational pilot who was now instructing. King and crew were later posted to 490 Squadron.

24 May, 1944

U-476, a type VIIC submarine, commanded by Oberleutnant Otto Niethmann, sunk.

Catalina 'V', 210 Squadron, on patrol 2345–1240 hrs.

Capt F.W.L. Maxwell, SAAF	Pilot
FO J.A. Wickson	2nd pilot
FO A.H. Jackson	Nav
PO K. Fraser	Eng
F/Sgt R. LeCheminant	WOP
PO E. Coulson-Smith	WOP
PO E.H. O'Toole	WOM/AG
F/Sgt L. Conway	Rigger
Sgt F.G. Williams	FME
Sgt E.H. Shrubsole	AG(spare)

At 0716 hrs, in position 6503/0459, sighted a fully surfaced U-boat at 5 miles. As aircraft closed in it was met by a heavy flak barrage, but the D/Cs went down, No. 6 falling very close alongside. The boat was seen to spin round, almost 360 degrees, stop and then sink, with its bows right out of the water. Just as it disappeared, it came to the surface again as if its tanks had been blown. The bows, foredeck and conning tower were all out of the water, but then the boat once again sank, stern first, taking nearly 10 minutes to do so. The scene was then covered by a snow squall.

U-476 had just joined the Arctic Flotilla and had left Bergen for Narvik four days earlier. It was so severely damaged in this attack that it foundered, 21 of her crew being rescued by U-990, which was herself sunk on the 25th (see 15 Group).

Captain Maxwell and his crew were posted to 202 Squadron at Gibraltar on 3 August, 1944.

24 May, 1944

U-921, a type VIIC submarine, commanded by Oberleutnant Alfred Werner, damaged.

Sunderland 'S' DW111, 423 RCAF Squadron, on patrol 0330–1648 hrs.

F/L R.H. Nesbitt	Sgt J. Gingrich
FO R.J. McManamy	Sgt E.G. Knibbs
FO G.W. Caldwell	Sgt C. Ramsden
FO T.R. Howe	Sgt V.E. Tilley
PO G.F. Tomlinson	Sgt P. Woollatt

At 0850 hrs instructed to home on to the Catalina of 210 Squadron which had just attacked (and sunk) U-476 (see previous entry). The Catalina was sighted at 1000 hrs and then began a routine patrol of the area. At 1419 hrs an SOS message was picked up and a moment later the second pilot sighted what he took to be a large puff of smoke or splash, 10–15 miles to the north. Aircraft investigated and the front gunner spotted a wake of a U-boat. Closing to attack, letting down from 2000 feet, they flew by some wreckage. The U-boat now opened fire and taking evasive action, Nesbitt carried out an attack, dropping five D/Cs (the sixth failing to release). About 1½ minutes later the boat began to submerge and nothing else was seen. After circling for some time, the aircraft inspected the earlier wreckage, which appeared to be from an aeroplane.

U-921 had joined the Arctic Flotilla on 21 May and was on her way from Kristiansund to Trondheim when attacked and damaged. Several of her crew were injured. She did not make her first war patrol until 2 July, from Narvik, and was sunk on her third, on 30 September, by a FAA Swordfish of 813 Squadron from the escort carrier *Campania*.

24 May, 1944

U-675, a type VIIC submarine, commanded by Oberleutnant Karl-Heinz Sammler, sunk.

Sunderland 'R' ML736, No. 4(C) OTU, on patrol 0739–1708 hrs.

FO T.F.P. Frizell, RAAF	Captain.
WO Macdonald (NZ)	1st pilot
FO M. Angelo (NZ)	Nav
and crew	

Sighted a fully surfaced U-boat at 5 miles in position 6227/0304 at 1349 hrs. Aircraft circled to allow time for the starboard bomb carrier to be wound out by hand. U-boat opened fire with 20mm cannon, but it was out of range. When ready, the Sunderland attacked, and the U-boat opened fire with a large gun from the conning tower. Frizell began an approach, undulating by as much as 300 feet, and his aircraft was not hit. The shells were falling below the aircraft, for as he saw the gun fire, so Frizell pulled up each time. Coming in with the sun behind him, six D/Cs were released – but one failed to fall – from around 20 feet! The No. 4 D/C actually landed on the deck of the sub, forward of the conning tower, rolling off into the water. After the explosions, the bows lifted into the air until they were almost vertical. As it began to sink an explosion occurred in the boat and it disappeared from view. Mushrooms of air bubbles came to the surface, followed by wreckage of oil drums, planking and bodies. The Sunderland's port outer engine was now giving trouble, so Frizell decided to return to base. Peter Frizell remembers: 'It was the old "Empire Day" when I was sent out to patrol off the coast of Norway with a trainee crew. The position arose because of the shortage of squadron aircraft, which were mostly engaged in pre-D-Day ops. For most of the war there had been a Totally Restricted Bombing Area off the Norwegian coast, as our own submarines were always likely to be operating there. A day or so before, this had been lifted, and the area covered as much as possible by our own aircraft, hoping to catch the Germans unawares. They had, of course, been fully aware that they would not be attacked there. The ruse was successful, as others as well as myself were successful in attacking U-boats in the next week or so.

'It was quite a pleasant day, with broken overcast, and we were happily flying along just within sight of the coast when one of the gunners called a sighting of a ship not far away. On turning, I could see that it was a U-boat, fully surfaced, and of course dived for it, "hell-for-leather", hopping into the captain's seat, which had been occupied by the trainee captain. Despite the fact that we had been warned some time before that submarines, newly equipped with extra guns, might stay up and fight, I could hardly believe this would happen.

'I went in for a quarter attack, which we had practised *ad nauseam* in training with a towed target, only to find that the U-boat could turn inside us easily. During the run-in, the bomb-bay called up to say that the bomb racks would not extend electrically, and would have to be wound out by hand. As this takes some time, I had to abort the attack, in the process coming under fire from cannon and the 5 in. gun. I then circled as close as possible, and called for the rear gunner and others to announce the instant they could see a flash from the 5 in. gun. I figured that light travels much faster than a shell, and thus climbed, dived or turned each time he fired, and managed not to be there when a shell arrived! At the same time the front gunner announced a jam, which he eventually cleared.

'I was worried that the thing would crash-dive after the first abort, but he stayed on the surface. As soon as the green lights came on for the correct extension of the bomb racks, we made another run, but again he put me in an unfavourable position to attack and we broke off to try again. I had always sworn that I would not waste precious depth charges on a bad approach. Next time we managed to out-guess him and finished up in a perfect quarter attack position. The D/Cs all released properly and we continued on past the target without turning, to allow the rear-facing camera to operate. Next thing I heard was a yell from the rear gunner, which I interpreted as one of distress, and thought we must have missed. However, the yell turned out to be one of jubilation, and on turning, we could see what is evident from the subsequent photos.

'We had flown through quite a lot of flak, but no one seemed to be hurt. As we approached again, the U-boat went into a vertical dive, stern first and blew up. We flew around for some time, taking hand-held photos of the wreckage and bodies, etc., and when there seemed little point in remaining, set course for base. I feared that we would soon be chased by fighters, as we had sent out a sighting report, as, no doubt, had the U-boat.

'We seemed unharmed, except for a fuel pressure warning light. We inspected the underfloor area on the way home, but no holes were evident. At the time, I remember, I was more upset at returning in some sort of triumph from that trip, to see most of my original crew, with whom I had flown a full tour, sitting around in the Messes, looking most disconsolate. They had been with me for so long out over the Atlantic and the Bay, and had never had a success, and on this day had not been with me. Such is Fate!'

U-675 was on its first patrol, having sailed from Kristiansund on 18 May, heading for the North Atlantic.

Flying Officer Peter Frizell was an instructor at the OTU, having recently completed a tour of operations with 423 RCAF Squadron. An Australian, he received the DFC for his attack, and in June was promoted to flight lieutenant. MacDonald and crew were later sent to 490 Squadron.

26 May, 1944

U-958, a type VIIC submarine, commanded by Kapitänleutnant Gerhard Groth, damaged.

Mosquito 'N' HR262

Lt J.M. Jacobsen	Pilot
S/Lt L. Humlen	Nav

Mosquito 'E' HP904

Lt H. Engebrigtsen	Pilot
Lt O.G. Jonassen	Nav

333 Norwegian Squadron, on patrol 0815–1215 hrs.

Airborne from Leuchars but slightly delayed as 'E' had one engine overheat, so had to delay till around 0830 hrs. An hour later a surfaced U-boat was spotted in position 6135/0328 and attacked with cannon fire from 500 feet, the sub putting up defensive fire. Strikes were seen all over the U-boat, 'N' tracking over the target from stern to bow while 'E' flew in from its starboard beam. Before a second attack could be made, the sub crash-dived.

U-958 had left Bergen the previous day for her first patrol and had to return because of damage and casualties. She sailed on patrol in June and was then withdrawn from operational duties in July.

Hans Engebrigtsen and Odd Jonassen were accidentally shot down by RAF Spitfires on 11 June, 1944. They came down in the sea, the injured pilot being rescued, but Jonassen was lost. Jacobsen and Humlen were to have further success against U-boats in June (see later).

3 June, 1944

U-477, a type VIIC submarine, commanded by Oberleutnant Karl Joachim Jenssen, sunk

Canso 'T' (A) 9816, 162 RCAF Squadron, on patrol 1745–1010 hrs.

F/L R.E. MacBride	Pilot
FO J.K. Guttormson	2nd pilot
FO W.C. Lawrence	Nav
Sgt C.G. White	Eng
Sgt T.C. Harper	2 Eng
PO D.G. MacDonald	WOP/AG
F/Sgt G.W. King	WOP/AG
PO G.P. McNulty	WOP/AG

Flying from Wick, found and attacked a U-boat at 0211 hrs, dropping four D/Cs from 60 feet. The D/Cs straddled the boat, which was enveloped in explosions, and appeared to be lifted bodily out of the water, losing forward movement as it swung to port. When the explosions cleared, the boat submerged on an even keel, but five survivors were seen in the water and an oil patch developed covering an area of one mile by 400 yards. The total patrol time covered 16 hours 25 minutes.

U-477 was on her first war cruise, having sailed from Kristiansund on 28 May. A schnorkel boat, she sank in position 6359/0137, off the Norwegian coast.

Flight Lieutenant MacBride received the DFC in August, while later in the year, Flying Officer Gordon Patrick McNulty also received the DFC.

11 June, 1944

U-980, a type VIIC submarine, commanded by Kapitänleutnant Hermann Dahms, sunk.

Canso 'B' 9842, 162 RCAF Squadron.

FO L. Sherman	Pilot
FO G.W. Besley	2nd pilot
FO J.L. Harrison	Nav
F/Sgt F.R. Dreger	Eng
Sgt J.E. Roberts	2 Eng
F/Sgt M.A. Gislason	WOP/AG
FO R.R. Ward	WOP/AG
FO F.W. Lawrence	WOP/AG

At 1515 hrs a U-boat was sighted on the surface and was immediately attacked, the aircraft losing height from 1000 feet. The front and starboard blister gunners began firing at 800 yards, while the boat too began firing, keeping its stern to the incoming Catalina. Four D/Cs went down from 50 feet, one falling midway between the bow and conning tower. As the plumes subsided, a trail of oil was being left by the boat. A gun duel then ensued between boat and aircraft, but the boat was now much lower in the water and it sank at 1532 hrs, leaving wreckage and about 35 men in the water.

U-980 had been on her first patrol, having left Bergen on 3 June. She went down in position 6307/0026, north of the Shetlands.

The very next day this crew took off from Wick in this same aircraft, at 2200 hrs. It flew to an area in the vicinity of 6330/0000. At 0120 hrs on the morning of the 13th, a flash report was received, stating that they had sighted a German sub in position 6410/0011. After this nothing else was heard and it must be assumed they were shot down during the subsequent attack. Laurance Sherman's immediate DFC was Gazetted in July.

13 June, 1944

U-715, a type VIIC submarine, commanded by Kapitänleutnant Helmut Rottger, sunk.

Canso 'T' A 9816, 162 RCAF Squadron.

WC C.StG.W. Chapman	Pilot
FO J.M. McRae	2nd pilot
FO D.J.C. Waterbury	Nav
F/Sgt H.C. Leatherdale	Eng
Sgt R.F. Cromarty	2 Eng
WO J.J.C. Bergevin	WOP/AG
F/Sgt G.F. Staples	WOP/AG
WO F.K. Reed	WOP/AG

At 1012 hrs two periscope feathers were seen from 2000 feet, 3 miles off. Aircraft closed and attacked from 50 feet. The U-boat surfaced and began turning to starboard while the aircraft circled a couple of miles away. The boat remained only half-surfaced and still turning and then began to settle by the bows, then the stern went steeply into the air, its screws not turning, and several men were seen in the water. The aircraft began to fly over the sub to take pictures and the captain saw a German run to man the guns. The aircraft jinked as the gun fired, but an explosion was heard in the aircraft and the port engine began to leak oil, leaving a trail of smoke. The engine was shut down, but it would not feather, and fuel could not be jettisoned due to the risk of fire. The aircraft lost height and finally hit the waves at 45 knots. The hull had two or three large holes in it and the flying boat sank within 15–20 seconds. All the crew safely boarded the dinghies, but one exploded while the other had two holes in it. They decided to have two men in the damaged one at a time while the rest stayed in the water, and they would change over frequently but as time went on this became impossible. A Liberator appeared, but flew away, and later a Warwick flew over and dropped a lifeboat, which fell about 150 yards away. Flying Officer Waterbury stripped down to his Mae West and swam for it, but it took him an hour of hard endeavour to bring it back. Meanwhile, Flight Sergeant Leatherdale, who was being held up, lost his grip and was lost. The seven others got into the lifeboat which had been damaged and was half under water. Another Warwick arrived and dropped a Lindholme dinghy, but when trying to pull one of the weaker men in, a hole was torn in it. The lifeboat's sail was raised with difficulty and the crew tried to reach a second Lindholme dinghy, but it drifted away. Reed and Staples were now in a bad way and everything possible was done for them. They were all sitting up to their armpits in water and these two had to have their heads supported above the water. Finally an Air Sea Rescue launch arrived and took all the men on board, but Reed and Staples died.

U-715 was on her first patrol. A schnorkel boat, she had sailed from Stavanger on 8 June, and went down in position 6245/0259, north-east of the Faeroes.

Wing Commander Cecil St George William Chapman, the squadron commander, received an immediate DSO, and all the other surviving members of the crew received DFCs and the DFM. The Canso had been the same aircraft flown by MacBride in the sinking of U-477, ten days earlier.

14 June, 1944

U-290, a type VIIC submarine, commanded by Oberleutnant Helmut Herglotz, damaged.

Mosquito 'H' HP864, 333 Norwegian Squadron, on patrol 1355–1610 hours.

Lt E.U. Johansen	Pilot
2/Lt L. Humlen	Navigator

This crew sighted the submarine at 1500 hrs in position 6106/0325 and positioned themselves for an attack, which commenced 15 minutes later. The sub was turning to port and firing from the conning tower, keeping its beam to the aircraft, but finally Johansen made his approach from the stern, firing from 1200 yards, which silenced the German gunfire. One D/C was dropped, which exploded alongside the bows, which were thrown up as it continued to turn to port. The U-boat then dived, leaving some oil and a couple of bodies on the surface.

U-290 was on her first patrol, sailing from Egersund on 1 June, returning damaged on the 16th. She did not sail again until August, when she moved into the Baltic.

Lauritz Humlen had been involved in the attack on U-958 on 26 May, so this was his second success. Both he and Erling Johansen would have further success, two days later.

16 June, 1944

U-998, a type VIIC/41 submarine, commanded by Kapitänleutnant Hans Fiedler, damaged (but lost to the German Navy).

Mosquito 'H' HP864, 333 Norwegian Squadron, on patrol 1815–2030 hrs.

Lt E.U. Johansen	Pilot
2/Lt L. Humlen	Navigator

Three Mosquito aircraft of the squadron were sent out at two-hourly intervals to search for German submarines. They sighted a U-boat at 1904 hrs, on the surface, in position 6101/0300, 8 miles away. Johansen immediately lifted into cloud and six minutes later broke out to attack, when the boat was 2 miles on the port bow. Cannon fire scored strikes on the conning tower and the two D/Cs went down from 100 feet. The boat was seen to rock and start a small circle, leaking oil, which spread to 3000 yards, with dark objects in it – thought to be bodies. The boat continued to zigzag, then submerged leaving wooden wreckage. Then the bows came up and the aircraft fired again, and a few minutes later they disappeared backwards, the boat seeming to be on its side. The Mosquito was slightly damaged by return fire, and when circling the area, seagulls were seen over the oil patch.

It was thought U-998 had gone to the bottom, but she limped into Bergen on the 17th, having sailed on this her first patrol, from Kiel, on the 12th. The boat was so badly damaged that she was paid off on 27 June, so in effect, 333 Squadron can claim a kill. Hans Fiedler had previously commanded U-564.

16 June, 1944

U-804, a type IXC/40 submarine, commanded by Oberleutnant Herbert Meyer, damaged.

Mosquito 'R' HP860, 333 Norwegian Squadron, on patrol 2209 hrs.

Lt J.M. Jacobsen	Pilot
2/Lt P.C. Hansen	Navigator

This was the third Mosquito to fly this evening, searching the area 6163/0304. A corrupted radio message was received at base at 2259 hrs that the Mosquito was either attacking or being attacked, but the crew failed to return. In actual fact the aircraft was attacking a U-boat which it sighted, but return fire hit the Mosquito's port engine and split open the wing. Jacobsen had no choice but to crash land on to the sea, where he and Per Hansen got into their dinghy. They spent 30 hours in the dinghy until, amazingly, they were rescued by another U-boat and taken to Bergen and into captivity. They were released by American troops in April 1945.

U-804 was informed that U-998 had been attacked and damaged, and went to investigate. The U-boat reported seeing a twin-engined aircraft which fired off the correct colours of the day when the boat began firing at it. The U-boat ceased fire, but then the aircraft dived to attack, cannon and machine-gun fire hitting the conning tower, seriously wounding three men and slightly wounding five others. Due to the casualties, the captain had to abort and put into Bergen. Three days later she sailed for Farsund, where she was to have a schnorkel fitted. U-804 was sunk on 9 April, 1945, on passage to Herton, by a Mosquito Strike Wing.

Lieutenant Jacob Jacobsen had damaged U-958 on 26 May, 1944.

17 June, 1944

U-423, a type VIIC submarine, commanded by Oberleutnant Klaus Hacklander, sunk.

Catalina 'D' FP183, 333 Norwegian Squadron, on patrol 1320–1850 hrs.

Lt C.F. Krafft	Pilot
Lt K.J. Garstad	2nd pilot
P/Off K.K. Gilje	3rd pilot
2/Lt K.J. Johnansen	Nav
P/Off T.F. Johannessen	Eng
P/Off K.K. Svendsen	WOP/AG
P/Off A.M. Fritzvold	WOM/AG
P/Off A.L. Bjerkset	WOP/AG
P/Off E. Vetvik	FME/AG
P/Off R.K. Hauge	FMA/AG

Sighted a surfaced U-boat at 1643 hrs in position 6306/0202 and attacked with six D/Cs. The boat opened fire during the approach but the aircraft was not hit. The boat was straddled, with three D/Cs either side, Nos. 3 and 4 falling close against the vessel. It sank 6 minutes later, leaving 40 survivors, wreckage and oil on the surface.

U-423, a schnorkel boat, was on her first war patrol, having left Kiel on 9 June, and went down

15 Group

Flying Officer William Roxburgh, DFC, of 206 Squadron, who sank U-489 on 25 March, 1943, flying a Fortress aircraft. (IWM)

Flight Lieutenant Douglas Gall, of 201 Squadron, sank U-440. (D.M. Gall)

Wing Commander R.B. Thomson, DSO, DFC, of 206 Squadron. He sank U-417 on 11 June, 1943, but then he and his Fortress crew were in turn shot down by the U-boat and spent three days in their dinghy before being rescued. (IWM)

Flying Officer Al Bishop, DFC, 423 RCAF Squadron. Shot down in the act of sinking U-489 on 4 August, 1943, he and five survivors of his 11-man crew were rescued by a destroyer. (A.A. Bishop)

U-643, crippled by attacks from Z/68 and T/120 Squadrons, later blew up and sank, 21 survivors being picked up by HM ships. (J. Luker)

Seated in front of a 120 Squadron Liberator are Flying Officer Denis Webber and his crew, who helped sink U-643 on 8 October, 1943. Front row, l to r: Sgt J.G. Jeans, PO H.L. Matthews, FO D.C.L. Webber, FS J. Luker; back row: FO Barker (not present during the attack), Sgt A.J. Allan, F/Sgt H. Lea, Sgt J. Bradley. (J. Luker)

Wing Commander B.E. Peck, DFC, shared in the destruction of U-470 on 16 October, 1943, when a flight lieutenant with 120 squadron. (B.E. Peck)

Flight Lieutenant Paul Sargent, RCAF, 422 Squadron, drowned when he went down with his Sunderland after damaging a U-boat on 17 October, 1943, and had to crash land on the sea. (RCAF)

Sergeant Max Painter, 612 Squadron. On 10 February, 1944, he damaged U-545 so badly she had to be scuttled when returning from her first war patrol. An Australian, he was later commissioned and received the DFC.

Sunderland EK591 'U' of 422 RCAF Squadron at anchor at Castle Archdale in 1944. On 10 March, 1944, she sank U-625 when being flown by Flight Lieutenant S.W. Butler, RAF, who received the DFC. (Public Archives of Canada)

Flying Officer P.W. Heron, DFC, 407 RCAF Squadron, who sank U-283 on 11 February, 1944. (RCAF)

U-625 under attack by Flight Lieutenant Sidney Butler, 422 RCAF Squadron, west of the mouth of the River Shannon. There were no survivors. (IWM)

18 Group

Flying Officer Peter Frizzle, RAAF. While instructing a new crew at No. 4 Coastal OTU he attacked and sank U-675 on 24 May, 1944. Having already completed a tour with 423 RCAF Squadron, he later received the DFC. (T.F.P. Frizzle)

U-675 under attack by Peter Frizzle in a Sunderland of 4 OTU, north-west of Stadlandet, Norway. (T.F.P. Frizzle)

David Hornell and some of his 162 Squadron crew. Front, l to r: Sgt F. St Laurent, Sgt D.S. Scott, FO G. Campbell, F/Sgt I.J. Bodnoff. Rear: FO F.W Lawrence, FO S.E. Matheson, F/L D.E. Hornell, SL W.F. Poag. (Poag and Lawrence were not involved in the final mission). Hornell sank U-1225 on 24 June, 1944, but was shot down in the attack. Scott and St Laurent died and Hornell died later, but for his courage he received a posthumous Victoria Cross. (Public Archives of Canada)

David Hornell's flying boat in which he won the VC, Canso 9754, 162 RCAF Squadron. (via R.C. Bowyer)

Wing Commander C.StG.W. Chapman, CO of 162 RCAF Squadron. He sank U-175 on 13 June, 1944, but not before the boat's gunners brought him and his Catalina down. Three of his crew died, but he and the others were later rescued, Chapman being awarded an immediate DSO. (RCAF)

Flight Lieutenant Geoffrey Parker, DFC, 86 Squadron, who sank U-317 off Norway, 26 June, 1944. (via Mrs Jean Parker)

U-317's last moments beneath Parker's Liberator. (via Mrs Jean Parker)

Flying Officer Syd Norris, 86 Squadron and co-pilot to Geoff Parker. (S. Norris)

U-317 with D/Cs overshooting in the first attack and the boat blowing up after the second. (S. Norris)

Geoff Parker and some of his crew, l to r: Nip Hogan, WOP/AG; Des Carter, DFM, 2nd Nav; Geoff Parker; Tom Garrett, WOP/AG; Taffy Jones, Nav. (S. Norris)

John Downey and crew, 244 Squadron. They attacked and damaged U-763 on 24 September, 1943. Downey, with another crew, sank U-2365 on 5 May, 1945. Rear: Bob Lowe, L.G. Hall (?), John Downey, H. Sutton, Mike Kowalchuk. Front: R.H. Griffin (?), Vic Acourt, R.A. Ranson (?), Bert Butler. (J.C.T. Downey)

John Cruickshank won the second anti-U-boat VC for an attack on U-347 on 17 July, 1944. The boat was sunk and Cruickshank badly wounded, but he retook the controls and helped land the Catalina when they returned to base at Sullom Voe. Rear row, l to r: Sgt Stockton, FO J. Coulson, FO J.A. Cruickshank, FO J.C. Dickson, Sgt F.J. Appleton. Front: Sgt S.B. Harbison, Sgt Westby, Sgt Wallis, F/Sgt J. Smith, Sgt C.J. Webber. Only Dickson, Appleton and Harbison were with him on the VC action, although the others were all with him when he attacked and damaged U-267 on 7 July, 1943. (F.J. Appleton)

Flight Lieutenant J.H. Jamieson and Flying Officer N. Earnshaw of 248 Squadron, with their Mosquito. Earnshaw, flying a Whitley, had helped damage U-415 in 1943 (612 Sqn), and as part of the Banff Strike Wing helped to sink U-251 on 19 April, 1945. (N. Earnshaw)

Mosquito RS625 NE-D on 143 Squadron. Flown by S/Ldr D.C. Pritchard and F/L W. Bower on 9 April, 1945, they had helped sink U-804. (DeHavilland)

Wing Commander M.A. Ensor, DSO, DFC, 244 Squadron. He sank U-579 on 5 May, 1945. In November 1942, flying with 500 Squadron, he had sunk U-259, although his Hudson was so badly damaged he and his crew were forced to bale out. (M.A. Ensor)

U-804 under attack by Mosquito aircraft of the Banff Wing, 6 April, 1944. (ACM Sir C. Foxley-Norris, via R.C. Bowyer)

Art Bruneau and his crew, 547 Squadron, 1945, involved in the battles over the Kattegat in May 1945. Front row, l to r: FO M.J. Lee, FO A.A. Bruneau, WO E.J. Moody, FO F. Bell. Rear: FO C. Hodgson. PO M.M. Stewart, F/Sgt G. Mooney, FO R. Fallon, FO G.R. Maxwell. Bob Fallon had earlier flown a tour with 120 Squadron and been involved in the sinking of U-279 in October 1943. (Via R. Fallon)

north-west of Stadtlandet.

A week later, Carl Fredrik Krafft and FP183 would be involved in a famous rescue.

20 June, 1944

U-743, a type VIIC submarine, commanded by Oberleutnant Helmut Kandzior, damaged

Liberator 'K' FK231, 86 Squadron, on patrol 1121–0010 hrs.

FO E.D. Moffit (Aust)	Pilot
PO S.W. Whitby (Aust)	2nd pilot
FO H. Pearson	1 Nav
Sgt K. Richardson (Aust)	2 Nav
Sgt J. Moffat	Eng
F/Sgt D. O'Beirne	AG
Sgt L.H. Mason (Aust)	WOP/AG
Sgt J.G. Williams (Aust)	WOP/AG

At 1855 hrs in position 61 North by 25 East, Moffit sighted the wake of a surfaced U-boat. This was confirmed through binoculars and an attack carried out, but the six D/Cs overshot, as when the aircraft was committed, the sub took sharp evasive action. On a second attack the boat again took similar action and no D/Cs were dropped. On the third run in, two D/Cs straddled. The U-boat now seemed in trouble as the Lib circled, but then the boat went down. During these attacks, gunners from the boat and the aircraft kept up a gun duel and hits were made on the conning tower, and sustained in the tailplane and fuselage of the aircraft. The hydraulics were also hit, but Moffit landed safely at base.

U-743 was on her first patrol, sailing from Kiel on 15 June. A schnorkel boat, it was damaged in this attack and had to put into Bergen the following day. It did not sail again until 18 August, when it sailed to Trondheim, then left for the North Channel on the 21st. She was sunk on 9 September by a corvette and a frigate, escorting convoy ONF 252, in position 5545/1141.

Flying Officer Moffit and his crew took off in Liberator FL931 'M', at 0256 hrs on 26 June, 1944, and failed to return.

24 June, 1944.

U-1225, a type IXC/40 submarine, commanded by Oberleutnant Ernst Sauerberg, sunk.

Canso 'P' 9754, of 162 RCAF Squadron, on patrol from Wick 0930 hrs.

F/L D.E. Hornell	Pilot
FO B.C. Denomy	2nd pilot
FO S.E. Matheson	Nav
Sgt D.S. Scott	Eng
Sgt F. St Laurent	Eng
F/Sgt I.J. Bodnoff	WOP/AG
F/Sgt S.R. Cole	WOP/AG
FO G. Campbell	WOP/AG

At 1900 hrs, after nearly ten hours of patrol, Hornell was on his way home when a surfaced U-boat was seen 5 miles away, in position 6300/0050, north-west of the Shetlands, making a terrific wake. Closing in, flak was encountered, severe as the aircraft got close. The gunners in the Cat opened fire on the run-in, but one jammed, so only one gunner was able to fire. The aircraft was hit and the starboard engine began to stream oil, while a fire had started in the trailing edge of the wing. The aircraft was vibrating badly and at about 300 yards from the boat, the engine had to be feathered, and Hornell had great difficulty in controlling the machine. Nevertheless, four D/Cs went down from 50 feet which straddled the boat successfully. Struggling with the controls, both pilots got the Canso up to 250 feet, but the fire continued on the starboard wing, and it was soon realized that they would have to ditch. Both pilots got the flying boat to a stalled landing, bouncing twice. Flight Sergeant Cole, who was on the radio, had been flung out of his seat and stunned when the aircraft had first been hit by the flak. Campbell got back and continued to send SOS messages, but it was thought that the radio had been knocked out. After landing, the badly damaged Canso sank to wing level in 8 to 10 minutes, and had sunk totally in 20. No one had been injured in the ditching, but the crew had then to endure 21 hours in the sea. The eight men shared a four-man dinghy, and at first they took it in turns to sit in it while four men stayed in the water. Later they all tried to huddle in it, although Scott's legs trailed in the water. They were sighted, quite by chance, by a Catalina of 333 Norwegian Squadron (FP183 'D'). This was flown by Lt C.F. Krafft, who had sunk U-423 just a week earlier, in this same aircraft. His crew saw the signal flares while on a patrol, and then continued to circle the area until 1145 hrs – they had taken off at 1930 hrs the previous evening! The Norwegians also saw an oil patch about three miles away, as well as some 35–40 survivors, but these gradually disappeared as the day progressed. A Wellington arrived at 1100 hrs and dropped a lifeboat but the men in the dinghy were unable to reach it. Finally at 1500 hrs on the 25th, a High Speed Launch picked them up, guided by the flying boat, but two of the Canadian crew, Scott and St Laurent, had died in the sea and Hornell died some 20 minutes after rescue.

U-1225, a schnorkel boat on its first patrol, had left Kiel for the North Atlantic on 17 June.

For his gallant attack and his courage while in the dinghy, David Hornell, aged 34, was awarded a posthumous Victoria Cross. Bernard Denomy received the DSO, Ed Matheson and Graham Campbell the DFC, while DFMs went to Joe Bodnoff and Syd Cole.

26 June, 1944.

U-317, a type VIIC/41 submarine, commanded by Oberleutnant Peter Rahlff, sunk.

Liberator 'N' FL916, 86 Squadron, on patrol from Tain 2045 hrs.

F/L G.W.T. Parker	Pilot
F/Sgt S. Norris	2nd pilot
F/Sgt D. Jones	1 Nav
F/Sgt D. Carter (NZ)	2 Nav
Sgt B.J. Hunt	Eng
F/Sgt A H Hogan (Aust)	WOP/AG
F/Sgt M Garrett (Aust)	WOP/AG
Sgt A S Powell	WOM/AG
PO F S Hanlin	AG (Passenger)

Liberator 'N' had previously taken off at 0543 hrs, flown by Flight Lieutenant D. Gauntlett, but he had been forced to return an hour later due to a petrol leak from the starboard wing tank. Once repaired, Parker then took over this aircraft that evening. At 2320 hrs, on a 'Blue Peter' patrol, a U-boat was sighted 5 miles away in position 6203/0145. Parker made two attacks and on the second run, three D/Cs were dropped, which fell along the starboard side. The boat rolled over to port and began to sink. Bodies were seen to be floating in a large patch of oil. However, the Lib had been hit by the sub's gunfire, the No. 3 engine's oil and fuel tanks being holed. Parker headed for home, and being unable to get down at Tain due to mist landed safely at Stornoway. Syd Norris, the second pilot, recalls:

'Before taking off we were warned that the weather at Tain would probably prevent us returning there, so our later signal to fly to Stornoway was no surprise to us. Even at 2320 hrs it was very light when Des Carter and I sighted the U-boat and Geoff sounded the alarm. After that, all the hours of practice paid off; the bomb doors were opened, I wrote the "first sighter" message, and Taffy Jones armed the D/Cs. We sought the slight cloud cover and immediately we broke cloud and re-sighted the target, it was obvious that the U-boat captain was determined to fight it out.

'Undulating, we soon came under fire and I can vividly remember the tracer. Des Carter opened fire on the front gun. Our first D/Cs undershot and we circled to port, the U-boat manoeuvring to keep its stern towards us. On our second attack the flak was more intense and more accurate. The No. 3 engine was put out of action on the run-in and the propeller had to be feathered. Des was equally accurate on the front gun for he silenced their guns. Members of our crew saw the D/Cs entering the water, and then the great explosion that blasted parts of the U-boat into the air, and watched as it heeled over. As Geoff turned the aircraft again to port he and I saw the water subsiding with no trace of the U-boat.

'As we tracked over a patch of oil, we counted about 15 survivors in the water and we sent our message: "Sub sunk, RTB, survivors." Followed by: "RTB, 3 engines," and then "UB sunk 6203 0145, 15 survivors." U-317 was on her first cruise, sailing from Egersund on 21 June for a patrol off the Norwegian coast. She went down north-east of the Shetlands. There were no survivors from the boat's 50 crew.

Flight Lieutenant Geoffrey William Tyndall Parker and Flight Sergeant Desmond Carter, who manned the front gun, received an immediate DFC and DFM. 'Farmer' Parker had joined the RAF in 1940, aged 27 and flew with 269 Squadron in 1941–42. He died in 1988. The Liberator was more seriously damaged than the crew knew. Geoff Parker flew it back to Tain with just Syd Norris, Taffy Jones and Sandy Powell, and when it was stripped down for repair it was found that a flak shell had gone right through the main spar and the Lib should never have been flown.

28 June, 1944

U-396, a type VIIC submarine, commanded by Kapitänleutnant Hilmar Siemon, damaged.

Catalina 'Q', 210 Squadron, on patrol 0945–0046 hrs.

FO J.C. Campbell	Pilot
F/Sgt H.O. Williams	2nd pilot
Lt A. van der Bijl	1 Nav
FO E. Anderson	2 Nav
Sgt L.G. Law	FME/AG
Sgt J. McLean	WOP/AG
F/Sgt W. Thirlwell	WOP/AG
Sgt R.J. Thomas	WOM/AG
Sgt A. Smith	WOP/AG
Sgt C. Gasken	AG

At 1519 hrs, in position 6234/0046, a strange ship's balloon was sighted at 800 feet and the aircraft shot it down. At 1957 hrs, at 750 feet, a radar contact at 4½ miles dead ahead produced a sighting 2 minutes later of a U-boat at one mile. Flak came up, but this mostly exploded behind the Lib as it flew in. D/Cs were dropped which fell over and beyond the boat's conning tower and as the aircraft circled round to port, the boat seemed blown off its course. A second attack with machine-gun fire was met by gunfire, and soon afterwards the boat submerged. Another wake was also seen 1½ miles away, but this too disappeared.

U-396, from Kiel, where it began its first patrol on 20 June, had to put into Bergen on 3 July, with damage. It was eventually lost on its fifth patrol, which began from Bergen on 20 March, 1945, sunk by 86 Squadron.

30 June, 1944.

U-478, a type VIIC submarine, commanded by Oberleutnant Rudolf Rademacher, sunk.

Liberator III 'E' FL924, 86 Squadron, on patrol 0730–0028 hrs.

FO N.E.M. Smith	Pilot
FO G.F. Aspinall	2nd pilot
F/L J.D. Symonds	1 Nav
F/Sgt E.A. Brown (Aust)	2 Nav
Sgt F. Chiltern	Eng
WO J. Hamilton	AG
WO A.A. Tulip	WOP/AG
Sgt E.A. Horton	WOP/AG

This U-boat was first seen and reported by a Canso of 162 RCAF Squadron (9841), flown by F/L R.E. McBride, who had sunk U-477 earlier in the month. He had attacked, but the D/Cs failed to release, so they homed in 86 Squadron's Liberator, despite having been damaged by the U-boat's defensive fire. Smith arrived at the location at 2115 hrs, sighting the fighting U-boat in position 6327/0050. He immediately attacked with six D/Cs, which straddled, lifting the bows out of the water. The U-Boat then sank stern first. The Lib had also been hit by flak, damaging No. 4 engine. After circling an increasingly large patch of oil and seeing survivors in two dinghies, Smith set course for home.

U-478 was on her first patrol, having left Kiel on 20 June. She was a schnorkel boat.

Flying Officer Smith received an immediate DFC. Smith was later promoted to flight lieutenant and Brown and Chilton were commissioned.

15 July, 1944.

U-319, a type VIIC/41 submarine, commanded by Oberleutnant Johann Clemens, sunk.

Liberator 'E' EV947, 206 Squadron, on patrol 0550 hrs.

FO D.W. Thynne Pilot	
FO A.G. Echlin, RCAF	
FO L.B. Mollard, RCAF	F/Sgt C. McRobb
FO J.E. Taylor, RCAF	FO A.A. Desilets, RCAF
PO W.W. Preston	Sgt R. Fitch
FO A. Forsyth, RCAF	Sgt N. Hilton

This Liberator failed to return from its patrol. At 2025 hrs on 16 July, the body of Sergeant Hilton was picked up by a High Speed Launch, in position 5742/0455, having been seen in a dinghy the previous day. On the 15th a large oil patch was seen nearby by Liberator 'B' of 206 Squadron.

U-319 had sailed from Stavanger on its first patrol, to the south-west coast of Norway, on 5 July, and went down south-west of the Lister Light.

17 July, 1944

U-347, a type VIIC submarine, commanded by Oberleutnant Johann de Buhr, sunk.

Catalina 'Y' JV928, 210 Squadron, on patrol 1345–0405 hrs.

F/L J.A. Cruickshank	Pilot
F/Sgt J. Garnett	2nd Pilot
Sgt S.I. Fidler	3rd pilot
FO J.C. Dickson	Nav
F/Sgt S.B. Harbison	Eng
WO W.C. Jenkins	WOP
F/Sgt H. Gershenson	WOP
F/Sgt F.J. Appleton	WOM/AG
Sgt R.S.C. Proctor	WOP/AG
F/Sgt A.I. Cregan	Rigger

A year had past since Cruickshank and his crew had attacked and damaged U-267 (see 19 Gp) and John Appleton was still a member of his crew. He recalls that, despite official reports of this attack, which state the radar picked up U-347 at 15 miles, John, who was on the radar set, saw it at 43 miles! He reported the blip at 40 miles and at first they thought it was a cruiser, then perhaps a destroyer, finally a possible sub. They approached through patches of sea mist and Dickson went into the bomb aimer's position in the nose. Paddy Harbison was at the front gun, and once they got into visual contact John took up position behind Cruickshank, looking ahead as they ran in. Despite some flak, the Catalina was not hit, but the D/Cs did not release owing to some corrosion in the mechanism. Coming round for another attack, the U-boat's fire became more accurate. John remembers looking out as flak bursts exploded ahead of them, while cannon shells streaked towards them. Just as they were about to release the D/Cs, a 3.7mm shell hit beneath the bomb aimer's position, killing Dickson instantly. The exploding shell wounded Harbison in both legs, injured Garnett in the left hand and seriously wounded Cruickshank in the chest and legs. Appleton, his goggles up, instinctively put his left hand over his eyes, collecting numerous splinters in hand and fingers. Despite this, and a 3-inch gash in the top of his head, he was unaware of any injuries until after they had landed. As the radar compartment and apparatus were also badly smashed about, his injuries could have been serious had he remained there.

After the attack, John bound Garnett's hand and then tried to help Cruickshank, but the Skipper fell forward. He was helped back to the bunk area but refused morphine. John did what he could for him, and then fell asleep in the next bunk, obviously reacting to his own head wound. When the other two pilots got them back to base (Sullom Voe) – it was Fidler's first operational trip – Cruickshank insisted on being helped back to the cockpit, and both he and Jack Garnett landed the Catalina safely, running the damaged Cat up on to the beach. Help and medical assistance were awaiting them, Cruickshank being given a blood transfusion in the cockpit. Only then did John Appleton know of his own injuries when someone referred to his blood-covered face. The blood on his hand he took to be Cruickshank's.

U-347, which was destroyed by Cruickshank's attack, had been in Stavanger at the beginning of April 1944 and moved to Bergen on 9 May. It joined the Arctic Flotilla and began its second patrol from Narvik on 3 July. It went down in position 6835/0600, west of the Lofotan Islands.

John Cruickshank was awarded the Victoria Cross for his gallant attack and for refusing medication that might have precluded him from helping to land the flying boat. Jack Garnett received the DFM. Dickson, a former policeman, was a good navigator who never let anyone else navigate – not even new navigators under training! His son had been born a month earlier but he did not live long enough to see him.

This was the second of only two VCs awarded to Coastal Command. Hornell's had been awarded for an action just three weeks earlier, also a Catalina (Canso) pilot.

17 July, 1944.

U-361, a type VIIC submarine, commanded by Kapitänleutnant Hans Seidel, sunk.

Liberator III 'U' FK223, 86 Squadron, on patrol 1426–0441 hrs.

PO M.G. Moseley	Pilot
F/Sgt W. McRae	
WO P.H. Carpenter	Sgt J. Boffey
PO R.B. Watson	WO R. Evans
F/Sgt M.C. Blee (Aust)	Sgt H.V. Hill
WO A. Lamb	

Flying at 400 feet under a cloud layer over a calm sea with patches of sea fog, a U-boat was sighted at 12 miles in position 6836/0833. Moseley immediately climbed into the cloud, flew on for 4 miles, then broke for a look, then lifted back. He noticed a splash in the water as he did so, which was presumed to be gunfire. After a further 4 miles, they came out, AA fire bursting about them. They went back into cloud and emerged again at 1½ miles, re-entered and came out finally when just 800 yards away. The front lookout opened fire as the Lib flew in, surrounded by flak. Six D/Cs went down from 125 feet, which appeared to straddle the surfaced boat, then Moseley turned to port. The rear gunner saw the conning tower amidst the explosions, then it went down. A large patch of black oil stained the surface and then some survivors and wreckage could be observed. The Lib tracked over the spot and among the many oil-covered objects, at least six men were thought to be there. They circled for an hour and a half, then set course for home. Damage to the Lib amounted to hits to its upper fuselage, rear turret and loop aerial.

The assessment was that the attack was good, 'probably resulting in a kill'. U-361 was certainly lost, ending its third patrol, which had begun on 27 June from Narvik. The boat had joined the Arctic Flotilla in early 1944.

Pilot Officer Michael George Moseley was awarded the DFC.

18 July, 1944.

U-742, a type VIIC submarine, commanded by Kapitänleutnant Heinz Schwassmann, sunk.

Catalina 'Z', 210 Squadron, on patrol 0635–2120 hrs.

FO R.W.G. Vaughan	Pilot
F/L J. Sinclair	2nd pilot
FO N. Wheatley	3rd pilot
FO J.G. Mills	Nav
F/Sgt P.L. Ludgate	Eng
F/Sgt J. Maule	FME/AG
WO C.J. Webster	1 WOP
Sgt G. Gibbons	2 WOP
FO K.S. Freeman	WOM/AG
F/Sgt S.M. Audifferen	Rigger

Shortly before 1500 hrs an object, thought to be a ship, was observed at 15 miles, but then seen to be a surfaced U-boat, in position 6825/0951. Closing in, flak was met at 3 miles and the PBY sustained hits, but a good straddle was made. Pulling round to port, the boat was seen to disappear, but leaving 35–40 survivors in the water with some small yellow dinghies. There was also a large oil patch and some bodies. Vaughan was then told of a serious oil leak in the starboard engine and a fuel leak in the port tank. Two of his crew had also been wounded, Flying

Officer Freeman and Flight Sergeant Maule. On the flight home, they were losing fuel at 100 gallons an hour, and then one engine had to be closed down. At 1945 hrs they were down to two hours of fuel and as the hull seemed to be damaged too, it was decided to beach the Cat at Heinkel Cape. They landed at 2125 hrs, running up on to the beach. They had flown the last 500 miles on the port engine.

U-742 had joined the Arctic Flotilla on 12 May, 1944, and made her first patrol on the 20th. Her second and last began from Narvik on 4 July.

Flying Officer Ronald William George Vaughan received an immediate DFC.

19 July, 1944

U-968, a type VIIC submarine, commanded by Oberleutnant Otto Westphalen, damaged.

Liberator III 'R' FL930, 86 Squadron, on patrol 0529–2120 hrs.

F/L W.F.J. Harwood	Pilot
FO H.C. Tyas (Aust)	2nd pilot
F/Sgt P.L. Tutty	1 Nav
WO W.K. Bridges (Aust)	2 Nav
Sgt R.G. Knowles	Eng
F/Sgt R.D. Bennett (NZ)	WOP/AG
F/Sgt L.T.C. Holm (Aust)	WOP/AG
F/Sgt J.B. Sproule (Can)	WOP/AG
PO E. Addison	AG

Reached their patrol area at 1126 hrs and just 14 minutes later, in position 6939/0901, a fully surfaced U-boat was found and attacked. In the first attack, six D/Cs were released which overshot by 40 feet, and in the second the last two D/Cs undershot by 30 feet. Continuous flak was experienced, which was finally silenced by the nose gunner. The Lib, however, was not hit and the aircraft circled, unable to do any more than watch. Finally the boat submerged at 1215 hrs.

U-968 was on her second patrol from Narvik, and despite the distance the RAF crew thought their D/Cs had over- or undershot, the boat had been damaged and was forced to return to its base. She eventually sailed on six war cruises and was at sea when the war ended, returning to Trondheim on 10 May, 1945. Otto Westphalen was a Knight's Cross holder.

19 July, 1944

U-716, a type VIIC submarine, commanded by Oberleutnant Johannes Dunkelberg, damaged.

Liberator 'F' FL985, 59 Squadron, on patrol 1243–0213 hrs.

FO R.C. Penning	Pilot
FO A. Johnston	
FO P.A. Richardson	Sgt G.T. Rogers
FO R. Webb	Sgt J.E. Berry
Sgt A.J. Waterfield	Sgt J.H. Walton

On its way to the patrol area in Norwegian waters, and flying at 1400 feet, the starboard beam gunner sighted a fully surfaced U-boat 6 miles away, at 1912 hrs. Simultaneously a radar contact was made, position 7019/0602. The Liberator lost height and was met by intense flak on the run-in, which was returned by the front gunner. Using the Mk 3 bombsight, six D/Cs were dropped from 100 feet. The last two were seen to overshoot but the others exploded around the sub. Two minutes later the Lib returned to release its last two D/Cs from 75 feet, falling one on either side. Brown smoke had been seen coming from the base of the conning tower after the first attack, which increased in volume after the second. The boat remained on the surface for some time but finally went under at 1941 hrs. Two of the Lib's crew saw black objects in the water where the boat had disappeared.

U-716, on its fifth patrol, sailed from Hammerfest on 17 July and was forced to return damaged on the 21st. It made at least one more war patrol under Oblt Hans Thieme and was in Trondheim at the war's end.

19 July, 1944

U-387, a type VIIC submarine, commanded by Kapitänleutnant Rudolf Buchler, damaged.

Sunderland 'O' EJ155, 330 Norwegian Squadron, on patrol 1744–0700 hrs.

Lt B. Thurmann-Nielsen	Pilot
2/Lt B. Ullebust	2nd pilot
QM A. Titlestad	Nav
2/Lt T. Fidjeland	Eng
QM A. Knutsen	WOP/AG
QM T. Johnsen	WOP/AG
QM G. Ulversoy	FMA/AG
QM S. Lanjord	AG
QM H. Hansen	AG
QM E.O. Kruse	WOM

A radar contact at 2310 hrs, in position 6833/0720, 18 miles, sent Sunderland 'O' off to investigate. At 3½ miles they sighted a fully surfaced U-boat, and Bredo Thurmann-Nielsen immediately pulled up into cloud to avoid being seen. At ¾ of a mile he broke cloud at 600 feet and dived on the boat, sending six D/Cs down, two falling on the port side, four on the other. The sub emerged from the explosion plumes, turning to starboard and opened fire, which forced the Sunderland to take evasive action. The boat seemed to be on an uneven keel with decks almost awash and some 6 minutes later the boat went down. Heavy rain and low cloud prevented the Norwegian crew seeing any wreckage or oil.

U-387 was on her seventh war patrol, having left Narvik on 12 July, putting into Trondheim, damaged, on the 30th. She completed at least 10 patrols before being sunk on 9 December, 1944, north of Kola inlet, by the corvette *Bamborough Castle*.

20 July, 1944

U-863, a type IXD/42 submarine, commanded by Kapitänleutnant Dietrich von der Esch, damaged.

Mosquito VI 'N' HR262, 333 Norwegian Squadron, on patrol 1555–1830 hrs.

Lt R. Leithe	Pilot
PO N. Skjelanger	Nav

Two Mosquitoes were flying an anti-U-boat Rover patrol off the Norwegian coast and found a German flak-ship. This was attacked by aircraft 'K' (HP858), at 1700 hrs off Fedje island. Then Lieutenant Rolf Leithe spotted a U-boat on the surface 100 yards astern of the flak-ship. He attacked, coming in over the island, opening fire from 500 yards, and at 100 feet in height, with cannon and machine guns, then dropping two Mk XI D/Cs from 50 feet. The navigator saw them explode 20 feet astern of the sub.

U-863 had sailed from Bergen the previous day on her first cruise and returned damaged on the 21st. She sailed again on the 26th and made her way, via Iceland, to South American waters. Here she was sunk on 29 September, south-east of Pernambuco, by two US Navy Liberators, one VP 107, operating from eastern Brazil.

25 July, 1944

U-244, a type VIIC submarine, commanded by Oberleutnant Mackeprang, damaged.

Mosquito VI 'E' HP904,

2/Lt S. Breck	Pilot
2/Lt P. Hjorten	Nav

Mosquito VI 'F' HR 116,

PO J.A. Stiff	Pilot
F/Sgt H.E. Bussey	Nav

333 Norwegian Squadron, on patrol 1133–1508 hrs.

Flying an anti-U-boat patrol off the Norwegian coast, sighted a surfaced U-boat at 1329 hrs, at 8 miles, in company with an escort vessel. The aircraft attacked and when the escort ship opened fire, Breck fired off German recognition signals and the flak stopped. When Breck then opened fire at 1000 yards, the flak recommenced. Hits were scored on the U-boat's conning tower and also on the deck of the escort, forward of the bridge. As Breck tracked over the sub, two D/Cs were dropped, but only one explosion plume was seen, between the conning tower and the stern. Meanwhile, Pilot Officer Stiff attacked with cannon and machine guns, scoring hits on both vessels, with a big explosion on the escort's forward deck. He also dropped two D/Cs on the sub from 50 feet.

U-244 had sailed from Kiel to Kristiansund, on 18 July, arriving on the 23rd. The same day she left for the Atlantic after refuelling, but was damaged by 333 Squadron and had to return. She went on to make five cruises, her fifth ending in her surrender on 12 May, 1945.

Second Lieutenant Sigmund Breck was killed on 10 December, 1944.

27 July, 1944

U-865, a type IXC/40 submarine, commanded by Oberleutnant Stellemacher, damaged.

Liberator 'R', 86 Squadron, on patrol 1212–0133 hrs.

FO G.G. Gates	Pilot
FO B.S. Bury	2nd pilot

WO G.F. Hough (Aust)	1 Nav
WO H. Pordage (Aust)	2 Nav
Sgt B.T. McCabe	Eng
F/Sgt I.R. Noble (Aust)	WOP/AG
F/Sgt R.J. Peck (Aust)	WOP/AG
F/Sgt J.P. Mellon (Aust)	WOP/AG
PO J.C. Edwards	AG

The Lib reached its patrol area at 1617 hrs and at 2003 sighted a fully surfaced U-boat in position 6440/2020. In the attack, six D/Cs were released, which overshot, but the sub appeared to pass between the plumes. Flak was encountered and the Lib's Nos. 1 and 2 engines were hit and caught fire. The Lib's gunners, too, fired into the conning tower and it was believed that some casualties were inflicted. The boat was last seen turning in a tight circle, but Gates had then to head for home. The fires were put out, and despite the damage they flew home and landed successfully.

U-865 had begun her first patrol from Kiel on 20 June, but had to put into Trondheim with defects on 5 July. While here she was fitted with the schnorkel apparatus and sailed again on the 27th, only to be damaged by 86 Squadron. She returned to Trondheim on the 28th. In August she sailed again but had to return due to further defects, finally commencing her second cruise on 8 September. She failed to return, being lost south-east of Iceland, possibly to a ship-laid minefield.

18 September, 1944

U-1228, a type IXC/40 submarine, commanded by Oberleutnant Friedrich-Wilhelm Marienfeld, damaged.

Liberator 'R', 224 Squadron, on patrol from Milltown till–0319 hrs.

FO P.M. Hill	F/Sgt R.T. Frayne
WO K. Saywell	F/Sgt R.W. Beck (NZ)
FO E.S. Liddle	WO A.J. Phillips (NZ)
Sgt W.V. Johnstone (Aust)	Sgt W. Irvine
WO H. Smolenski (NZ)	Sgt K. Ashworth

A radar contact was picked up at 2142 hrs at 15 miles. The Lib flew on until 10 miles from target, when course was altered for a home-in. The Leigh Light went on at one mile from the target, illuminating a large, fully surfaced U-boat, dead ahead, in the rear edge of the light's beam. The bomb aimer, who was also operating the light, was too busy to align the bomb sight, so the D/Cs were dropped by eye from 200 feet, when flying in at 200 mph. They fell some 30 feet over the boat. The pilot quickly turned to come in again for a front gun attack, but although the radar contact was maintained for several minutes, it then disappeared at 2 miles and nothing further was seen.

U-1228 had sailed for her second patrol, from Bergen, the previous day, returning damaged on the 20th. She surrendered on 9 May, 1945, on her fourth cruise, in mid-Atlantic, to HM ships.

19 September, 1944

U-867, a type IXC/40 submarine, commanded by Kapitänleutnant von Muhlendahl, sunk.

Liberator 'Q', 224 Squadron, on patrol 1220–2015 hrs.

F/L H.J. Rayner	F/Sgt S.H. Whiter
WO E.C. Browning	F/Sgt W. Robinson
PO M.H. Evans (Aust)	Sgt R.J. Munro
WO L.C. Kenney (Aust)	Sgt W.S. Newlands
FO H. Lord	F/Sgt A.M. Bell

This boat had been found and attacked on the 18th by Warrant Officer H.A. Corbin, CGM, of 248 Squadron, off the Norwegian coast. The next day, at 1625 hrs, 224 Squadron's Liberator picked it up on radar at 15 miles, and homed in. Seven minutes later Rayner sighted the boat, fully surfaced on the starboard beam, and came in down-sun. The boat began a sharp turn to port and Rayner tightened his turn, then dropped six D/Cs, which overshot. The sub was putting up some very accurate flak, but this had ceased when the front and mid-upper gunners had opened up from 1000 yards. Photos taken later showed two dinghies in the water, close to the U-boat, when the first D/Cs exploded. After the attack, the boat appeared stationary and five minutes later it sank on an even keel. Completing a second circuit, the RAF crew saw one large and several small dinghies, containing about 50 men, floating in a patch of oil. Pieces of timber and a tarpaulin were seen amongst the dinghies.

U-867 had been on her first patrol, having sailed from Kristiansund on 12 September. Attacked by 248 Squadron and then by 224 Squadron, she was badly damaged and the commander had to scuttle after Rayner's attack. She went down in position 6215/0150, west of Stadlandet.

24 September, 1944

U-763, a type VIIC commanded by Oberleutnant Karlheinz Schroter, damaged.

Liberator 'A' EW308, 224 Squadron.

SL J.C.T. Downey	Pilot
FO M. Kowalchuk	2nd pilot
FO H. Sutton	Nav
Sgt V. Acourt	Eng
F/Sgt A.H. Butler	WOP/AG
Sgt R.H. Griffin	WOP/AG
Sgt R.A. Ranson	WOP/AG
Sgt A.R. Wilson	WOP/AG
FO R.W. Lowe, DFC	

John Downey recalls: 'The events were fairly straightforward compared with most attacks at that time. The U-boat was fully surfaced and we, flying a box patrol over a calm sea, picked him up on ASV at some distance (7 miles). Probably he had just surfaced. We homed straight in, but bent the course a bit to avoid attacking with the aurora borealis behind us, because it was particularly bright that night. I'm sure the U-boat was taken completely by surprise, because it took no evasive action and didn't fire a shot. When we switched on the Leigh Light at about ¾ of a mile the deck crew were in the conning tower staring straight back up the beam. I can see them now. Our D/Cs fell across the stern and although our photo-flash failed to work, so that there was no attack photo, the rear gunner said that the stern was lifted out of the water. A photo taken on a run over the spot immediately afterwards showed a huge bubble. The sinking was confirmed in November 1944.'

The attack was timed at 0415 hrs, in position 6100/0407, and Downey and his crew circled until daylight, when a thin streak of oil and an oil patch could clearly be seen.

After the war it was assessed that John Downey had attacked and sunk U-855 (Oblt Prosper Ohlsen), who had been weather reporting in the Atlantic and was on his way home. Subsequent investigation indicates that U-855 hit a mine about 18 September in position 6310/1230. Downey, in fact, attacked and damaged U-763, the only U-boat in the vicinity of his attack, and whose war diary confirms the details of the Lib's approach, etc..

U-763 was in fact *en route* from La Pallice to Bergen, which she reached the next day. Repairs kept her there for two weeks before she could sail on to Kristiansund. She was finally destroyed in a Russian air raid in Koenigsberg on 21 January, 1945.

In her three earlier patrols she had sunk just one ship. However, she had been a dangerous adversary of Coastal Command. On her first patrol from Kiel beginning 14 December, 1943, her gunners had shot down Liberator 'F' (BZ795) of 53 Squadron (Flight Lieutenant D.A. Bell), who failed to return on 4th February after sending a flash report that he was about to attack a U-boat. The next day she shot down Halifax 'R' of 502 Squadron (Flying Officer F.T. Culling-Mannix, RNZAF) as he made an attack. On her second patrol from St Nazaire, on 10 June, she was recalled to base, but was found and attacked by Beaufighters of 248 Squadron, but made La Pallice.

John Downey was to damage U-2365 so severely on 5 May, 1945, that she scuttled.

30 October, 1944

U-1061, a type VIIF submarine, commanded by Oberleutnant Otto Hinrichs, damaged.

Wellington XIV 'R' NB839, 407 RCAF Squadron, on patrol 2346–1025 hrs.

FO J.E. Neelin	Pilot
FO L.W. Creaser	2nd pilot
FO K.D. Taylor	Nav
PO F.L. Davey	WOP/AG
PO R.M. Sheppard	WOP/AG
PO E.J. Goodman	WOP/AG

Liberator 'A' 224 Squadron, on patrol 1630–0547 hrs.

F/L W.S. Blackden	Sgt L.J. Weeks
F/Sgt G. McConghy	Sgt J.E. Elley
F/L E.J. Stretton	Sgt A. Liggins
FO A.L. Greenwood	Sgt P.C. Martin
F/Sgt A. Diack	Sgt J. Tracey

On patrol from Wick, the Wellington picked up a radar contact at 0209 hrs, in position 6143/0342 – range 5 miles. She homed in and illuminated the conning tower of a U-boat, which was attacked with six D/Cs. As aircraft circled another aircraft, thought to be a Liberator, it made an attack run. Flak could be seen in action against the other aircraft, and later a large orange glow from a fire was seen which lasted for at least a minute. Radar contact was maintained and 'R' called up and homed 'T' of 407 Squadron. A parachute flare from the Lib was also seen to be dropped, but nothing further was observed until some hours later. By this time it was daylight and

three large oil slicks could be made out. It was later felt that there were in fact two U-boats, but whether this was true or not could not be resolved at the time.

The Liberator was from 224 Squadron, who had also picked up a radar contact at 0221 hrs, 15 miles. Homing in, it picked up the Wellington too and then while still some miles away, a Leigh Light was seen and two Marine Markers. Having gone down to 200 feet, the navigator, in the front turret, spotted at one mile a vessel in the diffused moonlight and at ¾ of a mile the Leigh Light illuminated a fully surfaced U-boat, which began to fire at the aircraft. The Wellington was still in evidence from a red light under its fuselage. At 0245 hrs, Blackden made an approach out of the dark side of the sky, the front guns and the U-boat blazing away at each other. The flak weakened and then the D/Cs were falling as the U-boat appeared to start a crash-dive. By now there were other aircraft in the vicinity, but the U-boat had gone.

U-1061, a torpedo transporter, had been in Narvik in mid-April 1944 and made three transport cruises during mid-1944. At the end of October, she was on passage from Bergen to Trondheim when she was severely damaged by air attack. Unable to dive, she made for Maloy Sound on the surface. Later, under a new CO – Jager – she ran aground near Alvo on 7 February, 1945. Towed into Bergen with considerable hull damage, she was still in Trondheim harbour when the war ended.

4 November, 1944

U-1060, a type VIIF submarine, commanded by Oberleutnant Herbert Brammer, sunk

Liberators 'Y' and 'H', 311 Czech Squadron, on patrol 0400–1420 hrs.

FO F. Pavelka	SL A. Sedivy
F/L J. Osolsobe	Sgt J. Stark
F/Sgt F. Klemens	FO J. Francu
Sgt F. Maly	F/Sgt P. Gibian
Sgt J. Novak	Sgt R. Soudek
Sgt V. Novak	F/Sgt E. Fleischamnn
Sgt D. Nemeth	Sgt A. Hayek
F/Sgt J. Szarkozy	F/Sgt S. Dubrava
Sgt M. Rikovsky	WO A. Pegrimek

Halifaxes 'D' and 'T', 502 Squadron, on patrol 0405–1407 hrs.

F/L W.G. Powell	SL H.H.C. Holderness
FO N. Haynes	DFC AFC
FO N.H. Shacknell	F/L J.ET. Wray

FO G.E. Tapping (Can)	F/L G.D. Bateman
Sgt J. Rogers	FO A.J. Evans
F/Sgt L.W. Baker (Can)	F/Sgt F. Hardy
F/Sgt K. Bennet	Sgt M. Harrison
F/Sgt J.C. Hall (Can)	PO S. Watson

U-1060, a torpedo transporter, was between Narvik and Bergen on 27 October when it was attacked by a Firefly of 1771 Squadron, Fleet Air Arm, from the carrier *Implacable*. Damaged, it ran aground on the nearby island of Fleina. Here it was attacked and bombed by 311 and 502 Squadrons. Later it was seen to keel over and settle in deeper water. Flak from shore guns and some nearby ships engaged the RAF aircraft without inflicting damage.

U-1060 had on board 28 of the crew from U-957, damaged in a collision with a German ship on 19 October, west of Tromso. Its commander, Oberleutnant Schaar (Knight's Cross), had to abandon her, being picked up by Brammer's boat. From the two boats a total of 61 men died.

20 March, 1945

German U-boat, possibly sunk.

Liberator VIII 'B' KH340, 86 Squadron, on patrol 1915–0420 hrs.

F/L N.E.M. Smith, DFC	Pilot
FO J.F. Grist	2nd pilot
PO E.A. Brown (Aust)	1 Nav
PO J.H. Keene	2 Nav
FO F. Chiltern	Eng
F/Sgt A.F. Wood	WOP/AG
F/Sgt S. Spicer	WOM/AG
Sgt E.A. Horton	WOP/AG
Sgt T.W. Rothwell	AG
PO A.M. Pollock	AG

Soon after the patrol began, a radar contact was picked up and homed towards, but it then disappeared. It was regained at 1½ miles, but again lost. During a third run the contact was resumed, again at 1½ miles, but lost almost immediately. Finally, in position 5944/0516, a marker and 'Purple' sonobuoy pattern was dropped, followed by two acoustic torpedoes when a positive contact was made. Nothing further seen.

It had been thought that the victim was U-905 (Oblt Herbert Schwarting) on her way to the Atlantic on her second patrol, having left Trondheim on 13 March. She failed to return and was credited to 86 Squadron. It is now known that it was not U-905, but the identity of the submarine attacked is not certain.

If this was indeed a sinking, it was Flight Lieutenant Smith's second success, having sunk U-478 on 30 June. Brown, Horton and Chiltern had been with him on that earlier operation.

29 March, 1945

U-1106, a type VIIC/41 submarine, commanded by Oberleutnant Erwin Bartke, sunk.

Liberator 'O', 224 Squadron, on patrol 0342–1430 hrs.

F/L M.A. Graham	Sgt A.G. Dulieu
F/Sgt R. Steed	Sgt T. Owen
F/L J. Timmins	Sgt G.A. Shuttleworth
FO G. Shakespeare	F/Sgt B.S. Bennett
F/L S.A. Goodacre	FO R.J. Lidbury
Sgt L. Peterson	

From Milltown, they reached their patrol area at 0514 hrs. Just over 4½ hours later, in position 6144/0223, flying at 1000 feet, they sighted a wake at 3 miles. Homed to one mile and sighted a positive schnorkel, and made an attack. As the D/Cs exploded, the stern of the U-boat rose to the surface, but then disappeared. At 1020 hrs, laid a sonobuoy pattern from which the sounds of banging and machinery noises could be heard. There was also an intermittent propeller beat, but this was mostly drowned out by the noises.

U-1106, a deep-diving schnorkel boat, failed to return from her first patrol, which commenced from Kiel on 23 March.

9 April, 1945

U-804, a type IXC/40 submarine, commanded by Oberleutnant Herbert Meyer, sunk.

U-1065, a type VIIC/41 submarine, commanded by Oberleutnant J. Panitz, sunk.

34 Mosquito aircraft, led by Squadron Leader H.H. Gunnis, DFC – 143, 235 and 248 Squadrons. (The Banff Strike Wing.)

SL H.H. Gunnis DFC	Pilot	
F/L M.F. Southgate DFC		'V' of 248 Squadron.
	Nav	
FO A.A. McIntosh	Pilot	

FO A.J. Thorogood	Nav	'L' of 248 Squadron.
SL D.C. Pritchard	Pilot	'D' RS635, 143
F/L W. Bower	Nav	Squadron.
F/L P.R. Davenport	Pilot	
FO R.T. Day	Nav	'C' 235 Squadron.

Flying an anti U-boat Rover patrol with an escort of Mustang fighters, the Banff Wing flew to the Skagerrak. Shortly after their arrival in the area, two U-boats were seen in position 5805/1110. 143 Squadron, led by Pritchard, and 235 Squadron, led by Davenport, made strafing attacks, while 248 orbited, but who then attacked the leading boat. Rockets, cannon and machine guns raked both targets. Meanwhile, the second sub submerged, leaving oil and debris, and later the first U-boat appeared to be sinking by the stern. Soon after McIntosh's attack, the sub blew up, throwing debris into the air which damaged four of the attacking aircraft. A camera Mosquito, from the RAF Film Unit, flown to film the sortie, was seen to turn on to its back and spin into the sea from 1000 feet. One aircraft from each of 235 and 248 Squadrons had to make for Sweden with engine trouble, followed soon afterwards by a second 248 aircraft, flying on one engine. A third submarine was then seen (see next entry).

U-804 was on passage from Kiel to Horten, having sailed on 6 April, and went down north-east of Skaw. It had been damaged back in June by 333 Squadron (see earlier).

U-1065 had made no war cruises, and also went down during this passage trip from Kiel to Horten.

Squadron Leader Gunnis received a bar to his DFC in August 1945, while McIntosh received the DFC in May.

9 April, 1945

U-843, a type IXC/40 submarine, commanded by Kapitänleutnant Oskar Herwartz, sunk.

Mosquito 'A', 235 Squadron.

FO A.J. Randell	Pilot
FO R.R. Rawlins	Nav

This crew went after the third U-boat seen, in position 5741/1126 (see previous entry). The U-boat opened fire as the Mosquito made its run-in, but then Randell released his eight rockets and let fly with his cannon and machine guns. A second attack

with cannon and machine guns from the opposite side met with far less gunfire. After the attack, smoke and steam were coming from the boat in considerable quantities. It made no attempt to dive and was still smoking on the surface when the Mosquito flew off at 1725 hrs.

U-843 had made three cruises between October 1943 and April 1945. On the second one, she had been damaged by an aircraft attack on 10 April, 1944, south-west of Ascension Island, in the Indian Ocean, on her way to Batavia. Her third cruise had been from Djakarta, commencing on 3 December, arriving in Bergen on 3 April, 1945. On the 4th she sailed for Kiel, but met the Banff Wing. She had sunk one ship.

19 April, 1945

U-251, a type VIIC submarine, commanded by Oberleutnant Franz Sack, sunk.

U-2502, a type XXI submarine, commanded by Leutnant Heinz Franke, damaged.

U-2335, a prefabricated boat, commanded by Leutnant Karl Dietrich Bethin, damaged.

22 Mosquito aircraft from 143, 235, 248 and 333 Squadrons, led by Wing Commander A.H. Simmonds.

At 1631 hrs, an 'M'-class minesweeper was seen, followed by four U-boats, but the leading sub then submerged. An attack was ordered from east to west, the boats being some 200 yards apart. Three aircraft of 143 Squadron attacked the second boat with 24 rockets and cannon fire, then made a second cannon run. The boat began smoking and several dinghies were seen alongside it. The third boat, U-2502, was seen to be stationary, as was the fourth, U-2335, which then appeared to sink. 248 Squadron reported seeing four submarines, but one submerged before the attack. 248 had attacked the last two boats, and although they fought back, one seemed to sink. One aircraft of 248 was damaged and headed for Sweden, while another was hit over Denmark on the way home and force landed in that country. In one of the 248 Squadron aircraft was Flying Officer Norman Earnshaw, who in 1943 had attacked and damaged U-415 as an NCO pilot with 612 Squadron. He remembers: 'We were one of a fairly large number of

Mosquito aircraft on patrol in the Kattegat area which sighted a convoy comprised of four U-boats with attendant escort vessel in line astern. The "vic" formation of which I was part was ordered to attack the last U-boat in the line – now identified as U-2335. Our aircraft was "DM-S" RF615, which I flew at least 21 times between March 1945 and January 1946. In a copy of the *Lancashire Evening Post*, I was quoted concerning this attack – "We took on the last U-boat in the line and got at least four cannon hits on the conning tower. Large pieces of the boat were flying through the air as we passed over and we could see the escort vessel burning as we came away." Whilst we were attacking this U-boat, others were attacking the other U-boats – there were aircraft all over the place in various stages of attack. Flight Lieutenant J.H. Jamieson was my navigator from October 1944 to the end of the war and we completed 25 operational trips together over the Norway area. This trip was our 23rd.'

U-251 had made six of her nine cruises under KvtLt Timm with the Arctic Flotilla in 1942–43 before a long refit which commenced in June 1943, in Trondheim. This passage trip began on 17 April and the whole crew perished.

U-2502 received only slight damage, while U-2335, on her first cruise, managed to limp into Kristiansund despite extensive damage.

23 April, 1945

U-396, a type VIIC submarine, commanded by Kapitänleutnant Hilmar Siemon, sunk.

Liberator VIII 'V' KH224, 86 Squadron, on patrol 1243–2324 hrs.

F/L J.T. Lawrence	Pilot
Sgt E.F. Taylor	2nd pilot
F/L R.A. Dalton (NZ)	1 Nav
FO G.B. Gray	2 Nav
PO C.S.A. Withers	Eng
WO V.G. Binns	WOP/AG
WO J.R. Landry (Can)	WOP/AG
Sgt A. Quinton	WOM/AG
F/Sgt K.M. Rupert (Can)	AG
FO W.R. Young (Can)	AG

It took just over an hour to reach their assigned patrol area, but immediately they did so they picked up a radar contact at 4½ miles, but lost it after closing in to half a mile. A sonobuoy pattern was laid, but without positive results from sounding or the torpedoes that were also dropped. Aircraft was then ordered to hunt another U-boat in position 6040/0500, but a square search revealed nothing.

U-396 was on her fifth war cruise and failed to return. She had been on a weather reporting trip and was on her way home when lost. She was credited to 86 Squadron in position 5929/0522, north-west of Cape Wrath.

2 May, 1945

U-2359, a type XXII prefab submarine, commanded by Oberleutnant G. Bischoff, sunk.

33 Mosquitoes of the Banff Wing, led by Squadron Leader A.G. Deck, which comprised 143, 248, 235, 404 and 333 Squadrons with an escort of Mustangs.

SL A.G. Deck	Pilot	'Z' RS501 – leading 143
WO P.B. MacGregor	Nav	Squadron.
F/L D.E. Luckwell	Pilot	'L' – leading 248
FO M.L. Coulstock	Nav	Squadron.
F/L G.R. Mayhew, DFC	Pilot	'A' – leading 235
FO S.W. Farrow	Nav	Squadron.

The Wing had been briefed to hunt for U-boats believed moving north in the Kattegat, taking off at 0615 hrs. At 0854 hrs, sighted two U-boats in line astern, half a mile apart, in position 5729/1124. Deck ordered an attack and five of 143 Squadron went down on the leading boat, firing 38 rockets, scoring at least 12 hits, plus cannon damage. Two others of 143 attacked the second boat with 16 R/Ps, scoring at least two hits, then four Mossies attacked it with cannon fire. 248 Squadron, led by Squadron Leader Luckwell, also attacked the second boat and scored rocket hits and cannon strikes. 235, led by Flight Lieutenant G.R. Mayhew, DFC, also attacked the second boat, scoring eight and possibly 16 R/P hits. This sub was seen to sink after much debris had been thrown into the air, leaving an oil patch, wreckage, dinghies and survivors in the water. An attendant minesweeper was also attacked and left burning. It later sank. Three aircraft were damaged by flak or debris, one, from 235, having to head for Sweden. However, in this Mosquito were FOs Randell and Rawlins, who had been successful against U-843 on 9 April. 404 and 333 Squadrons acted as air cover and did not attack.

U-2359 had not made any patrols and was sunk on this passage trip from Kiel to Horten, going down north-east of Laeso Island. The second boat, also a prefabricated type XXII, was damaged.

On 5 May, 1945, there were a number of German submarines trying to make for Norway across the Kattegat. Coastal Command Liberators flew patrols over the area all day and claimed a number of successes. After the war the claims were assessed and credited to various squadrons and crews. Most of these assessments have now been changed. The following list of successful attacks is the latest position regarding U-boat losses on this extraordinary day.

5 May, 1945

U-3523, a type XXI prefab submarine, commanded by Oberleutnant Werner Muller, sunk.

Liberator 'L', 311 Czech Squadron, on patrol 1558–0221 hrs.

WO J. Benes	Sgt J. Gazdarica
F/Sgt F. Bret	F/L V. Kocman
FO A. Sverma	Sgt J. Schellong
F/Sgt A. Kasal	WO A. Sipek
F/Sgt J. Jedlicka	

At 2032 hrs, obtained a radar contact in position 5727/1038, and upon investigation spotted a submerging submarine. Two attacks were made, and on the second a direct hit was made and an explosion seen. Oil then began to appear on the surface, and upon closer inspection the upturned hull of a U-boat could be seen just below the surface.

U-3523 was sunk on a passage trip from Kiel. L/311 was originally assessed to have sunk U-2365.

5 May, 1945

U-3503, a type XXI prefab submarine, commanded by Oberleutnant Hugo Deiring, sunk.

Liberator 'T' KK250, 206 Squadron, on patrol 1525–0216 hrs.

F/L G.H.G. Thompson	PO L.D. Hurst
F/L P.R. Harbot	PO R. Walker
FO W.E. Phillips	F/Sgt H. Mansfield
PO D. George	F/Sgt B. Jones
PO R.L. Jones	F/Sgt R.J. Plummer
PO W.W. Sawchuk	

At 2154 hrs sighted a fully surfaced U-boat, 1½ miles to starboard. No radar contact had been made, so it was thought that the boat had only just surfaced. Aircraft made a tight turn to port and, as they ran in, the Lib's front gunner began firing. The D/Cs went down as the boat began to dive. The aircraft circled the spot for an hour, during which time oil and debris came to the surface, seen clearly in the now failing light.

According to survivors, U-3503 was badly damaged on the 5th and on the 8th the captain was forced to scuttle the boat off Gösteborg, in position 5739/1140.

5 May, 1945

U-579, a type VIIC submarine, commanded by Oberleutnant Schwarzenberg, sunk.

Liberator 'T', 224 Squadron, on patrol 1226–2101 hrs.

WC M.A. Ensor, DSO, DFC	Pilot
RO R.N. Hind	2nd pilot
FO W.J. Smith	Nav
WO J.J. Lawson	
F/Sgt J.N. Lemming	
FO M.P. McCarthy	
Sgt E.H. Sutcliffe	
Sgt J.R. Elliott	
WO J.A. Huxtable	
WO J.H. Smith	

Patrolling the inner Kattegat for escaping submarines, at 1632 hrs, just 15 minutes after reaching the patrol area, a radar contact was made at 8 miles. The contact was then seen to be two or three U-boats in line astern. Another Liberator was seen in the area, making an approach and obviously preparing for an attack. Ensor and another of his crew then saw two more subs, 6 miles off. The first boats were now 3 miles away, with the other Lib making for the second one. Ensor headed for the first which seemed to have turned and was beginning to go down. He attacked it at conning tower depth with D/Cs, his rear gunner seeing the second and third D/Cs straddle the tower, which was just about under the water. A couple of minutes later oil and bubbles came to the surface, followed by yellow planking and other debris. A sono pattern was laid and sounds of escaping air were so loud that movements of the other U-boats in the area could not be heard. Mike Ensor recalls: 'There was nothing remarkable about this attack. We were flying below 1000 feet in the area and homed on a radar contact, which, when sighted, was a surfaced U-boat, and I also saw another. We made a standard daylight attack from under 100 feet and sank it with six torpex depth charges spaced 100 feet apart. It had started to submerge when we attacked. I later felt a bit guilty about the loss of life so close to the end of the war, although we did not know how close it was on that day.'

U-579 was later confirmed as going down in position 5606/1106, the position noted in 224's attack report. The boat had been commissioned in Hamburg in July 1941 but damaged by fire in October and paid off. Later she became a training boat and did not see any operational service.

Wing Commander Ensor had received a bar to his DFC in March 1945. This was his second confirmed sub kill, having sunk U-259 in November 1942.

5 May, 1945

U-1168 a type VIIC/41 submarine, commanded by Kapitänleutnant Hans Hugo Umlauf, sunk.

Liberator VI 'K', 547 Squadron, on patrol 1231–2255 hrs.

FO A.A. Bruneau (Can)	Pilot
FO M.J. Lee	2nd pilot
FL W.M. Thorvaldson (Can)	3rd pilot
FO R. Fallon	Eng
FO G.R. Maxwell (Can)	WOP/AG
PO M.M. Stewart (Can)	
F/L H. Tunstall	
WO F.K. Brown	
F/Sgt G. Mooney	AG
Sgt J. Peck	

The other Liberator seen by Mick Ensor was this one, flown by Art Bruneau, who relates: 'I only qualified as a 1st pilot in late March or early April 1945. Then an epidemic of "pink-eye" developed and our crew, which seemed particularly affected, was unable to do sufficient training to undertake operations until 5 May. Even then we had several non-regular crew members. Thus a rather patched up crew, with a 1st pilot on his first operational trip as skipper, had the good fortune to sink a U-boat – something many crews did not have a chance to do through many months of operations.

'The loss of so many German sailors so close to the end of the war was a futile exercise. However, we did not know that at the time and we were doing what we had been trained for.

'On the 5th, a number of aircraft were detailed to seek out U-boats attempting to sail from the Baltic to the Norwegian fjords. We were to fly at low level over Denmark, where, although the Germans had surrendered, they were still shooting at aircraft! The flight over Denmark was exciting. Many Danish flags had just been raised for the first time in years and people on the roads were waving to us.

'Not long after reaching the Kattegat, we picked up two submarines on radar at about 14 miles and soon saw them visually. Having seen sunk shipping sitting on the sea bed with masts and funnels out of the water we realized that U-boats would not submerge. As we approached, both subs opened fire, which seemed heavy to me, and which we of course returned. We took pretty severe undulating evasive action and the German gunners must have been terrified and not too accurate – in any event we were not hit. We attacked the leading U-boat at low level, and as we passed over, the rear gunner reported that it had broken in half. We made a wide turn to try to get at the second sub, but it had changed its course to a direction which would have allowed us to get at it quite directly but the rear gunner did not report this and by the time we got on the line of attack, another aircraft [Ensor] was already attacking.

'Soon after we had to start for home because of petrol level and, as final excitement, made a rough landing at Leuchars in foul weather.'

Maurice Lee was the second pilot, and recalls: 'We took off from Leuchars and set course for the Skagerrak, passing over Denmark on the way. We were a bit apprehensive about this as there were several airfields, and Bob Fallon took photos of the German aircraft on the ground with a hand-held camera. When we arrived in the Skagerrak there were two U-boats on the surface and, I believe, two Liberators, including ourselves. One U-boat promptly dived, but the other started firing at us with their mounted cannon, luckily, due to evasive action, not scoring any hits on us. Evasive action in a four-engined Lib, at 50 feet, is not very easy!

'We pressed on and the sub dived, but we were soon over the spot where it went down and dropped our depth charges in a line. We circled round and saw oil and debris on the surface, but no survivors, so we were not sure whether we had sunk it or they had blown out the oil and debris. After that we continued our search but found nothing more in the sea, so returned to base.'

Bob Fallon, the Flight Engineer, was on his second tour, having flown with 120 Squadron, and been on a successful U-boat sinking in October 1943 (U-279). He had been commissioned and recommended for a pilot's course, but had preferred to remain on ops, so had moved to 547 Squadron at RAF Leuchars.

Bob, also known to everyone as Paddy, remembers: 'It was a fine sunny day as we flew over the German Aalborg aerodrome. There was some excitement aboard when we saw three Me 109 aircraft, engines running, on the end of the runway. We were somewhat relieved that they did not come up and chase us. Denmark looked a picture, so neat and tidy. From the beam window we saw an old chap cycling and when he saw us he started to wave, but lost control and went clean over the handlebars!

'I was on the flight deck when ahead we saw two very large U-boats. They saw us too and both opened fire. The black smoke from their exploding shells was rolling over our wings. The skipper ordered me to the beam gun position as the WOP/AG was required to send off some signals. I fired a short burst from the 0.5 machine gun, but nothing came in my line of fire. The skipper released the D/Cs and we circled to observe results. The leading U-boat had crash-dived. The area of our attack was a mass of debris and was visible from a distance of seven miles. Another Liberator came on the scene and dropped his D/Cs in the middle of our muck heap. I saw them explode and am quite sure that No. 1 U-boat was no longer in the area, hence no kill.

'We resumed our patrol but had no more fun and games for that day.'

U-1168 was sailing from Kiel to Norway and went down off Flensburger fjord. She had been commissioned in Danzig in January 1944, but had not seen operational service.

The original assessment indicated the sub was U-2521, but according to survivors this boat was sunk on the 4th.

Art Bruneau received the DFC.

5 May, 1945

U-534, a type IXC/40 submarine, commanded by Kapitänleutnant Herbert Nollau, sunk.

Liberator VIII 'G' KH347, 86 Squadron, on patrol 0859–1902 hrs.

WO J.D. Nicol	Pilot
FO L.N.A. Collins (Aust)	2nd pilot
FO L.C. Fowler	1 Nav
FO N. Baker	2 Nav
WO L.E. Sanson (Aust)	WOP/AG
Sgt C. Williams	WOM/AG
F/Sgt V.A. Seery (Aust)	WOP/AG
F/Sgt E.H. Collett (Aust)	WOP/AG

Reached their Kattegat patrol area at 1313 hrs and within 20 minutes had picked up a radar contact in position 5635/1158, 4½ miles, when at 1000 feet. Homed in and sighted three fully surfaced U-boats in staggered line astern, dead ahead. A Lib of 547 Squadron made two attacks on one of them, but overshot both attempts, but the second one may have caused damage. This aircraft was then hit by flak and crashed into the sea. This was E/547 flown by F/L G.W. Hill. Only one survivor observed and he was picked up by a rescue ship from a nearby lighthouse. Nicol saw the U-boat which had been attacked while diving, and the centre one was already submerged, but the third was still fully surfaced and was attacked with six D/Cs. These overshot and strong flak was met, but subdued by the front and rear gunners. A second run and four D/Cs went down, after which the rear gunner saw the sub sinking stern first and about 40 survivors, dinghies and wreckage were later photographed. Nothing further seen of the other two boats. Nicol then helped guide the rescue ship to the survivor of the downed Liberator.

U-534 had made two cruises, from Bordeaux to the Atlantic in the summer of 1944, and then the trip to Kiel in the autumn. She had left Kiel on 4 May for Norway, and went down east of Anholt Island, in position 5645/1152, where her wreck was later discovered.

5 May, 1945

U-2365, a type XXIII prefab submarine commanded by Oberleutnant Uwe Christiansen, sunk.

Liberator 'S' KG959, 224 Squadron, on patrol 0858–1910 hrs.

SL J.C.T. Downey, DFC	Pilot
F/Sgt Pollington	2nd pilot
FO H. Sutton	Nav
F/Sgt V. Acourt	Eng
F/Sgt R.H. Griffin	WOP/AG
Sgt R.A. Ransom	WOP/AG
F/Sgt A.H. Butler	WOP/AG
WO L.G. Hall (Aust)	
WO Thompson	
F/L Guthrie	
F/Sgt Wilkinson	

'While on this patrol the aircraft spotted some MTBs

and later a Danish three-masted schooner. At 1408 hrs, an oil slick and six dinghies containing German sailors were seen, and a rowing boat picking up some survivors, in position 5650/1152. Later saw a white Liberator submerged with its wheels protruding from the surface, with two other Liberators circling (Nicol was one of them). They also saw the lone suvvivor of the Liberator (E/547 Sqdn) swimming to an approaching rowing boat.

At 1529 hrs, in position 5650/1120, homed in and then flew over a fully surfaced U-boat, but saw it too late to attack. The U-boat began to submerge but then resurfaced. Aircraft attacked with D/Cs, but most overshot. On a second attack the D/Cs failed to release, which happened again on a third attack. John Downey recalls: 'The attack was a complete balls-up and was assessed very critically by Captain Peyton-Ward and Co. When we first sighted the U-boat it was travelling so fast we thought it was a speed boat (big wake) and therefore turned on too late to get lined up, toppling the gyros in the Mk 14 bombsight in the process of a very steep turn. The D/Cs missed by miles and only our gunfire could have done any damage. The boat crash-dived but almost immediately reappeared and, since there was much discoloration of the sea surface, we thought (afterwards) that it must have ricocheted off the bottom in shallow water. However, we had another go, quite well lined up this time, but the bomb-aimer had mis-selected his switches and nothing came off the racks. He then re-submerged and stayed down.'

It is now known that U-2365 was damaged and later the captain was forced to scuttle. In 1956 the sub was raised from position 5650/1120, the spot where Downey had attacked her.

John Downey, a flight commander on 224 Squadron, was thought to have sunk a U-boat the previous September, but later investigation showed the sub had only been damaged.

6 May, 1945

U-2534, a type XXI Prefab submarine, commanded by Kapitänleutnant Ulrich Drews, sunk.

Liberator VIII 'G' KH347, 86 Squadron, on patrol 1324–0220 hrs.

F/L T.H.E. Goldie, DFC	Pilot
PO S. Hedley	2nd pilot
F/Sgt E.W. Payne	Nav
F/Sgt W.G. Tarr	2nd Nav
F/Sgt R.S. Ash	Eng
PO J.K. MacKenzie (Can)	WOP/AG

WO N. Robinson	WOP/AG
F/Sgt H.P. Plant	WOP/AG
F/Sgt D.R. Gould	FME/AG
PO N. Mather	WOP/AG

Reached the same patrol area which had produced success the previous day for this same aircraft (Nicol), at 1743 hrs. Fifty minutes later two radar plots were investigated and then in position 5755/1053 a periscope and schnorkel were seen 2½ miles away. An immediate attack was made with six D/Cs and the explosions forced the U-boat to rise, its conning tower clearly seen above the sea. Black objects were blown into the air and later much wreckage could be seen. Two streams of bubbles and oil also seen five minutes later.

U-2534 had been on her way from Kiel to Norway when attacked and sank in position 5752/1049.

6 May, 1945

U-1008, a type VIIC/41 submarine, commanded by Oberleutnant Hans Gessner, sunk.

Liberator VIII 'K' KH290, 86 Squadron, on patrol 2121–0749 hrs.

F/L M.C. Kay	Pilot
FO V.M Willrich (Can)	2nd pilot
FO J. Stead	Nav
Sgt M. Mallace	Eng
Sgt E. Margerison	WOM/AG
FO D.F. Medhurst	WOP/AG
Sgt C.A. Burley	WOP/AG
Sgt W.J. Bibby	AG
Sgt J. O'Farrell	AG

At 0255 hrs, a radar contact was investigated, but aircraft got too close to the target before the light was put on so flew off. At 0310 hrs, a wake was sighted a quarter of a mile away, within the Leigh Light beam, but they were still in an unfavourable position. Coming round again, the light went on to illuminate a periscope and schnorkel and six D/Cs were dropped from 270 feet. The Lib's gunners also fired into the target, and coming round once again an oil patch was seen, which later extended to half a mile.

U-1008 had sailed from Kiel on the 6th, heading for Norway and went down in position 5622/1110, after being scuttled by her crew.

7 May, 1945

U-320, a type VIIC/41 submarine, commanded by Oberleutnant Emmerich, damaged.

Catalina IV 'X', 210 Squadron, on patrol 0330–1650 hrs.

F/L K.M. Murrey	Pilot
FL W.C. Robertson	2nd pilot
FO F. Weston	3rd pilot
FO C. Humphrey	Nav
FO J.H. Moore	Eng
F/Sgt P.C.A. Alway	FME/AG
F/Sgt D. Fowler	1 WOP
F/Sgt I.W. Evans	2 WOP
F/Sgt L.W. Rose	WOM/AG
F/Sgt G. Swift	Rigger

At 0445 hrs, in position 6132/0132, a schnorkel and periscope, with white smoke, was seen. An attack was carried out one minute later, some 6 seconds after the boat had submerged. Four D/Cs fell and were seen to explode and later an oil patch was seen. At 0820 hrs a sono contact was made, with sounds of hammering as if repairs were being carried out. Two oil streaks developed each 120 feet long, and two hours later the hammering sounds could still be heard. At 1410 hammering and engine noises, but after contact of 11 hours the Catalina had to leave.

U-320 had not been on the surface following Germany's surrender, as all U-boat commanders had been ordered to do, so was attacked. She was badly damaged, and despite attempts at repair she had to be scuttled south-west of the Norwegian coast on 9 May.

---

19 Group

30 October, 1941

U-81, a type VIIC submarine, commanded by Oberleutnant Johann Krieg, damaged.

Catalina 'Z' AH545, 209 Squadron on a Cross Over patrol – 0800–1845 hrs.

FO D.M. Ryan	Pilot
PO D.H.C. Fry	2nd pilot
FO G.B. Windeler	Obs
and crew.	

At 1444 hrs this crew sighted the U-boat on the surface on a course of 090 degrees, 15 knots. U-boat fired off a three- or five-star pyrotechnic and began turning to port. Catalina circled and exchanged gunfire with it and an explosive shell hit the tail-plane, smashing the IFF and dinghy air bottle. The crew then sighted a Hudson aircraft. The U-boat commenced to dive at 1509 hrs and the Hudson attacked. The Catalina then attacked with four depth charges (although one hung up), by which time the U-boat had fully submerged. Circled for 15 minutes, seeing considerable oil and bubbles for 3 to 4 minutes.

Hudson 'H', 53 Squadron, on patrol 1140–1710 hrs.

PO Henry	Pilot
FS R.W. Gellard, DFM	Obs
Sgt Davy	WOP/AG
Sgt Turner	WOP/AG

Dived to attack from 600 feet and at 300 released three depth charges, estimating a hit. Aircraft circled and observed a large white patch of foam but very little else.

U-81, on its way to the Mediterranean, returned to Brest for repairs. It had already made two war cruises, the first from Kiel to Norway in July 1941, then sailing to Brest from Trondheim on 28 August. It eventually left for the Mediterranean on 4 November and made its base at La Spezia. It carried out an unknown number of cruises in the Med, being involved in the sinking of the *Ark Royal* on 13 November, 1941, under Capt Freidrich Guggenberger. It was eventually destroyed at the submarine base at Pola by a USAAF raid on 9 January, 1944.

Denis Mervyn Ryan later served with 210 Squadron, and in 1943 won the DFC as a flight lieutenant.

30 November, 1941

U-206, a type VIIC submarine under the command of Kapitänleutnant Herbert Opitz, sunk.

Whitley V 'B' Z9190 of 502 Squadron, on patrol 0609–1619 hrs.

FO R.W.G. Holdsworth	Pilot
Sgt W.H.A. Jones	2nd pilot
Sgt G. Gray	
Sgt W. Gill	
Sgt G.A. Smee	

During a sweep at 1215 hrs, an S/E contact was made at a distance of 5 miles while flying at 1800 feet. Sighted the submarine at 3 miles while aircraft was losing height. The U-boat crash-dived when the aircraft was 1½ miles away and was fully submerged when still one mile off. Flying Officer Holdsworth decided it was too late to attack along U-boat's course so turned to the right and released a stick of three D/Cs across U-boat's probable track and ahead of the submarine's swirl. After the attack the water turned a dirty brown colour. The aircraft then circled to port and came down the U-boat's track and released a second stick of three D/Cs, 100 yards ahead of the swirl. Nothing further seen, although the aircraft remained in the vicinity for 32 minutes.

However, the U-boat had gone to the bottom in position 4655/0716. It had left Trondheim on 5 August 1941, arriving at St Nazaire on 10 September. It made a patrol from there between 30 September and 28 October, but then had been ordered to proceed to the Mediterranean, sailing on 29 November. The next day it encountered Flying Officer Holdsworth and his crew.

Flying Officer Holdworth became tour-expired in February 1942 and was promoted to Flight Lieutenant. Sgt Jones was later commissioned and with 58 Squadron in 1943 was part of a crew which sank U-663 on 6 May.

1 December, 1941

U-563, a type VIIC submarine, commanded by Oberleutnant Hartmann, damaged.

Whitley 'T' Z9124, 502 Squadron, on patrol from Limavady, 0651–1638 hrs.

FO W.W. Cave	Pilot
Sgt A.E. Coates (NZ)	2nd pilot
Sgt J. Hall	
Sgt K. Nelson	
PO H. Pearce	
Sgt A. Cheshire	

At 1148 hrs in position 4700/1135, a submarine periscope and forward part of a conning tower was sighted, while flying at 4500 feet, at a distance of 2 miles. FO Cave dived and at 1000 feet, turned to starboard. Reducing height to 100 feet, he had turned the Whitley on to a reciprocal course to the U-boat and released six D/Cs in one stick. Three were seen to explode forward of the U-boat, one right on the bows, one on port amidships and the last on the starboard quarter. The rear gunner saw the

U-boat completely obliterated by water for 4–5 seconds. Aircraft turned to port and made two circles, firing at the U-boat with its machine guns from front and rear turrets, tracer being seen to hit the conning tower. Five separate machine-gun attacks were made and a man was seen to dive into the conning tower. The U-boat then submerged, being almost stationary. There was some traces of oil on the surface of the sea and a few minutes later a large spout of oil and air bubbles were seen, about 50 feet in diameter. Fifteen minutes later the conning tower reappeared for about 30 seconds, then disappeared.

U-563 had left Brest on the 29 November, 1941 to sail to the Mediterranean and was forced to return to Lorient on 2 December following its encounter with 502 Squadron. It was eventually sunk on its eighth war cruise, on 31 May, 1943, having itself sunk five ships including the destroyer HMS *Cossack*, on 23 October, 1941.

FO Cave later received the DFC and flew with 59 Squadron, but was killed in a flying accident in May 1943. Sgt Coates was later commissioned and was reported missing on 15 September, 1942.

1 April, 1942

U-129, a type IXC submarine commanded by Kapitänleutnant Nicolai Clausen, damaged.

Whitley VII 'F', 502 Squadron. On patrol 1839–0510 (1/2 April).

F/Sgt V.D. Pope	Pilot
Sgt R. Green	2nd pilot
Sgt W.H. Ison	Obs
F/L W.O'M. Brayton	
Sgt A. Crawford	
Sgt P.G. Sharpe	

Seventeen minutes before midnight, in position 4630/0635, a U-boat was sighted on the surface at 700 yards range. Flight Sergeant Pope attacked at 1150 hrs from the U-boat's starboard quarter, releasing six 250 lb D/Cs from 50 feet. The first two exploded short of the submarine, two aft of the conning tower, but the last two not seen as the crew were busily watching the earlier explosions. Following the explosions, a burst of air bubbles, the length of the U-boat, was seen on the surface and a further convulsion took place three minutes later. Aircraft stayed in the vicinity for 27 minutes before continuing patrol. At 0107 hrs a signal ordered a return to the attack position to carry out a search, but nothing further was seen.

U-129 was on its fourth war cruise, having sailed from Lorient for the Caribbean on 25 January, 1942. It was on its way home when damaged by 502 Squadron, limping into Lorient on 5 April, the damage keeping the vessel in harbour until 20 May when it made its next patrol. In all U-129 was to make 10 patrols, including one in the Gulf of Mexico in June 1942. It was eventually scuttled by its then CO, Ltn. von Harpe, in Lorient harbour, 19 August, 1944.

Flight Sergeant Victor Danial Pope received the DFM, the first for the squadron, and was commissioned. Sergeant Ison too received a commission in June 1942.

14 April, 1942

U-590, a type VIIC submarine, commanded by Oberleutnant W. Kruer, damaged.

Whitley VII 'M' of 502 Squadron, on patrol from St Eval, 0730–1659 hrs.

FO E. Cotton	Pilot
PO A.J.W. Birch	2nd pilot
F/Sgt J.B. Murray	
F/Sgt R.F. Spears	WOP/AG
F/Sgt C.F. Hodgkinson	
Sgt R. Miles	

Obtained several radar contacts during patrol which materialized as Spanish fishing vessels. Then at 1021 hrs, a contact at 9 miles to port turned out to be a fully surfaced U-boat. The aircraft was at 1000 feet, and the U-boat was 5 miles ahead in position 4909/1201. It was attacked while it was in the act of crash-diving, Cotton releasing six 250 lb D/Cs from between 30 to 40 feet, spacing 50 feet. All explosions were seen across U-boat, just abaft of the conning tower. Aircraft circled for 14 minutes, but nothing further seen. The aircraft then flew 30 miles away and returned 30 minutes later, but still nothing could be seen or detected.

U-590 was on its way from Kiel to St. Nazaire, having sailed on 4 April. It arrived damaged on the 17th, following its encounter with 502 Squadron. It later carried out a total of seven war cruises, the last to South American waters on 8 June, 1943. On 9 July, it was sunk in position 0322/4838, north-west of the River Amazon by an aircraft of VP 94 Squadron, US Navy.

Flying Officer Edward Cotton later received the DFC and was promoted to Flight Lieutenant. Tony

Birch went to 58 Squadron and sank the Italian submarine *Tazzoli* on 16 May, 1943. Murray was promoted to Warrant Officer and Spears was later commissioned.

4 June, 1942

The Italian Submarine *Luigi Torelli*, commanded by Tenente di vascello Augusto Migliorini, damaged.

Wellington 'F' ES986

SL J.H. Greswell	Pilot
PO A.W.R. Triggs RAAF	2nd pilot,
PO S.J. Pooley	Nav
Sgt E.A. Walker	
Sgt E. Roberts	
Sgt D.W. Archibald	

Squadron Leader Greswell sighted two U-boats and selected one, attacking in a shallow dive from a distance of ¾ mile. At a height of 50 feet he dropped four 296 lb Torpex Mk 8 D/Cs with Mk 3 pistols, set to explode at 25 feet, with a spacing of 35 feet. Three exploded, one on starboard quarter about five yards from the hull, the other two on the port side. The second U-boat was about 12 miles from the first one, and was attacked from 150 feet with machine-gun fire, scoring hits on the hull and conning tower.

The squadron had only become operational during this month, the first patrols having been flown on the night of 3/4 June.

This Marconi class submarine was to receive further damage three days later, see next entry.

J.H. Greswell later became Air Commodore, CB, CBE, DSO, DFC. Triggs became a Flight Lieutenant, MBE, DFC, and later flew with 23 RAAF Squadron.

5 June, 1942

U-71, a type VIIC submarine under the command of Korvettenkapitän Walter Flachsenberg, damaged.

Sunderland 'U' W3986, 10 RAAF Squadron, on patrol 1125–2350 hrs.

F/L S.R.C. Wood	Captain
FO H.D. White	1st pilot
PO D. Griffiths	2nd pilot
PO H. Winstanley	Nav
Sgt C.E. Nicholls	1st WOP
Sgt T.N. Price	2nd WOP

AC1 R.A. Reid	Rigger
Cpl W.L. McPerry	Armouror
Sgt P. McCombe	Fitter I
Cpl C.A. Whitley	Fitter II
LAC C.H. Mills	Rear Gunner
Sgt G.C. Reid, RAF	Sub spotter

The crew reached their patrol area at 1545 hrs and almost at once got an S/E contact at 8 miles on the starboard bow. One minute later, while at 5000 feet a fully surfaced U-boat was seen at 8–10 miles. Wood brought the Sunderland down to 50 ft, as the U-boat began to dive, attacked and released eight D/Cs, which appeared to straddle the target 130 yards ahead of the predicted track, 25 seconds after it had crash-dived. A minute later the U-boat came back to the surface bow first and, on settling, seemed to be down by the bows, which were awash with the stern raised and it had a list of 15 degrees to port. With the U-boat stationary, the Sunderland made several machine-gun attacks. The boat then began to move and some men appeared on the conning tower, but quickly disappeared when the rear gunner again opened fire. Then one man was seen by the heavy forward gun and then the U-boat opened fire with both cannon and the deck gun, scoring several hits on the aircraft. The U-boat then got under way and dived. The Sunderland remained nearby for two hours, but saw nothing further.

When leaving the area at 1935 hrs, a Focke Wulf 200 was sighted on the port quarter one mile away. It began firing on the Sunderland and made three attacks, the last damaging the Sunderland, cutting the power lines to the rear turret. Temporary repairs brought the turrret back into operation as another attack was made, although the turret had to have some manual help. In this attack the FW 200 was hit by the midships gunners and it broke off the attack. Two of the Sunderland crew had been slightly injured and the aircraft itself had five large and 18 small holes from cannon shell hits; the R/T aerial was shot away and both flaps were damaged.

U-71 was on its seventh war cruise, having left La Pallice on 4 June, whence it was forced to return on the 6th. It sailed again on the 11th only to return again after being depth charged by RN ships. In all it made 12 patrols, the last between 27 March and 30 April, 1943, when it became a training boat. It was finally scuttled in Wilhelmshaven in May 1945. It sank the tanker *Dixie Arrow* on 26 March 1942.

Flight Lieutenant Wood (later Wing Commander) later received the DFC. He and Griffiths were involved in the damaging of an Italian submarine on 1 September, 1942.

7 June, 1942

The *Luigi Torelli*, damaged during 172 Squadron's attack, was found again on the 7th by two Sunderlands of 10 RAAF Squadron, and sustained more damage.

Sunderland 'X' W3994 on Patrol 0125–1345 hrs.

PO T.A. Egerton	Captain
PO M.S. Mainprize	1st pilot
Sgt G. Strath	2nd pilot
PO T. Fairway	Nav
PO J.H. Portus	2nd Nav
Sgt H.W. Knight	Fitter I
Cpl A.W. Reeves	Fitter II
Sgt M.R. Delaney	1st WOP
Sgt C. Keane	2nd WOP
LAC E.G. Luck	Rigger
PO A.H. Steele	Rear Gunner
LAC M.K. Miller	Armourer

Sunderland 'A' W4019 on Patrol 0140–1215 hrs.

F/L E.StC. Yeoman	Captain
PO J.P. Roberts	1st pilot
PO R. Carson	2nd pilot
PO White	Nav
Sgt G.F. Horgan	Fitter I
AC L.T. Hogg	Fitter II
Sgt J.M. Lawrie	1st WOP
Sgt W.H. Isle	2nd WOP
AC1 W.E. Menzies	Rigger
Sgt J.A. Harrison	Rear Gunner
LAC S. Pile	Armourer
PO C. Austin	Pilot under instruction

At 0712 hrs, Pilot Officer Egerton was at 1500 feet when a U-boat was sighted 5 miles away. There were also four or five small boats in the area, the nearest being ¼ mile from the sub. As the Sunderland approached and manoeuvred to attack the submarine opened fire at 3000 yards, with a heavy gun. The attack was made out of the sun at an angle of 30 degrees to the U-boat's course, on the port bow, with one stick of D/Cs. One large explosion was observed alongside the boat's stern, then it began to zigzag through the spray at reduced speed. During the run-in the front gunner had scored many hits from the turret and now the rear gunner opened fire. However, the Sunderland was hit also and two of the crew received shrapnel wounds. A message of the sighting had already been sent to base and at 0740 hrs, Flight Lieutenant Yeoman's aircraft arrived on the scene.

He and his crew had been flying along the Spanish coast by Cape Mayor when they saw the other Sunderland and then the submarine. As they approached and began to circle, the submarine opened fire on them too, hitting the aircraft's tail. Yeoman brought the Sunderland into an attack, the front gunner opening fire as they closed. Eight D/Cs were released (although one failed to fall), and the last two were considered to have exploded under the submarine amidships, the others some yards on the starboard beam. The sub was seen to be lifted from the water and then turned to port and ejected from the stern what appeared to be a torpedo. Due to lack of fuel Yeoman had soon to turn for home. Shortly afterwards, an Arado seaplane was seen coming in towards the Sunderland's stern, so Yeoman flew low over the sea as the rear gunner opened fire from 400 yards. The Arado too opened fire, but then sheared away to come round for a second attack. Both tail and midships gunners fired at the German plane, which then turned and disappeared.

The *Luigi Torelli* had sailed from La Pallice on 2 June for the Bahamas in company with the Italian submarine *Morosini*. It was so badly damaged by these attacks that it was beached in Santander, Spain, and an air reconaissance showed the vessel to have a large hole amidships.

Pilot Officer Tom Egerton received a Mention in Despatches for his part in the attack. He later became a Squadron Leader, DFC. Pilot Officer Mainprize later received the DFC for his part in the sinking of U-563 on 31 May, 1943. Pilot Officer Roberts was part of a crew which sank U-465 on 7 May, 1943, and when captain of his own crew sank U-426 on 8 January, 1944, and received the DFC. Flight Lieutenant Yeoman, Pilot Officer Carson, Sergeant Isle and Aircraftmen Hogg and Menzies were all lost on 9 August, 1943.

11 June, 1942

U-105, a type IXB submarine of 1051 tons, commanded by Kapitänleutnant Jurgen Nissen, damaged.

Sunderland 'W' W3993 of 10 RAAF Squadron, on patrol 0515–1815 hrs.

F/L E.B. Martin,	Captain
PO J. Hazard	1st Pilot
PO G.G. Rossiter	2nd Pilot
PO J.S. Rolland	Nav
PO A. Meaker	Nav U/I
Sgt E. Brill	Fitter I
Cpl W. Fitzgerald	Fitter I
Sgt E. Biggs	1st WOP
Sgt G. Coysh	2nd WOP
LAC D. Graham	Rigger
Sgt M. Mattner	Rear Gunner
LAC G. Hore	Armourer.

At 0930 hrs whilst at 2000 feet, a fully surfaced U-boat was sighted 5 miles away on the port bow. Martin dived from dead astern, and at approx 40 feet dropped six D/Cs. All exploded on or adjacent to the U-boat, which was then seen stopped in the water, with a list to starboard. It then seemed to wallow, with first the stern and then the bows up, but then began to move slowly forward, turned to port and submerged. A minute later it resurfaced and the Sunderland attacked with two anti-submarine bombs in two separate attacks from the stern, dropping one bomb on each run from 600 feet, while both front and rear gunners opened fire as the U-boat's gunners also fired, the latter scoring a hit in the port wing tip. After the second bomb, some light grey smoke was seen coming from the conning tower, but the aircraft had then to leave the area due to a low fuel state.

U-105 was on its seventh war cruise, having left Lorient on 7 June. It was forced to enter the Spanish port of Ferrel on the 12th for urgent repairs, then left for Lorient on the 28th, which it reached the next day. Its next patrol did not take place until 23 November – to Trinidad. In was sunk on its ninth patrol to West Africa, which it began on 16 March, 1943. On 2 June, 1943, off Dakar, it was destroyed by 141 Free French Squadron escorting convoy SL 130, in position 1415/1735.

Flight Lieutenant Eric Martin and Pilot Officer Meaker were both killed in action on 31 July, 1942. Pilot Officer Jacques Hazard (a Free French pilot) was reported missing on 21 June. Rossiter sank U-465 on 7 May, 1943, while Pilot Officer Rolland was part of the crew of 461 Squadron which sank U-461 on 30 July, 1943.

23 June, 1942

U-753, a type VIIC submarine, commanded by Korvettenkapitän Alfred Manhardt von Mannstein, damaged.

Whitley 'C' Z9135, of 58 Squadron, on patrol 1050–2025 hrs.

F/Sgt W. Jones	Pilot
Sgt H. Hughes	2nd pilot
Sgt C.J. McNelly	Obs (Can)
Sgt F.G. Andrews	WOP/AG

| Sgt A. Hoey | WOP/AG |
| Sgt K. Broome | WOP/AG |

On anti-submarine patrol over the Bay of Biscay, sighted a U-boat at 1610 hrs, on the surface. As the attack was made the U-boat dived, but was still visible under the water as the Whitley passed over to drop the D/Cs. These fell 20–30 yards ahead of the swirl some 5 seconds after the sub went under.

A high fountain of water and then several patches of oil resulted and 5 minutes later the boat returned to the surface and the crew manned the guns. The Whitley was hit by gunfire, but the front and rear gunners also opened fire, and one man was seen to fall overboard and others collapse in the conning tower. U-boat later disappeared at a steep angle without any apparent forward movement, leaving just an oil patch. Much later radio messages, calling for assistance, were intercepted from the damaged U-boat.

U-753 was on its third war cruise, having left La Pallice on 22 April. It was returning from the Caribbean when badly damaged by Jones and his crew, but made it into harbour on the 25th. In all, U-753 made six patrols, but was sunk near convoy HX 237, north-east of the Azores on 13 May, 1943, by 423 Squadron.

Jones and his crew had been posted to the squadron in mid-June and this was only their second anti-submarine patrol.

6 July 1942

U-502, a type IX C/40 submarine, commanded by Kapitänleutnant Jurgen von Rosenstiel, sunk.

Wellington 'H' of 172 Squadron, on patrol 2239–0745 hrs.

PO W.B. Howell (US)	Pilot	Sgt F.A. Smith
Sgt G.E. Whitley		PO J.N. Robinson
PO E. Hebden		Sgt J.H. Philcox

Picked up a S/E contact at 7 miles and at 0445 hrs, when one mile from the contact, the Leigh Light was switched on, illuminating a U-boat on the surface. Four D/Cs were released from 50 feet across its bows from starboard to port as it was in the act of crash-diving, the decks and conning tower still visible. The rear gunner opened fire as the Wellington passed over and as the spray from the exploding D/Cs subsided, he saw a swirling mass of water. The aircraft returned and dropped flame floats, the crew seeing the water to be of much darker colour than

the rest of the sea. The Wellington remained in the vicinity till 0513 hrs, but made no further contact.

U-502 was returning from the Caribbean on its fourth war cruise, having left Lorient on 22 April. It was later confirmed as sunk in position 4610/0640. Its first patrol had been between September and November 1941 and the boat had been credited with sinking 16 Allied ships.

Pilot Officer Howell, an American, received the DFC, and was later a Captain in the US Navy. This was the first successful attack by a Leigh Light aircraft, and the first by a Wellington.

12 July, 1942

U-159, a type IXC submarine, commanded by Kapitänleutnant Helmut Witte, damaged.

Wellington 'H' of 172 Squadron, on patrol 2215–0635 hrs.

PO W.B. Howell (US)	Pilot	Sgt F.V. Smith
Sgt G.E. Whitley		PO J.H. Robinson
PO E. Hebden		Sgt J.H. Philcox

At 0100 hrs in position 4642/0455, 'H' was flying at 1000 feet when an S/E contact was made at 7 miles. Howell reduced height to 300 feet and at ¾ of a mile the Leigh Light was turned on to illuminate a fully surfaced U-boat. The U-boat immediately opened fire as Howell came in to drop four D/Cs from 100 feet across the vessel. The rear gunner fired 400 rounds as they flew over the explosions and saw a red glow through the spray. The U-boat was not seen again, although a search was carried out for over two hours.

U-159 was returning to Lorient from the Caribbean, having sailed on 14 May. It had been a successful second patrol, for it had sunk 10 ships, and Helmut Witte received the Knight's Cross. He was lucky to survive Howell's attack, but he did and brought his damaged submarine into Lorient on the 13th. During the period May to December 1942, Witte sank a total of 21 Allied ships. On 12 June, 1943, U-159 sailed again for the Caribbean under the command of a new skipper, Oblt H. Beckmann, and was sunk in position 1558/7344 east-south-east of Jamaica by a Mariner aircraft of VP 32 Squadron, US Navy.

This was Wiley Howell's second successful attack in a week.

17 July, 1942

U-751, a type VIIC submarine, commanded by Korvettenkapitän Gerhard Bigalk, sunk.

Whitley 'H' of 502 Squadron, on patrol 0802–1805 hrs.

PO A.R.A. Hunt	Pilot	Sgt E.S. Kingsford
F/Sgt I.S. Currie		Sgt G. Sutcliffe
Sgt C.W. Crouch		Sgt S.A. Bailey

Lancaster 'F' R5724 of 61 Squadron, on patrol 0730–1810 hrs.

F/L P.R. Casement	Pilot
Sgt I.A. Woodward (NZ)	2nd pilot
FO Wright	Nav
F/Sgt A.B. Hay	Nav
Sgt W.T. Upton	WOP
Sgt T.A. Jeffries	AB
F/Sgt L.G. Galloway	AG
Sgt J.B. Aitken	AG

The U-boat was sighted on the surface in position 4513/1222 and the Whitley pilot altered course and dived, releasing D/Cs from 50 feet across the conning tower. After the attack the U-boat moved slowly and began to circle to port. Then two 100 lb anti-submarine bombs were dropped from 600 feet, but they undershot by 75 feet, and several machine-gun attacks were also made. After 50 minutes the U-boat disappeared stern first, sliding back under the water.

An hour later, the Lancaster of 61 Squadron sighted an oil patch and then saw the U-boat, which had resurfaced, about a mile away. Flight Lieutenant Casement made two attacks, the first with D/Cs, and when it was obvious the boat was not able to dive, he climbed to 700 feet and dropped his anti-submarine bombs. Meanwhile his gunners picked off several of the U-boat's crew who were trying to man the guns. The U-boat then slid stern first under the water and its crew began to abandon ship.

Peter Casement, later Group Captain, DSO, DFC & Bar, whose squadron was briefly attached to Coastal Command from Bomber Command, recalls: 'Our detachment to St Eval was brief and a relatively relaxing interlude in a rather hectic Bomber Command summer. Flying Officer Wright was not a member of my own crew, but a member of one of the resident Coastal Command squadrons at St Eval who was sent along with us to assist in the niceties of Coastal Command procedures of which we knew nothing, as this was our first patrol.

'As to the action itself it was all very straight-forward. I had a well-tried and experienced crew and we had no great problem in attacking what – eventually – turned out to be a sitting duck. There was some anxiety about gunfire from the boat and I believe one propeller spinner was holed.

'We were, of course, unaware that 502 Squadron had been involved earlier and I think we were mildly surprised that the U-boat had not dived, and it only dawned on us later that it was probably disabled already. Despite a good deal of local excitement (first sortie by Bomber Command detachment, etc) I have to say that I do not recall this event with any particular sense of satisfaction. No great skill was demanded, or daring.'

U-751 was leaving on its seventh war cruise when damaged and sunk by these two crews, having left St Nazaire on the 14th. It was sunk in position 4514/1222. It had sunk five Allied ships and Bigalk was a recipient of the Knight's Cross.

Pilot Officer A.R.A. Hunt received the DFC in August 1942. In 1944, Squadron Leader Casement was a flight commander on 120 Squadron, Coastal Command.

27 July, 1942

U-106, a type XB submarine commanded by Kapitänleutnant Hermann Rasch, damaged.

Wellington 'A' of 311 (Czech) Squadron, on patrol 0918–1941 hrs.

SL J. Stransky	Pilot	PO Hrebadka
Sgt Vycha		Sgt Halada
Sgt Havranek		Sgt Bukancik

At 1530 hrs, while at 1500 feet, a U-boat was spotted 2 miles away, whilst the Wellington was above three tunnymen, one of which altered course towards the U-boat. The U-boat made no attempt to dive as the aircraft attacked but opened fire with twin guns abaft the conning tower. The aircraft released four Torpex D/Cs from 40-50 feet as the front gunner fired into the submarine. As the aircraft turned for a second attack the U-boat could be seen listing slightly and almost stopped. Two more D/Cs went down from 10 feet, one exploding right alongside the boat. The U-boat then went under without any forward motion, and although the crew saw the conning tower hatch still open, the lower hatch must have been closed as no bubbles or debris came up. Only a patch of green/grey oil was left visible in position 4625/0928.

U-106 was just leaving on its seventh patrol,

having left Lorient on the 25th. It limped back on the 28th. Its first patrol was made in January 1941 under Ltn Oesten and its last CO was Oblt Wolfdietrich Damerow. Exactly a year later, U-106 was off on its tenth cruise but was sunk by 228 and 461 Squadrons on 2 August, 1943.

Squadron Leader Stransky received the DFC in August and the 3rd Class of the Czech War Cross. Sergeant Halada received the 1st Class Czech War Cross.

10 August, 1942

U-578, a type VIIC submarine, commanded by Korvettenkapitän Rehwinkel, sunk.

Wellington 'H', of 311 Czech Squadron, on patrol 1105–2106 hrs.

FO J. Nyult Pilot	Sgt Trmka
Sgt Sotola	Sgt Kubin
Sgt Mocek	Sgt Kokes

Nyult and his crew found this U-boat at 1440 hrs, but it made no attempt to dive. The Wellington attacked, but only dropped three D/Cs when Nyult found he was overshooting the target. They exploded at 10, 25 and 60 feet from the submarine. Three men could be seen in the conning tower and the front gunner of the Wellington opened fire on them at 300 yards. The U-boat began firing too. As the Wellington came in again to drop the three remaining D/Cs, the U-boat was in the act of diving. The conning tower and stern were still visible when the second attack was made. When the aircraft circled the scene, a large patch of oil, 100 yards in diameter, appeared, which after 35 minutes had grown to 150 yards.

U-578 was on its fourth war cruise, having set off from St Nazaire on the 6th for a patrol in the North Atlantic. It went down in position 4559/0744. Its first war cruise was made in January 1942. It had sunk seven ships.

31 August, 1942

U-256, a type VIIC submarine commanded by Kapitänleutnant Odo Loewe, damaged.

Whitley 'B', of 502 Squadron, on patrol 0703–1728 hrs.

FO E.G. Brooks	Sgt G. Geary
PO D. Evans	F/Sgt J. Wilson
F/Sgt R. McDonald	Sgt J.S. Coates

Whitley 'O' Z9144 of 51 Squadron, on patrol 1310–2302 hrs.

F/L E.O. Tandy	F/Sgt L.O. Weakley
Sgt W.J. Musson	Sgt K. Dandeker
Sgt E.V.J. Purnell	Sgt R.G. Sharland

The 502 Squadron crew were just investigating two Spanish trawlers and some tunnymen at 1449 hrs when they picked up an S/E contact at 18 miles on the port bow. Proceeding through cloud and reducing height, the Whitley broke cloud to find the U-boat almost underneath them. They circled and attacked, selecting eight D/Cs, but three failed to release. When they came round again the U-boat had gone.

Flight Lieutenant Tandy and his crew were on their outward leg from Bishop's Rock at this time, but at 1725 hrs they received a message that a U-boat had been attacked in position FNWY/5506 at 1450 hrs when it was on a course of 90 degrees. Tandy set course for this position and upon arrival found a U-boat on the surface 3 miles off. Tandy attacked down-sun and the U-boat began to dive when the aircraft was one mile away. With the front gunner firing at the disappearing target, the D/Cs were dropped 80–90 yards ahead of the swirl some 19 seconds after the boat had gone below the waves. Nothing further was seen of the U-boat although the aircraft remained in the area for 19 minutes, adopting baiting tactics. Five unidentified aircraft were also seen in the vicinity of the attack and this, together with a slight problem with the Whitley's port engine, decided the crew to turn for home.

U-256 was on its first cruise, sailing from Keil on 28 July to proceed to Lorient via the North Atlantic. It was on its run into the French port when it was seriously damaged in this attack. Because of the severe damage, the boat was nearly scrapped, but it was then adapted into a flak-boat. Its next war cruise came over a year later, sailing on 4 October, 1943, but was damaged by surface craft on 1 November. On its third cruise, having been reverted to normal armament, it shot down a Wellington of 407 Squadron in early 1944. On its fourth patrol it was damaged by 53 Squadron on 7 June 1944. In late 1944 it sailed to Bergen, where it was paid off in October.

Flight Lieutenant Edward Bertram Brooks received the DFC in April 1943.

1 September, 1942

The Italian Liuzzi Class submarine *Reginaldo Giuliano* commanded by Capitano di Corvetta Vittore Raccanelli, damaged.

Sunderland 'U' W3986, 10 RAAF Sqn, on patrol 0600–1815 hrs.

F/L S.R.C. Wood, DFC
PO Austin
PO D. Griffiths   2nd pilot
PO Gerrard
and crew

Sunderland 'R' W3983, 10 RAAF Sqn, on patrol 0605–1735 hrs.

F/L H.G. Pockley DFC
PO Gore
PO K.M. McKenzie
PO Skinner
and crew

When 'U' first sighted the vessel through cloud it was thought to be a ship but when identified, Wood dived to attack, whereupon the U-boat opened fire. He dropped four 250 lb D/Cs from 400 feet and an explosion was seen between conning tower and bows on the port side. A second attack was attempted, then Sunderland aircraft from 10 and 461 Squadrons were seen approaching. In contacting these, it was agreed to make a concerted attack, but before this could be carried out, 'U' was ordered to continue its patrol.

Sunderland 'R' made an approach towards the submarine through cloud, but was then ordered not to attack. Meanwhile, the sub opened fire with its forward gun. Aircraft circled and as the U-boat remained on the surface, Pockley decided to attack and dived from 1500 feet, dropping two 250 lb bombs. The Sunderland met intense return fire, its own gunners firing back. Made a second attack with one bomb, which exploded just astern of the sub, and the rear gunner estimated casualties amongst the U-boat crew. The Sunderland sustained some flak damage. Then an attack by 'R' and the 461 aircraft was agreed, but then base ordered both aircraft to continue with their patrols.

The submarine was damaged and a message, in Italian, was intercepted, which stated: 'Captain killed and casualties among crew. Require immediate air protection. Viva. First Lieutenant.' Whether the danger from enemy fighters was the reason the Sunderlands were withdrawn is not known.

F/L Pockley was killed in action on 25 March, 1945, and McKenzie on 17 May, 1943.

2 September, 1942

The *Reginaldo Giuliano*, damaged the previous day, sustained further damage.

Wellington 'A', 304 (Polish) Squadron, on patrol 0630–1548 hrs.

FO M. Kucharski   Pilot   Sgt T. Jasinski
FO S. Zurek   Sgt B. Kocyk
FO Z. Jaroszynski   S. Zesko

Sighted the U-boat at 1140 hrs in position 4430/0442, fully surfaced, 5 to 7 miles on the port bow. Aircraft attacked and released six D/Cs, the explosion of two completely obscuring the vessel. The aircraft's gunners fired on the run-up and several members of the deck crew were seen to collapse. No return fire was experienced, but two five-star red cartridges were fired as the Wellington approached. The submarine stopped and the Wellington dropped two separate 500 lb anti-submarine bombs, which undershot by 20 and 10 yards. The boat was now leaving a large oil patch and was listing to port, and about ten men were seen in the sea. The Wellington's gunners continued to fire at the boat and more men were seen to collapse or fall into the water. When the aircraft finally had to leave, the sub was down by the bows and surrounded by a large oil slick. No attempts to dive or man the guns had been made.

The *Reginaldo Giuliano* eventually got under way and put into the Spanish port of Santander, severely damaged and with a number of casualties. The boat had a final score of three ships sunk.

FO Kucharski later became a Squadron Leader and received the 1st and 2nd bars to the Cross of Valor.

3 September, 1942

U-705, a type VIIC submarine, commanded by Korvettenkapitän Karl-Horst Horn, sunk.

Whitley 'P' Z6978 of 77 Squadron, on patrol 1135–2055 hrs.

F/Sgt A.A. MacInnes   Sgt K.J. Seeley
F/L A.W. Martin   Sgt E. Billett
Sgt D. Mole   PO K.A. Adam

The sub was sighted from 2500 feet at 5 miles, S/E not being carried. The Whitley crew attacked with D/Cs, released from 50 feet, the U-boat appearing to be taken completely by surprise. The rear gunner and wireless operator definitely saw one of the D/Cs hit the boat's port saddle tank amidships and another explode within 20 feet of the port side. Three men were also seen in the conning tower wearing leather jerkins and peaked caps. Two more were between the tower and the forward gun, while three more stood on the aft part of the tower. The front gunner fired from point blank range as the aircraft approached and the rear gunner fired as they flew over. A steep turn heralded a second attack, the boat now being stationary but half-submerged. Four minutes later the boat went under but glare from the sun made it difficult to see any oil patches.

U-705 was on its first patrol, having sailed from Kiel for the North Atlantic on 1 August. It went down in position 4642/1107.

No. 77 Squadron was a Bomber Command unit loaned to 19 Group of Coastal Command, and based at RAF Chivenor from May to October 1942. An earlier assessment gave credit for the sinking of this submarine to another Whitley of 77 Squadron, Z9461 'V', PO T.S. Lea. However, it has now been established that this attack had been upon U-660, which was not damaged.

20 October, 1942

U-216, a type VIID minelaying submarine, commanded by Kapitänleutnant Karl-Otto Schultz, sunk.

Liberator 'H' FL910, 224 Squadron, on patrol 0935–1855 hrs.

FO D.M. Sleep	F/Sgt N.R. Johnson
Sgt S.E. Patton	PO J.E. Edwards
Sgt R. Rose	F/Sgt J. Clifford

At about 1600 hrs on the return flight, a fully surfaced U-boat was seen and it was attacked along its course, with six 250 lb D/Cs from 30 feet. They exploded on impact and the explosion damaged the Liberator, especially its elevators. It went into a steep uncontrollable climb, almost stalling, but the climb was brought under control by both pilots. The rear gunner had seen debris and wreckage fly up from the U-boat and watched as the elevators had disintegrated. The Lib was extremely tail-heavy and the anti-submarine bombs could not be jettisoned owing to damaged gear. Later the Engineer managed to release them manually. All loose gear was thrown

overboard and the flight home was accomplished by both pilots, continually relieved, bracing hands and knees on the control columns, while all the crew positioned themselves in the nose of the aeroplane to help balance it. About an hour before landing, the control column had to be tied forward with straps. The wireless had been knocked out and the electrics had failed. The Scilly Isles were sighted at 1840 hrs and the crew decided to try a crash landing at Predannack. When over the aerodrome, the elevator controls broke loose and in the crash landing Sergeant Rose suffered a broken leg. The Liberator was destroyed by fire, but the rest of crew got clear with just scratches and cuts.

U-216, which was on its first patrol, sailing from Kiel on 29 August for the North Atlantic, was destroyed in the attack and sank in position 4841/1925, with all hands, on her way to a Biscay port.

For his skill and courage, Flying Officer Sleep received the DFC.

24 October, 1942

U-599, a type VIIC submarine, commanded by Kapitänleutnant Wolfgang Breithaupt, sunk.

Liberator 'G' FK225, 224 Squadron, on patrol from Beaulieu 1050–2242 hrs.

PO B.P. Liddington	Pilot
Sgt L. Race	2nd pilot
Sgt J.E. Armstrong	Nav
F/Sgt R.A. Denney	
F/Sgt S. Burr	
Sgt F.T. Hamlyn	
PO W.J. McCaffery	

Air cover for convoy KX2, which was not met. At 1650 hrs sighted fully surfaced U-boat and attacked. As the Liberator came in a man was seen running towards the conning tower from the forward deck. After the attack the man was not seen and a dark patch of oil came to the surface 20 seconds after the U-boat had gone under. A further search for the convoy was commenced an hour later, but it was not located.

U-599 had sailed from Kiel on its first cruise on 27 August for a patrol in the North Atlantic. In was sunk in position 4607/1740 west-north-west of Cape Finisterre, on its way to a Biscay port.

10 November, 1942

U-66, a type IXC submarine, commanded by Capt Richard Zapp, damaged.

Wellington VIII 'D', 172 Squadron, on patrol 1745–0212 hrs.

FO D.E. Dixon	PO J. Burbridge
PO D.J. Ashworth	Sgt G. Cornfield
Sgt G.C. Bell	Sgt T.W. Young

At 2108 hrs in position 4613/0740, the U-boat was spotted when the aircraft was at 1000 feet, after making an S/E contact from 6 miles. The Leigh Light was switched on at half a mile and the U-boat made clearly visible just off the port bow. Four D/Cs were dropped across the boat's bows from 100 feet and the rear gunner fired 100 rounds as the aircraft flew over. The submarine began to make a half-circle to port and remained on the surface with reduced speed. 'D' remained in contact until 2320 hrs, when it had to return to base.

U-66 had left Lorient the previous day to begin its seventh war cruise and had to put back to port on the 11th. Its first cruise had been carried out in May and June 1941. It was damaged again on 3 August, 1943, by aircraft from the USS *Card* and was finally sunk on 6 May, 1944, on its tenth patrol, in position 1717/3229, west of the Cape Verde Islands. Its destruction was shared by an aircraft from the escort carrier USS *Block Island*, which damaged her, before the US destroyer *Buckley* rammed and boarded. Its new CO for her last voyage was Capt Seehausen. U-66 sank five ships off the US coast in early 1942, and in all was credited with 29 sinkings. Zapp received the Knight's Cross.

27 November, 1942

U-263, a type VIIC submarine, commanded by Kapitänleutnant Kurt Noelke, damaged.

Halifax II 'J' 405 (Canadian) Sqn, on patrol 0605–1708 hrs.

F/L C.W. Palmer	PO K.A. Decher
FO G.A. Sweany	F/Sgt J. McDonald
F/Sgt J.L. Taylor	F/Sgt L. Lasuchner
Sgt H.J. Anderson	

Hudson 'Q' FH260 233 Sqn, on patrol 0916–1555 hrs (24 Nov).

Sgt E.H. Smith	WO T.A.N. Watt
Sgt D.H. Beniston	Sgt H. Pike

Sergeant Smith attacked this U-boat at 1135 hrs on the 24th in position 3634/1200, and his D/Cs, dropped from head-on, seemed to explode all around the vessel. Oil and bubbles seen after the submarine had dived continued for several minutes. This attack was assessed as causing damage. (233 Sqn were Gibraltar based and details of this attack also appear under Gibraltar based aircraft.)

The U-boat was then found and attacked on the 26th by F/L F.G. Tiller of 59 Squadron in Henday's Bay at 1730 hrs. This brought the Canadian Halifax crew after her, by which time the U-boat had been met by two escort vessels. The ships were seen at a distance of 6 miles in position 4335/0255 and as the bomber approached the escort ships opened fire. It was 1115 hrs when Palmer attacked down-sun from the U-boat's starboard side, releasing six D/Cs from 200 feet while the boat was still on the surface. The U-boat had begun a turn, but the D/Cs fell towards its stern. No results were seen and the Halifax had to clear from the intense flak. Making a second attack, four D/Cs fell across the U-boat and again Palmer had to take avoiding action from the escort's fire, which shot away the machine's trailing aerial. When the Halifax came out of cloud shortly afterwards, the U-boat had disappeared.

U-263 was on its first patrol, sailing from Kiel on 27 October. Having been damaged West of Gibraltar, it limped into La Pallice on 29 November, having been damaged again by 405 Squadron as it entered the Bay of Biscay to pick up an escort. It did not sail again until 19 January, 1944, when it sortied out for the North Atlantic. Fate was against it for it hit an RAF-laid mine on the 20th and sank in position 4610/0114. It had sunk two ships during its maiden voyage.

No. 405 RCAF Squadron was another Bomber Command squadron on loan to Coastal Command for a period. Flight Lieutenant Palmer received the DFC and was later a Wing Commander and CO of 405 Squadron. He was reported missing on bomber operations, 26 September, 1944. Flying Officer Sweany later became a Squadron Leader, DSO, DFC, during his service with Bomber Command.

10 February, 1943

U-519, a type IXC submarine, commanded by Kapitänleutnant Gunter Eppen, sunk.

Liberator 'T', 2 Squadron, USAAF.

1st Lt W.L. Sandford   Pilot
and crew

It was a rainy and hazy day when this American crew picked up a radar contact at 3-4 miles at 0910 hrs and homed in to sight a U-boat on the surface in position 4705/1745, with two or three men seen on the bridge. The aircraft circled for position, but the U-boat had gone down by the time the Liberator reached it, although the top and rear gunners fired into the swirl. At 0928 hrs the aircraft had resumed the patrol when the left waist gunner saw a U-boat and at the same time an S/E contact was made on it at a distance of 4 miles. Sandford attacked as the U-boat was going under, its stern and deck still exposed. Six D/Cs went down, but they overshot, the rear gunner seeing one explode 30 feet to the starboard of the boat as he was firing. The conning tower broke surface and the decks were again awash. The Lib circled and made a second attack from 200 feet with three D/Cs. On the third run-in the navigator thought the boat was listing to starboard and seconds later it disappeared on an even keel as three more D/Cs went down. Later a brown patch appeared at the spot.

The Royal Navy assessed at the time that this attack 'possibly damaged' the U-boat and that the 'U-boat crew must have had a frightening few minutes'. However, it is now known that U-519, on its second war cruise, was sunk at this time, in position 4705/1834. It had begun this patrol on 30 January. Its first patrol, from Kiel to the Azores, ended in Lorient on 29 December.

No. 2 Squadron, USAAF, was one of several American squadrons attached to Coastal Command during the war. Lieutenant Sandford, not under Coastal Command control, later sank U-524 south of Madeira (Kapitänleutnant Freiher von Steinaacher) on 19 March, 1943.

19 February, 1943

U-268, a type VIIC submarine, commanded by Oberleutnant Ernst Heydemann, sunk.

Wellington VIII 'B' MP505, 172 Squadron, on patrol 2319–0710 hrs.

FO G.D. Lundon   FO J.G. Prideaux
FO G.B. Aldred   FO N. Barnett
Sgt C.H. Smith   Sgt D.M. McLeod

Flying over a smooth sea with visibility in the moon's glow at 10 miles under a 10/10ths cloud base of 2000 feet, an S/E contact was made at 4 miles on the port bow. Lundon homed in and a wake was sighted 20 miles dead ahead and at 0150 hrs, at one mile, a U-boat was seen in position 4703/0556. The Leigh Light was switched on at ¼ mile, which took the submarine by surprise as three men could be seen in the conning tower and three more around the forward deck gun, all cowering in the searchlight's beam. With no gunfire from the sub, Lundon released four D/Cs, one of which exploded 20 feet from the boat's port quarter, another just ahead of the conning tower, and a third close to the port bow. The boat appeared to stop in relation to the flame float which went down with the D/Cs, and as the aircraft circled the U-boat disappeared, leaving just an oil patch and bubbles, seen in the moon's glow. The Wellington circled around till 0255 hrs, by which time the oil patch had grown to 100 yards in diameter.

U-268 went straight to the bottom. It had moved from Kiel to Stavanger between 2 and 6 January, 1943, and then sailed on this, its first patrol, from Bergen on the 10th. It was making its way to its French base after sailing in the North Atlantic, where it had sunk one ship.

20 February, 1943

U-211, a type VIIC submarine, commanded by Kapitänleutnant Karl Hause, damaged.

Liberator 'C', 1 Squadron, USAAF.

Lt Wayne Johnson   Pilot
and crew

While at 1600 feet over a rough sea, the navigator in the nose sighted a broad wake of a fully surfaced U-boat three miles away in position 4930/2155. The pilot dived to attack at 1342 hrs, entering cloud, but then emerging when only 1–1½ miles from the boat. The navigator opened fire with the front gun, seeing strikes, and then the pilot released six Mk XI D/Cs from 200 feet. The crew's S/E operator, who was lying on the catwalk above the bomb doors, trying to get photos, saw the D/Cs splash into the water, four to starboard and another to port, as the U-boat was beginning to submerge. Others saw the explosions and the bows lift and 15 seconds later the U-boat had gone down. The Liberator circled a large patch of oil and bubbles until 1347 hrs, when baiting procedure began. Returned to the scene at 1424 hrs, but still nothing was visible. The crew had seen what they described as something resembling an octopus painted on both sides of the conning tower.

The Royal Navy assessed this as possible serious damage, and so it was. U-211, on it third war cruise, had only left Brest on the 13th and had to put back on the 25th. It was later converted to a flak boat and on its fifth war cruise was sunk by 179 Squadron on 19 November, 1943. It had sunk three ships, including the destroyer HMS *Firedrake* on 16 December, 1942.

26 February, 1943

U-508, a type IXC/40 submarine, commanded by Kapitänleutnant Georg Staats, damaged.

Liberator 'Z' AL507, 224 Squadron.

SL P.J. Cundy	Pilot
FO R. Sweeney	2nd pilot
FO R.R. Fabel, DFC	Nav
F/Sgt W. Owen	Eng
Sgt A. Graham	AG
Sgt H. Richardson	WOP/AG
F/Sgt I.A. Graham	WOP/AG
F/Sgt E. Cheek	WOP/AG

Over a calm sea with visibility 12–15 miles, a contact was made on the Mk V S/E at 1101 hrs, at 30 miles. Aircraft homed in and at 2000 feet saw a U-boat on the surface 6 miles away, in position 4133/2149. The submarine began to dive as the Liberator made its run-in from the boat's starboard beam, releasing four D/Cs, but without any visible results being seen. After circling the patrol was continued at 11.30 hrs.

This action was assessed as very nearly a good attack, but probably resulted in no damage, although the German crew would have been shaken up. However, U-508, which had sailed on this its third

war patrol from Lorient on the 22nd, was damaged and eventually had to cut short its cruise and return home. It was later sunk on its sixth patrol, which began on 9 November, 1943, being sent to the bottom three days later in position 4600/0730 by a Liberator of VP 103 Squadron US Navy, but not before the Liberator was shot down by the U-boat. Georg Staats received the Knight's Cross.

Peter Cundy had earlier flown with 53 Squadron and with this crew had been flying with 120 Squadron, so they were an experienced crew. Collectively and individually they were to achieve further success in the U-boat war. They had left 120 to take this Liberator II (AL507) nicknamed 'Dumbo' for Special Duties in the USA, returning with it in October 1942 and posted to 224 Squadron, who were converting from Hudsons to Liberators at Beaulieu. Peter Cundy recalls his attack on U-508: 'We were flying at about 6000 feet in clear blue sky above a calm sea when we spotted a U-boat almost immediately below. U-boats crash-dive in about 30 seconds, but we managed to get down somehow and dropped four depth charges across the swirl. Afraid our airspeed was too high, but this was not surprising under the circumstances. Shortly afterwards the U-boat's bows appeared and she hung vertically like a fishing float for about 4 minutes and then sank. We had no more depth charges to release, having successfully attacked (too late) another U-boat earlier in the day. Also, as our aircraft did not have gun mountings for the beam positions (nor self-sealing fuel tanks for that matter) the only further damage we could have inflicted was via the tail turret, which for various reasons could not have been very effective. In the event, and to our consternation, approximately 20 minutes later the U-boat slowly came to the surface and eventually got under way and headed eastwards at about six knots.'

3 March, 1943

U-525, a type IXC/40 submarine, commanded by Kapitänleutnant Hans-Joachim Drewitz, damaged.

Wellington 'B' MP505, 172 Squadron, on patrol 2251–0742 hrs.

F/Sgt J.L. Tweddle	Pilot
Sgt H.L. Gregory (NZ)	2nd pilot
Sgt J.W. Buxton	Nav
Sgt L. Harrop	WOP/AG
Sgt A.A. Turner	WOP/AG
Sgt D.A. Radburn	WOP/AG

An S/E contact was picked up when flying at 500 feet on a track of 133 degrees, just off to starboard at 6 miles. The Leigh Light was switched on when at ¾ mile from target, illuminating a fully surfaced U-boat which had already started to submerge when aircraft was ¼ mile away and at 250 feet. Tweddle got down to 60 feet and dropped the D/Cs across the boat's bows. Two bright blue flashes were seen either side of the conning tower and although the Wellington circled for ten minutes, nothing else was seen.

U-525 had been out on a long first patrol, sailing from Kiel to the North Atlantic on 15 December, 1942. She was making for Lorient when she was damaged by 172 Squadron. She was lost on her third patrol which began on 27 July, 1943 to the West Indies. On 11 August, she was sunk in positon 4129/3855 west-north-west of Flores near the Azores by aircraft from the escort carrier USS Card covering convoy UGS 13.

Duncan Radburn, remembers: 'It was me who saw the blue flashes on each side of the conning tower and I fired a hundred rounds off for good measure. It was a well executed attack and I was pleased to learn after the war that U-525 had to return to base badly damaged.'

Sergeants Buxton, Les Harrop and 'Ches' Turner were later members of another crew involved in the sinking of U-459 on 24 July, 1943. Turner was the sole survivor of that crew when their aircraft was shot down in that action (see later).

21 March, 1943

U-332, a type VIIC submarine, commanded by Oberleutnant Eberhard Huttemann, damaged.

Wellington XII 'T', 172 Squadron, on patrol 1937–0230 hrs.

FO I.D. Prebble Pilot	Sgt D.K.R. Rowley
PO J.G. McCormack	Sgt T.C. Moynihan
FO G.O. Whatnall	Sgt W.J. Clemow

At 2201 hrs an S/E contact was made and 4 minutes later in position 4647/0370, having reduced height to 200 feet, the Leigh Light illuminated a fully surfaced U-boat one mile ahead. Owing to gunfire the light was switched off and the rear gunner fired four or five bursts as the aircraft flew over the boat. The aircraft turned, but the radar contact faded and was then lost. Some time later another radar contact was made 2½ miles off. At 2255 hrs in position 4520/0800 a U-boat was spotted in the moonlight so the Light was not required. Six D/Cs went down

from 100 feet and explosions completely obscured the boat. Coming in again the sea was empty except for a swirl where the U-boat had been. Circling once again, the conning tower of the U-boat came to the surface, but then it disappeared leaving a bubbling patch of water some 11 minutes after the first attack.

U-332, from La Pallice was on its way home from its sixth patrol, having been operating in the North Atlantic. It reached port on the 24th, damaged. It sailed for its seventh patrol in April, but was sunk by 461 Squadron on 2 May.

22 March, 1943

U-665, a type VIIC submarine, commanded by Oberleutnant Hans-Jurgen Haupt, sunk.

Wellington XII 'G' MP539, 172 Squadron

FO P.H. Stembridge	Pilot
PO J. Boyd	2nd pilot
FO P. Dene	Nav
PO E.C.C. Goodman	WOP/AG
F/Sgt D. Hobden	WOP/AG
Sgt R. Webb	WOP/AG

Peter Stembridge retired as a Group Captain. Before his untimely death in November 1988 he told me: 'Soon after midnight on 22 March, height 1000 feet and visibility one mile, we had an ASV III contact at 7 miles. We homed and at one mile, height 350 feet, turned on the Leigh Light; at half a mile we sighted a U-boat in the act of crash-diving, conning tower and stern still visible. I dropped six D/Cs from a height of 70 feet, ahead of the conning tower swirl, the stern being still visible. Due to the angle of attack, the D/Cs had more of a cluster effect than a spaced "stick" and the rear gunner reported what appeared to be one large explosion with the full length of the U-boat visible in the trough caused thereby; as he could not see the conning tower or hydroplanes, he thought the U-boat was keel uppermost. He fired a burst of about 50 rounds from his guns for good measure! I made a wide circle and came back at 250 feet over the flame floats 3 minutes later, with the Leigh Light on. We saw two separate patches of very large bubbles, but no sign of any part of the U-boat. It was confirmed in due course that we had sunk U-665.'

U-665 had indeed been sunk, in position 4647/0958. It was on its maiden voyage, sailing from Kiel on 20 February and making its way to a French port from its North Atlantic patrol area, where it had sunk one ship.

Flying Officer Stembridge and his crew had several encounters with U-boats, and he would receive the DFC. Their first attack was made on 22/23 December, 1942, which was assessed as causing 'serious or lethal damage', but it had not. Now however, the crew had been more successful.

10 April, 1943

U-376, a type VIIC submarine, commanded by Kapitänleutnant Friedrich Marks, sunk.

Wellington XII 'C', 172 Squadron, on patrol 2027–0314 hrs.

PO G.H. Whiteley	Pilot	Sgt R. Cross
Sgt A. McNiven		Sgt P.H. Philcox
Sgt S.G. Hoad		Sgt B.P. Hitchman

Flying on a track of 240 degrees, at 2500 feet, an S/E contact was made at 2244 hrs at six miles to port. An almost complete turn was made to starboard and contact again picked up. Homing in and reducing height to 600 feet, the Light was exposed at ¾ of a mile, which illuminated a U-boat in position 4648/0900. An attack was made from the boat's starboard quarter and D/Cs released from 25 feet which were seen to straddle the target, although only three were definitely seen to explode, one close to the starboard quarter, the other two on the port beam. Circling back to the area nothing was seen and no radar contact made.

However, the attack had been lethal and U-376 perished. This U-boat had left Kiel in March 1942 as part of the Arctic Flotilla and had carried out a number of war patrols. During one of these, she had been part of a three-boat Wolf Pack which had attacked convoys PQ 14 and QP 10 in March 1942. In January 1943 U-376 sailed from Bergen to St. Nazaire and sailed on her last patrol on 6 April from La Pallice. She had sunk two ships.

10 April, 1943

U-465, a type VIIC submarine, commanded by Kapitänleutnant Heinz Wolf, damaged.

Catalina 'M', 210 Squadron, on patrol from Pembroke Dock, 1922–1115.

F/L F. Squire	Pilot	
Sgt Ridley		
		Sgt A.E. Fielder

FO Atkinson	Sgt Simpson
FL Talbot	Sgt G. Miller
F/Sgt C.L. Jones	Sgt G.S. Brown
F/Sgt S.H. Leigh	FO Adamson

Flying on an 'Enclose' patrol, a U-boat was sighted at 2241 hrs on a course of 230 degrees, estimated speed 15 knots. An S/E contact had been picked up at 4 miles on the starboard side and the Catalina turned to investigate.

Contact was then lost, but the aircraft circled and the radar contact re-established. Flight Lieutenant Squire dropped four D/Cs from between 50 and 70 feet, but saw nothing further after the attack.

U-465, however, had been damaged. It had sailed from Lorient on the 7th and had to return, arriving back on the 14th. She had been damaged by two aircraft of 120 Squadron on her second cruise, in February 1943, and on her fourth, which began from St. Nazaire on 29th April, 1943, she was sunk by 10 RAAF Squadron on 7th May.

Flight Lieutenant Frank Squire later became a squadron leader and ended the war with the DSO and DFC.

26 April, 1943

U-566, a type VIIC submarine, commanded by Kapitänleutnant Hans Hornkohl, damaged.

Wellington XII 'R', 172 Squadron, on patrol 2050–0346 hrs.

Sgt A. Coumbis	Pilot	Sgt G.W. Young
Sgt N.P. Walker		Sgt H. Hever
FO C.D.J. Ashworth		F/Sgt G.C. Bell

Flying in the Derange area of the Bay, over a rough sea with visibilty 3 to 4 miles and 10/10ths cloud at 1700 feet, an S/E contact was obtained at 2325 hrs at 4 miles. Aircraft homed and lost height. When at 200 feet and ¾ of a mile away, the Leigh Light was switched on, illuminating a U-boat with its decks awash in position 4629/0921. Coumbis attacked, releasing six D/Cs from 50 feet, straddling the boat's bows, the rear gunner seeing three large explosions. They circled and switched the light back on at 2 miles, again picking up the U-boat between two flame floats. The enemy vessel began to open up with erratic and wild gunfire so the light was switched off and evasive action taken. After 12 minutes the radar contact faded so the patrol was resumed.

U-566 had sailed from Brest earlier on this day and had to limp back there on the 29th, thereby ending prematurely its seventh patrol. On its fifth patrol in late 1942, it had been damaged by 233 Squadron. It was sunk on its 9th patrol in October 1943 by 179 Squadron.

Sergeant Alex Coumbis was to achieve another success in July.

29 April, 1943

U-437, a type VIIC submarine, commanded by Oberleutnant Hermann Lamby, damaged.

Wellington 'H' HP630, 172 Squadron

FO P.H. Stembridge	Pilot
PO J. Bird	2nd pilot
PO P. Dene	Nav
PO E.C.C. Goodman	WOP/AG
F/Sgt D.H. Hobden	WOP/AG
Sgt R. Webb	WOP/AG

Liberator 'D' 224 Squadron, on patrol 0519–1440 hrs.

F/L A.R. Laughland	Pilot	
Sgt G. Cochrane		FO P. Caldwell
Sgt D. Pess		FO T.E. Kubein
Sgt H. Kehler		F/Sgt A. Jeffrey
Sgt H.R.A. Berry		Sgt R. Heelis

The late Group Captain Stembridge recalled: 'Just past midnight we detected an ASV III contact at 8 miles (position 4508/0943); at 1½ miles I sighted a wake and at ¾ mile we illuminated a fully surfaced U-boat. I dropped six D/Cs from a height of 100 feet, pulling out of a comparatively steep diving turn, so again the D/Cs had more of a cluster effect than a spaced "stick" as had happened on 22 March. During our attack the U-boat opened fire with cannons and/or machine guns. This time the rear gunner, although he reported a single large explosion due to the near cluster effect, saw no sign of the U-boat after that attack run. We made a wide circle and flew back towards the flame floats. Again we encountered heavy cannon fire from the position of the attack but could not positively sight the U-boat. We remained in the vicinity for over an hour, having dropped a Marine Marker to replace the flame floats. During this time the ASV contact remained almost stationary and three lighted fishing boats, observed within 7 miles, also remained stationary all the time we were there. We had, of course, sent the

appropriate messages to our "Control" (Plymouth). We were pretty sure that, by this stage of the Battle of the Bay, the U-boats were well aware that our Leigh Light Wellingtons carried only one stick of D/Cs. The ASV contact then disappeared so we resumed our patrol. The immediate Intelligence Assessment of our attack was "damaged, perhaps sunk", but I heard long afterwards that the U-boat was the U-437. We had damaged it and it was attacked again by the daytime aircraft.'

It was found again by 224 Squadron in the Derange area, at 0804 hrs, in position 4554/1022, when the Liberator picked up an S/E contact at 8 miles. They then sighted the surfaced U-boat at 4 miles, which began to submerge. They attacked, releasing six D/Cs, 25 seconds after the boat had gone down. Seeing nothing further, Laughland carried out baiting tactics, returning at 1040 hrs to regain radar contact at 18 miles and again strongly at 5 miles. Three minutes later they saw the U-boat on the surface 2 miles away with three men on the conning tower and one near the forward gun. An attack from 50 feet sent down six D/Cs, which straddled the submarine, which went down after being lifted, leaving oil in a broiling mass of water 300 feet across, wood and canvas also being observed. After 15 minutes, with nothing else seen, the Liberator turned for home.

Although assessed a probable kill, U-437, on its sixth patrol, having left St Nazaire three days earlier, had to put back into harbour, severely damaged. It did not sail again until August. It eventually made 12 war cruises by the end of September 1944, being destroyed in a bombing raid on Bergen on 4 October 1944. It had claimed just one ship sunk.

Russell Laughland later received the DFC for his anti-submarine work.

1 May, 1943

U-415, a type VIIC submarine, commanded by Oberleutnant Johannes Werner, damaged.

Wellington 'N', 172 Sqn

Sgt P.W. Phillips	Pilot
Sgt N.J. Harris	2nd pilot
Sgt H.A. Bate	Nav
Sgt A.A. Turner	WOP/AG
Sgt W.H. Ware	WOP/AG
F/Sgt G.W. Duncan	WOP/AG

U-71 under attack by F/L S. R.C. Wood of 10 RAAF Squadron, 5 June, 1942. She was on her seventh patrol and had to abort her mission and return to port damaged. (R.C. Bowyer)

502 Squadron crew, St Eval, 1943. Front: Sgt D.A. Radburn, Sgt Roy Phillips, F/Sgt D.L. Mumford. Rear: Sgt E. Bruton, PO E.L Hartley. Duncan Radburn was involved in an attack on U-525 on 3 March, 1943, while with 172 Squadron, and Hartley later flew with 58 Squadron. Doug Mumford also had his own crew with 172 Squadron. (D.A. Radburn)

Flying Officer Peter Stembridge of 172 Squadron. He sank U-665 on 22 March, 1943. (P.H. Stembridge)

Peter Stembridge and his crew went on to help damage U-437 on 29 April, 1943. l to r: Peter Dene, Peter Stembridge, Denis Hobden, Jim Boyd, Bob Webb, Eddie Goodman. (P.H Stembridge)

Sergeant Peter Phillips, 172 Squadron, damaged U-415 on 1 May, 1943.

F/L E.C. Smith and crew, 461 RAAF Squadron, helped damage U-415 on 1 May, 1943, and then sank U-332 the very next day. Front: L. W. Cox, J.C. Grainger, J. Gamble, R. MacDonald. Middle: R.V. Stewart, H. Smedley, J. Barrow. Rear: C.J. Dawson, F.B. Gascoigne, E.C. Smith, E.R. Crichter. (J. Barrow)

Jim Stark and his crew (58 Squadron), who sank U-528 on 11 May, 1943. l to r: 'Tich' Jones, 'Red' Roy, Frank Burroughs, Jim Stark, J.P. Young, Ernie Abbey (missing from photo: Frank Hopper). (J.B. Stark)

Sergeant Alex Coumbis, 172 Squadron. Damaged U-566 on 26 April, 1943, and then sank U-126 on 3 July. (D. Hobden)

Peter Cundy and crew, 224 Squadron. They sank U–628 on 3 July, 1943, and several of the crew took part in other successes with the squadron. l to r: FO Ron King, Peter Cundy, DSO, DFC, Lt. Col Farrant (armament expert), Sgt Jock Graham, Sgt D. Doncaster, Sgt Eddie Cheek, Sgt Ian Graham, Sgt Ken Owen, FO Perry Allen. Most of the crew were later decorated. (P.J. Cundy)

Peter Cundy, DSO, DFC, with the inventor of the Leigh Light, Wing Commander H. deV. Leigh. The Leigh Light in this picture, taken in 1945, is under the starboard wing of a 220 Squadron Liberator. (P.J. Cundy)

The Leigh Light in action. Many a U-boat was caught in these beams and it must have given many U-boat crews the shock of their lives as the night sky suddenly lit up and illuminated them as they travelled on the surface. (IWM)

Clutterbuck and his first crew as they came together at 3 OTU. l to r: Sgt W.W.A. Cole, Sgt Jock Hulbert, FO A.R.D Clutterbuck, FO A.R. Burns, Sgt J.J.M. James, Sgt N. G. MacDougal. (Whitley aircraft in background). Joining 58 Squadron, they converted to Halifax IIs and added two more crew members. Clutterbuck and his crew attacked one of three U-boats on 13 July, 1943. (A.R. Burns)

Eric Hartley and his crew, 58 Squadron. Seated: Sgt M Griffiths, FO E.L Hartley, Sgt G.R. Robertson. Standing: Sgt A.S. Fox, (?), F/Sgt K.E. Ladds, FO T.E. Bach, Sgt R.K. Triggol. In sinking U-221 on 27 September, 1943, they were shot down and spent 11 days in a dinghy, together with Group Captain R.C. Mead. Griffiths and Triggol did not survive; Hartley and Ladds were decorated. (E.L. Hartley)

Eric Hartley and the survivors of his crew are rescued by HMS Mahatra. G/Capt Mead had the 'fore & aft' cap and battledress. (E.L Hartley)

Ian Gunn and his crew, 612 Squadron. They attacked and damaged U-966 on 10 November, 1943. Front: Reg Sadler, Ian Gunn, Louis Jaffre. Rear: Roy Wingfield, Gil Bayliss, Bernard Dennehay. (I.D. Gunn)

Wing Commander J.B. Russell, DSO, CO of 612 Squadron, who with this crew damaged U-373 on 3 January, 1944. Standing: F/Sgt George Underhill, W/C John Russell, F/L Skyrme, FO Johnny May. Front: Charles Brignall, H.M. Bedford. (C.V. Brignall)

U-271 under attack by Lt C.E. Enloe of VP103 Squadron, USN, 28 January, 1944.

F/L R.D. Lucas and his 461 RAAF Squadron crew, who sank U-571 on 28 January, 1944. Rear: FO H.D. Roberts, F/Sgt C.D. Bremner, F/L Richard Lucas, FO R.H. Prentice, F/Sgt G.H. Simmonds. Front: F/Sgt Bunnett, Sgt J.R. Brannen, Sgt D. Musson, Sgt D.N. Walker, F/Sgt W.J. Darcy. (D. Musson)

Flight Sergeant Don Bretherton and crew, 612 Squadron. They attacked and damaged U-629 on 12 March, 1944. Front: Ian Green, Don Bretherton, Don Sullis. Back: Bob Campbell, Martyn Dally, Len Cole. (J.M. Dally)

The second attack of 461 Squadron's Sunderland 'D' on U-571, position 5241/1427 – 28 January, 1944.

U-426 sinking after the attentions of FO J.P. Roberts and his 10 RAAF Squadron crew, 8 January, 1944.

Les Baveystock, DSO, DFC and bar, DFM. Flying with 201 Squadron, he sank U-955 on the night of D-Day, and on 18 August sank U-107. (L.H. Baveystock)

Baveystock's flares go down over U-955 in the early hours of 7 June, 1944. (via R.C. Bowyer)

Flight Lieutenant Stanley Nunn and his navigator FO J.M. Carlin, 248 Squadron. Nunn led a formation of Mosquitoes, which attacked and sank U-821 on 10 June, 1944. (S.G. Nunn)

U-821, stern down, under attack by FO K. Norrie, 248 Squadron. Ushant is on the horizon. (S.G. Nunn)

Flying Officer K.O. Moore (right), seen here with WO Johnston McDowell, his navigator, of 224 Squadron. Ken Moore was the only pilot to sink two U-boats in one patrol, on the night of 7/8 June, 1944 – U-629 and U-373. Moore received an immediate DSO, McDowell the DFC. (IWM)

Stanley Nunn's Mosquito, LR347 T-Tommy, in which he attacked U-821 on 10 June. This picture was taken exactly one month later, 10 July, as he returns on one engine following an attack on German shipping. The flight ended with a no-wheels, no-flaps landing at Portreath. (S.G. Nunn)

Flight Lieutenant W.B. Tilley and crew, 461 Squadron RAAF, after sinking U-243, 8 July, 1944. l to r: George Bishop, Lindsay Penny, Bill Aitkenhead, Lance Cooke, Gil Casey, Dick Prentice, Don Hunt, Mick Mattner, Bill Tilley, Ivor Wood, Roy Felan, Les Walker. Note pigeon box in the hand of Don Hunt. (10 RAAF Sqn)

I.F.B 'Wally' Walters, DFC, 201 Squadron, who attacked and sank U-1222 on 11 July, 1944, received a bar to his DFC. (I.F.B Walters)

F/L Bent's 201 Squadron crew just before Les Baveystock took it over. With them Baveystock sank U-107 on 18 August, 1944. Rear: A.R. Cottrell, W. Parsons, Danny McGregor, PO Macaree, E.A. Bulloch. Middle: FO Wiles, FO Ian Riddell, F/L Bent, Brian Landers, Les Baveystock. Front: Alec Howat, Jack Paton, E. Perran. (B.W. Landers)

Wellington XIV of 304 Polish Squadron (QD-V) being loaded with depth charges. 304 Squadron sank two U-boats and damaged two others. (J.B. Cynk via R.C. Bowyer)

Sunderland 'M' DV968 461 RAAF Sqn

F/L E.C. Smith	Captain
FO C.J. Dawson	1st pilot
PO D.A. Sinclair	2nd pilot
F/L F.B. Gascoigne	Nav
Sgt L.W. Cox	Eng
Sgt R.V. Stewart, RAF	Fitter
F/Sgt H. Smedley, RAF	WOM
F/Sgt J. Gamble	WOP/AG
Sgt J. Barrow, RAF	WOP/AG
Sgt R. MacDonald, RAF	Fitter
PO E.R. Critcher	AG

Whitley 'E', 612 Squadron.

F/Sgt N. Earnshaw	Pilot
Sgt M.G. Millard	2nd pilot
PO L.R. Green	Nav
Sgt L.J. McQuiston	WOP/AG
Sgt L. Shaw	WOP/AG
Sgt B. Dennehey	WOP/AG

Just after midnight, Sergeant Phillips found a U-boat in position 4445/1157 in the beam of his Leigh Light following a radar contact. The U-boat opened fire with cannon, but six D/Cs were released, two falling on one side, four on the other. With the light off, Phillips circled and came in again but this time the light only revealed sea foam and bubbles which lasted for about four minutes. Unknown to the Wellington crew, flak had punctured their port tyre, although they did know their hydraulics had been slightly damaged. On landing at Predannack, the useless tyre caused a crash landing, but none of the crew were hurt.

The attack had damaged U-415 and she was found again at 1136 hrs by 461 Squadron and dived immediately. When first sighted the boat was 6 miles from the Sunderland and by the time Smith was over the spot the U-boat had crash-dived. A further salvo of D/Cs further damaged the sub and it began to limp towards the Spanish coast.

At 1525 hrs that afternoon, U-415 was located again, this time by 612 Squadron, in fair weather with visibility ranging from between 10 and 20 miles. The U-boat was 5 miles to port, the Whitley at 3000 feet. As the Whitley began to approach and lose height so the U-boat's gunners began to fire but then it started to dive. With decks awash, the sub was given six more D/Cs, but they fell 200 yards off to the right. Coming round for a second try, two further D/Cs went into the water where the U-boat had gone down, resulting in a gush of oil coming to the surface. The Whitley pilot was Norman Earnshaw, who recalls: 'The attack on U-415 was eventful to say the least. It stayed on the surface and took hard

evasive action, steering in a tight turn, which made our positioning for a good attack very difficult. Anti-aircraft gunfire from the conning tower and deck was directed at our aircraft throughout our run-in – I can recall watching many tracer shells coming directly towards us, but thankfully not hitting the aircraft. The first attack, a string of six depth charges, exploded some distance away from the U-boat, which then submerged, giving me an opportunity to make an unopposed and a more calculated and timed second attack ahead of the conning tower wake. Perhaps it was this second attack with our remaining two depth charges which caused the damage.

'The fact the U-415 stayed surfaced and fought back came as no surprise since we had been warned to expect this response at the time. It was nevertheless disconcerting since the Whitley aircraft was quite a large target and not at all fast. In a shallow dive it would perhaps achieve a speed of around 150 knots. It was not unknown for a U-boat to shoot down attacking aircraft!'

U-415 was damaged again but it had been lucky to survive the attentions of three Coastal Command aircraft during the day. It was on its first war sortie, having left Brest on 7 March, but it made port on 5 May. Following this cruise, U-415 went on to make eight cruises but was lost on 14 July, 1944, outside Brest harbour, when it struck an RAF-laid mine. It had sunk four ships during its career.

Norman Earnshaw was to have a further encounter with U-boats in 1945, by which time he was piloting a Mosquito. E.C. Smith had a further encounter the very next day!

2 May, 1943

U-332, a type VIIC submarine, commanded by Oberleutnant Eberhard Huttemann, sunk.

Sunderland 'M' DV968, 461 RAAF Squadron, on patrol 1354–0213 hrs.

F/L E.C. Smith	Captain
PO C.J. Dawson	1st pilot
PO J.C. Grainger	2nd pilot
FL F.B. Gascoigne	Nav
Sgt L.W. Cox	Eng
F/Sgt H. Smedley,	RAF WOM
F/Sgt J. Gamble	WOP/AG
Sgt J. Barrow, RAF	WOP/AG
Sgt R. MacDonald, RAF	Fitter
Sgt R.V. Stewart, RAF	Fitter
PO E.R. Critcher	AG

Having been damaged on 21 March, 1943, U-332 sailed again from La Pallice on 26 April, only to give Smith and his crew their second U-boat sighting in two days. At 1915 hrs in the Derange area they spotted the U-boat at 10 miles, in position 4448/0858. Smith approached the area in cloud, coming out just 4 miles off, and during the attack, the U-boat began firing at one mile range. He made two attacks, dropping four D/Cs each time, scoring good straddles. Oil appeared after the first attack and after the second the crew of the sub were seen to jump over the side as the vessel went down stern first. As the Sunderland circled at least 15 men were counted in the sea.

Flight Lieutenant Smith, already having flown with 228 Squadron, later received the DFC. He became a squadron leader and saw considerable service with Maritime squadrons. U-332 had sunk nine ships in her career of seven war patrols.

John Barrow remembers this day: 'When the attack took place I was on what might be called an off-duty period, which meant that I had to watch the action from a porthole. The things that come most easily to mind were the German gunners with the AA fire, and Sergeant McDonald returning fire with the VGO from the front turret. After a while it became apparent that the gunners did not intend to be left on deck, and dashed for the conning tower.

'When I saw the sub circle after we had dropped everything on it, I wondered if we had done enough to sink it, but then one end went into the air and then the whole thing vanished, leaving about 15 survivors in the water, some of whom were waving. "Gas" Gascoigne was taking pictures like mad, and I can hear him now, saying, "Just another one!" as we circled round and round. We seemed to be there for ages.

'In July 1943 the Skipper and Nav finished their tours and the crew broke up. Flying with Flying Officer Craft on 30 August, Stewart, Smedley and Gamble were killed. I missed that trip through illness, as did "Tich" Cox, as he was on a gunner's refresher course. We were both rather fortunate. Flying Officer Grainger was killed whilst flying with Flying Officer Dowling on 13 August, but Pilot Officer "Russ" Critcher was with Flight Lieutenant I.A.F. Clarke's crew when they sank U-106 on 2 August.'"

5 May, 1943

U-663, a type VIIC submarine, commanded by Kapitänleutnant Heinrich Schmid, sunk.

Halifax 'S' HR745, 58 Squadron, on patrol 0435–1300 hrs.

WC W.E. Oulton	Pilot	Sgt E.G. Andrews
PO W.H.A. Jones	2nd pilot	Sgt A. Hoey
FO B.S. Gibson		Sgt W.M. Graham
Sgt S. Webster		

A submarine was located early in the patrol and D/Cs were dropped on the swirl the boat left, 10-15 seconds after it went under, from 100 feet. Nothing else was seen so the patrol was continued. At 1015 hrs another U-boat was seen, which began a turn to port, at the same time opening fire with cannon and machine-guns, hitting the Halifax in the wings. A further salvo of D/Cs was dropped, two of which actually hit the conning tower, but without any sign of damage. However, U-663, which was the first boat attacked (in position 4643/0952), went straight to the bottom, giving the CO of 58 Squadron the first of his three U-boat kills. The second U-boat attacked (in position 4633/1112) had been U-214, which, although undamaged, resulted in her CO being injured.

U-663 was on its third patrol, having left Brest for the Atlantic on this same day. In its previous cruises it had sunk two ships.

Pilot Officer Jones became an aircraft captain during this month and in August received the DFC.

6 May, 1943

U-214, a type VIID minelaying submarine, commanded by Kapitänleutnant Rupprecht Stock, damaged.

Whitley 'K' BD189, No. 10 OTU, on patrol 1129–2040 hrs.

Sgt S.J. Barnett	Sgt L. Whitworth
Sgt T.H. Pike	PO E.A. Price
Sgt G.O. Sharpe	Sgt H.A. Weber

At 1805 hrs in the Derange area, the U-boat was seen 3 miles off and Barnett attacked. As they came in they saw another aircraft astern of the U-boat and then the boat began to open fire. The Whitley's front gunner replied until his guns jammed, but Barnett let go his D/Cs at 300 feet then pulled up into cloud.

When he came out of the cloud neither the U-boat nor the aircraft could be seen, and whether this was a German Ju 88 fighter or a Sunderland of 228 Squadron which had witnessed the attack is not certain.

U-214 had sailed from Brest the previous day on this its fifth cruise. It not only suffered some damage from the D/C attack, but casualties had been sustained on the bridge from the front gunner's machine-gun fire. It had to return to harbour, arriving on the 10th. It was sunk on its 11th cruise by a Royal Navy frigate, 22 July, 1944, under Oblt Gerhard Conrad.

No. 10 Bomber Command Operational Training Unit had been loaned to Coastal Command and its Whitley aircraft took a large share of patrols over the Bay of Biscay. In theory it gave its embryo crews some good operational experience before going on to bomber squadrons for ops over Germany, but they sustained heavy losses. Barnett and his crew were lucky to survive being shot down by two Ju 88s over the Bay on 17 May. They were rescued by a fishing boat and landed at Vigo in Spain, later being repatriated to England via Gibraltar.

7 May, 1943

U-465, a type VIIC submarine, commanded by Kapitänleutnant Heinz Wolf, sunk.

Sunderland 'W' W3993, 10 RAAF Squadron, on Derange patrol 0435–1655 hrs.

F/L G.G. Rossiter	Captain
FO M.H. Jones	1st pilot
FO J.P. Roberts	2nd pilot
FO W.C. Felgenhaur	Nav
gt A.F. Leggett	WOP
Sgt K.L. Dowling	WOP
Sgt W.C. Moser	Fitter 2E
Sgt E.C. O'Brien	Fitter
Sgt F.K. Cowled	Rigger
Sgt G.C.E. Hore	Armourer
SF/Sgt R.F. Mattner	AG
FO A.L. Coombes	Nav U/T

After sighting one U-boat, which went down before it could be attacked, another fully surfaced boat was found and attacked at 1228 hrs in position 4706/1058. Four D/Cs straddled the target forward of the conning tower, and during the attack both front and rear gunners scored hits on the sub. A second attack sent another four D/Cs around the U-boat, after

which it began to circle and leave a trail of oil. It then slowly settled by the stern, then went under, leaving a large oil patch 250 x 500 yards in diameter.

U-465 had sailed from St Nazaire on 28 April for its fourth patrol, following the repairs sustained on 10 April.

Flight Lieutenant Geoffrey Rossiter was awarded the DFC. He rose to Wing Commander rank and commanded 40 RAAF Squadron in 1945. For Flight Sergeant R.F. Mattner and Flying Officer Roberts, this was the second time they had been involved in a successful attack.

11 May, 1943

U-528, a type IXC submarine, commanded by Oberleutnant Georg von Rabenau, sunk.

Halifax II 'D' HR942, 58 Squadron, convoy patrol 0305–1253 hrs.

PO J.B. Stark	Pilot
PO H.W. Burroughs	2nd pilot
Sgt J.E. Abbey (Can)	AG
WO G.A. Roy (NZ)	Nav
PO G.P. Ruickbie	
Sgt J.P. Young	Eng
F/Sgt E.D. Jones	1st WOP/AG
F/Sgt K. Hopper	2nd WOP/AG

Jimmie Stark recalls: 'We took off about 3 am and rendezvoused with the convoy (OS 47) about 0600 hrs. As I approached the convoy I fired the "colours of the day" to identify myself – too bad to be shot down by our own navy! I flew up the centre of the convoy to where I thought the merchantman, on which the commodore of the convoy was stationed, was situated. By Aldis lamp, this ship signalled the code word "Cobra". This indicated to us what sort of search we had to carry out – all the searches had code names of snakes. 'Cobra' meant a square search round the convoy.'

Two hours later (0931 hrs), a U-boat was sighted, but it submerged before an attack could be made. Stark flew to the commodore's ship to report, and then returned to the former position and saw a fully surfaced U-boat in position 4655/1444, which he attacked from the port bow. The D/Cs straddled the boat and its stern seemed to lift and roll before disappearing. A large piece of debris was thrown into the air by what seemed to be a secondary explosion and then the boat went down, only for the bows to reappear again, then it again went under. An oil patch began to stain the surface of the sea, 100 yards across, an iridescent light colour with a dark centre. At 0950 hrs, having seen nothing further, the pilot returned to the convoy and made a further report, but received no acknowledgement, although the convoy then changed course. When PLE was reached, Stark saw a corvette heading towards the scene of the attack. The escort vessels HMS *Mignonette* and *Fleetwood* continued the attack on the damaged submarine, which they finished off and picked up 15 survivors. Jim Stark continues: 'After we had made the attack we returned to the convoy to report, which we did by R/T. I thought I would be bawled out for doing this, but the message would have taken too long by Aldis lamp. The only code word we used on the R/T was "Hearse" which was the code name for a U-boat.

'When we landed back at St Eval, the debriefing officer, I remember, was very excited about the "kill" and kept pumping the crew for more information. The crew were quite keen to give the information, but when we all had to stay in the debriefing room until the photo section had developed our photos we got fed up because we had our minds on lunch, which we still had to have – and we had been airborne since 3 am!'

U-528 was on its first patrol, having left Kiel on 15 April for the North Atlantic It had been damaged on 28 April by a USN Catalina and was limping towards the Bay of Biscay, but was sunk near the convoy on its way (see also Iceland).

This was Pilot Officer Stark's 52nd anti-submarine patrol and he was rested before the end of May. He did, however, receive the DFC.

15 May, 1943

U-463, a type XIV tanker submarine, commanded by Korvettenkapitän Leo Wolfbauer, sunk.

Halifax 'M' HR746, 58 Squadron, on patrol 1208–2125 hrs.

WC W.E. Oulton Pilot	Sgt H.A.C. Cooke
PO N.A. Lyes	Sgt B.D. Wyatt
PO R.W. Bee	Sgt L. Brewis
Sgt R.A. Berniston	Cpl J.P. Lusina

This U-boat was spotted in position 4528/1020 at 1810 hrs and carefully stalked from out of the sun. Oulton finally attacked from the port quarter, the D/Cs appearing to explode right under the boat. The bows slowly came up out of the water until they hung vertically. Two minutes later the U-boat sank, still in this vertical position, leaving a patch of light blue oil which spread around a froth of greenish-white water.

This was U-463's sixth patrol, having left Bordeaux on the 12th for the Atlantic to refuel boats already operating at sea. It was the first 'Milch Cow' – as these supply boats were called – that had been sunk.

This was Wilf Oulton's second kill.

15 May, 1943

U-591, a type VIIC submarine, commanded by Kapitänleutnant Hans-J. Zetzsche, damaged.

Whitley 'M' LA822, 10 OTU, on patrol 0805–1632 hrs.

F/Sgt G.W. Brookes	PO J.T. Saunders
F/Sgt J.H. Walton	Sgt K.G. Sewell
Sgt S. Fontley	F/Sgt H.G. Reid

At 1127 hrs this crew found a surfaced U-boat in position 4649/1156 and dropped five D/Cs from 50 feet. The nearest of these exploded and lifted the boat, then she went down leaving nothing but brown scum on the water. The Whitley's gunners had fired at three or four men seen in the conning tower. An hour later, Brookes was still in the area and found this or another U-boat in position 4615/1150, which was only 20 miles from the first position. As he closed in to drop his last depth charge, the boat began to fire at him, his gunners replying, scoring hits on the conning tower and hull. The single D/C went down (it had hung up in the first attack) and exploded 150 feet on the sub's port beam. The Whitley was hit and slightly damaged as it flew over its target, which began to slowly submerge.

U-591 had previously served with the Arctic Flotilla in 1942 and this was her third patrol from St Nazaire. Sailing on the 12th, her commander was wounded in the attack, by machine-gun fire, and the mission had to be abandoned in order to get him to hospital. In February 1943 she had sunk two ships from the convoy SC 121 and in all she sank six ships before she herself was sunk on 30 July, 1943. This occurred in position 0836/3434 off Pernembuco, Brazil, by a Ventura of VB127 Squadron, US Navy, on her fourth patrol, when commanded by Ober-leutnant zur See Reimer Zeissmer.

Brookes attacked another submarine on 22 May, but return fire from the boat frustrated the attack, although the rear gunner saw one man fall into the sea when he opened fire.

16 May, 1943

The Italian Tazzoli class submarine *Enrico Tazzoli*, commanded by Korvettenkapitän Fecia di Cossato, sunk.

Halifax 'R' HR774, 58 Squadron, on patrol 1431–2345 hrs.

FO A.J.W. Birch	Pilot
PO R.H. Collishaw	2nd pilot
F/Sgt W. Hale	Nav
Sgt J.R. Shaw	Eng
F/Sgt W. Cawthorne	Sig
Sgt J.D. Rice	AG
F/Sgt T.H. Linton	AG

At 2003 hrs, in position 4557/1140, the U-boat was sighted well on the port beam and the pilot stalked it out of the sun. An attack was made just after it had crash-dived, one D/C falling 100 feet ahead of the swirl, the others in the swirl and wake. A pool of blue oil was later observed with something floating in it.

The *Tazzoli*, after service in the Mediterranean, sailed from La Pallice on 19 November, 1942, returning on 2 February, 1943. Her next patrol began on 16 May. She sank at least 18 ships, including four on her first Atlantic patrol.

Tony Birch had been a second pilot when U-590 was damaged in April 1942.

24 May, 1943

U-523, a type IXC/40 submarine, commanded by Kapitänleutnant Werner Pietsch, damaged.

Whitley 'J' BD414, 10 OTU, on patrol 0715–1648 hrs.

Sgt S.C. Chatton	Sgt W.A. Reffin
Sgt C. Langford	Sgt W. Archibald
Sgt L.R.G. Armitage	Sgt L.V.J. Smith

The aircraft was at 6000 feet at 1122 hrs when it surprised a U-boat in position 4626/1053, having picked out the wake at 3–4 miles. Attacking through cloud, Chatton was down to 2000 feet when one mile off and as he came in his front gunner began firing. There were several men seen in the conning tower and one crumpled up. The rear gunner also opened fire as they flew over, and after the D/C explosions subsided, the boat appeared to have stopped, but then dived.

U-523 had sailed from Lorient on the 22nd, returning from this damaging attack on the 26th. It was supposed to have been her second patrol, her first having been made in March and April. Her next cruise was not until August, but her captain was recalled because of the severe losses being sustained in the Bay. She sailed again later that month but was sunk by the destroyer HMS *Wanderer* on the 25th, her CO and 37 crew being taken prisoner. She had one Allied ship to her credit.

24 May, 1943

U-441, a type VIIC submarine converted to a flak ship, commanded by Kapitänleutnant Klaus Goetz von Hartmann, damaged.

Sunderland 'L' EJ139, 228 Squadron, on patrol 1400 hrs.

FO H.J. Debden	FO C.L. Houedard
FO A.H. Pelham-Clinton	FO W.C. Haylock
F/Sgt F. Capes	F/Sgt R. Cooper
F/Sgt B. Crossland	Sgt L. Whatley
Sgt E. French	Sgt W. Easson
Sgt A. Scales	

This aircraft took off from Pembroke Dock to fly a patrol in the Derange area of the Bay of Biscay and found U-441, a boat designed to stay on the surface and fight attacking Coastal Command aircraft. The Sunderland was shot down in the attack and all the crew were killed, but Debden had managed to place his D/Cs around the U-boat, damaging her.

U-441 had sailed from Brest on the 22nd (her fifth patrol) and was forced to return, arriving on the 26th. She would be sunk by 304 Polish Squadron in June 1944, on her 10th cruise.

Flying Officer Debden had previously served with 209 Squadron in 1941.

31 May, 1943

U-563, a type VIIC submarine, commanded by Oberleutnant Gustav Borchardt, sunk.

Halifax 'R' HR774, 58 Squadron, on patrol 1100–1958 hrs.

WC W.E. Oulton	Sgt J.H. Oliver
Sgt R.S. Crick	Sgt D. Jackson
FO R.M. Cooper	Sgt J. MacKinley
Sgt G.J. Stoddart	

Sunderland 'X' DD838, 228 Sqn, on patrol 1359–2215 hrs.

FO W.M. French
FO R.W. Fox
Sgt C. Black
Sgt D. Norman
Sgt J. Armstrong
F/Sgt W.J. deBois

FO A.S. Pedley
Sgt D. Skinner
Sgt P. Brown
Sgt T. Kilsby
Sgt S. Baker

Sunderland 'E' DV969, 10 RAAF Sqn, on patrol 1345–2135 hrs.

F/L M.S. Mainprize	Captain
Sgt C. Clark	1st pilot
FO D.M. Ryan	2nd pilot
Sgt A.W. Reeves	Eng
FO C.N. Austin	Nav
Sgt M.R. Delaney	WOM
Sgt A.C. Carrett	WOP/AG
Sgt I.V. Spiers	Rigger
Sgt L.J. Lang	Armourer
Cpl B.C. Leech	Eng U/T
Sgt F.C. Callander	AG
LAC B.E. Steer	Fitter

The U-boat was sighted by Wing Commander Oulton at 1545 hrs and stalked through cloud. He then attacked, achieving a straddle, which left the boat in obvious trouble. A second attack with remaining three D/Cs was made, oil being seen trailing from the sub on the run in. With no more D/Cs, Oulton ordered his gunners to fire. One and a half hours later, 'J' of 58 Squadron arrived (PO E.L. Hartley), but his D/Cs fell short.

At 1650 hrs, 'E' of 10 Squadron received instructions to search for the damaged U-boat and later came upon the scene with the two Halifax aircraft still circling. The Sunderland attacked twice, dropping four D/Cs each time. After the first attack the U-boat stopped, and after the second it began to sink, the crew appearing on the deck in life jackets.

The 228 Squadron Sunderland then arrived (position 4700/0940) and also made two attacks, seeing bodies thrown into the air, following which 30–40 seamen could be seen in the water. Bill French then saw a second U-boat and attacked with machine-gun fire, but it dived.

U-563 was on its eighth war cruise, having sailed from Brest for the Atlantic two days earlier. It had sunk five ships, including the destroyer HMS *Cossack* on 23 October 1941.

This was Wilfred Oulton's third success during May and he received both the DFC and DSO. Maxwell Stanley Mainprize was also decorated later, receiving the DFC, and William Maynard French too received the DFC, whilst Flight Sergeant William John deBois received the DFM. By one of those odd chances of fate, Oulton's three successful sinkings had all ended with the number 63. U-663, U-463 and now U-563.

31 May, 1943

U-621, a type VIIC submarine, commanded by Kapitänleutnant Max Kruschka, damaged.

Liberator 'Q', 224 Squadron, on patrol 1251–2128 hrs.

FO R.V. Sweeny (US)	Pilot
PO E. Allen	2nd pilot
FO R.W. King	Nav
F/Sgt I.A. Graham	WOP/AG
F/Sgt C. Owen	Eng
F/Sgt E. Cheek	WOP/AG
Sgt A. Graham	AG

Making an S/E contact at 8 miles at 1845 hrs, the aircraft homed in to find a U-boat in position 4724/1059. They approached through heavy cloud and when breaking through, the U-boat was right below, which opened fire. Sweeny circled at 1500 feet 1000 yards away, the gunners firing back, then attacked from 50 feet, dopping six D/Cs. There were several men in the conning tower, all clearly seen as the aircraft flew over. The D/Cs appeared to overshoot, but oil was seen on the water and then the U-boat was submerging. A second attack sent six more D/Cs down ahead of the swirl, 4 or 5 seconds after the boat went under. The Liberator circled for 15 minutes, but nothing further was seen.

U-621 had left Brest on 22 April for its 4th patrol and was returning from a cruise to the Azores when it was damaged, but it made port on 3 June. It was later sunk by a Canadian Destroyer on 18 August, 1944, having sunk a total of 12 Allied ships.

Bob Sweeny, Owen, Cheek and the two Grahams had been part of Peter Cundy's crew and were continuing their success against the U-boats. Sweeny, an American, soon received the DFC. Bob Sweeny and his brother Charles had helped form the famous Eagle Squadron in 1940 and Bob had been adjutant before training as a pilot. In 1937 he had been the British amateur golf champion while at Oxford.

1 June, 1943

U-418, a type VIIC submarine, commanded by Oberleutnant Gerhard Lange, sunk.

Beaufighter 'B' T5258, 236 Squadron, on patrol 0910–1307 hrs.

FO M.C. Bateman	Pilot
F/Sgt C.W.G. Easterbrook	Nav
Lt Cdr F.J. Brookes	Obs

Flying out from Predannack, a wake was sighted by Brookes just after 1100 hrs, through binoculars, at a distance of 10 miles when the Beau was at 3500 feet. Lt Cdr Brookes was a Royal Navy U-boat warfare specialist, who was about to see U-boat warfare at close quarters. Bringing the boat to the attention of Bateman, the RAF pilot saw that it was diving, so he immediately attacked, firing four 25 lb rockets. After the attack all that could be seen was a green patch of water, but later a second green patch, twice the size of the swirl, was visible. The attack was estimated as successful but there was no evidence of a definite kill.

Because rocket projectiles were still on the secret list, Bateman's report had to state that he had used depth charges and it was not until September that he heard from the Assessment Committee that his 'seriously damaged' U-boat had been upgraded to a 'Confirmed'.

U-418, on its first cruise, had indeed been sunk, in position 4705/0855. It had sailed from Kiel on its first patrol on 24 April and was inbound for its new French base from the North Atlantic when attacked.

Mark Bateman, promoted to Flight Lieutenant, was awarded the DFC. (For a first-hand account of his attack, see *Conflict over the Bay* by N.L.R. Franks, Wm. Kimber & Co, 1986.)

13 & 14 June, 1943

U-564, a type VIIC submarine, commanded by Oberleutnant Hans Fiedler, sunk.

Sunderland 'U' DV967, 228 Squadron, on patrol 1330 hrs.

FO L.B. Lee	Sgt R. Shaw
FO D.F. Hill	Sgt R. Smith
PO G. Lough	Sgt J. Fraser
FO A.K. McDougal	Sgt A. Carmichael
FO R.J. Agur	Sgt D. Davies
Sgt V. Goldstone	

Leonard Bertrand Lee and his crew met U-564 over the Bay, but was shot down in the attack which inflicted damage on the vessel, and the crew all died. The attack was made in position 4430/1500 at 2000 hrs. The next day the damaged submarine was spotted by:

Whitley 'G' BD220, 10 OTU, on patrol 0949 hrs from St Eval.

Sgt A.J. Benson (Aust) Pilot	Sgt G.T. Graves
PO T.J.J. Lee	FO A. Kingsley
Sgt R.L. Rennick	

At 1439 hrs a radio message was received from Benson that he had spotted two U-boats in position 4417/1025. He shadowed them until 1645 hrs, having carried out homing procedure, and was then given permission to make an attack. After the attack on one of the boats, he again radioed that his aircraft had sustained damage and that his hydraulics were u/s and he was heading for home. However, his starboard engine had also been hit and stopped at 1920 hrs. A Whitley did not fly very far on one engine and soon he was sending out an SOS, but he failed to return. The crew survived a crash landing in the sea and were rescued after three days by a French fishing boat, which landed them in France, where they were taken prisoner.

For U-564, the 13th proved unlucky, but the 14th was more so. Until then it had survived nine patrols and had commenced the tenth, from Bordeaux, on 9 June.

It had sunk a total of 33 ships. Most of the patrols had been made under the command of Leutnant Reinhard Suhren (previously 1st officer aboard U-48), who had been decorated with the Knight's Cross with Swords and Oak Leaves.

Following Benson's attack, Oberleutnant Fiedler and 18 survivors were rescued by U-185.

Benson was promoted to Warrant Officer and heard in prison camp of his award of the DFM.

14 June, 1943

U-68, a type IXC submarine, commanded by Oberleutnant Albert Lauzemis, damaged.

U-155, a type IXC submarine, commanded by Oberleutnant Fritz Altmeier, damaged.

Mosquito 'B' HJ648, 307 (Polish) Squadron.

SL S. Szablowski	Pilot
Sgt M. Gajewski	Nav

Because of losses while crossing the Bay, U-boats began a period of sailing in groups for self-protection. Leading a formation of four aircraft, five U-boats were spotted at 0930 hrs in position 4450/0850. The leader ordered line astern and directed an attack on the second U-boat. As he attacked he saw strikes on the conning tower and then he attacked the third boat and again saw cannon hits. The squadron leader's port engine was then hit by the combined return fire from the U-boats, which stopped. The second Mosquito found his cannons would not fire and broke away, and by then the defensive fire was so great that the other two aircraft decided not to attack, especially as their leader was now heading away with one engine leaving a trail of smoke. Szablowski flew the 500 miles back to England on one engine and made a belly landing at Predannack.

Both U-boats had been damaged in the attack and had to abort their cruises and return to Lorient. They were on their seventh and sixth patrols respectively. U-155 went on to complete ten patrols, but U-68 was lost on 10 April, 1944, sunk by aircraft from the Escort Carrier *Guadalcanal*, having sunk 27 ships. Five of these had been off Freetown in early 1942 under Karl-Friedrich Merten. U-155 sunk 18 in her career, her commander having received the Knight's Cross.

21 June, 1943

U-462, a type XIV supply submarine under the command of Oberleutnant Bruno Vowe, damaged.

Mosquito aircraft of 151 and 456 Squadrons.

SL B.D. Bodien DFC	Pilot

FO R.W. Simpson	Nav	HJ655 'V' (151)
PO J.D. Humphries	Pilot	
PO H.J. Lumb	Nav	'W' (151)
FO A.D. Boyle	Pilot	
Sgt H.M. Friesner	Nav	'X' (151)
WO G.F. Gatenby	Pilot	
F/Sgt J.M. Frazer	Nav	DZ299 'D' (456)

These four Mosquito crews had flown out from Predannack shortly after 1000 hrs and at 1215 hrs found the U-boat on the surface in position 4535/0815, heading out across the Bay. Each in turn made an attack run over the boat, inflicting cannon and machine gun damage, and causing casualties to the men in the conning tower.

Having sailed for the Atlantic two days earlier, the damage and casualties forced the skipper to abort his supply sortie and head U-462 back to port.

It sailed again on 28 June, only to meet and be damaged by 224 Squadron on 2 July. It was later sunk on 31 July.

Joe Bodien was on an anti-Ju 88 'Instep' patrol when he happened across U-462, indeed, only two days earlier he had shot down a Ju 88. Gatenby had damaged another in the same action, as did Humphries, although he later had to make a crash landing at base.

2 July, 1943

U-462, see above.

Liberator 'J', 224 Squadron on patrol 0910–2112 hrs.

WO E.J.J. Spiller, DFC	Pilot
Sgt R. Pierce	2nd pilot
F/Sgt R.H. Humphrey	Nav
PO E. Bentley	Eng
Sgt F.T. Holland	WOP/AG
Sgt J.R.L. Thompson	WOP/AG
F/Sgt J. Mackin	WOP/AG
F/Sgt R.A. Denny	WOP/AG

At 1402 hrs, radar contact was made at 19 miles, but at 3 miles it disappeared. Another contact made at 1530 hrs at 18 miles and 15 minutes later two U-boats were sighted and attacked with D/Cs and bombs. Spiller broke cloud at 1000 feet when 10 miles from the target, picking them up visually at 2 miles, in position 4337/1005. The attack was made on the leading boat, through light flak, while the second boat began to dive. After attacking this boat,

Spiller turned to attack the second, which by this time had gone down. Then a third attack was made on the leading boat, which was also going under. Due to confusion over the R/T the pilot released the last D/Cs as the bomb aimer dropped the anti-submarine bombs. Circling the area, air bubbles were seen rising to the surface and then an oil patch, but nothing else.

As previously mentioned, U-462, damaged yet again, had to abort her mission and return to base, which she did on the 7th.

3 July, 1943

U-126, a type IXC submarine, commanded by Oberleutnant Siegfried Kietz, sunk.

Wellington 'R', 172 Squadron, on patrol 2239–0639 hrs.

F/Sgt A. Coumbis	Sgt G.W. Yung
FO C.S. Rowland	Sgt J.F. Wilmer
FO D.J. Ashworth	Sgt H. Hever

At 0237 hrs an S/E contact was obtained at 13 miles to port and Coumbis homed in and illuminated a German U-boat at ¾ of a mile when he was at a height of 150 feet. Eight minutes had elapsed between the sighting and the D/Cs going down – from 50 feet – falling on either side of the sub. The rear gunner fired and saw the explosions around the boat, but when Coumbis came round again 1½ minutes later, their Light only saw an empty sea except for their flame floats.

However, U-126 had made the final plunge. It was returning from West Africa hoping to complete its sixth war cruise, but found only the bottom of the Bay in position 4602/1123. The attack was witnessed by U-154, who reported the sinking to base. U-126 had been a successful boat until then, having been away from Lorient since 20 March. In 28 months of active service it had sunk one Allied ship for each of them.

Alex Coumbis was a Rhodesian, and this was his second success over the Bay. A married man, sadly he was later killed in a flying accident in Wales.

3 July, 1943

U-386, a type VIIC submarine commanded by Oberleutnant Fritz Albrecht, damaged.

Liberator 'D' BZ731, 53 Squadron, on patrol 0543–1935 hrs.

WO L.L. Esler	Sgt A.H. Nopper
F/Sgt J.L. Knight	Sgt A.W.G. Brown
F/Sgt W.R. Kinsman	Sgt R.C. Laver
F/Sgt A. Campbell	

This squadron had become operational on Liberators in June at Thorney Island with a detachment at St Eval. On this day Esler was flying in the Musketry patrol areas when, in the afternoon, a radar contact at 20 miles sent him to locate a submerging U-boat, but no attack was made. Later, another contact at 12 miles brought him to position 4450/0950, at 1430 hrs. Here they found and attacked a boat, their D/Cs making a good drop. The U-boat rolled as five of the D/Cs exploded along its port side then disappeared. During the run-in cannon fire was experienced and at least one round was fired from the large forward gun. After the attack large oil patches were all that could be seen.

U-386 had sailed from St Nazaire on 29 June and had to return on 8 July without completing its second war cruise. It was sunk on its fourth, by a British frigate on 19 February, 1944, having sunk just one ship.

3 July, 1943

U-628, a type VIIC submarine commanded by Kapitänleutnant Heinrich Hasenchar, sunk.

Liberator 'J' FL963, 224 Squadron, on patrol 0916–1830 hrs.

SL P.J. Cundy, DFC	Pilot
PO E. Allen	2nd pilot
FO R.W. King	Nav
F/Sgt I.A. Graham	WOP/AG
Lt Col Farrant	Passenger
F/Sgt E. Cheek	WOP/AG
F/Sgt C. Owen	Eng
Sgt A.H. Graham	AG
Sgt D. Doncaster	AG

At 1256 hrs, in the Derange area, when investigating what looked to be an oil patch, the second pilot spotted the periscope of a U-boat, but no attack was made. Then at 1402 hrs an S/E contact was made at 10 miles ahead and a minute later they sighted the wake of a U-boat and attacked with 35 lb anti-submarine bombs and then with D/Cs. Peter Cundy recalls: 'Colonel Farrant's presence was because he was trying to promote the acceptance of a new anti-submarine bomb. These weapons were dropped at the same height and speed as D/Cs, but in sticks of 18, and a direct hit was essential. In this particular case our bomb load consisted of one stick of these little chaps and four D/Cs. On the first run the bombs were released by Ian Graham, whose turn it was at the time to be in the bomb-aimer's position.

'We sighted the enemy several miles away and I pushed the stick forward. The U-boat was not asleep and opened fire with all armament while we were still a mile away and as the range closed he scored hits on us. My gunners were not idle and returned a hot fire and one of the U-boat crew was seen to fall over the side. We had a hole in a fuel tank and petrol was flowing over the engine exhaust. I thought we would have a fire any moment, but we carried on and dropped our load, one D/C bouncing off the conning tower into the sea.

'Once again we flew over and our second stick of D/Cs straddled it, hiding the U-boat in the huge plumes of the explosions, which merged into a single, gigantic fountain of water. As I circled round we saw that the U-boat had disappeared and all we could see was a dark brown patch of oil. Then several bodies rose to the surface. My navigator saw six men who appeared to be swimming. I then saw another four and another of my crew saw three more, but only one seemed to be wearing a Mae West.' Flight Sergeant Eddie Cheek remembers: 'After the attack, Peter put the aircraft into an orbit about the U-boat, and we could see bodies and wreckage in the water. While this was in progress I went aft to see how things were in the after compartment. The port beam gunner and Colonal Farrant were looking through the hatch at the terrible results of our attack. I then noticed the Colonel was undoing his Mae West and I felt obliged to ask him what he was doing! He told me he was going to throw his life-vest to "Those poor devils down there". As we had yet to determine the extent of our own damage I was constrained to tell him that there might well be a need for it by these "poor devils up here!"

'Our damage included cannon strikes on the starboard wing, fin, rudder and one petrol tank. The aerodynamics of the aircraft were not seriously impaired and we made an uneventful return to St Eval.'

U-628 was lost with all hands on the start of this her fourth cruise, having left Brest on the 1st. She went down in position 4411/0845, without being able to add to her previous score of eight ships sunk.

Peter Cundy received the DSO and later Eddie Cheek was awarded the DFM.

5 July, 1943

U-535, a type IXC submarine commanded by Kapitänleutnant Helmut Ellmenreich, sunk.

Liberator 'G' BZ751, 53 Squadron, on patrol 0626–2203 hrs.

F/Sgt W. Anderson (NZ)	F/Sgt G.H. Sheeran
Sgt G.B. Tomlinson	Sgt C. Coley
WO I.C. Bradshaw	Sgt W.R. Robinson
Sgt R.N. Lord	

A search was carried out in the Musketry patrol area in company with four Navy sloops of Captain Walker's 2nd Escort Group, but nothing was found despite an earlier report of a U-boat by 10 RAAF Squadron. Finally PLE was reached, and the Liberator set course for base. Then not one but three U-boats were sighted and Anderson attacked. The first attack was spoilt when the U-boat he selected began to evade and on the next attack the D/Cs failed to release. However, on the third attack, two D/Cs fell to port and six to starboard of the boat just aft of the conning tower. All three U-boats were putting up a barrage of flak and the Liberator was hit in the wings, tail and rear fuselage, and the beam gunner was wounded. However, the D/Cs found the mark and U-535 went to the bottom.

The U-boat had sailed from Kiel on 25 May and after a patrol to the Azores was inbound for a French port when attacked and sank in position 4338/0913 just after 1700 hrs. Thus ended its first war cruise. Its companions, U-170 and U-536, which had joined together for mutual protection, sailed away.

7 July 1943

U-267, a type VIIC submarine, commanded by Kapitänleutnant Otto Tinschert, damaged.

Catalina 'B' FP277, 210 Squadron, on patrol 0655–0000 hrs.

FO J.A. Cruickshank	Pilot
FO J. Coulson	2nd pilot
FO J.C. Dickson	Nav
Sgt S.B. Harbison	Eng
Sgt Westby	WOP/AG
Sgt Wallis	WOP/AG
F/Sgt J. Smith	WOP/AG
Sgt F.J. Appleton	WOM/AG
Sgt C.J. Webster	FME/AG
Sgt Stockdon	Rigger

This was a patrol to the west of Portugal and lasted for 17 hours 5 minutes. Sergeant John Appleton recalls: 'We had flown down from Hamworthy (Poole Harbour) to Gibraltar on 21 June and flew convoy escorts well out into the Atlantic. These convoys were probably destined for the Med, due to the invasion of Sicily [10 July]. On the 7th we were airborne at 0655 hrs. I cannot recall the time, but I was in the starboard blister admiring the clouds and wave tops. The crew up front reported on the intercom that they had seen something suspicious. We homed in and I heard it identified as a submarine. When I first saw it it was a couple of miles ahead on our starboard side. It made no attempt to dive nor did it fire at us. I was assuming that Cruickshank was keeping his distance and planning to attack down the sub's track, but he seemed to fly too far before turning.

'I clearly recall suddenly seeing the spray and splashing as the sub's valves opened and it began to dive. I called on the intercom, "Skipper, its diving; turn 180 starboard quick!" This he did and we flew straight down the sub's track. I saw the D/Cs drop, but thought the sub's hull was too far under. One of the engineers in the port blister and I both fired our .5in Brownings at the conning tower, which I thought was just about awash by then. It is very hard to point the blister gun straight down and I think we both doubted if we were very effective, but I do clearly remember looking into the bridge of the sub from about 50 feet.'

U-267 had sailed from St Nazaire for its third patrol on 4 July and was forced back there, arriving on the 13th. The damaging attack occurred in position 4145/1136. Its first patrol began on 12 January, 1943 and it went on to complete six before

it was sent to Stavanger in October 1944. In February 1945 it hit an RAF-laid mine when on its way to Oslo and had to be towed into Flensburg.

For John Cruickshank and some of his crew, a year later saw an action for which this gallant pilot was to win the Victoria Cross.

8 July, 1943

U-514, a type IXC/40 submarine, commanded by Kapitänleutnant Hans-J. Auffermann, sunk.

Liberator 'R' BZ721, 224 Squadron, on patrol 0853–1948 hrs.

SL T.M. Bulloch, DSO, DFC★	Pilot
F/Sgt N.E. Lord	2nd pilot
FO D.E.H. Durrant	Nav
Sgt A.G. Dyer	WOP/AG
F/Sgt D. Purcell	WOP/AG
Sgt R. McCall	Eng
FO F.B. Lewis	WOP/AG
F/Sgt L. Larkin	AG
FL C.V.T. Campbell	Passenger

Following his successes from Iceland with 120 Squadron, Terry Bulloch had a sort of a roving commission at this stage of the war. He now had a Liberator which was equipped with rockets and was attached to 224 Squadron for operational trials.

Patrolling above a calm sea with unlimited visibilty, Flight Lieutenant Campbell, an Armament Specialist, was looking at some Spanish fishing vessels through binoculars when he spotted a U-boat right in amongst them. He yelled a warning to Bulloch, who immediately turned into the attack with his new weapons. Losing height he approached the U-boat, seeing five or six men on the bridge. He fired a pair of rockets at 800 feet, a second pair at 600 feet and a salvo of the last four at 500 feet, from a height of 500 yards. The navigator, in the nose, saw splash entry of the rockets definitely between the conning tower and the bows. The rear gunner later saw one rocket emerge from the sea beyond the U-boat. Front, rear and port beam guns (Campbell) fired into the boat as they flew over it. The U-boat was seen to submerge, only to reappear with its tail up by about 20 degrees. At 1320 hrs the boat went down.

Colin Campbell remembers: 'What was not in the (official) report was that about 1545 hrs, a signal was received from 19 Group to the effect that a group of enemy aircraft was heading into the area of attack. As we were near PLE, course was set to westwards and then to base. 'N' of 210 Squadron had departed for Gibraltar some time previously. 'Q' of 53 Squadron was intercepted by a group of Ju 88 fighters and shot down in visual distance of the Second Escort Group, which steamed to the position but found no survivors.

'Also not recorded for security reasons was that "R" was carrying a Mk 24 mine and half-load of D/Cs. Bulloch decided after the RP attack to drop the mine, and within a few minutes of doing so an object was observed on the sea surface making a wake and travelling at quite a few knots. We overflew this object, which was closely observed by the crew and photographed by McColl. It was not possible to determine whether it was the U-boat endeavouring to surface or, perhaps, the acoustic homing torpedo. Bulloch decided to attack the object with, I think, a brace of D/Cs. When these exploded the aircraft experienced a heavy blast and the rear gunner reported a large flash. It was later considered that this was the torpedo gone wrong and that the D/Cs had counter-mined it. The Mk 24 US-developed acoustic torpedo was TOP SECRET and was only then coming into use by the heavy anti-sub squadrons under the greatest secrecy. That Bulloch attacked and destroyed this mine – even in error – was absolutely correct, for if it had been picked up, say, by a fishing vessel, this important contribution to the defeat of the U-boats could have been rendered useless, for all the U-boat under attack had to do was dive deep quickly and shut down its engines.'

U-514, on its fourth patrol, having left Lorient bound for South Africa, went down in position 4337/0859.

This was yet another success for Terry Bulloch.

12 July, 1943

U-441, a type VIIC submarine converted into a flak ship, damaged.

Beaufighters of 248 Squadron, on patrol 1030–1634 hrs.

F/L C.R.B. Schofield	Pilot	
Sgt J.A. Mallinson	Nav	'B'
Lt G.C. Newman (FF)	Pilot	
FO O.C. Cochrane	Nav	'V'
FO P.A.S. Payne	Pilot	
FO A.M. McNichol	Nav	'A'

The weather was fine with occasional showers. U-414 had sailed again, hoping to lure an unsuspecting Coastal aircraft into range of its deadly gun batteries. Unfortunately for von Hartmann, he was located by three equally deadly Beaufighters at 1405 hrs in position 4506/0854. Diving through a hail of gunfire, the three Beaus attacked with their 20mm cannon. At one stage there appeared to be up to 18 men on the deck and in the conning tower, but they disappeared. One man was later seen in the water and another lying on the deck. All fire from the boat ceased, enabling the RAF aircraft to press home their attacks and an explosion was seen just aft of the conning tower followed by another, some smoke and a brilliant red flash, which was probably some unused ammunition being hit. Each aircraft made a total of five attacks over a period of 15 minutes, the navigators of 'A' and 'V' also firing their rear guns. Finally the U-boat dived, apparently quite under control.

U-441 had sailed from Brest on the 8th and had to return on the 13th with damage and heavy casualties among the men who had been at the guns and on the bridge during the attack. Ten men had died and a further 13 were wounded. Also, during the patrol the Beaufighters engaged and shot down two Ju 88s.

13 July, 1943

U-607, a type VIIC submarine, commanded by Oberleutnant Wolf Jeschonneck, sunk.

Sunderland 'N' JM708, 228 Squadron, on patrol 0304–1635 hrs.

FO R.D. Hanbury	F/Sgt B. Lacey
PO T. Pearson	F/Sgt E. House
PO W.K. Knights	F/Sgt N. Wilson
F/Sgt A. Beal	Sgt A. McFarlane
F/Sgt G.A. Williames	Sgt F. Akers

At 0746 hrs in position 4502/0914, three U-boats were sighted on the surface just outside the Musketry area. Gunfire was exchanged as the aircraft circled while calling other aircraft to the scene. One U-boat then detached itself from the others and the aircraft attacked with seven D/Cs and the explosions blew off the boat's bows and conning tower. It sank immediately, leaving 25 men in the water. A dinghy was dropped and six men were seen to scramble into it. The Sunderland was later shadowed by a Ju 88, but not attacked.

This fifth and last cruise by U-607 began three days earlier from St Nazaire, its task being to lay mines off Jamaica. She had sunk five ships. The

Captain was the half-brother of General Hans Jeschonneck of the Luftwaffe. It was also his 24th birthday! He and some of his men were rescued by HMS *Wren* of the Second Escort Group the next day. The other U-boats were U-613 and U-445, both on their fourth patrols. Only Graf von Treuberg's U-445 was to return, U-613 being lost on 23 July to US ships and carrier-borne aircraft.

In the same action a Halifax of 58 Squadron (HR691 'O') piloted by Flying Officer A.R.D. Clutterbuck tried to co-operate with Hanbury, Clutterbuck having located the boats earlier. Flying Officer A.R. Burns was Clutterbuck's co-pilot, and he relates: 'Both aircraft stayed outside the range of flak. One U-boat inexplicably veered away from the formation right into the path of the Sunderland. Whilst we were observing their attack in which we could confirm portions of the boat blown off, another U-boat commenced to submerge towards the same area. We attacked and during this time I was taking photographs, but our target went below the surface and our stick straddled the estimated track in front of the wake and point of submersion. We saw bodies and oil and wanted to think we had been successful; Clutterbuck was convinced, but most of us were unsure. We could not stop to debate, confirm or gather any more information. Whilst circling we had been talking of our need to break off and return home because at the time of sighting we were almost at the end of our patrol. Clutterbuck (he was always known as just Clutterbuck), it should be said, received the DFC for this action.'

(For a personal account by G.D. Williames, see *Conflict over the Bay*.)

20 July, 1943

U-558, a type VIIC submarine, commanded by Kapitänleutnant Gunther Krech, sunk.

Liberator 'F' 19 Squadron USAAF, on patrol 0740 from St Eval

Lt C.F. Gallimeir	Pilot
Lt Rosoff	Nav
and crew	

Halifax 'E' DT642 58 Squadron, on patrol 0900–1755 hrs.

F/L G.A. Sawtell	Pilot
PO J.M. Clark	

F/Sgt T.R. Urquhart	
Sgt B. Hilldon	
PO R.W. Marshall	AG
Sgt W.A. Tennant	
Sgt B.E. Mitchell	AG
Sgt L.C. Matthews	

At 1010 hrs the American crew had an S/E contact and 15 minutes later spotted two U-boats in position 4530/0945, 6 miles ahead. They caught the boats by surprise and singled out one for attention, attacking with D/Cs from 600 feet. Lieutenant Rosoff opened fire with the front gun as they closed in, then the top and waist guns began firing. Finally the U-boat's gunner replied, hitting the Liberator, wounding one of the air gunners in the leg. Seven D/Cs went down, exploding close by the boat's port side. More flak came up and Charles Gallimeir was about to make a second attack when he found he had sustained damage to the port inner engine, which cut out.

At this moment the 58 Squadron Halifax came on the scene. The U-boat was rolling heavily and was down by the stern. At first the Halifax merely exchanged gunfire with the Germans as more of the crew came up on deck. A number were hit by the RAF fire and fell into the water. The U-boat appeared to be settling and Sawtell then made his attack, thinking the new men coming up were going to man the guns. Eight D/Cs went down from 50 feet. Bodies were thrown into the air by the explosions and the boat keeled over, 12 feet of its bows visible through the spray. The U-boat stopped firing as they ran out of ammo and no more could be hoisted from below, the boat being now full of deadly chlorine gas as sea water was now getting into the batteries. The German crew began to abandon ship. Gallimeir did not see the end of the U-boat. He was struggling towards England, which he reached safely.

Gunther Krech, holder of the Knight's Cross, survived. Six men had got into a dinghy which had been launched, while 30 more clung desperately to its sides. Most of these men died, many as a result of the bad gassing. On the 25th, five survivors, including Krech, were rescued by the Canadian warship *Athabascan*.

U-558 was on its way back to Brest from the Azores on its 10th patrol. She had been active for almost two years and had sunk 20 ships. The best patrol had been its seventh between August and October 1942, when 16 ships were sunk, which resulted in Krech's Knight's Cross. Now 41 of her crew had perished only Krech, his second lieutenant and three ratings having survived.

Geoffrey Sawtell later received the DFC, while

two of his gunners, Robert Marshall and Banks Earle Mitchell, received the DFC and DFM respectively.

24 July, 1943

U-459, a type XIV tanker submarine, commanded by Korvettenkapitän Georg von Wilamowitz-Moellendorf, sunk.

Wellington 'Q', 172 Squadron, on patrol 1230 hrs.

FO W.H.T. Jennings	Pilot
FO J.G. McCormack	2nd pilot
F/Sgt J.W. Buxton	Nav
FO J. Johnston	WOP/AG
F/Sgt L. Harrop	WOP/AG
Sgt A.A. Turner	AG

At 1750 hrs the Wimpy was about to turn to a new course when an S/E contact was made 6 miles to starboard. The aircraft went into cloud and came out to see a U-boat on the surface which was obviously going to stay up and fight. Jennings brought his Wellington down to 100 feet, but at 1000 feet from the target it was badly hit and the pilots may also have been killed or injured. In any event the Wimpy carried on and ploughed right into the submarine. The sole survivor, Sergeant Turner, found himself in the sea when the aircraft disintegrated. Struggling on to a dinghy which had inflated but was upside down, he could see the U-boat with its crew on deck. Debris was all around, and indeed, at least one depth charge had landed on the boat, but exploded in the sea when it was pushed off by the Germans. The U-boat was out of control, smoke pouring from the stern and settling. Then a Wellington of 547 Squadron, piloted by Flying Officer J. Whyte, saw the damaged boat, attacked and its D/Cs exploded about her. The crew began to abandon ship.

From Bordeaux, U-459 had begun its sixth patrol on 22 July. Its CO was not among survivors picked up by the destroyer *Orken*. These comprised five officers and 32 men. The destroyer crew also heard the shouts of Sergeant Turner and rescued him too. U-459 had resupplied boats 75 times during its five earlier cruises including 15 boats off Bermuda in April 1942. It carried 700 tons of oil.

Sergeant Turner, who was later a player for Charlton Athletic Football Club, had been part of the crew which damaged U-525 in March 1943.

28 July, 1943

U-404, a type VIIC submarine commanded by Oberleutnant Adolf Schoenberg, sunk.

Liberator 'W', 224 Squadron, on patrol 1200–2115 hrs.

FO R.V. Sweeny	Pilot
PO E. Allen	2nd pilot
FO R.W. King	Nav
F/Sgt I.A. Graham	WOP/AG
F/Sgt E. Cheek	WOP/AG
Sgt C. Owen	Eng
Sgt A.H. Graham	AG
Sgt D. Doncaster	AG

Liberator 'N', 4 Squadron USAAF

Lt A.J. Hammar and crew	Pilot

At 1430 hrs a square search was made for a reported U-boat, but nothing was seen. Later saw a D/C explosion some 25 miles ahead and flew to investigate, although nothing showed on the ASV Mk V. Then a signal was intercepted and more D/C plumes seen and then they saw a U-boat with a Liberator circling it. Sweeny went straight in and dropped seven D/Cs from 150 feet. Flak from the boat set the Liberator's No. 4 engine on fire. D/Cs straddled the target, which disappeared below, but immediately reappeared on an even keel but then went down again. When the water settled about ten bodies could be seen in life belts where the U-boat had been.

U-404 had been attacked earlier by Major McElroy of the 4th Squadron USAAF, and then Lieutenant Arthur Hammar had picked up the message and at 1752 hrs had seen the U-boat on the surface five miles off. He straddled it with eight D/Cs then made a second attack, two men falling overboard as the American gunners opened fire. The B.24 was hit in the port outer engine and also in the tail and fuselage. It had been their D/C plumes that Sweeny had seen, and he arrived just as Hammar was breaking off the action with his damaged aircraft.

U-404 went down in position 4553/0925 at 1807 hrs. There were no survivors. It had sailed from St Nazaire four days earlier for the North Atlantic. In earlier patrols it had sunk 18 ships, including the destroyer HMS *Veteran* on 29 June, 1942.

The American B.24 reached England safely. These American Army Air Force squadrons had recently been attached to Coastal Command to give additional support to the anti-U-boat war. Sweeny and his crew also got home, although they had to jettison all movable equipment. They landed at St Mawgan and returned to St Eval by road. Bob Sweeny later received the DFC, while the two Grahams in the crew were awarded DFMs. Eddie Cheek thought he would spend his 21st birthday (29 July) in a dinghy eating Horlicks tablets, but luckily he didn't. He and Ronald King later received the DFM and DFC respectively.

29 July, 1943

U-614, a type VIIC submarine commanded by Kapitänleutnant Wolfgang Strater, sunk.

Wellington VIII 'G', 172 Squadron, on patrol 0721–1435 hrs.

WC R.G. Musson	F/L L.H. Burden (Can)
WO R. Reynolds	Sgt B. Todd
F/L E. Carr	Sgt G.R. Manley-Tucker

Flying at 1200 feet in cloud, an S/E contact was picked up at 6½ miles, which looked like a possible U-boat surfacing. Keeping in cloud, Musson turned and broke cloud only when ¾ of a mile from the contact. They quickly spotted a fully surfaced U-boat, at which the front gunner began firing, although nobody could be seen in the conning tower. Six D/Cs went down from 50 feet, while the aircraft was in a gentle glide, clearly seen by the rear gunner to form a perfect straddle, with four to starboard and two to port. The No. 4 D/C exploded close to the boat's starboard bow and No. 5 to port just by the conning tower. The rear gunner fired 400 rounds as he watched the plumes obscure the target, but as the spray cleared the boat was gone. Aircraft flew back over the scene two minutes later, finding a spreading oil patch and survivors in the sea, some wearing life jackets and yellow skull caps. All were waving or shaking their fists. Musson remained close by for 15 minutes by which time the patch was 200 x 50 yards, then resumed the patrol.

U-614 went down at 1050 hrs in position 4642/1103, having sailed on its third war patrol from St Nazaire on the 25th, bound for the North Atlantic. It had one ship to its credit.

Rowland Gascoigne Musson was a pre-war airman. On 24 August, 1943, he took off for a patrol from Chivenor shortly before midnight. For some unexplained reason, the Wellington crashed two miles inland from Clovelly, its D/Cs exploded and all on board were killed. In addition to Musson, Carr,

Todd and Burden, the squadron Gunnery Officer, who had been with him when U-614 was sunk, all died.

30 July, 1943

U-461, a type IV supply submarine, commanded by Korvettenkapitän Wolf Stiebler, sunk.

Sunderland 'U' W6077, 461 RAAF Squadron, on patrol 0248–1827 hrs.

F/L D. Marrows	Captain
PO P.C. Leigh	1st pilot
F/Sgt P.E. Taplin	2nd pilot
FO J.S. Rolland	Nav
Sgt G.M. Watson, RAF	Eng
Sgt A.N. Pierce	Fitter
PO P.T. Jensen	1 WOP
F/Sgt H.H. Morgan	2 WOP
Sgt D.C. Sydney	AG
Sgt R.L. Webster	3 WOP
Sgt F. Bamber	Rigger
J. Tainer	U/T

Air patrols this day caught three surfaced U-boats heading out across the Bay. Dudley Marrows and his crew sighted them at 1148 hrs, with a Halifax and a US Liberator circling nearby. Combined fire from the U-boats were keeping the aircraft at bay, but then as the Lib tried an attack and took the attention of the German gunners, Marrows attacked and straddled one boat with seven D/Cs and the boat disappeared under plumes and scum. Heavy fire from the other boats was returned by nose and tail gunners, and when the area cleared, survivors could be seen in the water. The Sunderland flew over taking pictures, and a dinghy was dropped, some of the Germans being seen to get into it. One D/C remained, but an attempt to attack a second boat was driven off by heavy flak. The Sunderland had been hit and a fire did break out, but it was put out with an extinguisher. On the flight home, another U-boat was seen, but although an attack was made, the final D/C still could not be released. They landed and refuelled at the Scilly Isles before flying back to base.

U-461 went down in position 4542/1100 at five minutes after midday. This had been her sixth war cruise, having sailed from Bordeaux three days earlier for the Atlantic to supply Wolf Packs already operating there. It was a strange twist of fate that led Sunderland U/461 to attack and sink U-461!

Dudley Marrows received the DFC for his attack.

Forty years later, he and some of his crew met Wolf Stiebler when he was their guest during a visit to Australia. (For a detailed account of this action, and those of the Halifax and Liberator, as well as personal narratives, see *Conflict over the Bay* by N.L.R. Franks). Marrows and his crew were shot down by Ju 88s in September 1943 but survived and were rescued from their dinghy. Marrows later received the DSO.

30 July, 1943

U-462, a type XIV supply submarine, commanded by Oberleutnant Bruno Vowe, sunk.

Halifax II 'S', 502 Squadron, on patrol 0715–1645 hrs.

FO A. van Rossum (Dutch)	PO J.A. Ridock
F/Sgt C.D. Aidney (Fiji)	F/Sgt R.E. Wiggall
F/L A.W. Martin	F/Sgt F.S. Fraser
FO G.W. Leadson	Sgt A. Sills

The aircraft received a U-boat sighting report, changed course, made radar contact at 36 miles and found the 2nd Escort Group heading for the three U-boats which were 20 miles further on. Another Halifax of 502 Squadron and then the Sunderland arrived, and then both Halifax aircraft, with 600 lb bombs, made attacks. One bomb dropped by 'S-Sugar' landed close to the stern of the boat and later smoke was seen to come from the conning tower as the sub began to circle. Meanwhile, the Sunderland attacked another U-boat and then the Liberator made an attack. Van Rossum made two further bombing runs and finally the U-boat stopped in the water. Slowly she began to sink, and men started to jump overboard. As the conning tower began to submerge, so the first shells from the approaching Escort Group began to fall nearby. Meantime, the US Liberator had been hit and damaged by flak from the third U-boat – U-504 – and he had to limp away, while yet another Lib, O/53 Squadron, had also arrived and it too was hit by flak and damaged. As the ships came on to the scene, U-504 dived, but she was hunted by the surface ships and sunk.

U-462 went down at 1210 hrs in position 4508/1057. She was on her fifth cruise, having left with the others from Bordeaux on the 27th for the Atlantic.

Flying Officer van Rossum received the DFC early in 1944.

1 August, 1943

U-454, a type VIIC submarine, commanded by Kapitänleutnant Burkhard Hacklander, sunk.

Sunderland 'B' W4020, 10 RAAF Squadron, on patrol 1001 hrs.

F/L K.G. Fry	Captain
FO H.R. Budd	1st pilot
FO J.M. Curtis	2nd pilot
FO J.H. Portus	Nav
PO A.M. Welch	Nav U/T
Sgt H.B. Lydeamore	Eng
Sgt F.O. Pettersson	Fitter
F/Sgt B.E. Cook	WOP/AG
F/Sgt R.G. Welfare	WOP/AG
Sgt J.E. Fryer	Fitter
Sgt J. Haslam	Armourer
Sgt D.I. Conacher	AG

Patrolling the Musketry area, the aircraft sighted five sloops on a U-boat hunt and joined them. The aircraft observed a submarine from 1700 feet, passed over it and made a steep turn to starboard, then came in for an attack at 50 feet. Six D/Cs fell three either side of the target, and during the approach the nose gunner was returning fire from the U-boat's gunners. The Sunderland was hit in the starboard inner engine and starboard main petrol tank. Petrol began flooding the bridge area when the aircraft was still half a mile away. The cockpit area was a shambles and it is probable that both pilots were hit on the run-in. With one engine on fire the Sunderland lost what height it had after the attack, and plunged into the sea. Only six of the Australian crew survived – Portus, Pettersson, Cook, Welfare, Haslam and Conacher. Among the dead was Pilot Officer Welch, a trainee navigator on his first operational trip. The six survivors were picked up by HMS *Wren* of the Escort Group.

U-454 was sunk; indeed she had broken in two. She had sailed from La Pallice on 29 July, for her fifth patrol. HMS *Kite* picked up 14 of her crew from the water, including her captain. She had gone down in position 4536/1023 at 1442 hrs. She had sunk the destroyer HMS *Matabele* on 17 January, 1942, as well as two M/Vs, one being the ammunition ship *Harmatrio*.

Ken Fry, a farmer from South Australia, was just nine days short of his 30th birthday.

1 August, 1943

U-383, a type VIIC submarine, commanded by Kapitänleutnant Horst Kremser, sunk.

Sunderland 'V' JM678, 228 Squadron, on patrol 1450–2350 hrs.

F/L S. White	Sgt B. Hodgeman
FO A. Neville-Stack	F/Sgt T. Robney
FO K.A. Mooring	Sgt W. Champion
PO F. Jackson	Sgt R. Glazier
F/Sgt E. Kampton	Sgt W. Carteen
Sgt F. Baker (Aust)	

Sighted a surfaced U-boat in showery weather while on a Musketry patrol at 2002 hrs. The aircraft attacked and U-boat returned rapid and accurate gunfire while taking violent evasive action. The flying boat's gunner replied and scored hits in the conning tower. The first run was spoilt by the evasive tactics and flak shot away the aircraft's starboard float and smashed the starboard aileron, as well as putting holes in the fuselage and below the front turret. On the second run, seven D/Cs went down, and when the spray cleared the boat was seen to be listing heavily to port. Men were then seen jumping into the sea. The Sunderland could no longer turn because of its damaged aileron, so headed for home.

U-383, on her fourth patrol, leaving Brest for the Atlantic on 29 July, sank in position 4724/1210, but not immediately after the attack. Despite seeing men apparently abandoning ship, Kremser still had some measure of control and radioed base reporting his boat seriously damaged. Two other U-boats were sent to her aid as well as three torpedo boats, but U-383 foundered during the night before further radio calls could be made.

Flight Lieutenant Stanley White received the DFC. On 30 July, it had been him who had actually found the three U-boats sunk by Marrows, Van Rossum and the 2nd Escort Group.

2 August, 1943

U-706, a type VIIC submarine, commanded by Kapitänleutnant Alexander von Zitzewitz, sunk.

Liberator 'T', 4 Squadron, USAAF

Lt J.L. Hamilton
and crew

Hampden 'A', 415 Squadron RCAF, on patrol 0553–1225 hrs

SL C.G. Ruttan	FL C. Ellwood
PO A.G. Smith, DFM	Sgt W.C. Norquay

This U-boat was spotted by Squadron Leader C.G. Rutton RCAF, flying on a Musketry patrol, at 0903 hrs. Despite heavy gunfire, the Canadian attacked, but results from his six D/Cs could not be determined. However, the boat had been damaged, as survivors later confirmed. The Liberator now arrived on the scene, having picked up a radar contact at 20 miles and then had seen the Hampden at 10 miles. Hamilton went straight into the attack from the sub's starboard side, from the sun. Yet the German gunners hit the B.24, but it did not stop 12 D/Cs being dropped from 50 feet. When the explosions subsided the boat was going down by the stern and at least 15 men were in the sea amidst oil and wreckage. The Americans flew back over the spot and dropped a dinghy, and some of the survivors were seen to clamber in. Later a Catalina and a Sunderland arrived and helped to direct HMS *Waveney* of the 40th Escort Group to the scene, and she picked up the survivors.

U-706 went down in position 4615/1025 at 0920 hrs. She had not survived her fifth patrol, which had begun from La Pallice on 29 July. She had sunk two ships.

Rutton was given command of 415 Squadron on this very day, and the following spring he was awarded the DSO.

2 August, 1943

U-106, a type IXB submarine, commanded by Oberleutnant Wolfdietrich Damerow, sunk.

Sunderland 'N' JM708, 228 Squadron, on patrol 1100–0106 hrs.

FO R.D. Hanbury	FO D. Pearson
F/Sgt A. Beal	F/Sgt B. Lacey
F/Sgt T. Kilsby	F/Sgt E. House
F/Sgt N. Wilson, DFM	F/Sgt R. Webster
Sgt W. Harris	Sgt D. Norman
Sgt R. Morrison	

Sunderland 'M' DV968, 461 RAAF Squadron, on patrol 1242–0045 hrs.

F/L I.A.F. Clarke	FO J.C. Amiss
Sgt D.M. Jorgenson	F/Sgt P. Pfeiffer

F/Sgt L. White	Sgt R. Jeffries
WO R. Hattam	F/Sgt J.H. Royle
F/Sgt L.G. Studman	FO E.R. Critcher
F/Sgt J.H. Poulton	

This U-boat was attacked by Wing Commander J.C. Archer of 407 RCAF Squadron at around 0930 hrs, but the D/Cs did not appear to damage the German, but it had been slightly damaged and turned for France. The crew then effected repairs and the captain called base for assistance. The Germans put up aircraft and redirected subs and torpedo boats, looking vainly for U-383 (see earlier). Some hours later a 228 Squadron aircraft saw the three torpedo boats, reporting them as destroyers. This brought a response from Group, in the shape of Reader Hanbury of 228 and Irwin 'Chic' Clarke of 461 Squadron, while not far away were the ships of the 40th Escort Group. A Halifax and a Liberator also joined in to shadow the three boats, and later the U-boat was seen in the distance. Hanbury flew in and began a gun duel with the enemy gunners. Chic Clarke also joined in and in turn both aircraft dropped six D/Cs around the stricken boat. Now severely hit, Damerow gave the order to abandon ship, while five men continued to man the AA guns. As the German crew took to dinghies and life rafts, the two aircraft continued their gun duels, some sailors falling into the sea. At 2040 hrs the U-boat blew up, littering the sea with debris and four dinghies full of survivors. The 40th Escort Group later picked up 37 men, including Damerow.

This ended the 10th patrol of U-106, which had begun from Lorient on 29 July. She had been successful in the past, having sunk a total of 20 Allied ships.

This was Hanbury's second success in one month.

2 August, 1943

U-218, a type VIID minelaying submarine, damaged.

Wellington 'B', 547 Squadron, on patrol 1227–1941 hrs.

PO J.W. Hermiston	Pilot
F/Sgt F.G. Duff	2nd pilot
PO L.G. Speyer	Nav
Sgt W. Owens	WOP/AG
Sgt J.W. Horwood	WOP/AG
Sgt L. Davies	WOP/AG

Early in this Easter Monday patrol, the crew spotted

two RN destroyers but were fired on so gave them a wide berth and flew on. At 1519 hrs, at 1800 feet, Bill Owens in the front turret spotted a U-boat in the heavy swell, which just seemed to pop up from nowhere. It was only about a mile away and Owens could see a large white dragon painted on its conning tower. An almost immediate D/C drop overshot so the aircraft proceeded to make several machine-gun attacks before the boat finally went under.

In the event, U-218 was undamaged, but the combined gunfire of Bill Owens and the rear gunner, Sergeant Davies, inflicted several casualties amongst the men in the conning tower. She had sailed from Brest – for Trinidad – on 29 July, but had to abort her mission and return to base for medical treatment for her wounded. She was later converted to a schnorkel boat.

Pilot Officers Hermiston and Speyer and Flight Sergeant Duff did not survive the war. Bill Owens completed his tour and later flew on Air Sea Rescue Warwicks.

7 September, 1943

U-669, a type VIIC submarine, commanded by Oberleutnant Kurt Kohl, sunk.

Wellington XII 'W' HF115, 407 RCAF Squadron.

PO E.M. O'Donnell	F/Sgt R.C. Gaudet
Sgt A.D. Moreton	F/Sgt I.E. Smithson
F/Sgt C. Grant	F/Sgt K.A. Keelar

Flying at 1500 feet, with visibility 2 miles, an S/E contact was picked up to port at 8 miles, and the aircraft turned and lost height rapidly. At ¾ of a mile the Leigh Light was turned on, illuminating a U-Boat, low in the water, but not submerging, in position 4536/1013. Not being in a favourable position for attack, O'Donnell swept behind the boat, turning to port, followed by flak fire from the conning tower. The rear gunner replied as the light went off. Circling, the Wellington came in again and at 2 miles picked out the wake of the sub, which was now steering a zigzag course. The light went on at one mile and the U-boat then began to go under, but the tower was still above water when the D/Cs fell around it, at 0241 hrs. One D/C hung up, but the other five did their work, although coming back over the spot the sea was clear except for the flame floats.

U-669 went straight to the bottom, leaving no sign of its loss. She was on her second cruise, which began from St Nazaire on 29 August, bound for the

North Atlantic. Her first had been from Kiel in May 1943. There were no recorded sinkings by her.

O'Donnell, flying with Grant, Gaudet and Smithson, failed to return from a sortie from Limavady on 11 March, 1944, in Wellington HF311.

27 September, 1943

U-221, a type VIIC submarine, commanded by Kapitänleutnant Hans Trojer, sunk.

Halifax 'B' HR982, 58 Squadron, on patrol 1138 hrs.

FO E.L. Hartley	Pilot
GC R.C. Mead	2nd pilot
FO T.E. Bach (Can)	Nav
Sgt G.R. Robertson	Eng
F/Sgt K.E. Ladds	M/U gnr
Sgt R.K. Triggol	R/Gnr
Sgt A.S. Fox	WOP
Sgt M. Griffiths	Fnt gnr

On patrol to the Percussion area at 50 feet, below 10/10ths cloud at 800 feet, over a calm sea, sighted a U-boat at 6 miles, dead ahead, in position 4700/1800. Made an attack at 1713 hrs, releasing eight Mk XI D/Cs, which straddled the boat just aft of the conning tower, from port bow to starboard quarter. Just before they were released, however, the Halifax was caught by flak from the sub, which hit the No. 2 fuel tank and set the starboard wing on fire. As the burning aircraft flew over the U-boat, the rear gunner reported plumes either side of the target's stern and then the bows rose into the air before slipping back into the water and going under. However, by this time, Eric Hartley was struggling with his crippled aircraft and was forced to make a crash landing about 3 miles from the scene of the attack. He was unable to release the remaining D/Cs and had no flaps, so he hit the sea at 110 kts. The tail broke off and water rushed in through the front as the Halifax went up on its nose. Group Captain Mead, Holmesley South's Station Commander, Bach and Ladds had taken up position in the rest area, Robertson, Fox and Griffiths against the rear spar. Triggol was in transit from the rear and was not seen again. The others all clambered out and made for the dinghy, but Griffiths was badly dazed and despite a struggle to save him he slipped away and was drowned. Due to the speed of the events, no emergency equipment was saved, and as their rapid SOS had been sent at such a low altitude and base was 700–800 miles away, the surviving six men guessed they had a long wait for rescue. In the event it was to be 11 days before rescue came – 8 October!

The six men survived on barley sugar, malted milk and Horlicks tablets, chocolate, condensed milk, chewing gum and a few pints of water. Finally, on the afternoon of the 8th, Ken Ladds sighted the mast of a ship and they fired off three signal cartridges. Two destroyers came into view, and about 20 minutes later HMS *Mahratta*, homeward bound from Gibraltar, picked them up. They were not searching for them, and it was pure chance they were spotted.

U-221 had been on her fifth patrol, having left St Nazaire on 20 September for the North Atlantic. Her first had been from Kiel a year earlier. She had sunk 12 Allied ships, including a claim for eight ships from convoy SC104 during 12–13 October, 1942, although only five were actually lost.

Eric Hartley, whose 27th operational trip this was, received an immediate DFC and Ken Ladds, on his 47th op, and who helped to keep the men's spirits up in the dinghy, received the DFM.

7 November, 1943

U-123, a type IXB submarine, commanded by Leutnant Reinhard Hardegan, damaged.

Mosquito XVIII 'I', 248 Squadron, on patrol 0818–1129 hrs.

FO A.J.L. Bonnett, RCAF	Pilot
FO A.M. McNicol	Nav

This crew was on detachment from 618 Squadron and the aircraft was equipped with the new 6-pounder 'Tsetse' gun (57mm). The first two Tsetse-gunned Mosquitoes taken on by 248 were HX902 and HX903 in October 1943. On patrol over the Bay, they found a surfaced U-boat in position 4715/0438 at 0945 hrs. Turning to come down to attack on track, Bonnett opened fire at 1600 yards while at 1500 feet, until he was down to 200 yards at 200 feet. Eight rounds of 57mm were fired and strikes were seen on the foredeck, between the conning tower and the deck gun, then aft of the conning tower. Yellow-coloured smoke came from the boat, and some gunfire was aimed at the Mossie, one bullet hitting the oil tank. A second attack was made, but the Tsetse gun jammed, so Bonnet fired with his machine guns.

U-123, on its way home from Trinidad, whence it had sailed from St Nazaire in mid-August, returned damaged on this same day. Because flak from the boat had ceased after the first attack it was assumed that the heavy gun had inflicted casualties as well as damage in the U-boat. This was her 13th patrol, its last beginning in January 1944, to West Africa. The boat, which had sunk 37 ships, was finally scrapped in August 1944. It had begun its career back in September 1940 under Leutnant Moehle. It was the first U-boat to sink an American ship off the US coast after America declared war on Germany – outside New York on 12 January, 1942. On its next cruise to the US seaboard it sank at least eight ships, probably more.

Bonnett and McNicol were again successful on 7 June, 1944.

10 November, 1943

U-966, a type VIIC submarine, commanded by Oberleutnant Ekkehard Wolf, sunk.

Wellington IX 'B', 612 Squadron, on patrol 0001–1025 hrs.

WO I.D. Gunn	Pilot
Sgt L. Jaffre (French)	2nd pilot
F/Sgt G. Bayliss	Nav
Sgt B. Dennehy	WOP/AG
Sgt R. Wingfield	WOP/AG
Sgt R.G. Sadler	WOP/AG

Liberator 'E', VPB 103 Squadron USN

Lt K.L. Wright and crew	Pilot

Liberator 'E', VPB 110 Squadron USN

Lt J.A. Parrish and crew	Pilot

Liberator 'D', 311 Czech Squadron

F/Sgt Zanta and crew	Pilot

612 Squadron picked up the U-boat at 0409 hrs on radar, sighted it on the surface 4 miles away and from 100 feet dropped six D/Cs, but they fell a little short, and after an exchange of gunfire the boat submerged. Ian Gunn recalls: 'I remember sighting the U-boat in the moonpath from about 200 feet and we didn't give him any warning by using the Leigh Light. But he did shoot back! I should say that the

U-boat dived about three minutes after the attack. We flew over the area for nearly two and a half hours afterwards and searched a radius of 5 or 6 miles but we saw nothing more.'

Lieutenant Wright received a signal that the U-boat was in position 4439/0908 but on the way two Ju 88s were seen, so the B.24 flew off for a while, during which time further signals suggested the boat was making for Ferrol. Making a landfall at Ferrol, Wright set course for the boat's last position and at 1140 hrs made radar contact. He attacked and released five D/Cs – one hanging up – and on a second run dropped a 600 lb D/C. The boat was then seen to be down by the stern and leaving a trail of oil. After the exchanges of gunfire one sailor was seen hanging over the side of the conning tower.

Later it was located by Lieutenant Parrish. The sea was breaking over the conning tower and it was still down by the stern. As the aircraft circled and reduced height the U-boat began to open fire. Coming in out of the sun with forward guns blazing, the B.24 dropped six D/Cs, the explosions rolling the U-boat over to its port side, but it straightened up before making a complete circle. It was now about 12 miles off the Spanish coast and again began to head in that direction.

Flight Sergeant Zanta's crew picked up a radar contact and later saw the U-boat 3 miles off the Spanish coast. Aircraft circled to confirm its nationality as the boat opened fire and made full speed towards the coast. Another Lib was seen circling and contact established by R/T. At 1345 hrs Zanta, whose aircraft was fitted with rockets, attacked, firing the first pair of R/Ps at 1000 feet, then a second pair, but both pairs failed. The last four did fire at 600 feet and the rockets were seen to enter the water, level with the bows, 50 feet from the boat, and were not seen to emerge. Nothing else seen but the boat did appear to slow down.

U-966 had sailed from Kiel to Bergen between 9 and 13 September, 1943, then from Trondheim on its first cruise to the Atlantic on 5 October. Making its way to a Bay port it was damaged by 612, and then when trying to make the Spanish coast it was attacked and again damaged by the attentions of the two American and the Czech Liberators. She eventually beached herself near De Santafata Bay, where she was blown up by the crew who then came ashore in their dinghies.

This had been the second U-boat attacked by Ian Gunn, (a Scot), having achieved a near miss on one back on 2 May, flying a Whitley (BD676 'G'). His second pilot, Louis Jaffre, was a Free French pilot.

12 November, 1943

U-508, a type IXC/40 submarine, commanded by Kapitänleutnant Georg Staats, sunk.

Liberator 'C', VPB 103 Squadron, USN

Lt R.B. Brownell	Pilot
Ens D.A. Schneider	2nd pilot
CAP(AA) R.K. Poole	Nav
AMM1/c W. English	
AMM2/c G.B. Simpson Jr	
ARM1/c B.R. Holladay	
ARM3/c W.N. Meroney	
AOM2/c C.K. McClung	
AOM2/c L. Eitel	
SEA1/c W.C. Rodgers Jr	

On the night of the 12th this crew was on patrol, but nothing else was heard of them after they gave a flash report. A search the following day revealed two oil slicks, one large and one small, 5 miles apart. It was assumed that they attacked and sank the U-boat but were themselves shot down by it.

U-508 was on its sixth war cruise, sailing from St Nazaire on 9 November, for a patrol in the North Atlantic. On the night of the 12th, she encountered the American Navy B.24, and although the Liberator was shot down, its D/Cs claimed the U-boat, which sank in position 4600/0730. U-508 had sunk a total of 12 Allied ships.

The whole crew received posthumous awards; Ralph Brownell the Navy Cross, Danial Schneider and Ridgeway Poole, DFCs, and the rest Air Medals.

13 December, 1943

U-391, a type VIIC submarine, commanded by Oberleutnant Gert Dueltgen, sunk.

Liberator 'B' BZ814, 53 Squadron, on patrol 0015–1350 hrs.

SL G. Crawford, AFC	F/Sgt B.G. Barton (NZ)
FO D.G. Biggs (Can)	F/Sgt R.A. O'Kane (NZ)
F/Sgt R.J. Martin	Sgt A. Stoten
Sgt K.V. Jones	PO L.G. Renn
WO H.A. Corns	

Half an hour after take-off, the aircraft was contacted by Group to hunt for a U-boat in position 4544/0930. Flight Lieutenant J. Barton (BZ793 'R') of the same squadron had found a contact but had had to leave the search. At 0413 hrs a square search began

from there, but the radar was not working satisfactorily so was switched off every three minutes. However, a contact was made at 1656 hrs, but when homing, the radar and intercom temporarily failed. When the Leigh Light was switched on a U-boat opened fire as it was held in the beam to starboard and hit and damaged the Liberator. With the light off, Crawford turned to attack from up-moon. The flak had stopped, but began again as the aircraft approached, the Lib's gunners also opening fire. Six D/Cs made a good straddle and afterwards two bodies were seen in the water and a small radar contact obtained for a moment, suggesting the U-boat's bows or stern at the moment of plunging below the waves.

U-391 was on its first cruise, having sailed from Kiel on 2 October for the Azores. It went down when trying to reach its new French base.

Squadron Leader Crawford, AFC, was awarded the DFC. However, he and his crew, with the exception of Sergeant Jones and Pilot Officer Renn, failed to return from a sortie over the Channel on the night of D-Day, 6 June, 1944.

2 January, 1944

U-445, commanded by Oberleutnant Rupprecht Fischler Graf von Treuberg, damaged.

Halifax 'A' HR792, 58 Squadron, on patrol 2005–0625 hrs.

FO T.A. Griffiths Pilot	F/Sgt S. Greig
F/L F.S. Jackson	F/Sgt G. Frape
FO H.E. Quinn Nav	Sgt D. Laffy
Sgt G. Martlew	F/Sgt J. Scott

The aircraft obtained an SE contact at 9 miles and homed in, opening the bomb doors at 4 miles shortly after 0200 hrs. At 1½ miles, 3 x 4in. HI flares were dropped and a U-boat was sighted dead ahead in position 4531/0719, from 600 feet. Reduced height to 300 feet and released five D/Cs – the sixth hung-up. The navigator had already begun to fire from 1000 yards with the nose gun, and the U-boat also fired, red and green tracer coming up, but this ceased when the aircraft had fired. As they circled after the attack, the boat seemed to be submerging and then the radar blip was lost. The assessment made no mention of any conclusions of this attack although the excellent radar and approach work was praised.

U-445 was on its fifth patrol, having to return to St Nazaire, whence it had sailed on 29 December. Its first cruise was in November 1942 and its last – ninth – began on 22 August, a trip from Lorient to Norway. It was sunk two days later by the frigate HMS *Louis*.

Flying Officers Griffiths and Quinn both received DFCs for this attack, the former having flown 34 A/S patrols, the latter, 39. In this attack, HI flares had been used for the first time.

3 January, 1944

U-373, a type VIIC submarine, commanded by Oberleutnant Detlef von Lehsten, damaged.

Wellington 'L' MP756, 612 Squadron, on patrol from Chivenor 1644–0138 hrs.

WC J.B. Russell DSO	Pilot
FO J.T.A. May	2nd pilot
F/L Skyrme	Obs (Nav)
F/Sgt G.H. Underhill	WOP/AG
F/Sgt C.V. Brignall	WOP/AG
FO H.M. Bedford	WOP/AG

Liberator 'H', 224 Squadron, on patrol from St Eval 1847–0843 hrs.

FO H.R. Facey (Can)	Pilot
F/Sgt N.L. Pickerhill	
FO F.H. Hackman (Can)	Nav
PO L.H. Skellern (NZ)	
WO D. Terrington	
WO W. Holmes (Can)	
WO G.P. Angus (Can)	
F/Sgt R. Lidbury	
Sgt J. Butler	

On Percussion patrol a radar contact was made by L/612, and after homing in, a surfaced U-boat was seen in the Leigh Light, D/Cs being dropped from 75 feet, 80 feet ahead of the swirl left by the crash-diving sub. Five minutes later another radar contact was picked up at 8 miles and homing in the U-boat was found again. With no more D/Cs, the Wellington circled some way off and homed in H/224 Squadron. After watching their attack, the Wellington set course for home at 2338 hrs.

The Liberator received the homing message at 2120 hrs and when it reached position 4602/0819, Flying Officer Hackmann, in the nose, sighted a U-boat. The captain felt he was tracking too far astern for a good attack so made a turn and was immediately fired upon by the sub, the Lib's gunners replying. A circle was flown, and without use of the Leigh Light an attack was made at 2215 hrs with eight D/Cs. The rear gunner thought they overshot slightly, but as the aircraft flew off, an orange glow was seen on the water which lasted for several minutes. Flying back, the Liberator again came under heavy fire. Then three radar contacts appeared, but investigation found no other sightings. When the Liberator again came to the scene of the attack, and found the Marine Marker, there was no sign of the U-boat.

Charles Brignall relates: 'On this day we did our usual Air Test in the morning, "L" had been newly serviced and everything seemed to work. That afternoon we took off at 1645 hrs and I recorded in my log-book "Attacked U-boat (my first seen) suspect damaged it. Slight AA fire." I seem to remember that the night was fair to fine, certainly no great worry, and that the attack was fairly early in the patrol, as it was, I think, before we ate our sandwiches, etc. Bedford was on the radar and I was on the wireless set at the time and so saw and heard nothing much of the actual "do". Johnny May was our second pilot, Bedford our number one WOP/AG/ASV and George Underhill and myself the other two.'

U-373, on its 11th patrol, had left La Pallice on New Year's Day. It was not to be her year. She returned damaged on the 4th and did not sail again until 7 June, 1944. She was sunk the next day – by 224 Squadron.

John Russell was the commanding officer of 612 Squadron and became tour expired on 25 January. Flying Officer Bedford was the Squadron Gunnery Officer and completed two tours of operations before going to No. 6 OTU. Johnny May later became a first pilot and Charles Brignall was later commissioned. Harold Facey received the DFC later in the year.

4 January, 1944

U-629, a type VIIC submarine commanded by Oberleutnant Hans-Helmut Bugs, damaged.

Wellington 'B' HF185, 304 (Polish) Squadron, on patrol 0407–1140 hrs.

FO H. Czyzun	Sgt K. Baranski
FO W. Siewruk	Sgt F. Bak
FO J. Kolano	F/Sgt W. Czerpak

At 0545 hrs a radar contact was made 7 miles to port. Investigated and found a surfaced U-boat, which was immediately attacked with six D/Cs, the nearest falling 25 feet from the target, while the air gunners fired 1200 rounds into it. The boat submerged, and although Markers were dropped and the aircraft remained in the area until 0732, nothing further was seen.

U-629 had earlier been part of the Arctic Flotilla. On 22 November, 1943, she had left Bergen for Brest and had rescued the crew of U-284 sunk on 21 December. Damaged by Czyzun and his crew, U-629 did not sail again until March.

5 January, 1944

U-415, a type VIIC submarine, commanded by Oberleutnant Johannes Werner, damaged.

Halifax 'R' HR983, 58 Squadron, on patrol 1615–0330 hrs.

F/L I.J.M. Christie	F/Sgt W.A. Rabig (Aust)
F/Sgt J.M. McCubben (Aust)	F/Sgt H. Finley (Aust)
F/L A. Swain	F/Sgt F. Chadwick
Sgt W. Heron	Sgt L. Griffiths

Visibility was 5 miles up moon when at 2257 hrs a radar contact at 22 miles put Christie and his crew on to a course that brought them to a U-boat. As they had already homed in to several trawlers on this night, they half expected to find yet another. However, in position 4644/0516 they spotted a wake and then the U-boat itself. They released three HI Mk 3 anti-submarine flares from 800 feet, which brought cannon fire from the sub, but this was aimed at the flares, allowing the Halifax to approach closer before it too attracted gunfire. At 2305 hrs six D/Cs were released from 150 feet, the nearest exploding 30 feet away. Another flare was released, bringing further gunfire and the RAF gunners too began firing. The boat then submerged, and although the Halifax remained in the area for over 3 hours nothing further was seen.

Despite the official assessment being thought to have caused nothing more than a severe shaking for the U-boat crew, U-415 had been damaged, but made port the next day. She had sailed on her fourth patrol on 21 November and was on her way back to Brest when attacked. She had earlier been damaged on her first patrol (see earlier) by three aircraft of Coastal, and was destined to be damaged on her fifth and sixth patrols in 1944 before being sunk by a mine.

8 January, 1944

U-426, a type VIIC submarine commanded by Kapitänleutnant Christian Reich, sunk.

Sunderland 'U' EK586, 10 RAAF Squadron, on patrol 0700–1542 hrs.

FO J.P. Roberts	Captain
FL S.W. Ashdown	1st pilot
FO W.R. McPharlin	2nd pilot
FO G.E. Rowe	Nav
Sgt L.J. Portwine	Eng
F/Sgt N.C. Dyer	2nd Eng
F/Sgt F.K. Randles	1 WOP/AG
Sgt E.G. Robinson	2 WOP/AG
F/Sgt A.J. Spence	AG
F/Sgt E.R. Goold	AG
Sgt J.S. Morris	Armourer(AG)

Flying a Percussion T.2 patrol a large U-shaped oil streak was sighted but nothing was seen and the patrol resumed. At 1154 hrs a U-boat was sighted with its decks awash 12 miles on the starboard bow in position 4647/1042. As the aircraft commenced attack the boat became fully surfaced and opened fire on the Sunderland, but when the front gunner opened up the flak ceased at 600 yards. However, the D/C trolley failed to run out and the attack was aborted, but when flying over the boat, six bodies could be seen lying in the conning tower. Six D/Cs were dropped in a second run-in from 50 feet, straddled the stern and the boat slowed down. It then began to list to starboard and sink stern first. Men were seen climbing from the conning tower and the bows rose in the air, followed by a large explosion. The U-boat sank, leaving about 40 men in the water, surrounded by debris and dinghies.

U-426 was on its second patrol, leaving Brest on 3 January for the North Atlantic. It had arrived from Bergen in November. Reich and 36 of his crew were lost.

Flying Officer Roberts, now the captain of his own crew, having been involved in earlier successful attacks, now had his own success. He received an immediate DFC.

28 January, 1944

U-571, a type VIIC submarine, commanded by Oberleutnant Gustav Luessow, sunk.

Sunderland 'D' EK577, 461 RAAF Squadron, on patrol 0836–1640 hrs.

F/L R.D. Lucas	Captain
FO R.H. Prentice	2nd pilot
F/Sgt C.D. Bremner	Nav
Sgt D. Musson, RAF	Eng
F/Sgt G.H. Simmonds, RAF	Mechanic
Sgt D.N. Walker, RAF	WOM
F/Sgt S.T.G. Bunnet	WOP/AG
F/Sgt W.J. Darcey	WOP/AG
FO H.D. Roberts	AG
Sgt J.R. Brannan (Can)	AG

Sergeant Danny Musson, the British Flight Engineer with this crew, remembers: 'The early morning of the 28th was, as was usual, dark, dank and miserable. The wind off the trots smelled of seaweed and oily mist. We were called at 0600 hrs, sleepily dressed and made our way to the aircrew mess. Later, while Dick Lucas, Prune Prentice, Col Bremner and Dave Walker went to briefing, the remainder of us collected flying rations and, via the dinghy, made our way aboard EK577, known affectionately as "Old Hopalong", to check the equipment.

'Our patrol was uneventful, watches changing on the hour, until 1300 hrs – position 5241/1427, about 500 miles from base. Lucas on "stick", Simmonds in nose, Bunnet on radar, Musson on engineer's panel, Walker on radio and Brannen in rear turret. Bunnet came up on intercom – "I think I have a contact on the starboard bow", immediately followed by Simmonds – "There's something down there – hell! he's shooting at us!"

'Lucas went straight into the attack, but the U-boat was "hosepiping" fire all over the place and violent evasive action had to be taken. At one point tracer was seen between the hull and starboard float. Simmonds let go with all he had and the conning tower stopped firing. The D/Cs went down and we swept over the U-boat – bodies could be seen in the conning tower area. This first attack was unsuccessful and Lucas came on the intercom, "Captain to all positions, I am going in again." Simmonds opened up again but there was no answering fire and down went the second lot of D/Cs.

'Someone came on the intercom – "Christ, she's still sitting there," then – "Look at that." The "That!" was the U-boat blowing up. There was a huge blast of white spray and she just disappeared. We made another run over what was now a quickly spreading oil slick in which floated wreckage and survivors, one of whom was waving. We made a further run and dropped a rubber dinghy and after it inflated we set course for base.

'Everything seemed to be functioning OK, no visible damage, but 15 minutes later the port inner oil temperature began to rise and a black streak of oil was visible on the underside of the engine housing. Knowing that if that engine had been hit it was likely that the port main petrol tank had also been hit, I decided to investigate. Leaving Joe Simmonds on the panel, I took off my Mae West and wriggled head first into the port wing among the struts and cross members, emerging some 15 minutes later covered in oil to report no fire damage. Next day we found and repaired a leaking oil union.

'When the films that Bremner had taken were developed, despite being temporarily knocked out when Lucas had made the first turn and he had lost his balance, it was found he had actually got a shot of the blow-up, and the Admiralty subsequently confirmed this as a "kill". We got a 48-hour pass in London (hic!)'

U-571 had gone down west of the mouth of the Shannon River off the west coast of Ireland. It had started its ninth war cuise from La Pallice on the 8th, and had sunk a destroyer on the 25th. On its previous patrol to West Africa it had suffered damage by an aircraft of 26 SAAF Squadron on 22 July. It had sunk a total of eight ships and Luessow had been skipper since its fourth cruise.

Flight Lieutenant Lucas, flying air cover to convoys SC 151 and ON 221, later received the DFC. After the war, he was a pilot with Qantas Airways. During the attack the bomb firing switch had failed to operate, so the second pilot's switch was operated by Prentice, who successfully released the D/Cs on the second run.

28 January, 1944

U-271, a type VIIC submarine, commanded by Kapitänleutnant Kurt Barleben, sunk.

Liberator 'E', VP 103 Squadron, US Navy.

Lt C.A. Enloe	Pilot
and crew	

On anti-sub patrol to convoy SC 151/ON 221, Enloe was at 2000 feet with a visibilty of 8 miles when a wake was sighted, followed by the U-boat itself, in position 5315/1552. He made an attack from out of the sun and the boat must have been caught by surprise, as only a few shots of flak came up. The front and top turrets fired back, hitting the deck and conning tower as six Mk IX D/Cs went down from 100 feet. They straddled just aft of the conning tower and the crew watched them explode as the Lib banked round. After being lifted by the stern, all forward motion from the sub ceased and then the stern began to settle. A 600 lb bomb was going to be dropped, but this was cancelled when it was seen that the boat was still on the surface, although air bubbles were filling the surrounding area. Then the boat went down leaving oil and more bubbles.

U-271 went down at 1147 hrs, west of Blacksod Bay, west of Ireland. She was on her third cruise, having left Brest on 12 January. There were no survivors from her 51 crew. For her second patrol in October 1943 she had been fitted out as a flak boat, but on this sortie her normal armament had been restored.

29 January. 1944

U-592, a type VIIC submarine, commanded by Oberleutnant Heinz Jaschke, damaged.

Liberator 'N', VP 110 Squadron, US Navy

| Lt H.H. Budd | Pilot |
| and crew | |

Shortly after 1350 hrs, a wake and then a U-boat was sighted in position 5107/1619 during a Percussion patrol. With the front and top gunners firing at the target, the second pilot, who had been in the left-hand seat when the boat was sighted, came in on a curve for the final run, releasing six Mk II D/Cs from 100 feet, but they fell short. He had involuntarily hit the release button as he was about to press it, making the drop just too soon. As the Lib flew over it was hit by a shell in the waist compartment. The American gunners kept up an intense return fire and the flak seemed to slacken for a short while. The Lib then circled out of range and Lieutenant Budd took command of the aircraft, but then the U-boat submerged. Soon afterwards two further aircraft of VP 110 arrived, but it was too late.

Nevertheless, U-592 had been damaged, and had to end her fourth patrol, which had begun on the 10th from St Nazaire. The boat started the return towards her Bay port, but two days later she was sunk by the sloops HMS *Starling*, *Wild Goose* and *Magpie* of the 2nd Escort Group, south-west of Cape Clear, position 5020/1729. Her first patrol began on 9 March, 1943, from Bergen.

30 January, 1944

U-364, a type VIIC submarine, commanded by Oberleutnant Paul-Heinrich Sass, sunk.

Wellington 'K' MP813, 172 Squadron, on patrol 2011 hrs.

F/Sgt L.D. Richards	Pilot
Sgt P. Horsefield	2nd pilot
Sgt C.J. Lowther	Nav
WO J. Pritchard	WOP/AG
Sgt R.C. Fisher	WOP/AG
Sgt A.B. Porter	WOP/AG

This crew took off to fly in the Percussion area, but no signals were received from them during the sortie and they subsequently failed to return. It is now understood that they discovered and attacked U-364 in the Bay of Biscay and sank her in position 4525/0515. However, the U-boat's defensive gunfire brought down the Wellington, and Leighton Richards and his crew perished.

U-364 had left Kiel on 23 November for its first war cruise to the North Atlantic and was making its way to a French port when sunk.

12 March, 1944

U-629, a type VIIC Submarine, commanded by Oberleutnant Hans-Helmut Bugs, damaged.

Wellington 'C', 612 Squadron, on patrol from Portreath, 2233–0950 hrs.

F/Sgt D. Bretherton	Pilot
Sgt I.W. Green	2nd pilot
F/Sgt D.W. Sulis (Aust)	Nav
Sgt R.A. Campbell	WOP/AG
Sgt L.J. Cole	WOP/AG
Sgt J.M. Dally	WOP/AG

At 0542 hrs, in position 4657/1055, a radar contact was made, lost, then re-established. An approach through low cloud and haze was made difficult as the aircraft did not have a radio compass, so the captain decided to fly lower than 500 feet as shown on the pressure altimeter. When ¾ of a mile away they flew into a clear patch and switched on the Leigh Light, but although a U-boat was seen, the aircraft was too high and had to go round again. The aircraft was then badly hit by the German's fire, which damaged the tail and rear turret. Sergeant Campbell, who had been on the radio, was disconnected from the R/T as he was due to change duties and it was some minutes before he realized that an attack was taking place. Sergeant Dally found himself in a similar situation. On the second run, Bretherton came down to between 50 and 100 feet and dropped five D/Cs, while the boat was still on the surface. (One D/C failed to drop). The boat appeared to come to a complete stop, but then it went down. Martyn Dally, who was initially on the radar, remembers: 'I picked up a signal on the radar screen and informed the skipper of the position of the blip relative to our course. The skipper changed course and reduced height to about 150–200 feet, having switched on the radio altimeter and lowered the Leigh Light ready for illuminating the target. I kept calling out the ranges to the skipper as we approached and I could also hear commands by him to other crew members. Suddenly the skipper ordered the Leigh Light to be switched on, but unfortunately the U-boat was not dead ahead as we expected. It was well off our run and certainly not in a position for us to drop our depth charges. The bombing run was aborted and we climbed away thinking we had missed our chance, as the U-boat would have immediately submerged.

'After levelling off, the radar screen no longer showed any sign of the U-boat and subsequently the three WOP/AGs decided it was time to change our positions. I think I handed over the radar to Bob Campbell, Len Cole went on W/T and it was my turn for the rear turret. I spent about 20–30 seconds looking out of the astrodome on my way back to the tail, but had not re-connected into the inter-com. Suddenly I felt the plane diving and turning so I plugged in to hear the radar operator giving homing instructions to the skipper. I realized we were already on the final approach and there was no time for me to get into the turret, so I jumped down to the waist guns, aft of the Leigh Light, and manned those in case I got a chance to use them. Before I could even get my breath I could hear from the running commentary that we were on the final run-in. Our front guns were firing and the U-boat was shelling us throughout the inward and outward run. Having dropped our D/Cs and banked sharply, I fired the waist gun at the receeding U-boat and saw the D/Cs explode in a good straddle.

'We circled, but each time we got within range of its guns it opened up on us. I now went to the rear turret and was met with an extreme amount of cold

air. On entering the turret I found quite a large hole through the floor and the Perspex hood above my head was shattered. This had been caused by a shell from the U-boat, and must have happened as we climbed away after dropping our D/Cs, and while I was on the waist guns!'

They remained circling the U-boat for some time until their fuel was running low, and finally had to make a run to England, crossing over the Brest peninsula – against normal safety rules – and landed at St Eval running out of fuel before taxiing was completed! They had been airborne for almost 12 hours.

U-629 had only just been repaired after being damaged on 4 January by 304 Squadron, having sailed on 9 March – its second patrol. It had to abort and return to Brest on the 15th. It would not sail again until D-Day, for its third and last cruise.

25 March, 1943

U-976, a type VIIC submarine, commanded by Oberleutnant Raimond Tiesler, sunk.

Mosquito XVIII 'L' (MM425?), 248 Squadron.

FO D.J. Turner	Pilot
FO D. Curtis	Nav

Mosquito XVIII 'I' (HX903?), 248 Squadron.

FO A. Hilliard	Pilot
?	Nav

Both on patrol 0700–1102 hrs.

Four aircraft of 248 Squadron led by Flight Lieutenant L.S. Dobson, in company with these two Mosquitoes of 248's Special Detachment, sighted a destroyer, two minesweepers and a U-boat in the Il de Yen area. The aircraft were at 50 feet above a calm sea. Turner made a total of four attacks with his 6-pounder Tsetse gun, while Hilliard made one. A good deal of flak came up from the small convoy, although the fire from the U-boat later ceased. Some ten hits were scored on the sub on the conning tower and forward deck near the water line. The U-boat remained on the surface during the attacks, but then submerged leaving an oil patch 100 x 30 yards. Time of attack, 0917 hrs, and cleared the area by 0928 hrs.

U-976 had left St Nazaire for this its second cruise on 20 March, but it was recalled to become part of Group 'Marder'. On its way back, having picked up its escort, it met 248 Squadron and was sunk in position 4648/0243. Survivors were picked up by these same escorting ships.

Turner and Hilliard were to find another submarine two days later.

27 March, 1944

U-960, a type VIIC submarine, commanded by Oberleutnant Gunther Heinrich, damaged.

Mosquito XVIII 'L' (MM425?), 248 Squadron.

FO D.J. Turner	Pilot
FO D. Curtis	Nav

Mosquito XVIII 'I' (HX903?), 248 Squadron.

F/L A. Hilliard	Pilot
?	Nav

Both on patrol 0655–1103 hrs.

Six aircraft of 248, led by Flight Lieutenant J.H.B Rollett escorted these two Special Detachment Mossies. As had been the case two days earlier, they were flying a sweep over the Il de Yen area of the Bay and found a convoy. It comprised nine armed trawlers, two U-boats and one Sperrbrecher plus a merchant ship. All aircraft attacked with good results, although one aircraft crash landed on return to base (F/Sgt L.A. Compton in 'X' LR363). Turner first sighted the convoy, then the U-boats. Both aircraft singled out the rear boat and at least four 6-pounder hits were seen. Heavy flak was experienced from the ships and Hilliard's aircraft sustained some damage.

U-960 was damaged, and when it was later sunk a prisoner from the crew confirmed that one 6-pounder shell had hit the conning tower and demolished the attack periscope and wounded 14 of the crew, four seriously. It too had been recalled, having originally sailed from La Pallice on 19 March, only to be damaged by the Mosquitoes. It sailed again on 27 April for the Mediterranean only to be sunk north-east of Tenes, Algeria, by American destroyers and RAF Wellingtons and a Ventura.

Douglas Turner and Desmond Curtis were both awarded DFCs.

28 April, 1944

U-193, a type IXC/40 submarine, commanded by Oberleutnant Ulrich Abel, sunk.

Wellington 'W', 612 Squadron, on patrol from Chivenor 2109–0818 hrs.

FO C.C. Punter (Aust)	Pilot	Sgt D. Casserley
FO G. Young		Sgt E.G. Dill
FO R. Hothersall		Sgt R. Crow

At 0040 hrs a contact was made in position 4540/1009 at 13½ miles. The aircraft had approached up-moon, but then the contact was lost at one mile. Baiting tactics were tried for an hour before patrol continued. On the return leg, at 0405 hrs, another contact was picked up, now in position 4544/0945, 11½ miles, but by now the moon had set. Homing in it was found that the Leigh Light turret was not working so the captain ordered the navigator into the front gun turret. At one mile the navigator saw a wake and then a U-boat. He opened fire, and in the light of the tracers Punter saw the boat too. He attacked from 50 feet and the rear gunner saw the bows lift out of the water and then the boat roll over on its side. There was no subsequent radar contact, but 15 minutes later the crew could see about 10 small bluish lights on the water.

U-193 was on her third patrol, leaving Lorient on 23 April. The first had been to the Azores and West Africa during May and July 1943, followed by a cruise to the Gulf of Mexico in October. After an air and surface attack on 9 February, she had hit the sea bed at 90 feet and sustained serious damage, forcing her into Ferrol for repairs. Oberleutnant Abel was the new skipper for the third and last patrol. It had sunk one ship.

Flying Officer 'Max' Punter received the DFC for this attack. He had attacked U-boats before and on one occasion had to fly his badly damaged aircraft home following one encounter.

4 May, 1944

U-846, a type IXC/40 submarine, commanded by Oberleutnant Berthold Hashagen, sunk.

Wellington 'M' HF134, 407 RCAF Squadron, on patrol 2147–0824 hrs.

F/L L.J. Bateman	Pilot
FO W.R. Keele	2nd pilot

WO A.D. Peter	Nav
WO J.W. Aulenback	WOP/AG
WO S.C. Miller	WOP/AG
Sgt T.I. Harries	WOP/AG

A radar contact was made at 7 miles at 0406 hrs when the aircraft was at 500 feet, in moonlight. The Leigh Light was not required, for when in position 4604/0920 a fully surfaced U-boat was observed. By now Bateman was down to 40 feet. The U-boat had already opened fire and the Wellington's front guns now jammed after firing one round. Bateman tracked over the boat and let go six D/Cs. Flak from the boat then ceased as aircraft flew off, later to return to the marine markers, but there was no sign of the sub except for an oily patch on the water. They circled this for some time before turning for home.

U-846, on her second patrol from Lorient (29 April), avoided an earlier meeting with fate on 2 May, when she had been attacked by a Halifax of 58 Squadron. The boat's gunners had succeeded in shooting down the RAF aircraft, but it did not fair as well when 407 Squadron located her.

Flight Lieutenant Bateman received the DFC.

24 May, 1944

U-736, a type VIIC submarine, commanded by Oberleutnant Reinhard Reff, damaged.

Wellington 'L', 612 Squadron, on patrol 2019 hrs.

FO K.H. Davies, RCAF	F/O C.E. Scott
F/Sgt K.S. Collins	WO J.A. Rooney
F/Sgt J. Bailey	Sgt H.C. Trump

Nothing was heard from this aircraft following its departure for a patrol over the Bay of Biscay. Ken Davies and his crew had arrived on the squadron on 11 May, and this was their first operational sortie.

It is believed this was the same U-boat which was attacked by 224 Squadron:

Liberator 'C', 224 Squadron, on patrol 2310–0604 hrs.

F/L E.W. Lindsay	FO A.R. Craine (Aust)
FO J.M. Francis (Aust)	WO W.J. Knill
PO J. Eglan	F/Sgt R.H. Cato (Aust)
PO G. Rumley	Sgt J.T. Dunn
Sgt J.G. Stebbings	

Flying at 300 feet an S/E contact was made at 22

miles, but this turned out to be Force 26. Then at 0035 hrs another contact was made at 12 miles, and closing in, began a run-in at 0056 hrs. Four minutes later, in position 4907/0441, the Leigh Light was switched on, illuminating a U-boat which was attacked with eight D/Cs. Nothing further was seen, although the navigator thought he saw some debris near the flame floats. Some time later a conning tower was seen in position 4903/0411, which was attacked at 0150 hrs with six D/Cs, but again nothing further was seen.

U-736 sailed from Bergen on 1 April for its first patrol and arrived severely damaged at Brest on 26 May. It did not sail again until 5 August, from Lorient, for the Channel. When she was sunk by HMS *Loch Killin* on 6 August, 1944, a prisoner said that it had been damaged by air attack on 24 May and that the boat was out of action for 2½ months as a result. Both giro and magnetic compasses were smashed, all W/T equipment was knocked out and a 3-foot long rent was made in the pressure hull just below the bow torpedo tubes. The next night the crippled boat was escorted into Lorient by five minesweepers.

7 June, 1944

U-995, a type VIIC submarine, commanded by Oberleutnant Johannes Baden, sunk.

Sunderland 'S' ML760, 201 Squadron, on patrol 1942–0848 hrs.

F/L L.H. Baveystock, DFC, DFM	Pilot
FO C.J. Griffith	2nd pilot
FO P.A. Hunt	Nav
FO A.V. Philp	1 WOP/AG
F/Sgt J.W. Hobson	
F/Sgt F. Foster	
F/Sgt D.E. South	
F/Sgt D.J.McC. Currie	
F/Sgt D. Sharland	
F/Sgt E. Watson	
F/Sgt J.C.L. Humphrey	
PO M.N. Anderson	passenger

This was the night of D-Day. Les Baveystock recalls: 'On the morning of 6 June when I awoke, Pembroke Dock was abuzz with the news that the big day had arrived. However, the crew of "S" already knew the fact, for on the afternoon of the 5th we had taken up our aircraft on a test flight over the Irish Sea. We had seen the huge naval force heading south towards the Channel.

'Colin Griffith, Peter Hunt and I were about to go down to the flight office to see what was in store for us, when I was summoned to the telephone. It was my wife with the news that my father had died just before midnight. I had been expecting it, but it was sad news nevertheless. On arrival at the office I found that we were scheduled for a special anti-submarine patrol that night. Later the CO agreed that I could have a few days' compassionate leave later in the week.

'At briefing we found that we were carrying out a "creeping line ahead search" along the track of a U-boat returning from the Atlantic that had been attacked on the night of the 5th by Johnny Posnett. It had been forced to stay submerged and thus Group Intelligence had a pretty good idea as to its position. We took off in daylight and arrived at our patrol area – north of Gujon, Spain, half an hour before midnight. Shortly before midnight, Dennis South, manning the radar, picked up a strong contact at 9 miles. The attack alarm was sounded and the wireless operator sent out a sighting report and our position.

'The D/Cs were run out and power to the engines increased. We turned on to the correct heading and lost height to 300 feet on our run-in. The blip remained steady and a ½-mile range I gave the order to commence dropping our 1.7 in. flares through the rear flare chute. As the first flare burst into parts each of one million candle power, no U-boat was visible. But seconds later we tracked over a large white foam-covered swirl where it had crash-dived. Unknown to us a 461 Squadron aircraft, in the same area, picked us up on their radar as we picked them up. We were on opposite courses, homing on to each other at a closing speed of some 300 mph. Suddenly the entire area was flooded with light as N/461 commenced dropping flares as he dived to his imagined target. The huge Sunderland passed directly under us – as shaken as we were!

'We now commenced baiting tactics by flying 4 miles off our flame float, then four miles south, and ditto east and west. We did this for one hour on the assumption that with low batteries our enemy would not travel more than that distance. With dawn breaking at 0500 hrs we felt sure the U-boat would stay submerged until 0300 hrs, when he would probably assume that we would have given up, but in this he was wrong. After the first hour we increased our distance from his last position to 8 miles and later to 12 miles.

'Usually the pilots changed positions every hour so as to stay fresh, but as the enemy might suddenly surface close to us I dare not risk a changeover. At 0300 hrs my tiredness was forgotten when Duncan Currie, on the radar, reported a blip at 11 miles. We intended to drop our flares at ½ mile, but before we were in range two streams of tracer opened up on us, so I gave the order to drop flares. We were at 300 feet and there was our U-boat dead ahead. As we came in his four cannons opened up on us. I dived and turned in to attack while our front gunner commenced firing. As I lined it up I opened up with our four fixed guns and the mid-upper also fired. The sky was a mass of criss-cross tracer and how we ever got through it without a single hit, I do not know.

'We dropped six D/Cs. Number 4 entered the water at just the right distance for its underwater travel to cause it to explode directly under the centre of the hull, and No. 5 was a dry hit on the hull, which fell alongside and exploded prematurely. As we climbed away from the attack the blip disappeared from the radar screen. With no further results and as our PLE arrived we returned to base.'

U-955 went straight to the bottom. The boat was on its first patrol from Bergen, sailing on 15 April, having been on a weather reconnaissance. It was sunk in position 4513/0830.

Les Baveystock received a bar to his DFC, while Dennis South and Duncan Currie were both awarded the DFM. Baveystock went to London to attend his father's funeral. Squadron Leader W.D.B. Ruth, DFC, took the crew (with the exception of Malcolm Anderson, the squadron intelligence officer who had only been along for the ride on a night op), while he was away. They failed to return and were reported missing, and it was later discovered they had been shot down when attacking another surfaced U-boat.

7 June, 1944

U-970, a type VIIC submarine, commanded by Oberleutnant Hans-Heinrich Ketels, sunk.

Sunderland 'R' ML877, 228 Squadron, on patrol from Pembroke Dock 1830–0702.

F/L C.G.D. Lancaster	F/Sgt N. Gough
F/L O.T. Brown	F/Sgt E. Greenhouse
FO P.A. Gibb	F/Sgt A. Versluys (NZ)
FO N.H. George	F/Sgt R. Raynel
PO F.G. Acres	WO T. Robey
Sgt R. Lang	

The average height flown on the sortie was 850 feet. At 1959 hrs the patrol area was reached and half an hour before midnight an S/E contact was picked up at 15 miles. At 2333 hrs a fully surfaced U-boat was seen by the light of flares and attacked from 100 feet with D/Cs, estimated to have straddled aft of the conning tower. The U-boat disappeared, but the attack had been a success.

U-970 sank in position 4515/0410 and the commander, two officers and 11 men were later rescued by the German rescue service. The boat had arrived from Bergen on 22 April and was despatched on this, its second patrol, on D-Day, from La Pallice.

Flight Lieutenant Charles Gordon Drake Lancaster was awarded the DFC later in the year.

7 June, 1944

U-415, a type VIIC submarine, commanded by Oberleutnant Johannes Werner, damaged.

Wellington 'G', 179 Squadron, on patrol from Predannack, 0121–0625 hrs.

F/L W.J. Hill	Pilot
FO W.H. Pope	2nd pilot
FO W. Banks	
FO L. Maude	
FO F.C. Whitehouse	
WO A.A. Stephenson	

At 0212 hrs in position 4827/0512, the second pilot sighted a periscope half a mile on the starboard bow and then a U-boat. A Liberator was also seen which attacked the U-boat with machine guns and rockets as the U-boat fought back. Both aircraft then attacked, but the boat went down. The Liberator was then seen to attack a second U-boat, seen silhouetted in the moonlight about 1½ miles ahead. The U-boat was seen smothered in fire from the Lib and then a third U-boat, unobserved until now, was seen when it opened fire on the Lib while the Wellington moved to the attack, securing a good straddle. At 0225 hrs the Wellington resumed patrol but five minutes later a brilliant flash was seen on the surface near where 'G' had dropped its markers. At 0319 hrs in position 4704/0310, a contact made at 17 miles and the aircraft went into cloud. At 0333 hrs heavy flak and machine-gun fire were seen through the cloud, and on coming down a number of enemy surface vessels were seen and their position radioed to base. Two hours later, two Mosquito aircraft were seen circling a large oil patch in which a marine marker was burning.

U-415 returned to Brest, from which it had sailed the previous day, the fourth time it had been damaged in action.

The Liberator had been from 53 Squadron (see following entries).

7 June, 1944

U-963, a type VIIC submarine, commanded by Oberleutnant Rolf W. Wentz, damaged.

Liberator 'L' BZ944, 53 Squadron, flying a 'Cork' patrol in the Channel from St Eval.

F/L J.W. Carmichael	Pilot
F/Sgt E.E. Stevens	
F/Sgt J.T. McKeown	Nav
FO A.C. Peters (Aust)	
FO V.R. White	
F/Sgt R.H. Curner (Aust)	
F/Sgt K.J. Campbell (Aust)	
FL J.W. Shaw	
F/Sgt I.E. Martin (Aust)	
Sgt V.H. Lusher	

Three radar contacts were made at 0404 hrs and the radar operator directed the pilot in order to isolate one plot and approach it from up-moon. The second pilot sighted U-boat's conning tower at 2 miles, silhouetted in the moonlight, and the aircraft attacked with six D/Cs by bombsight, from 100 feet, but the rear gunner estimated an overshoot. Flak from the boat was intense and both the front and rear turrets fired back. Carmichael circled for another attack, but by now flak was coming up from three subs, so he stood off and reported the boats' positions before attacking again, maintaining contacts on radar.

U-256, a type VIIC submarine, commanded by Kapitänleutnant Lehmann-Willenbrock, damaged.

At 0515 hrs, Carmichael made a second attack when again the second pilot picked out a U-boat when its wake was seen emerging from a patch of cloud shadow. By this time only one contact remained on the surface, so it was assumed the other two had dived. This boat was trimmed well down and the Lib approached up-moon, dropping six D/Cs slightly ahead of the conning tower from 50 feet. The rear gunner fired and saw the D/Cs explode, then saw a very large explosion and the bows lifted above the water. His impressions were clear-cut against the breaking dawn. During the run-in, the No. 3 engine was hit and a shell also exploded in the bomb bay, causing the marine marker to be dropped very close to the U-boat, and a fire seen was thought to be too large for it to be the marker. Nothing more was seen and with the damaged engine feathered, the Lib was flown home.

Both U-boats were damaged by these attacks, U-963 returning to Brest, from where it had sailed on the 6th – its fourth patrol. This submarine had shot down aircraft 'T' of 53 Squadron back on 5 February, 1944, now the squadron had gained some small measure of revenge.

U-256 was also on its fourth patrol and also put back into Brest in a damaged condition.

Flight Lieutenant John William Carmichael and Flight Sergeant McKeown were awarded an immediate DFC and DFM respectively, but before these were announced, both men, plus the rest of the crew, had failed to return from a subsequent mission. On the night of 6 June, Squadron Leader G. Crawford, who had sunk U-391 back on 13 December, 1943, had failed to return. Carmichael was promoted to squadron leader to fill Crawford's flight commander post. On the night of 13/14 June, Carmichael and his crew took off in Liberator 'C' (BZ818) at 2130 hrs. Later, base received a signal, 'About to attack U-boat...', but nothing further was heard from them.

7 June, 1944

U-989, commanded by Kapitänleutnant Harde Rodler von Roitberg, damaged.

Wellington XIV 'C' HF149, 407 RCAF Squadron, on patrol 2235 hrs.

SL D.W. Farrell, DFC	Pilot
FO W.P. Johnston	2nd pilot
FO A.D. Callender	Nav
F/L W.H. Brown	WOP/AG
FO E.C.N. Kent	WOP/AG
WO C.J. Hall	WOP/AG

Liberator 'M', 224 Squadron, on patrol 2139 hrs.

FO E. Allen, DFC (Can)	Sgt D.E. Froggett
PO M.E. Hayward (Can)	Sgt A.R. Croft
FL W.J. Ealer (Aust)	Sgt J. Mitchell
PO H.E. Pugsley	Sgt J.B.G. Gray
WO H. McIllaney	Sgt A. McLaughlin
F/L L.R. Aust, DFC, DFM	

Neither of these aircraft returned home.

U-989 was damaged in attacks by both of these aircraft, but the U-boat's gunners shot both aircraft down. It was only her second war cruise, having left

Brest on 6 June. Von Roitberg had previously been an officer on U-96. He was lost with his crew in U-989 on their fifth patrol on 14 February, 1945, north-west of the Shetlands, sunk by frigates of the 10th Escort Group in position 6136/0135.

Both Coastal crews were very experienced. Flight Lieutenant Brown in Farrell's crew was the squadron Gunnery Leader on his second tour, while Farrell was a flight commander and had already made attacks on submarines.

'Perry' Allen had been second pilot to Peter Cundy when they sank U-628 in July, 1943. Flight Lieutenant Leslie Roy Aust was a very experienced air gunner, having joined the RAF in 1937, and since the beginning of the war had flown five tours of ops, beginning in France in 1940.

7 June, 1944

U-212, a type VIIC submarine, commanded by Kapitänleutnant Helmut Vogler, damaged.

Mosquito XVIII 'O' NT225, 248 Squadron, on patrol 0533–0930 hrs.

FO A.L. Bonnett, RCAF	Pilot
FO A.McD. McNicol	Nav

Mosquito 'L' MM425, 248 Squadron.

FO D.J. Turner, DFC	Pilot
FO D. Curtis, DFC	Nav

Turner was leading this anti-submarine sweep when at 0729 hrs he sighted a wake and then a U-boat with decks awash, partly clear of the water. It began to zigzag as the aircraft attacked, but five or six hits with the 6-pounder gun were made near the water line and on the conning tower. Bonnett carried out a dummy attack after his gun jammed during their second runs in order to draw fire away from Turner. Light flak was experienced during the first two runs, but these ceased after the third. The boat went down leaving a patch of oil and one crewman in the water. Turner's aircraft was damaged in the port wing and engine nacelle. Low cloud, however, prevented the aircraft from diving at a sufficiently steep angle to ensure penetration of the pressure hull.

U-212 was on its third patrol, having left La Pallice on 6 June, whence it returned on the 8th. Its conversion to a schnorkel boat had been completed on 1 June. She had previously served with the Arctic Flotilla between January and October 1943. She was finally sunk on 21 July, on her sixth patrol, south-west of Beachy Head by the frigates *Curzon* and *Ekins*.

Bonnett and McNicol were both killed on 9 June, 1944, when returning from operations. They were involved in a mid-air collision over their base with the squadron CO, Wing Commander A.D. Phillips, DSO, DFC, who force landed safely. They had been flying HX903, which had previously been on successful sorties with the squadron. Wing Commander Phillips himself was reported missing on 4 July, 1944. For the team of Turner and Curtis, this was their third success against U-boats.

8 June, 1944

U-629 (Type VIIC) and U-373 (VIIC), commanded by Oberleutnant Hans-Helmuth Bugs and Oberleutnant Detlef von Lehsten respectively – both sunk.

Liberator 'G', 224 Squadron, on patrol 2214–0709 hrs.

F/L K.O. Moore (Can)	Pilot
FO J.M. Ketcheson (Can)	
WO T.J. McDowell	Nav
PO A.P. Gibb (Can)	Nav
WO W.N. Werbiski (Can)	WOP/AG
WO D.H. Greise (Can)	MU/AG
WO E. Davison (Can)	
WO W.P. Foster	WOP/AG
F/Sgt I.C. Webb	Rear Gunner
Sgt J. Hamer	F/Eng

At 0211 hrs while flying at 500 feet, a radar contact was made dead ahead at 12 miles. Moore turned slightly to port to place the target up the moonpath. At 3 miles a U-boat was sighted fully surfaced on a westerly course and a turn was made slightly to starboard to keep the target in the moonpath. The radar set was switched off at 2½ miles and the Leigh Light was not required. An attack was made at 0215 hrs, in position 4827/0547 from about 50 feet with six D/Cs, which straddled the conning tower, three falling each side. The U-boat appeared to be lifted out of the water and when the aircraft circled back oil and wreckage could be seen on the water. In the attack the front gunner, the navigator, Al Gibb, had opened fire and two of eight men seen in the conning tower were seen to fall.

Then at 0240 hrs another contact was picked up at 6 miles when at 700 feet. The aircraft homed in and at 2½ miles another U-boat was sighted by McDowell from the bomb aimer's position, but it was not in the moonpath, so Moore circled for a better position. Attacking from 50 feet, six D/Cs went down, four on the starboard, two on the port side, aft of the conning tower. As Moore circled position 4810/05311, the U-boat could be seen listing to starboard and then the boat's bows lifted to stick out of the water at a 45-degree angle. As the crew watched, the boat slid back into the sea and disappeared. Coming in again, the light was turned on and picked out three dinghies, while survivors could be seen swimming amidst oil and wreckage.

This was the first ever occasion in which a crew sank two U-boats in a single sortie, indeed, within half an hour! Kenneth Owen 'Kayo' Moore received an immediate DSO, while DFCs went to Johnston McDowell and Peter Foster, with a DFM for Sergeant John Hamer. Before take-off their CO had said there were several U-boats about and they should get at least two in an hour. Following this joking remark, Moore had laughingly said he'd probably get two in half an hour, never contemplating such an event could possibly come true.

U-629's first cruise began on 22 November, 1943, during which she rescued the crew of U-284, but was damaged on 4 January by 304 Squadron. Her third and last patrol began from Brest to the Plymouth area on 6 June. She had, prior to January, 1943, been with the Arctic Flotilla. One ship had been sunk by this submarine.

U-373 was on its 12th patrol, from Brest, whence it had sailed on 7 June for the Scillies. Its first patrol had been back in the autumn of 1941. She had been damaged twice, on her ninth sortie, by US escort carrier aircraft, on 23 July, 1943; and on 3 January, 1944, on her 11th cruise, by L/612 and H/224. She had sunk four ships.

8 June 1944

U-413, a type VIIC submarine, commanded by Oberleutnant Dietrich Sachse, damaged.

Halifax 'F', 502 Squadron, on patrol from Brawdy, 2205–0412 hrs.

FO J. Spurgeon	WO A. Watt (Can)
F/Sgt J. Cowan (Aust)	Sgt A. Davies
F/Sgt E. Ward	Sgt V. Efstathiou
Sgt H. Collingridge	Sgt R. Chittleboror

During the first part of the patrol, a radar contact turned out to be three small ships, one of which opened fire with machine guns. A second contact at 0145 hrs at 6 miles turned out to be a U-boat, fully surfaced, and in full view on this moonlit night. The

Iceland

Left 209 Squadron skippers Reykjavik, 1941. FO H.W.F. Edwards, F/L Bud Lewin, FO 'Squib' Squires, F/L John Wyllie (Nav officer), FO Wilf Nixon. In front is FO E.A. 'Ted' Jewiss. Jewiss had just been awarded the DFC for sinking U-452 on 25 August, 1941. Eddy Edwards and Bud Lewin were both involved in the capture of U-570 on 27 August.
(H.W.F. Edwards)

Squadron Leader J.H. Thompson, 269 Squadron. Flying a Hudson from Iceland, he captured U-570 on 27 August, 1941, and received the DFC.

Captured! U-570, which surrendered to Thompson, was towed to Iceland and later became HMS Graph.
(D. Lyall via R.C. Bowyer)

Terry Bulloch, DSO and bar, 120 Squadron, seen here in front of his special B.24 Liberator while attached to 224 Squadron.

Above Liberator III FL923 'V' – which sank U-189 on 23 April, 1943, when flown by FO J.K. Moffat.
(via N. Tingey)

Gordon Hatherley and crew, 120 Squadron, who sank U-635 on 5 April, 1943. Front:Sgt E.A. Day, FO G.L. Hatherly, FO A.G. McGregor, Sgt B. Threlfall. Rear: Sgt A.E. Bartley, Sgt E.H. Britton, Sgt E.B. Bailey.
(G.L. Hatherly)

*U-341 under attack by Frank Fisher and his crew,
10 RCAF Squadron, 19 September, 1943.
(via Mrs B. Shannon)*

*Flight Lieutenant R.F. Fisher, RCAF (2nd from right,
standing) who sank U-341 on 19 September, 1943, while
flying from Iceland in his 10 RCAF Squadron Liberator.
He was killed exactly one month later, when returning
home to Canada following the news of the death of his
brother in India. Others in his crew shown here are:
FO John Johnston, WO Jim Lamont, Frank Fisher,
FO Bruce Murray. Kneeling: WO Joe Barabanoff and
Sgt Eric Finn. All except Murray died in the air crash
one month later. (RCAF via Mrs B. Shannon)*

*John McEwen and crew, 120 Squadron. They sank U-279
(or possibly U-336) on 4 October, 1943. l to r: Bob
Fallon, A. Allwood, H.J. Bates, N.D. Hartnell, H. Dixon,
R.D. Ker, W.J.F. McEwen, Lt Leonard, USN. (R. Fallon)*

*U-279 under attack by McEwen and crew in position
6051/2826. (R. Fallon)*

Bryan Turnbull and his crew in Iceland. Al Hayes, Bryan Turnbull, Ron Copperthwaite. Front: Don Harborne, Noel Tingey, Mac McDonald, Jerry Storey. The Liberator is E-Enid – note the U-boat emblem painted below the pilot's window. This is probably the Lib flown by FO D.C. Fleming-Williams when he sank U-304 on 28 May, 1943, and damaged U-594 on 6 April (J.K. Moffat) – probably FL913. Bryan damaged U-135 on 8 February, 1943, then with Pop Oliver as 2nd pilot after Al Hayes left, damaged U-762 on 8 October and shared in the sinking of U-540 on 17 October. (B.W. Turnbull)

U-540 under attack by Bryan Turnbull and crew, 17 October, 1943. (B. W. Turnbull)

Liberator V, BZ880, 120 Squadron, 1944, clearly showing the Leigh Light under the starboard wing. (B. E. Peck)

Flying Officer Thomas C. Cooke, RCAF, of 162 Canadian Squadron, who received an immediate DFC for sinking U-342 on 17 April, 1944.

Gibraltar

Catalina 1B, AX-L, 202 Squadron, airborne from Gibraltar, 1941. Under Coastal Command control, 202 sank four U-boats, damaged four others and shared another with HM ships. (via A. Thomas)

Pilot Officer John Barling (right) and Sergeant Jack Forbes, 233 Squadron. Barling, with Forbes as his air gunner, sank U-605 on 14 November, 1942. (H. W. Thomson)

Flying Officer Hugh Thomson, RNZAF, observer to John Barling on 14 November 1942, when they sank U-605. (H. W. Thomson)

Flight Lieutenant H. R. Sheardown, RCAF, and his crew, formerly of 202 Squadron, but photo taken when with 117 RCAF Squadron, late 1943. The crew sank U-620 on 14 February, 1943, and damaged U-381. Back row, l to r: Jack McIntyre, Geoff Chew, Harry Sheardown, Jim Fletcher, H. Upson, FO Spinney (not with 202). Front: Art King, Reg Sprague, Doug Watkins, FO Dan O'Rourke (not with 202). O'Rourke and Spinney joined the crew when Jack Cox left to return to New Zealand. The crew flew together for over 1400 hours! (H. R. Sheardown)

Above American PBY (Catalina), as used by VP63 Squadron, USN. (USN)

U-134 under attack by Wellington 'J', 179 Squadron, flown by Flying Officer D. F. McRae, 24 August, 1943 – one of three U-boats accounted for by this Canadian pilot.

Lieutenant Russell Woolley and his crew, VP63, USN, some of whom were with him when U-761 was sunk on 24 February, 1944. Rear: Lt T. R. Woolley (second from left), AMM1/c Boyd Cummins (far right). Front, l to r: AOM2/c Lester Coker, ARM2/c James Cunningham, AMM2/c Billy Martin, (?), ARM1/c Bobby Henderson. (T. R. Woolley)

Lieutenant H. J. 'Jeff' Baker, USN, and three of his VP63 crew, engaged in the sinking of U-761. l to r: AMM1/c Earl Tanneberg, Lt Jeff Baker, ARM1/c Marlin Crider, Ensign William McSharry. (via H. J. Baker)

Lieutenant Ralph Spears, VP63, USN (as a Commander), shared in the sinking of U-392, 16 March, 1944. (R. C. Spears)

'Sniffer Wagner Spears' – Ralph Spears's dog, who was aboard his master's PBY-5 during the attack on U-392, 16 March, 1944. (R. C. Spears)

Lieutenant Van Lingle, VP63, USN Squadron (as a Commander), who shared in the sinking of U-392, 16 March, 1944. (V.A. Lingle)

Van Lingle's retro-bombs splashing into the water above U-392. Note smoke floats further astern. (V.A. Lingle)

Azores

Flight Lieutenant Rod Drummond and crew, 220 Squadron, who made the first successful U-boat sinking from the Azores (U-707) on 9 November, 1943. l to r: F/Sgt J.B. Fitzpatrick, Sgt F.D. Galloway, PO J.B. Brodie, F/L R.P. Drummond, F/L G.A. Grundy, FO R.D. Thompson, F/Sgt F. L. Fitzgibbon, Sgt L.S.G. Parker. Fitzgibbon had been involved in the sinking of U-575 on 13 March, 1943.

Fortress 'J' (FL459) of 220 Squadron. She sank U-624, U-633 and U-707, and shared in the sinking of U-575.

David Beaty's crew, 206 Squadron, who shared in the sinking of U-707 on 13 March, 1944. l to r: Jimmy Cunningham, Frank MacManus, John Johnston, Norman Draper, Jim Glazebrook, David Beaty, Leo Meaker. (J.J.V. Glazebrook)

Boeing B17F Fortress 'R', 206 Squadron (FA700), in which David Beaty and crew helped sink U-707. (J.J.V. Glazebrook)

Flight Lieutenant W.R. 'Pip' Travell, DFC, 220 Squadron, who helped sink U-707, 13 March, 1944. (W.R. Travell)

sub opened fire with cannon, and not being in the best position, Spurgeon had to make another run, but the bombs hung up, making it necessary to make a third run. They dropped 4 x 600 lb anti-shipping bombs in one stick, spaced at 16 feet apart. An explosion seen but not the results and because the Halifax had been hit in the port inner engine and made u/s, as well as damage being sustained to the tail, the pilot broke off the action, landing at Predannack.

U-413 had also sailed on the 6th, from Brest, returning damaged on the 9th. It was her seventh patrol. She had been damaged by air attack on her first war cruise in November 1942 by 608 Squadron. Her final sortie – eighth – did not begin until 2 August, but she was then sunk south-west of Beachy Head by three RN destroyers, on the 20th. She had sunk four ships including HMS *Warwick*.

10 June, 1944

U-821, a type VIIC submarine, commanded by Oberleutnant Ulrich Knackfuss, sunk.

Mosquitoes of 248 Squadron, on patrol 0825–1302 hrs.

F/L S.G. Nunn	Pilot	'T' LR347
FO J.M. Carlin	Nav	
FO G.N.E. Yeates	Pilot	'S' MM399
FO T.C. Scott	Nav	
FO K. Norrie	Pilot	'W' HR158
F/Sgt B.J. Palmer	Nav	
F/Sgt W.W. Scott	Pilot	'V' HP907
F/Sgt J. Blackburn	Nav	

Liberator 'K' EV943, 206 Squadron, on patrol 0510–1447 hrs.

F/L A.D.S. Dundas	Sgt A.L. Shamas, RCAF
FO M. Mays	Sgt E.C. Kemp
PO M. Clough	Sgt R. Mercer
PO J.W. Collyer	Sgt J. Welford
Sgt A.C. Ashbury, RCAF	WO D. Hawkins, RAAF
Sgt H.D. Reid, RCAF	

At midday, the four Mosquito aircraft, led by Flight Lieutenant Nunn, were in the area a few miles off Ushant. Group Captain Nunn recalls:

'Our brief was to locate and attack any surfaced U-boats attempting to enter or leave Brest. The patrol line was to be from north of Ushant, south to

the Isle de Sein. We were on task at 0900 hrs, flying at our normal operating height of 30 feet. As we were approaching the most northerly end of the patrol line at about midday a conning tower broke the surface about 2½ miles dead ahead. I immediately climbed the section to 500 feet and gave the order, "Attack, attack, attack!". By the time the first strikes hit the U-boat, it was fully surfaced.

'Each aircraft attacked in turn, either from stem to stern or broadside to the conning tower. Such was the weight of firepower directed at the U-boat that no attempt was made to bring the gun on the foredeck into action. It would seem that the crew had been taken completely by surprise and had failed to detect the aircraft before surfacing, because we were patrolling at such low level.

'Soon after the attack began there was a large explosion in or near the conning tower and a plume of black smoke rose into the air. This was probably the ammunition for the deck gun exploding. Not long after this the crew were seen jumping off the deck into the sea, and the boat began to settle by the stern.

'By this time all the aircraft had run out of ammunition. The bow of the U-boat was high in the water and the hull aft of the conning tower was submerged. It was obviously out of control and most, if not all of the crew had abandoned ship. As I began to make diving photographic runs over the stricken U-boat I caught sight of a Liberator some 6 miles away to the west.

'I instructed one of my aircraft to break away and endeavour to lead it to the scene of action. This it did and the Liberator made a run over the target and released a stick of D/Cs. These landed some way astern of the boat, which continued its aimless way. The Lib came in again and made another run, releasing a second stick which straddled the U-boat. When the eruptions subsided, the U-boat had gone. All that remained on the surface was a zigzag oil slick and a number of black blobs, which were survivors some distance from where the D/Cs had been dropped. Sadly, those in the water who had managed to survive thus far were to suffer further disaster later in the afternoon.'

Six of 248 Squadron were out that afternoon, led by Cdt Max Geudj, DSO, DFC, CdG, including two Tsetse gunned aircraft. They spotted a motor launch which it transpired had picked up survivors from the U-boat. One Mosquito, flown by Flight Lieutenant E.H. Jeffreys, DFC, flew low over the launch and was fired at by a single gun. The aircraft was hit in the port engine and staggered off towards France, but then crashed. The other Mosquitoes then proceeded to shoot up the launch and then the two 6-pounder aircraft also attacked, blowing the launch out of the water. Only one wounded sailor survived from the sub and launch crews.

U-821 was on its second patrol, leaving Brest on the 6th for the English Channel and the invasion fleet. It had arrived from Bergen via the North Atlantic on 12 April.

Both Stanley Nunn and Alexander Dundas later received DFCs.

11 June, 1944

U-333, a type VIIC submarine, commanded by Leutnant Peter Cremer, damaged.

Sunderland 'U' ML880, 228 Squadron, on patrol 1810 hrs.

F/L M.E. Slaughter (Can)	F/Sgt H. Chester
F/L D.H. Griffiths	Sgt J. Bleach
FO R.L. Griffin	Sgt G. Channing
FO L.C. Dadds	Sgt W. Patterson
WO J. Foubister	Sgt L. Segaloff
Sgt W. Carr	

The Sunderland was shot down in the attack, falling with one engine on fire and the rear gunner blazing away to the last.

However, U-333, on her 10th patrol, had been damaged in this attack and by an attack the previous night by Y/10 RAAF Squadron (F/L H.A. McGregor, RAAF). The radar was not working, the 3.7mm gun had jammed and various near misses had caused leaks in the hull. Cremer was forced to abort and return to La Pallice, which he did on the 12th. Cremer and U-333 were one of the most successful combinations of the German submarine arm. It sank several ships and Cremer held the Knight's Cross. U/228 was not the first aircraft this boat had shot down. B/172 fell to her gunners on the sixth patrol in 1943 and I/200 was shot down during a cruise to West Africa the same year. The boat finally went down, with its new skipper, Kapitänleutnant Hans Fiedler, off the Scillies on 31 July, 1944, sunk by ships of the 2nd Escort Group, on her 11th patrol.

12 June, 1944

U-441, a type VIIC submarine, commanded by Kapitänleutnant Klaus Gotz von Hartmann, damaged.

Liberator 'S', 224 Squadron, on patrol from St Eval 0105 hrs.

F/L J.E. Jenkison (NZ)	Pilot
F/Sgt K. Graves	
F/L A.M. McCleod (NZ)	Nav
F/Sgt T.F. Jones (Aust)	
PO C.C. Chitty	
WO F.J. Reid	
F/Sgt L. Starr	
F/Sgt L. Dixon	
Sgt R.T. Green	
Sgt A. Jenkins	

Jimmy Jenkison failed to return from this patrol to the West Channel area. It is understood he attacked and damaged a U-boat – probably U-441, which had left Brest on 6 June. Limping back to its base, it was attacked again and sunk on 18 June. Jenkison and his friend and fellow New Zealander Alan McCleod shared a room at St Eval.

13 June, 1944

U-270, a type VIIC submarine, commanded by Oberleutnant Heinrich Schreiber, damaged.

Wellington 'Y' MP789, 172 Squadron, on patrol from Chivenor 2149–0158 hrs.

PO L. Harris	Sgt W. Rodgers
F/Sgt D. Reedie	Sgt B. Warren
F/Sgt W. Davies	Sgt G. Haxell

A contact at 8 miles was picked up at 2338 hrs, in position 4750/0537. As they homed in they experienced heavy flak at one mile, and switched on the Leigh Light to illuminate a fully surfaced U-boat half a mile ahead. The front gunner opened fire, then six D/Cs went down, which straddled the boat's stern. Twice it was thought the boat had gone down, but suddenly it began firing again, causing Harris to take evasive action. Just on midnight a faint yellow glow was seen near the flame floats followed by a heavy explosion and a long streak of fire on the surface. A thick column of black smoke rose to 1000 feet. As both the W/T and radar became u/s, the aircraft left the position five minutes into the new day.

U-270 had begun its fifth war cruise from St Nazaire on the 6th, and having been damaged was forced to return, which it did on the 17th. Aircraft 'C' of 53 Squadron also attacked her on the 13th, but on this occasion, the sub's gunners shot it down. On her previous patrol she had been damaged – on 6 January, 1944, by 'U' of 206 Squadron. The U-boat shot that aircraft down too, but she was put out of action for several months. The damage that resulted from 172 Squadron's attack put paid to her career, for she was paid off on 1 July, 1944, but was sunk on a passage trip on 12 August (see later). She had sunk three ships.

18 June, 1944

U-441, a type VIIC submarine, commanded by Kapitänleutnant Klaus Gotz von Hartmann, sunk.

Wellington 'A' HF331, 304 Polish Squadron, on patrol 2115–0409 hrs.

F/L J. Antoniewicz	Pilot
FO Z. Spikowski	2nd pilot
F/Sgt L. Moller	Nav
F/Sgt J. Izycki	
Sgt S. Matias	
Sgt F. Szott	

At 2244 hrs this crew had to cut the patrol to regain time lost by avoiding shipping, and in addition, the radar had gone u/s. However, at 2255 hrs, they made a visual sighting of the wash of a U-boat while flying at 700 feet and the captain attacked, releasing six D/Cs from 100 feet. These straddled the U-boat across the conning tower, and on the run-in he saw a second U-boat in line abreast of his target boat, ¼ of a mile away, in the act of diving. Wreckage and oil was seen from the first U-boat as the aircraft circled after the attack.

U-441 had had a long career and was on her 10th patrol when sunk in position 4903/0448, north of Ushant Island. At one stage she had been a flak ship to bait aircraft into attacking her (see previously). She reverted to her normal armament for her eighth patrol at the beginning of 1944, and had sunk the warship *Gould*. In all she had sunk three ships before her last sortie, which had begun from Brest on 6 June.

20 June, 1944

U-971, a type VIIC submarine, commanded by Oberleutnant Walter Zeplien, damaged.

Wellington 'L' HF286, 407 RCAF Squadron, on patrol 2207–0828 hrs.

FO F.H. Foster	Pilot
FO E.R.B. Gray	2nd pilot
Sgt E.L. Read	Nav
WO J.E. France	WOP/AG
W/O J.K. Andrews	WOP/AG
W/O H.D. Godin	WOP/AG

A radar contact at 3 miles at 2325 hrs, sent the aircraft on to a homing course, and height was reduced to 200 feet in hazy conditions. At ½ mile both pilots saw a wake and then picked out a fully surfaced U-boat and turned to make an almost head-on approach. Six D/Cs were dropped from 100 feet which appeared to make a good straddle. The rear gunner fired as they went over and then he reported the boat submerging. Turning, they again picked up the boat on radar and saw that it was again fully surfaced but stopped, with a flame float burning right next to it. The boat began to open fire, which continued intermittently as the aircraft circled. However, the boat then went down and aircraft dropped two Mk II sea markers. On instructions from Control, they remained over the area until PLE was reached at 0631 hrs.

U-971 was on its first patrol, having sailed from Kristiansund for the Channel on 8 June. A schnorkel boat, it was damaged and was returning to port when it met disaster on the 24th (see later).

23 June, 1944

U-155, a type XI submarine, commanded by Oberleutnant Fritz Altmeir, damaged.

Mosquito 'P', 248 Squadron.

F/Sgt L.C. Doughty	Pilot
F/Sgt R. Grime	Nav

Six aircraft of 248 Squadron were on patrol between Ushant and Lorient when Doughty became separated from the others in bad light. He continued on alone along the French coast and between the Ile de Groix and the mainland he spotted a convoy of ships about to enter Lorient. Turning to take a look, having failed to contact the others by radio, Doughty flew along the starboard beam of the convoy, keeping close to the Garve Peninsula, which gave him cover. He made out one large and two smaller escort vessels and a U-boat. Flak now came up from batteries north-east of the Ile de Groix and Doughty decided to attack the sub, but now flak was also coming from the escort ships. He made his attack in a shallow dive, and made a short sighting burst followed by a long burst of cannon and machine guns. Strikes were seen all round the conning tower. Levelling out at 50 feet, he dropped two D/Cs in salvo and commenced violent evasive action. He quickly flew out of the flak, so was unable to see any results, and in fact his Mosquito did receive slight damage from two 20mm hits.

U-155 was just returning from its ninth patrol, having left Lorient on 11 March for West Africa. It was damaged in this attack, and was out of action until September when it sailed to Kristiansund. The boat was in Kiel harbour when the war ended.

Flight Sergeant Leslie Cook Doughty received an immediate DFM and was promoted to Warrant Officer.

26 June, 1944

U-971, a type VIIC submarine, commanded by Oberleutnant Walter Zeplien, sunk.

Liberator 'O', 311 Czech Squadron, on patrol 1409–2007 hrs.

FO J. Vella	F/Sgt J. Novosad
F/Sgt J. Klesnil	WO K. Gedus
FO R. Reimann	Sgt V. Hercik
FL M. Vild	WO I. Valnicek
F/Sgt L. Kondziolka	

The crew sighted the U-boat in position 4900/0540 and attacked with both rockets and D/Cs. The periscope of another sub was sighted in almost the same position and was also attacked in the same way. A destroyer was also seen turning into the attack and dropping D/Cs. Later a message was received that the U-boat had been destroyed and some survivors had been picked up by the destroyer.

U-971 had sailed on 8 June and was damaged by 407 Squadron on the 16th – its torpedo tubes being damaged. On the 17th she was attacked by 'L' of 228 Squaron and then 'D' of 502 Squadron. Finally, on the 24th, she was damaged by 311 Squadron's attack and went on to the sea bed. The captain decided to scuttle his damaged boat, despite the destroyers HMS *Eskimo* and HMCS *Haide* being

above. He came to the surface, scuttled, and 52 of his 53-man crew were safely rescued by the destroyers.

In March 1945, Vella and Vild received DFCs.

29 June, 1944

U-988, a type VIIC submarine, commanded by Oberleutnant Erich Dobberstein, sunk.

Liberator 'L', 224 Squadron, on patrol 2100–1041 hrs.

F/L J.W. Barling, DFC	Pilot
FO B. Benson (Can)	2nd pilot
PO R.H. Hurn	Nav
FO A.H. Jessell	2nd Nav
WO G. Skidmore	
F/Sgt L.H. Faulkner (Can)	Radar op.
Sgt W.J. Hamp	
PO H.J. Lewis	
Sgt E.T. Thomas	
Sgt E.C. Hannawin	Eng

At 0101 hrs, in position 4937/0350, a radar contact at 5 miles put the Liberator on course. The signal was weak and it was lost at 2 miles, but Barling continued on, positioning himself up-moon. Contact was renewed at 5 miles astern and Barling turned back, but again the contact was lost. Then several of the crew saw a schnorkel to port up the moonpath. Barling flew off 5 miles to gain better position and came back at 200 feet, the Leigh Light coming on at one mile and picking out the schnorkel. The navigator, in the nose, also saw what he thought was a periscope about 8 feet ahead of the schnorkel, both leaving feathers of water. Seven D/Cs went down at 0115 hrs. the bomb aimer being confident the straddle was good. Within 2 minutes oil and bubbles appeared which lasted about 10 minutes. As it flew to and fro, illuminating the area, the Lib crew saw an object about 30 feet long which resembled an upturned boat. When they finally left there was an oil patch stretching for over 2½ miles.

U-988 was on its first patrol, sailing from Bergen on 23 May to the English Channel. Later, the 3rd Escort Group arrived on the scene of Barling's attack and depth-charged a contact, but officially the sinking was credited to 224 Squadron and the frigates *Essington*, *Duckworth* and *Dommett*.

John Barling had received his DFC while serving with 233 Squadron and for sinking U-605 in November 1942. Benny Benson came from Chile and died in a car accident when he returned home after the war.

8 July, 1944

U-243, a type VIIC submarine, commanded by Kapitänleutnant Hans Maertens, sunk.

Sunderland 'H' W4030, 10 RAAF Squadron.

FO W.B. Tilley	Captain
FO G.M. Bishop	1st pilot
PO E.W. Felan	2nd pilot
FL I.A. Wood	Nav
Sgt L.L. Walker	Eng
Sgt W. Aitkenhead	2nd Eng
F/Sgt W.L. Penny	AG
F/Sgt L.E. Cooke	AG
F/Sgt G.G. Casey	AG
F/Sgt D.E. Hunt	1st WOP/AG
F/Sgt R. Prentice	2nd WOP/AG
F/L R.F. Mattner	AG

The aircraft was on patrol at 0750 hrs and at 1435 hrs, while on its fifth circuit of the area, a fully surfaced U-boat was sighted 6 miles away. Tilley headed for it while reducing height, the boat firing at 2 miles, the Sunderland replying with its fixed forward guns and nose turret. 1250 rounds swept the decks and the flak ceased. Six D/Cs went down from 75 feet, straddling the stern and conning tower. Circling at one mile range, the U-boat was seen settling with a list to port and making no forward headway. Again the boat opened fire, but then at 1500 hrs the German crew were seen to be launching dinghies. As this was happening, another 10 Squadron Sunderland arrived and then a US Liberator, both of which dropped D/Cs. The boat sank stern first, with the bow disappearing vertically. Survivors and dinghies remained in the water, and Tilley flew over and dropped another dinghy and a food pack. PLE was reached at 1622 hrs, when the aircraft made for base.

U-243 had sailed from Kiel to Norway in May 1944, then made a patrol between 8 and 11 June from Flekkefiord to Bergen. On the 11th it shot down an aircraft which flew over it, but when they later rescued the crew they found they had shot down a Ju 88!

On 15 June the crew sailed for the English Channel, meeting Tilley on 8 July. Hans Maerten was fatally wounded in the head during the first attack.

His boat went down in position 4706/0640, west of Nantes, and although Maerten and 38 crewmen were rescued by HMCS *Restigouche*, he later succumbed to his wound.

Flying Officer William Boris Tilley received an immediate DFC, while the front gunner, Flight Sergeant Lance Edmund Cooke, received an immediate DFM. On 27 August, Tilley landed his Sunderland to pick up three survivors of a 172 Squadron Wellington which had ditched during the night following an attack on a U-boat. For Flight Lieutenant Mick Mattner, now Squadron Gunnery Officer, this was his third successful attack on U-boats.

11 July, 1944

U-1222, a type IXC/40 submarine, commanded by Kapitänleutnant Heinz Bielfield, sunk.

Sunderland 'P' ML881, 201 Squadron, on patrol 0435–1915 hrs.

F/L I.F.B. Walters, DFC	Captain
F/L S.C. Buszard	1st pilot
Sgt J.B. Beck (Aust)	
FO E.H. Little (Can)	Nav
Sgt E.H. Adams	
Sgt E.A. Walters	
Sgt B.H. Perry	
WO C.B. Nicholson	
Sgt R. Swanson (Aust)	
WO G.B. Thompson	
Sgt E. Hinton	
Sgt W. Weese (Aust)	

Wally Walters was an experienced and long-serving airman and on this day he was supervising a new and inexperienced crew before they began operating on their own. They certainly received expert experience on this day.

Wally Walters recalls: 'The Form Green from Group briefed us to join the north-west corner of a rectangular search pattern running north-south between latitudes 47N and 45N and about 20 miles wide between longitudes 6 and 5 West. The joining time was to integrate with an input spacing of 20 minutes from other 19 Group aircraft in the pattern, which was flown anti-clockwise.

'During our first traverse of the pattern an inboard engine behaved erratically, so Group was warned that we may have to pull out and therefore upset the search pattern sequence. In the event the misfiring diminished and, by the time we had done one circuit, had cleared.

'We had not long turned south on the western leg when the second pilot poked his binoculars in the right direction and identified a schnorkel, then the U-boat, almost straight ahead, which was followed by the radar operator reporting a contact at 8½ nautical miles. I think the visual sighting was very commendable and reflected the high standard of this new crew.

'By the time we had lost height to the attack level – 50 feet – the U-boat had commenced a steep emergency dive in which the rusty green stern was clearly seen above the surface. Our subsequent photographs showed a perfect straddle. The submerging U-boat was bracketed by two and three D/Cs in the midships area. (No. 4 hung up). When the explosions subsided, there was widespread small wreckage and red discoloration of the sea in the target area, which at the time I thought could be decoy material. Subsequent intelligence identified the enemy as U-1222, which failed to return from a patrol in the Gulf of St Lawrence. There were no survivors.'

This had been U-1222's first war cruise. A schnorkel boat, she had sailed from Kiel on 13 April, 1944, for the Canadian seaboard and had made five unsuccessful attacks on five ships off Novia Scotia during May and June. On her return she was west of La Rochelle when fate put her in touch with 201 Squadron.

Walters received a bar to his DFC and his was the first successful attack on a schnorkelling submarine in daylight. Wally had already been in the RAF for 15 years by 1944, having begun his career as an apprentice WOM. He later served in the Middle East with 14 and 6 Squadrons and it was the mid-1930s before he became a pilot. In the summer of 1939 he was with 204 Squadron. During his first wartime tour he flew 98 operations. After a period as an instructor he joined 201 Squadron. By July 1944 his total ops had risen to 149, covering 1906 operational flying hours.

9 August, 1944

U-608, a type VIIC submarine, commanded by Oberleutnant Wolfgang Reisener, sunk.

Liberator VI 'C' EV877, 53 Squadron.

WC R.T.F. Gates, AFC	WO J. Chamerlain (Can)
F/L W.G. Payne	F/Sgt H.A. Stephen (Can)
Sgt L.A. Windress	Sgt K.J. Spackman
FO G.W. Nairn (Can)	Sgt A.S. Dantzic
Sgt A. Palmer	Sgt G.H. Cockburn
WO R.A. Scott	

Flying near the 2nd Escort Group, an oil slick was sighted and investigated. As aircraft approached, Gates and two of the crew saw the shape of a U-boat beneath the surface of the sea, just ahead of the mile-long oil streak, in position 4630/0308. Gates lost height to make another run, releasing a marker from 100 feet, then attacked from the stern of the oil slick, letting six D/Cs fall from 100 feet using the Mk II bombsight. They appeared to be dead on target and the rear gunner saw bubbles rising and a few minutes later more oil. At 1503 hrs the aircraft set off to contact the Escort Group, oil and bubbles still rising to the surface. Two further Sunderlands arrived over the area as the ships approached, and Gates then left to resume his patrol. Over an hour later, Gates returned to the scene to see large quantities of heavy orange-coloured grease amongst the oil and the ships informed him that the oil was increasing and that they had picked up some wooden planking. Later some survivors were picked up by the Group, who also saw the U-boat make its final plunge.

U-608 had left Lorient for its 10th patrol two days earlier. Its first patrol had been back in the summer of 1942 and in late 1942 she had laid mines off New York. Returning to Bordeaux in July 1943 – her fifth patrol, she had been damaged by 'L' of 86 Squadron. She had sunk four ships.

Wing Commander Gates had been on his last flight as CO of 53 Squadron. He received an immediate DFC, was promoted to Group Captain, and given an appointment with U-boat Operations at Coastal Command HQ.

11 August, 1944

U-385, a type VIIC submarine, commanded by Kapitänleutnant Hans Guido Valentiner, sunk

Sunderland 'P' ML741, 461 RAAF Squadron, on patrol 2220–0930 hrs.

PO I.F. Southall	Captain
FO R.R. Player	1st pilot
PO N.A. Wylie	2nd pilot
FO C.C. Pederick	Nav
F/Sgt J.T. Eshelby	
Sgt R. Rintoul	
WO N.A. Wyeth	
WO R.W. Norris	WOP/AG
F/Sgt J.H. Kendall	
F/Sgt K.W. Stevenson	AG
F/Sgt J.R. Hobbs	

The Sunderland was homed on to a radar decoy balloon apparently released by the U-boat, and this was reported to the nearby 2nd Escort Group. Then a real contact turned out to be a U-boat and Southall attacked. Six D/Cs went down, four falling to starboard, two to port. Some flak came up at them just after the attack and the rear gunner replied with about 100 rounds. After the D/C explosions subsided, the boat could be seen in the moonlight, not moving, but her gunners were putting up an accurate fire. Southall kept clear and when 2 miles astern of the boat the radar contact disappeared. The aircraft knew the Escort Group was only a few miles away and they were called to the scene, where a marine marker had been placed. For four hours the air and naval craft co-operated, before the aircraft had to leave. Later the boat was forced to the surface, where it was finished off by naval gunfire.

U-385 had been on its second war cruise, having left St Nazaire on the 9th for the Channel. It had been fitted with a schnorkel, but as one of the survivors recorded when he was interrogated after capture, the schnorkel had never worked properly, which had forced them to surface. When the Sunderland attacked, two D/Cs had caused serious damage. The starboard hydroplane was torn off, the rudder destroyed and the starboard screw put out of action. No. 5 torpedo tube was also damaged, which caused a serious leak. With foul air and unable to steer, the boat was forced to come to the surface early on the 11th even though it knew naval ships were waiting. No sooner had U-385 surfaced than shell fire hit the conning tower, causing more water to pour in. At 0641 hrs the boat sank in position 4616/0245, the crew being picked up by HM sloop *Starling*, which had fired the final shots at the sub.

Ivan Southall later received the DFC. After the war he wrote the famous book *They Shall not Pass Unseen*, the story of 461 Squadron.

12 August, 1944

U-981, a type VIIC submarine, commanded by Oberleutnant Gunther Keller, sunk.

Halifax II 'F', 502 Squadron, on patrol 0021–0948 hrs.

F/L J. Capey	Pilot
WO G. Bellicoff (Can)	2nd pilot
WO S.W. King	Nav
F/Sgt H.E. Lawson	WOM/AG
F/Sgt G.S. Rowe	WOP/AG
WO R.F. Upton (NZ)	WOP/AG
Sgt E.T. Foster	Eng
WO R. Cheetham	WOP/AG

Visibility was just 1–2 miles because of haze when a contact was made at 11 miles, which in fact

consisted of five blips, one being further astern of the others. They homed in on this rear contact, with the others near the Point de la Courbre, entering the mouth of the Gironde River. When abeam of the contact, three flares were released and two U-boats were seen in position 4541/0125. It was too late to make a direct attack on the boats, which were 100 yards apart. A second release of HI flares failed, so Capey made another run with Mk V flares at 2 miles. Losing height he came in and dropped 5 x 600 lb bombs from 7300 feet, while both boats fired at the Halifax. The rear gunner saw four bomb bursts around the U-boat's track and afterwards the boat attacked was seen to be making a tight circle to port, which continued until Capey flew off at 0639 hrs, seeing the second U-boat head for the Gironde, 25 minutes after the first sightings.

U-981, in company with U-309, was making for port, having only sailed from Lorient on the 7th, making for La Pallice. Two hours before the Halifax found them, U-981 had already run into trouble by hitting an RAF-laid mine. Capey's attack finished her off and Oberleutnant Mahrholz's U-309 picked up 40 of 52 crewmen when it sank at 0643 hrs.

Capey had joined the Squadron in April 1944, and received the DFC in December. The assessment of this attack was that it should have proved lethal, but it was not initially possible to know what had occurred as the aircraft had left. However, it was a kill, noted as the second and last success with a 600 lb A/S depth bomb.

12 August, 1944

U-270, a type VIIC submarine, commanded by Oberleutnant Heinrich Schreiber, sunk.

Sunderland 'A' ML735, 461 RAAF Squadron, on patrol 2025–0958 hrs.

FO D.A. Little	Captain
FO J.P. Bills	1st pilot
F/Sgt F.V. Robinson	2nd pilot
FO L.F. McInnes	Nav
Sgt C.I.M. Johnson, RAF	
Sgt E. Jones, RAF	
Sgt N.P. Smith, RAF	
F/Sgt R.C. Claxton	
F/Sgt R.E. Green	
F/Sgt L.R. Clough	
F/Sgt A.D. Dalglish	

Obtained an S/E contact at 6½ miles, turned to investigate and lost height. At ¾ of a mile, illuminated a fully surfaced U-boat, which opened fire with light tracer from four guns. The Sunderland's front gunner replied as the attack was made, in which six D/Cs were dropped from 300 feet, the boat's fire ceasing at ¼ of a mile. The Mk 3 bomb sight was used by McInnes and he got a straddle forward of the conning tower. The aircraft then lost contact, and when making a second run, nothing could be seen. An attempt to contact the nearby Escort Group failed although they turned up at 0130 hrs. Ten minutes later the Senior Naval Officer contacted the Sunderland to say that the boat had gone down and that they had picked up survivors.

U-270 had sailed with a scratch crew from Lorient on a passage trip to La Pallice, taking important members of the U-boat flotillas to safety, because of the advancing allied troops. She had a terrible journey, with almost constant alerts due to RAF aircraft, and was nearly attacked by a 179 Squadron aircraft on one occasion. When Don Little attacked, near misses damaged the pressure hull and in trying to dive the vents could not be opened. They continued on the surface, but water was coming in and eventually the order had to be given to abandon ship, despite the Captain's attempts to sail southwards. The boat sank at 0145 hrs and 71 of the 81 men aboard were picked up by destroyers. U-270 had completed five patrols and sunk three ships as well as shooting down two aircraft. She had in turn been damaged by air attacks on her last three cruises and been paid off at the beginning of July. She sank in position 4619/0256.

Don Little later received the DFC.

14 August, 1944

U-618, a type VIIC submarine, commanded by Oberleutnant Erich Faust, sunk.

Liberator 'G' EW302, 53 Squadron, on patrol 2213–0902 hrs.

F/L G.G. Potier, DFC	Sgt K.A. Kirkland (Aust)
Sgt K.S. Thue (Can)	Sgt J.K. Johnson
FO L. Cundy	Sgt W. Bond
FO T.K. Archer (Aust)	Sgt W. Strangward
WO F.E. Bailey (NZ)	Sgt E. Butterfield

When the radar operator picked up a contact at 7½ miles, it appeared to be a U-boat surfacing. Potier positioned himself and at 2356 hrs he was up-wind at 300 feet, turning into the attack from 11½ miles. When the Leigh Light went on it illuminated a surfaced U-boat in position 4722/0439. Both the

aircraft and the U-boat opened fire, an explosion and a fire being seen aft of the conning tower. Six D/Cs splashed down as well as flame floats and marine markers. The radar contact was held, but this slowly disappeared and in two fly-overs of the position, nothing could be seen. The Liberator homed a Wellington, which also illuminated the area, and both aircraft saw oil streaks in the vicinity of the markers.

U-618 had been badly damaged and was later finished off by the 3rd Escort Group's frigates *Duckworth* and *Essington*. It was sailing from Brest to La Pallice and had been *en route* for three days. It had previously sailed on seven patrols and sunk three ships. On its fifth patrol it shot down a 422 Squadron aircraft, but on its next cruise it was damaged when it hit an RAF-laid mine on 25 May 1944.

Gilbert Potier received a bar to his DFC. He had previously served with 210 Squadron and won the DFC with that unit in 1942. He had flown operations from the Shetlands, Russia and Gibraltar and by July 1944 had amassed a total of 1050 operational flying hours.

18 August, 1944

U-107, a type IXB submarine, commanded by Leutnant Fritz, sunk.

Sunderland 'W' EJ150, 201 Squadron, on patrol 1305–2150 hrs.

F/L L.H. Baveystock, DFC, DFM	Captain
FO B.W. Landers	1st pilot
FO D.D. MacGregor, RCAF	2nd pilot
FO I.C. Riddell	Nav
F/Sgt R. Paton	Eng
WO W. Parsons	WOM/AG
F/Sgt A.H. Howat	FME/AG
F/Sgt E.A. Bulloch	WOP/AG
F/Sgt A.R. Cottrell	AG
F/Sgt G. Davison *	
F/Sgt E. Perran	AG

This crew arrived at their patrol area at 1705 hrs and only 5 minutes later sighted a wake, 4 miles to port. Les Baveystock, who had sunk U-955 on the night of D-Day, recalls: 'I had made 16 flights with this, my new crew, by the time we found and attacked U-107. This attack was just too easy, it being a perfect day and an easy target. By this point in the war, Brest had been surrounded by the Americans and the enemy were using U-boats to carry out a shuttle service of high-ranking officers and technicians from Brest and La Pallice down to Bordeaux, and this was the purpose of our patrol on this day.

'At the time of the sighting I was literally caught with my pants down. I was sitting quietly communing with nature on the aircraft's "loo" when the silence was shattered by the alarm klaxon suddenly going off a few inches from my ear. Hastily I pulled up my trousers and scurried up the forward stairs like a bat out of Hell! I knew it was a submarine sighting by the klaxons sending out a series of "dots" in Morse code – S for Submarine. Brian Landers was in the captain's seat and MacGregor next to him. Quickly I was told that they had spotted a long, thin wake which with the aid of our binoculars was clearly seen to be caused by the periscope of a U-boat. travelling just under the surface. They had passed the spot and it was now on our port quarter.

'As the conditions of our attack were so perfect I decided to shorten the "stick" of our D/Cs from the normal spacing of 60 feet down to 50, which I did before taking over. Not wanting to waste time and possibly lose our U-boat, I let Landers continue making the approach and I motioned MacGregor to get out of the second seat. Still in my shirt sleeves with braces dangling, I leapt into his seat while a member of the crew leaned over from the rear and stuck my flying helmet on my head. Barely half a minute had elapsed since the wake had first been spotted.

'I continued to let Landers bring the aircraft round into position until the wake was again in view. When only about a mile away, the head of the periscope was clearly identified and I now took over control of the final approach from the second pilot's seat. I must accord Landers every credit for his part in the attack for he had positioned the aircraft just right. losing height down to about 200 feet, with airspeed and engine power just right and with the D/Cs run out ready to drop.

'I brought the aircraft down to a few feet above the sea and made my attack. The rear and mid-upper gunners reported a perfect straddle, with three D/Cs entering the water each side of the periscope. I climbed away and brought the aircraft round to have a good look and the sight was amazing. The whole of the surface of the sea for an area which must have been 100 feet in diameter was one white frothing mass of escaping air from which emerged thick oil and debris, including what was later identified by the Navy as German naval plotting sheets. This mass of violently escaping air continued to come up. It was our belief that the U-boat had most likely broken in two.'

Brian Landers remembers: 'On long patrols the three pilots adopted a watch system, one flying for an hour from the first pilot's seat, another keeping a look-out from the second pilot's seat and the third

being off duty in the ward room or having a meal. At the time, I was flying the aircraft, Danny MacGregor was in the second seat and Leslie Baveystock was downstairs – in fact, on the loo. Jock Paton, the Engineer, who was in the front turret at the time, and I, spotted the wake on the port bow simultaneously. After searching miles of ocean for hours day after day with practically nothing to report, I think it took a moment to sink in that the wake was across wind lanes and was therefore probably a submarine. I sounded the warning 'S' on the buzzer, ran out the bomb trolleys, increased revs and altered course for attack.

'Baveystock came up the small stairway between the pilots' seats pulling up his trousers and I signalled to him to get his helmet on so that he could plug into the intercom. This he did as he got into the second pilot's seat. By now we were making our run and Bav took control. He asked me to check that the D/Cs were properly selected and fused and I remember getting out of the seat to check this from the selector panel, which was on the bulkhead behind this seat.

'I remember clearly seeing the periscope as we went over and released six D/Cs. Unfortunately the automatic rear-facing camera did not work, so we did not get a picture of the straddle. We later observed oil and debris for a considerable period after the attack and homed in naval craft, which later picked up German plotting charts. Subsequently, Bavey wrote in the Squadron Line Book – "It was just like the towed target at Tenby" – and it was.'

U-107 was a successful U-boat, having sunk 39 ships under its previous COs, Kapitänleutnant Gunther Hessler in 1940–41 and Leutnant Gelhous in 1941–42, including 14 off Freetown in 1941 (Hessler). It had made 12 cruises to such places as West Africa, America and the Azores. At the end of August 1943 it had laid mines off Charleston and its last cruise had been to the coast of Nova Scotia. On this trip she had sailed from Lorient on 16 August, bound for La Pallice, and went down in position 4646/0339.

Les Baveystock received an immediate DSO following this sortie. Brian Landers later became captain of his own crew, and continued to fly with 201 till the end of the war.

* The squadron records Davison as part of the crew, but Brian Landers believes it was their usual PO Macaree.

30 December, 1944

U-772, a type VIIC submarine, commanded by Kapitänleutnant Ewald Rademacher, sunk

Wellington XIV 'L' NB855, 407 RCAF Squadron, on patrol 1644–0348 hrs.

SL C.W. Taylor, DFC	Pilot
F/L E.A. Blair	2nd pilot
FO K.S. Goodman	Nav
FO H.A. Cordell	WOP/AG
PO C. Cohen	WOP/AG
PO C.D. Myers	WOP/AG

A patrol over the English Channel brought a contact at 0208 hrs at 7 miles in full moonlight but with some haze on the sea. Three minutes later the pilot had homed to position 5005/0231, when both pilots saw dead ahead, at 1½ miles, a wake and then a schnorkel. They were too high to make an immediate attack so had to make another run-in, and when the Leigh Light went on a sub was spotted despite the haze. Six D/Cs were dropped and all were seen to explode by the rear gunner. Taylor turned and climbed to 1500 feet in order that a radio message could be sent to base. Circling the two flame floats – one dropped at each end of the D/C stick – nothing could be seen. When PLE was reached 47 minutes later, the sea was still empty and no further ASV contact had been made.

U-772 had been on its second patrol. Its first had been from Trondheim between August and October 1944, mainly weather reporting in the North Atlantic. Its final sortie began on 19 November, again from Trondheim, into the Channel. It had sunk a total of five ships. It went down south of Portland Bill.

24 February, 1945

U-927, a type VIIC submarine, commanded by Kapitänleutnant Juergen Ebert, sunk.

Warwick V 'K', 179 Squadron, on patrol 1715–0140 hrs.

F/L A.G. Brownsill	Pilot
F/L E.K. Paine	
F/Sgt Whichells	2nd pilot
FO R.W. Martin	Nav
F/Sgt A.P. Woodford	WOP/AG
F/Sgt H. Townend	WOP/AG
Sgt R. Olding	WOP/AG

(There is a note that a F/Sgt Coulter was on the ASV radar, but the Squadron records show the crew as listed above.)

In a fine, clear evening, south of the Lizard, a radar contact was made when at 600 feet. It was 2 miles off and the pilot lost height to pick up a visual sighting of a wake in position 4956/0444. A schnorkel with smoke was clearly seen, the aircraft being between the wake and the setting sun. At 100 feet, Brownsill flew up the wake, the schnorkel being some 5 feet out of the water, the sea breaking over it. From 70 feet they released six D/Cs, which made a perfect straddle of three each side of the boat, while both the front and rear gunners fired as they flew over. Flying back, the Leigh Light was switched on, picking out oil and debris on the water. The 3rd Escort Group was homed, arriving after midnight – the attack having been made at 2005 hrs.

U-927 was on its first patrol, having sailed from Kristiansund to the western Channel on 1 February.

This was the only success achieved by a Warwick aircraft, which had just begun to replace Wellingtons at this late stage of the war. Flight Lieutenant Antony Gerald Brownsill received the DFC on 6 May.

27 February, 1945

U-327, a type VIIC/41 submarine, commanded by Kapitänleutnant Hans Lemcke, sunk.

Liberator 'H', VPB 112 Squadron, US Navy.

Lt O.B. Denison	Pilot
and crew	

On patrol this aircraft picked up a U-boat's periscope at 1913 hrs but it disappeared before an attack could be made. Circling the area, they sighted an oil slick and commenced baiting tactics. It then homed in escort vessels of EG2, which arrived shortly afterwards. Guided to the last position of the sub, the ships took over the search and later sank her.

U-327 had left Kristiansund on 30 January for a patrol in the English Channel. It was attacked in the vicinity of convoy ONA 287, in position 4946/0547, south-west of the Lizard. Credit for the U-boat was shared between the Liberator crew and the ships of the 2nd Escort Group – the frigates *Labaun* and *Loch Fada* and the sloop *Wildgoose*.

11 March, 1945

U-681, a type VIIC submarine, commanded by Oberleutnant Werner Gebauer, sunk.

Liberator 'N', VPB 103 Squadron US Navy.

Lt R.N. Field Pilot	ARM3/c J.L. McLain
Lt N.L. Miley	AMM2/c R.R. Giarretto
Lt E.B. Tojek	ARM1/c M.F. Mechling Jr
AMM3/c C.A. Proctor	AMM1/c J.V. Hugo
AOM3/c C.W. Curet	ARM2/c R.J. Drack

On patrol around the Scillies and Land's End when Lieutenant Field sighted a fully surfaced U-boat 2 miles away in position 4953/0631, at 1026 hrs. He made a sharp turn to port and began to lose height and the boat could also be seen to be turning to port and diving. In order to get in a quick attack, Field ignored the fact that he was not in a good attack position, and dropped eight D/Cs from 100 feet, while the decks and conning tower were still visible. As Field turned back again, the crew could see the boat's bows out of the water and it then began to submerge. Shortly afterwards, several dinghies were spotted and also survivors in the water, together with oil and debris. Field made a second attack and the boat sank stern first. Two hours later a British ship arrived at the scene and at 1315 hrs two frigates also arrived. Between then they rescued 40 men from the water, one of the ships being HMS *Lochfadda*. Later a message was received from this ship: 'Congratulations on a first class knockout punch. Delighted to have been able to bring back the relics.'

U-681 had sailed from Kristiansund on 16 February for her first patrol. According to a survivor, she had sailed from Kiel on 7 February to Kristiansund, then to the Channel area. Off the Scilly Isles the boat had hit a rock near a lighthouse south of the Scillies (St Mary's sound) and began losing oil. The sub surfaced to abandon but was immediately seen by the Liberator and attacked. The boat began to sink by the stern and after the second attack an explosion lifted the bows and she went down stern first with the diesels still running, west of Bishop's Rock.

Lieutenant Russell Norman Field received both the American and the British DFC. Air Vice Marshal H F M Maynard, AOC 19 Group, in sending his congratulations, enclosed a piece of British DFC ribbon for Field, as this was probably difficult to obtain at Dunkeswell.

2 April, 1945

U-321, a type VIIC submarine, commanded by Oberleutnant Fritz Behrends, sunk.

Wellington 'Y' HF329, 304 Polish Squadron, on patrol 1132–2049 hrs.

WO R. Marczak	F/Sgt M. Fraczkiewicz
Sgt J. Tusiewicz	F/Sgt B. Skwarek
PO W. Dubiel	F/Sgt F. Kalinowski

At 1446 hrs, forty minutes after reaching their patrol area, south-west of Cape Clear, two radar contacts were made, one at 8 miles in position 4957/1306, the other – a brighter and bigger contact – 6 miles away. The Wellington made for the nearest target, but at 3 miles the contact disappeared. Flying on through a rain shower, the navigator in the nose saw a schnorkel and a periscope one mile dead ahead. These quickly went down, but at 1448 six D/Cs were dropped from 120 feet as the front gunner fired. Markers were dropped and R/T contact made with a nearby Liberator, but nothing else was seen.

However, U-321, on its first patrol, leaving Kristiansund on 17 March, sank in position 5000/1257, during a sortie to the south-west of Ireland.

25 April, 1945

U-1107, a type VIIC/41 submarine, commanded by Oberleutnant Fritz Parduhn, sunk.

Liberator 'K', VPB 103 Squadron, US Navy.

Lt D.D. Nott Pilot	Lt K.C. Robinson
Lt J.S. Walker	AMM3/c R.F. Mayer
AOM3/c J.G. Kirchdorfer	ARM1/c J. Jones
ARM1/c J.R. Alsop	AMM3/c M.J. Vaccher
AOM3/c R.L. Price	AMM1/c R.H. Roberts

At 1939 hrs, while on an anti-submarine patrol, sighted smoke, a schnorkel and then the wake, south-west of the Brest Peninsula. An attack was carried out, the schnorkel being seen to 'jump out of the water' after the explosion and subsequently a large oil slick appeared. Later one body was seen floating in the sea.

U-1107 had left Kristiansund for the Channel approaches on 31 March and was sunk south-west of Ushant, in position 4812/0542. She had sunk two ships.

Lieutenant Dwight Dee Nott received the American

DFC, while Air Medals went to the rest of the crew.

30 April, 1945

U-1055, a type VIIC submarine, commanded by Oberleutnant Rudolf Meyer, sunk.

Catalina 'R', VP 63 Squadron, US Navy.

Lt F.G. Lake   Pilot
and crew

At 1808 hrs while on a MAD Rover patrol, sighted a prominent arching white spray caused by a suspected schnorkel, at 2 miles. At ¾ of a mile a definite schnorkel was seen protruding from the water in position 4800/0630 which was about 60 miles from the 1st Escort Group. Attack was made from stern to bow from 100 feet, while the schnorkel, periscope and guy wire were clear of the sea. A strong MAD signal obtained and 24 retro bombs were dropped on signal. As aircraft turned, no M.A.D. signals were made but at 1813 hrs a boiling motion and air bubbles were seen and later an oil slick and some debris came to the surface. The aircraft remained until 1830 hrs and a 1500 yard sonobuoy pattern was laid but without result. When later the Escort Group arrived, they picked up a bottom asdic contact and took oil samples from the sea.

U-1055 was on its second patrol which began from Bergen on 7 April, for the Channel area. It went down south-west of Ushant, the last submarine sunk by 19 Group, Coastal Command.

Lieutenant Lake received the American DFC.

ICELAND

25 August, 1941

U-452, a type VIIC submarine, commanded by Kapitänleutnant Jurgen March, sunk.

Catalina 'J' AH553, 209 Squadron, on patrol 1630–1210 hrs.

FO E.A. Jewiss   Pilot
and crew.

Flying convoy cover, commenced search at 2008 hrs

and a few minutes later exchanged signals with an Icelandic trawler. It was some 10 hours later before a U-boat was sighted, on the surface a ¼ mile from the aircraft. Jewiss dived and dropped four D/Cs as it went down. The sub was blown to the surface and then sank stern first. Jewiss remained in the area until 0953 hrs, then set course for base. (Shared with the trawler, HMS *Vascama*.)

U-452 had left Trondheim just five days earlier on its first cruise. It went down in position 6130/1530.

Flying Officer Ted Jewiss was awarded the DFC in September, but was killed when taking off at 0400 hrs on 14 December, 1941.

27 August, 1941

U-570, a type VIIC submarine, commanded by Korvettenkapitän Hans Joachim Rahmlow, captured.

Hudson 'S', 269 Squadron, on patrol 0845–1515 hrs.

SL J.H. Thompson   Pilot
FO W.J.O. Coleman   Nav
Sgt Strode   WOP/AG
Sgt Drake   WOP/AG

From RAF Kaldadarnes the squadron had two aircraft on patrol, and one flown by Sergeant Mitchell located a U-boat, but his D/Cs failed to release. He homed in aircraft 'S', which attacked the boat at 1050 hrs in position 6213/1835 with four D/Cs. About 2000 rounds were also fired from the aircraft's front and belly guns. The U-boat started to dive then came back to the surface, bow down, and about a dozen men were seen on deck. The aircraft attacked with machine-gun fire until a white flag was waved from the conning tower. 30–40 of the crew then came on deck holding a large white board. Thompson signalled for assistance and was relieved by a Catalina of 209 Squadron at 1345 hrs, flown by Flying Officer E.A. Jewiss (AH553), and returned to base. Jewiss could see the white flag and when at 1745 another 209 Squadron aircraft arrived – Flight Lieutenant B. Lewin (AH565) – it was still being waved by a number of men on the deck. When Lewin arrived there was also an American Catalina and a Glenn Martin circling nearby. He spotted an approaching destroyer at 2100 hrs.

Later several ships arrived and the captured submarine was towed to Iceland by the trawlers *Westwater*, *Windemere* and *Kingston Agathe* in company with the destroyers *Burwell* and *Niagara*. U-570 was beached on the Icelandic coast, salvaged and then sailed to England, where it became HM Submarine *Graph*. Hans Rahmlow had previously been in U-58.

Squadron Leader James Herbert Thompson and Flying Officer William John Oswald Coleman were both awarded the DFC.

20 August, 1942

U-464, a type XIV supply submarine, commanded by Kapitänleutnant Otto Harms, sunk.

Catalina 'R', VP 73 Squadron, US Navy.

Lt R.B. Hopgood   Pilot
and crew

On the way to escort convoy SN 73, and after investigating a small Icelandic fishing vessel, this crew sighted a U-boat 1500 yards off the port bow in position 6125/1440 – 10 miles from the convoy. The sea was very rough with visibility no more than 2–5 miles. Hopgood attacked at 0610 hrs, with 5 x 325 lb USN depth bombs from 100 feet, and straddled the U-boat's conning tower, which remained on the surface. Swinging round the PBY-5A machine-gunned the boat, which also fired. Large quantities of oil could be seen, and while circling the PBY radioed the convoy, contacting HMS *Castleton*, directing her to the U-boat. By this time the sub had gone down, leaving survivors in the water, which were being picked up by a fishing boat. Later the *Castleton* arrived and took on 53 German seamen by 0815 hrs.

U-464 was on her maiden voyage, having left Kiel on 4 August, and went down south-east of South Point, Iceland.

2 September, 1942

U-756, a type VIIC submarine, commanded by Kapitänleutnant Klaus Harney, sunk.

Catalina 'B', VP 73 Squadron US Navy.

Lt J.E. Odell   Pilot
and crew

Escorting convoy SC 97 at 1200 feet under 10/10ths cloud with a rough sea, sighted a U-boat on the surface 10 miles off, in position 5808/2733. Odell attacked from 40 feet with 5 x 325 lb depth bombs

which straddled 30 feet ahead of the swirl. Oil was seen after the explosions and the Catalina made a second run dropping the sixth bomb, which had previously hung up. Aircraft circled for 20 minutes then rejoined the convoy. At 1910 hrs, 40 minutes after the attack, aircraft sighted a partly surfaced U-boat, which it attacked with machine-gun fire, but the boat quickly submerged.

Assessed only as being shaken up, U-756 had, however, sunk. It was on its first patrol, having sailed from Kiel on 15 August.

5 October, 1942

U-582, a type VIIC submarine, commanded by Korvettenkapitän Werner Schultze, sunk.

Catalina 'I' VP 73 Squadron, US Navy.

U-582 was on her fifth patrol, having left Brest on 14 September. Her first had been in late 1941–early 1942, to the Canadian seaboard. She had previously been thought to have been sunk by N/269 Squadron, but it was later assessed to have been sunk by this American Catalina, in position 5852/2142.

5 October, 1942

U-619, a type VIIC submarine, commanded by Oberleutnant Kurt Makowski, sunk

Hudson 'N'. 269 Squadron, on patrol 0931–1606 hrs.

FO J. Markham   Pilot
Sgt P.L. Keys   Nav
Sgt Milne   WOP/AG

Engaged on a creeping line-ahead search, in support of convoy ONS 136, sighted a fully surfaced U-boat at 1151 hrs, 5 miles away, while flying at 4000 feet. Aircraft dived to 20 feet and attacked while the boat was still on the surface with 4 x 250 lb Mk XI D/Cs and then with front guns. A patch of thin oil appeared which increased together with oil bubbles. Ten minutes later wreckage began to appear. Half an hour later oil and wreckage were still coming to the surface. Then W/269 arrived and confirmed seeing oil and debris.

U-619 went down in position 5841/2258, south of Iceland. This was her first patrol, having left Kiel on 10 September for the North Atlantic. She had sunk two ships.

Flying Officer Markham received the DFC. Markham had previously been credited with the sinking of U-582. but this had been reassessed as being U-619. U-582 is now credited to VP 73 Squadron, USN. U-619 had previously been credited to HMS *Viscount*.

12 October, 1942

U-597, a type VIIC submarine, commanded by Kapitänleutnant Eberhard Bopst, sunk.

Liberator 'H' AM929, 120 Squadron, on patrol 0842–1839 hrs.

SL T.M. Bulloch, DFC	Pilot
FO M.S. Layton	Nav
Sgt R.J. McColl	Eng
Sgt G.W. Turner	WOP/AG
Sgt J.S. Scouler	WOP/AG
Sgt G. Clayton	WOM/AG

Airborne from Reykjavik to escort ONS 136. At 1218 hrs an S/E contact was homed in on and 5 minutes later a U-boat was sighted in position 5647/2800, which was attacked. Half an hour later the Liberator made for the convoy – 37 MVs and 5 EVs – and informed the SNO by R/T of the attack and position. Bulloch finally left the convoy at 1516 hrs only to find another U-boat 24 minutes later in position 5722/2741. This too was attacked, although two D/Cs hung up.

U-597, on her second patrol, went down in Bulloch's first attack. She had left Brest on 16 September, and was lost with all hands.

This was Bulloch's first success, but would not be the last. He was soon to become established as the pilot with the greatest number of attacks against German U-boats, and many of his crew shared in his triumphs.

Liberator AM929 'H' was also to become top-scoring aircraft against German submarines.

1 November, 1942

U-664, a type VIIC submarine, commanded by Kapitänleutnant Adolf Graf, damaged.

PBY-5A Catalina 'A', VP 84 Squadron, US Navy.

Lt R.C. Millard	Pilot
Lt J.J. Walsh	2nd pilot
Lt D.S. Lee	3rd pilot
ARM1/c J.B. Vissage	Radio
ARM3/c J.I. Lund	Radio
AMM1/c C.C. Morgan	Mech
AMM2/c E.T. Gorny	Mech

Sighted a U-boat in the act of surfacing, 4 miles away, at 1303 hrs, west of Rockall. Aircraft, supporting convoy HX 212, immediately attacked in a dive from 2000 feet and released 2 x 650 lb and 2 x 325 lb depth bombs from 100 feet, 20 seconds after the boat had crash-dived. The explosions were in salvo, 100 feet from the swirl, but no oil or bubbles were seen. Position of attack, 5700/2500.

U-664 was on her first cruise, having left Kristiansund on 20 October, arriving at Brest on 10 November. She was eventually sunk on her fifth patrol, on 9 August, 1943, by aircraft from the US escort carrier *Card*, Graf being taken prisoner.

5 November, 1942

U-408, a type VIIC submarine, commanded by Kapitänleutnant Reinhard von Hymmen, sunk.

PBY-5A, Catalina 'H', VP 84 Squadron, US Navy, on patrol 0758 hrs.

Lt R.C. Millard	Pilot
Lt W.A. Shevlin	2nd pilot
Lt G.S. Smith	3rd pilot
Lt J.J. Walsh	Nav
AMM1/c J. Vasu	Mech
AMM2/c J.P. Smith	Mech
ARM1/c L.M. Neale	Radio
ARM2/c R.B. Carthen	Radio
AMM3/c K.A. Mattingly	Mech

Patrolling north of Iceland at 1120 hrs, a U-boat was sighted 4 miles off to port, the crew reporting they thought they saw 'U-10' painted on the conning tower. The Catalina attacked down track, releasing, from 125 feet, 2 x 650 lb and 2 x 325 lb depth bombs, which fell in a salvo while the U-boat was still on the surface, although its decks were almost awash. The eight or nine men seen in the conning tower when the bombs went down either jumped or were washed overboard. The boat was entirely hidden by the spray for a length of about 40 feet aft of the tower, and when it cleared, seven men could be seen in the sea together with quantities of wood splinters, oil and other objects. However, within 40 minutes the men in the sea had gone.

U-408 went down in position 6740/1832. She had left Kristiansund in May to join the Arctic Flotilla, but the number of war cruises made is not known.

Lieutenant Millard, who had damaged U-664 only four days earlier, received the American DFC. Millard went on to make a total of five sightings and three attacks, resulting in two U-boats sunk and one damaged. Lieutenant W.A. Shevlin became an aircraft captain and made three U-boat attacks, with at least one being damaged.

5 November, 1942

U-89, a type VIIC submarine, damaged.

Liberator 'H' AM929, 120 Squadron, on patrol 0445–2101 hrs.

SL T.M. Bulloch, DFC	Pilot
PO R.H. Thomson	2nd pilot
FO M.G. Layton	Nav
Sgt R.J. McColl	Eng
Sgt G.W. Turner	1 WOP/AG
Sgt J. Scouler	2 WOP/AG
Sgt R.H. Bishop	3 WOP/AG

On passage to convoy SC 107 at 0838 hrs, got a radar contact at 5½ miles, homed and sighted a U-boat's conning tower in position 5830/3252. However, the boat went down at least 30 seconds before the aircraft arrived, so no attack was made. The convoy was 32 miles away and it was reached at 0908 hrs. The earlier contact was reported to the SNO and then Bulloch carried out various sweeps till midday. At 1215 hrs R/T from an escort ship gave the aircraft a bearing from a strong H/F, D/F, so flew to investigate. A few minutes later, while at 3500 feet, sighted a U-boat 5 miles away and 14 miles from the convoy in position 5808/3313. Approach and attack made down-track, dropping six D/Cs while conning tower still visible, and 30 feet of stern rose into the air, both screws seen revolving. Then it disappeared, but a few minutes later air bubbles came to the surface. At 1245 hrs left the position as convoy requested aircraft to investigate another contact. At 1456 hrs another U-boat seen 25 miles from the convoy and attacked with two D/Cs, but nothing seen. Left convoy at 1745 hrs, the SNO saying 'Many thanks – come again tomorrow.'

U-89 was severely damaged in position 5820/3230, at 1330 hrs, and had to return to port. She was sunk by HM ships on 14 May, 1943, having sunk a total of five ships.

Terry Bulloch had received a bar to his DFC in October and on 1 December came the award of the DSO.

(This attack was thought to have resulted in the loss of U-132, commanded by KvtLt Ernst Vogelsang. It is now understood that this submarine was almost certainly lost before midnight on 3 November. In contact with SC 107, she sank three ships – the *Hobbema*, *Empire Linx* and *Hatimora*. The latter was carrying several hundred tons of high explosives and as she sank there was a tremendous underwater explosion as she blew up. Such was the explosion that many ships in the convoy thought they themselves had been hit, and it was registered by every U-boat in the area. It is assumed that U-132 was within lethal range of the explosion and thus became a victim of her own victim.)

10 December, 1942

U-611, a type VIIC submarine, commanded by Kapitänleutnant Nikolaus von Jakobs, sunk.

PBY-5A Catalina 'H', VP 84 Squadron, US Navy, on patrol 0500 hrs.

Lt Lowell L. Davis	Captain
Ens Early B. Abrams	2nd pilot
AP1/c William J. Bentrod	3rd pilot
Ens Wallace I. Pierce	Nav
ACMM(AA) A.W. Jones	PC (Mech)
AMM2/c N.C. Eichhorn	Mech
ACRM(AA) G.J. Brown	Radio
ARM3/c A.E. Haywood	Radio
Sea2/c C. Fisher	Gnr
Sea2/c J.J. McGuire	Gnr

On escort to HX 217, the second pilot sighted a U-boat on the surface at 6 miles at 1403 hrs, south-west of Iceland in position 5809/2244. Running in with the use of cloud cover, as the PBY broke cloud the sub fired from a cannon manned by two sailors in the tower, the PBY replying with .5 gunfire. Attacked while 6 feet of conning tower and some of the stern still showing, dropping a 650 lb Mk 29 D/C with a Mk 24 fuse, from 25 feet. The depth bomb exploded 12 feet to starboard and 8 feet abaft of the conning tower, which produced an oil patch which gradually spread over an area of ½ mile by 300 yards. A dead body was seen in the water and a few minutes later eight blimp-shaped objects surfaced, two of them bearing a man. Scattered bits of wood were also seen.

U-611 was on its first patrol, having sailed from Kristiansund on 1 October. It had been temporarily with the Arctic Flotilla, then sailed into the North Atlantic.

6 February, 1943

U-465, a type VIIC submarine, commanded by Kapitänleutnant Heinz Wolf, damaged.

Liberator 'X' FK236, 120 Squadron, on patrol 0323–2123 hrs.

SL D.J. Isted, DFC	Pilot
FO R.A. Crumpton	2nd pilot
F/Sgt D.J. Appleton	Nav
Sgt A. Richardson	Eng
F/Sgt R.T. Bedford	WOP/AG
F/Sgt T. Timoney	WOP/AG
F/Sgt A. Allwood	WOP/AG

On the way to convoy SC 118, sighted a U-boat 5 miles astern, but was not able to attack. At 1154 hrs they reached the convoy and reported the sighting. At first the Lib flew a 'Mamba' patrol, and finally left for base at 1459 hrs. At 1504 hrs, at 3000 feet, they sighted a surfaced U-boat 5 miles away in position 5433/2927, when 18 miles from the convoy. The aircraft went into cloud until abeam of the boat, then turned and dived into the attack. Six D/Cs were released from 40 feet as the boat was going down, No. 3 scoring a direct hit. Afterwards air bubbles could be seen and some oil, then the bows came up for a moment, then sank again. As PLE had been reached Desmond Isted turned for home, landing at Ballykelly.

At 1616 hrs, Flying Officer Fleming-Williams (in FL928) also saw and attacked a U-boat near this position (5430/2828), on his way to the convoy. He also dropped D/Cs and saw one hit the sub but ricochet into the air. Bubbles and oil seen and the boat went down on an even keel, leaving some wreckage on the water.

U-465 was damaged at this time while on her second patrol, having left St Nazaire on 16 January. It was forced to return, arriving on 18 February. She was later damaged on her third patrol by 210 Squadron, on 14 April, 1943, and finally sunk by 10 RAAF Squadron on 7 May, 1943.

Desmond Isted had received his DFC in December 1942 and was awarded a bar in March 1943. Flight Sergeants Don Appleton and Robert Bedford received DFMs. Bedford had previously flown 50 ops with Bomber Command.

8 February, 1943

U-135, a type VIIC submarine, commanded by Kapitänleutnant Siegfried Strelow, damaged.

Liberator 'K' FK220, 120 Squadron, on patrol 1043–0003 hrs.

Sgt B.W. Turnbull (NZ)	Pilot
Sgt A.E. Hayes	2nd pilot
Sgt D.A. Harborne	Nav
Sgt L.W. Lenz	Spare pilot
Sgt E. Storey	Eng
Sgt N.R. Tingey (NZ)	WOP/AG
Sgt R. Copperthwaite	WOP/AG
Sgt G. McDonald	WOP/AG

Airborne from Reykjavik, they were on their way to meet convoy SC 118, flying at 1000 feet through showers, when a U-boat was sighted at 15 miles. On emerging from cloud they found the boat right below them in positon 5632/2006 – 19 miles from the convoy. Turnbull flew on for a ¼ mile then turned to attack. Four D/Cs selected, but only one fell, 7 seconds after the boat had disappeared below, but it landed 15 feet to the starboard side of the swirl. Nothing further seen so continued to the convoy – 64 M/Vs and 3 E/Vs – which they reached at 1427 hrs.

Bryan Turnbull had already flown 32 ops with 206 Squadron on Hudsons before joining 120 Squadron. He recalls: 'One of my first flights with 120 was on 9 August, 1942, with Flight Lieutenant Willie Watson. I remember asking him what this, that and the other knobs and tits were for and finally, what a certain dial was for. "That", says Willie, "is the oxemeter." "And what does that measure?" I enquired. "The amount of bullshit!" says Willie. Five days later "Bull" Bulloch said I could join his crew as an extra second pilot to get some Liberator experience. Maurice Neville, Noel Tingey and I were all New Zealanders and felt very much at home with "Bull", who came from Belfast. I flew five sorties with him. Twice when I was keeping Bull's seat warm I had a sighting and shot out of the seat like a rocket – Bull was like a demon at the sight of a U-boat.

'My attack on 8 February was made in greater haste than usual as it looked as though it might crash-dive – they could disappear inside 45 seconds – no time was wasted. You will see Noel Tingey joined my crew when I became a first pilot. We later flew together in the Pacific, from Guadalcanal, with 40 RNZAF Squadron.'

U-135 was damaged by this single D/C and had to abort and return to St Nazaire, whence she had sailed on 24 January. She was lost on her next cruise sunk by HM ships near convoy OS 51, on 15 July 1943. She had sunk three ships. Strelow had previously been CO of U-435, 1941–42, and had taken command of U-135 for her last two patrols.

Bryan Turnbull was to have further successes.

15 February, 1943

U-225, a type VIIC submarine, commanded by Oberleutnant Wolfgang Leimkuhler, sunk.

Liberator 'S' FK232, 120 Squadron.

FO R.F.T. Turner	Pilot

(the crew is not listed in the Squadron records, but his usual crew at this time consisted of):

FO J.P. Dunlop	2nd pilot
WO R.J. Wells	Nav
Sgt B. Harvey	Eng
Sgt R.C. Baker	WOP/AG
Sgt P.W. Elder	WOP/AG
Sgt D.E. Farrant	WOP/AG

On a sweep round convoy SC 119, south-east of Greenland, over a moderate sea, sighted a surfaced U-boat 7–8 miles off, in position 5545/3109. Attacked and dropped six D/Cs from 70 feet while conning tower still visible, which straddled just aft of the tower. Oil and air bubbles seen and later wreckage came to the surface. Circled and then reported the attack to two nearby M/Vs, the *Shooting Star* and the *Sidney Star*.

U-225 sailed from Brest on 2 February, for her second patrol into the North Atlantic. By the 11th she was one of 11 U-boats ordered to form Group Ritter and attacks were made on convoy ON 166. She was believed to have sunk five ships.

Flying Officer Reginald Thomas Frederick Turner received the DFC later in the year and was promoted to flight lieutenant.

(It had previously been thought that this attack had been on U-529, commanded by KptLt Georg-Werner Fraatz, but it is now understood that he and his command were lost to unknown causes during February 1943. U-225 had been thought to have been sunk by the US cutter *Spencer* defending convoy ON166, on 21 February.)

5 April, 1943

U-635, a type VIIC submarine, commanded by Oberleutnant Heinz Eckelmann, sunk.

Liberator 'N', 120 Squadron, on patrol 1210–2230 hrs.

FO G.L. Hatherly	Pilot
Sgt B. Threlfall	2nd pilot
Sgt E.A. Day	Nav
Sgt E.A. Britton	Eng
FO A.G. McGregor	WOP/AG
Sgt E.B. Bailey	WOP/AG
Sgt A.E. Bartley	WOP/AG

Squadron Leader Gordon Hatherly recalls: 'We took off from Rejkjavik and set course to intercept convoy HX 231. At 1552 hrs we homed on to the convoy using Procedure B, as I recall, at 3000 feet, just in and out of the base of the cloud. Ten miles north of the convoy we sighted a U-boat, which appeared to me to be just surfacing. I gave the order to prepare for attack, open bomb doors, man guns, etc. In the meantime, I put the aircraft into a dive, losing height sufficiently rapidly to permit a low-level attack from 50 feet. The attack was carried out along the track of the U-boat as it sailed towards us. I carried out a visual attack (ie, we did not use the low-level bomb sight), releasing six D/Cs as the U-boat disappeared beneath the nose of the aircraft. The D/Cs fell along the track of the U-boat, straddling it, with two or three in close proximity to it, and exploded. The U-boat disappeared from view and we did not see it again during the time we remained in the area. We reported the attack to the SNO, who dispatched an escort vessel to investigate. We then carried out patrols as requested by the SNO until 1910 hrs, when we were recalled to base because of deteriorating weather at base.

'My crew and I subsequently visited Coastal Command HQ for an assessment of the attack by the joint RN/RAF assessment committee. The assessment was "Probable kill", as I recall, the highest category, when no survivors or wreckage were recovered from the immediate vicinity of the attack.'

Despite the 'Probable kill' assessment, no U-boat was subsequently credited to Gordon Hatherly and his crew, as none were known to have been lost on this date. When, later, German records became available, U-635, which was the U-boat attacked – and sunk – had previously been credited to HM frigate *Tay*, which had attacked a sub. This turned out to be U-306, which was not damaged and in fact not sunk until the end of October.

U-635 had been on its first war cruise, having sailed from Kiel on 16 March for the North Atlantic.

6 April, 1943

U-594, a type VIIC submarine,

commanded by Kapitänleutnant Friedrich Mumm, damaged.

Liberator 'E' FL913, 120 Squadron.

FO J.K. Moffatt	Pilot
(crew not listed in the squadron records but his usual crew at this time consisted of:)

F/Sgt L.W. Lenz	2nd pilot
Sgt V.C.S. Wilson	Nav
Sgt R.W. Barrett	Eng
F/Sgt F.H. Fitzjohn	WOP/AG
Sgt J.P. Hanton	WOP/AG
Sgt J.A. Earp	WOP/AG

While on escort to convoy HX 231, received a message from the SNO at 0923 hrs – 'Several submarines astern of the convoy.' At 1024 hrs, at 1000 feet below a 10/10ths cloud base, sighted a U-boat on the surface at 2½ miles in position 5811/2813, 12 miles from the convoy. Three men in the conning tower seemed to be taken by surprise as the aircraft, which had lost height, came in from 60 feet to release four D/Cs while the boat was still fully surfaced. Three fell short, but the fourth went over the hull. When the spray had gone, so too had the sub, but a few minutes later a large gush of air broke the surface and took on a bluish tinge. The aircraft circled then returned to report to the convoy. At 1208 hrs, flying below cloud base, another U-boat was seen, either trimmed well down or in the act of diving, in position 5808/2753, 30 miles from the convoy. At one mile the boat had dived, but Moffatt released two D/Cs from 50 feet 20 seconds after the U-boat had gone. No result seen.

The official assessment of these attacks were, 1. as being 'shaken-up', 2. as 'no damage'. However, U-594, on her fifth cruise, had been damaged. She had sailed from St Nazaire on 23 March, 1943 where she returned on 14 April.

She was sunk by 48 Squadron on her next patrol, off Cape St Vincent, on 4 June 1943.

For John Moffatt, this was the first of a number of successes he and his crew achieved. The Canadian 'Hoss' Lenz had previously flown with Bryan Turnbull.

23 April, 1943

U-189, a type IXC/40 submarine, commanded by Kapitänleutnant Hellmut Kurrer, sunk.

Liberator 'V' FL923, 120 Squadron, on patrol 1354–0047 hrs.

FO J.K. Moffatt	Pilot
F/Sgt L.W. Lenz	2nd pilot
Sgt V.C.S. Wilson	Nav
Sgt R.W. Barrett	Eng
F/Sgt F.H. Fitzjohn	WOP/AG
Sgt J.P. Hanton	WOP/AG
Sgt J.A. Earp	WOP/AG

From Reykjavik, on way to escort HX 234, sighted two U-boats at 4 and 8 miles respectively, in position 5950/3443, 32 miles from the convoy. Decided to attack the nearest boat, and dropped four D/Cs from 50 feet. The U-boat opened fire during the approach, but this ceased after the explosions. The boat also stopped and slewed round to port. Within a minute Moffatt was coming back for a second attack, putting two more D/Cs down from 50 feet. Later the boat was seen to be down by the stern and some 50 men were in the water. The aircraft circled for half an hour, having contacted the SNO, who said he could not spare a ship to go to the attack area.

U-189 was on her first patrol, one task being to report on the ice limits in the Denmark Straits and to the north of Iceland before proceeding into the North Atlantic. She had sailed from Kristiansund on 3 April, and with some irony, went down east of Cape Farewell! U-413, sailing nearby, heard the attack and reported the loss of U-189.

John Moffatt made three sightings on this flight and his double attack had been successful. His DFC was Gazetted on 1 June. In 1944, Robert Barrett was awarded the DFM.

28 April, 1943

U-528, a type IXC/40 submarine, commanded by Kapitänleutnant Georg von Rabenau, damaged.

PBY-5A Catalina 'G', VP 84 Squadron, US Navy.

Lt W.A. Shevlin	Pilot.
Ens A.M. Slingluff	2nd pilot
Lt E.S. Warner	Nav
AMM3/c D.L. Bronson	Gnr

AMM2/c R.J. Cranna	Mech
AMM1/c A.C.W. Polfus	Gnr
ARM2/c H.E. Schopf	Gnr
S2cV6 C. Fischer	Gnr

At 1443 hrs aircraft set course to search an area in which 172 Squadron, RAF, had made two sightings. On reaching the area a boat was spotted 4 miles off in position 6018/2953, 79 miles from convoy SC 127. Attacked from the boat's port beam, releasing four D/Cs from 150 feet which straddled slightly ahead of the bows.

U-528 on her first patrol, was damaged and had to head for a French port, but *en route* she ran into trouble when attacked by Jim Stark of 58 Squadron and the sloop *Fleetwood* on 11 May (see 19 Group).

14 May, 1943

U-640, a type VIIC submarine, commanded by Oberleutnant Heinz Nagel, sunk.

PBY-5A Catalina 'C', VP 84 Squadron, US Navy.

Lt P.A. Bodinot	Pilot
Ens D.S. Vieira	Nav
Lt F. Kleinbrink	
AOM3/c O.A. Chaney	
AMM1/c F.A. Cernek	Gnr
AOM 2/c G.B. Fotsch	Gnr
ACMM S.H. Morris	
ARM2/c L.F. Pellitier	Gnr
ARM2/c J.E. Peoples	Radio
AMM1/c L.W. Provow	Mech
AOM2/c J.E. Tarver	

At 0540 hrs, while on escort to convoy ONS 7, carrying out instructions from the SNO, sighted a surfaced U-boat 3 miles away in position 6032/3105, which was 16 miles from the convoy. In the attack the Cat dropped three USN D/Cs from 75 feet with the boat still on the surface, Nos. 2 and 3 straddling. After the explosions the speed of the boat was reduced to around 2 knots, while it trailed oil and bubbles. It then stopped completely and sank after wallowing and listing at a sharp angle. SNO advised and aircraft circled for 38 minutes. This crew actually attacked two U-boats on this sortie, the other being made in position 6025/3050.

This had previously been thought to have been U-657, but she is now known to have been sunk by the frigate *Swale* on 17 May. The official USN report recorded the use of three USN depth charges, but this boat was the first sunk by a Mk 24 mine. U-640

had sunk one ship, on this her first patrol, which had begun from Kiel on 1 May.

Three of this crew, Bodinot, Kleinbrink and Chaney, were killed later in the year.

17 May, 1943

U-646, a type VIIC submarine, commanded by Oberleutnant Heinrich Wulff, sunk.

Hudson 'J', 269 Squadron, on patrol 1907–0124 hrs.

Sgt F.H.W. James	Pilot
Sgt K.F. Healy	Nav
and crew	

Flying at 3500 feet above a calm sea, sighted a U-boat on the surface at 10 miles in position 6210/1430. As there was no cloud cover the Hudson went down to sea level and approached on the deck. Rising to 50 feet, it dropped four D/Cs and made a good straddle. A cloud of grey smoke which had an oily smell spread over the area of track. Ninety seconds after the boat went down, wreckage and debris were seen and when the aircraft left 23 minutes later, a large oil patch had spread and could be seen 5 miles away.

U-646 had left Trondheim on 12 May for her first Atlantic cruise, having made one Arctic patrol in April.

Sergeant James was promoted to Flight Sergeant and received the DFM.

19 May, 1943

U-954, a type VIIC submarine, commanded by Oberleutnant Odo Lowe, sunk.

Liberator 'T' FK223, 120 Squadron, on patrol 0207–1753 hrs.

F/Sgt W. Stoves	Pilot
Sgt E.A. Hughes	2nd pilot
F/Sgt S.F. King	Nav
Sgt C.J. Bell	Eng
F/Sgt T. McKie	1 WOP/AG
Sgt F.J. Fisher	2 WOP/AG
Sgt D.L. Caldecott	3 WOP/AG

If Bulloch made eight sightings on 8 December, 1942, Stoves came a close second by sighting six on this patrol. The first was at 0734 hrs when he saw and attacked a U-boat with 3 x 250 lb D/Cs which made a good straddle, then followed this up by dropping what was recorded as 2 x 600 lb D/Cs, but were in fact two acoustic torpedoes. After circling for 20 minutes, Stoves then saw two U-boats 2½ miles away, but with no further D/Cs could only make mock attacks, forcing the boats to dive. After returning to the convoy – SC 130 – another U-boat was seen at 0924 hrs, but this opened fire when the Lib dived at it, only submerging as the aircraft banked away, its rear gunner spraying the decks. At 1012 hrs came the fifth sighting and again the U-boat went under as the Lib moved towards it. The final sighting came at 1054 hrs with a repeat performance of mock attack and dive.

However, the first attack had sunk U-954, on her first cruise, sailing from Kristiansund on 8 April. On board was the son of Admiral Karl Doentiz, the commander in chief of Germany's U-boat arm. The boat went down in position 5509/3518, south-east of Greenland.

19 May, 1943

U-273, a type VIIC submarine, commanded by Oberleutnant Hermann Rossmann, sunk.

Hudson III 'M', 269 Squadron, on patrol 1205–1916 hrs.

FO J.N.F. Bell	Pilot
FO J.K. Renaut	Nav
and crew	

Carrying out baiting tactics after a first sighting, the Hudson descended through cloud and sighted a U-boat in position 5925/2433 at 1625 hrs. The aircraft went in to attack, releasing four D/Cs from 50 feet to estimate a good straddle of the conning tower. Considerable amounts of oil were then seen and the boat remained on the surface for several minutes as it made a turn to starboard. Five men in the tower manned a gun, which was trained on the Hudson as it stayed out of range, but then Bell made a run and fired with the front gun and one sailor collapsed. The turret gunner also fired and continued as they circled. Panic set in amongst the Germans and the gun was manned but not fired. A couple of minutes later the boat began to dive and the pilot again strafed the boat. After 15 minutes of circling, photos were taken of debris seen on the surface.

U-273 went down SW of Iceland, thus ending its first patrol which began on 8 May, in the vicinity of convoy SC 130.

Flying Officer Bell survived the war and later flew with British Airways.

20 May, 1943

U-258, a type VIIC submarine, commanded by Kapitänleutnant Wilhelm von Massenhausen sunk.

Liberator 'P' AM919, 120 Squadron, on patrol 0954–0115 hrs.

SL J.R.E. Proctor	Pilot
Sgt J. Leach	2nd pilot
FO M.P. Gallemaerts	Nav
Sgt N.G. Cotton	Eng
F/Sgt D. Binns	1 WOP/AG
Sgt H.E.J. Scammell	2 WOP/AG
Sgt J.F. Waite	3 WOP/AG

The activity around convoy SC 130 continued, when at 1712 hrs on the 20th, Proctor and crew spotted a U-boat at 8 miles in position 5518/2749. 17 miles from the convoy. Aircraft dropped four D/Cs from 200 feet whilst the conning tower and stern were still above water, and the rear gunner saw the boat lifted by the explosions. Later an oil patch was visible and air bubbles persisted for 20 minutes. This had been the second sub sighted and a third came at 1924 hrs, the aircraft attacking with machine gun fire, six men in the conning tower firing back. A second run with cannon scored hits and a 600 lb D/C went down. At 1934 hrs the SNO was advised that this boat seemed in difficulties and down by the stern, but heavy seas prevented a ship being sent. Shortly after leaving the convoy at 2143 hrs, yet another U-boat was seen, but although the aircraft dived, it was lost in the sun and haze.

Another 120 Squadron Lib, flown by Flight Lieutenant W.J.F. McEwen also made five sightings around this convoy and attacked one twice.

Von Massenhausen's U-258, on her fourth patrol, had left La Pallice on 7 April and failed to return. She had sunk two ships.

25 May, 1943

U-467, a type VIIC submarine, commanded by Kapitänleutnant Heinz Kummer, sunk.

PBY-5A Catalina 'F', VP 84 Squadron, US Navy.

Lt R.C. Millard	Pilot.
Lt E.B. Abrams	2nd pilot
CAP(AA) A.W. Lewis	Nav
AMM2/c E.M. Francis	Mech
ARM2/c A.W. Macy	Gnr
AMM2/c E.J. Molloy	Mech
ARM1/c L.M. Neale	Radio
AMM1/c J. Vasu	Mech

Sighted a U-boat on the surface and attacked with 3 x 350 lb D/Cs from 100 feet. The boat remained on the surface and opened fire on the American Catalina. Five minutes later Lieutenant Millard made a second attack, just after it had suberged – timed at 1801 hrs.

U-467 had previously been with the Arctic Flotilla, but after one cruise went into the Atlantic, from Bergen, on 20 May. It went down in position 6225/1452, south-east of Iceland.

Lieutenant Millard already had the American DFC for earlier U-boat attacks and soon afterwards also received the British DFC. In all Millard was to make five sightings and three attacks. Lieutenant Early Abrams had been second pilot to Lieutenant L.L. Davis when U-611 was sunk in December 1942. Vasu and Neale were also with Millard when he sank U-408 in November 1942.

28 May, 1943

U-304, a type VIIC submarine, commanded by Oberleutnant Heinz Koch, sunk.

Liberator 'E', 120 Squadron, on patrol 1554–0703 hrs.

FO D.C. Fleming-Williams, DFC	Pilot
FO R.A. Hayden	2nd pilot
FO J.H. Wilsher	Nav
Sgt R. Meyer	Eng
F/Sgt M.J. Brady	1 WOP/AG
Sgt H.F. Holland	2 WOP/AG
Sgt T.C. Stowell	3 WOP/AG

On passage to HX 240, flying at 7000 feet in 10/10ths cloud, sighted a U-boat on the surface at 5 miles, position 5450/3720. Aircraft turned to port and climbed into cloud before turning to starboard. On breaking cloud cover the boat was 2 miles dead ahead. Attack made from 100 feet with four D/Cs while decks and tower still visible. One minute later a gush of oil was seen followed by wreckage and pieces of wood. The oil spread to 300 feet in diameter and was still there 20 minutes later when Donald Fleming-Williams left the area.

U-304 had been on her first patrol, having sailed from Kristiansund on 27 April, bound for the North Atlantic. She went down with all hands.

8 June, 1943

U-535, a type IXC/40 submarine, commanded by Kapitänleutnant Helmut Elmenreich, damaged.

Hudson III 'K', 269 Squadron, on patrol 1040–1507 hrs.

Sgt R. Couchman	Pilot
Sgt J.M. Parrish	Nav
and crew	

Near convoy SC 132, flying over a calm sea at 2500 feet a U-boat was seen at 6 miles in position 6040/2055. Making use of cloud cover, the aircraft lost height and attacked, releasing four D/Cs from 80 feet. Two made a good straddle aft of the conning tower and four or five men were seen in the tower as the Hudson flew over. Flak fire exploded near the aircraft's tail and Couchman took evasive action. The boat was now going around in circles, trailing oil, but after 18 minutes it submerged, leaving a trail 2½ miles long. The Hudson came back to the scene half an hour later but could see nothing further.

U-535, on her first patrol to the Azores, was damaged and lost much oil. She was refuelled by other U-boats on her way to France, but before she reached safety was sunk by 53 Squadron on 5 July.

Time of attack, 1225 hrs, and the Assessment made comment, 'Well done – you deserve better luck next time.'

15 June, 1943

U-449, a type VIIC submarine, commanded by Kapitänleutnant Hermann Otto, damaged.

Liberator 'F', 120 Squadron, on patrol 1652–0738 hrs.

F/L S.E. Esler, DFC	Pilot
Sgt W.H. Duncan	2nd pilot
F/Sgt T.J. Kempton	Nav
PO G.M.L. Goodall	Eng
F/Sgt F.W.W. Wallace	1 WOP/AG
F/Sgt J. Blair	2 WOP/AG
Sgt C.A. Sherwood	3 WOP/AG

Sam 'Red' Esler was on patrol cover to ONS 10, carrying out a 'Cobra' patrol at 6200 feet when a U-boat was sighted 12 miles away in position 5713/3004. This was 43 miles from the convoy and Elser attacked in a steep dive despite gunfire from the Germans. Flak and cannon shells came at the Lib, whose front guns too fired, before four D/Cs went down from 100 feet. After the attack the boat could be seen down by the stern with grey smoke coming from the rear which lasted for several minutes. The boat did not appear to be in control and 8 minutes later it submerged. The aircraft had called for escort ships, and two destroyers did come to the scene later to carry out an asdic search.

U-449, on her first voyage, was damaged and had to make for France, but she was later found and sunk in the Bay of Biscay by the sloops of the 2nd Escort Group on 24 June, in position 4500/1159.

20 June, 1943

U-388, a type VIIC submarine, commanded by Oberleutnant Peter Sues, sunk.

PBY-5A Catalina 'I', VP 84 Squadron, US Navy, on patrol 0400 hrs.

Lt E.W. Wood	Pilot.
Ens O.S. Sigurdson	2nd pilot
CAP(AA) F.W.E. Fenzel	Nav
ARM1/c J.F. Piedi	
Cdr L.H. Goldsmith	Passenger
ARM3/c H.L. Parker	Radio
AMM2/c J.E. Armstrong	Gnr
AMM2/c A.Z. Clark	Gnr
ACMM J.D. Strickland	
AMM2/c R.G. Hesselbarth	Mech

At 1049 hrs, south-west of Iceland, on a sweep for convoy ON 189, sighted a surfaced U-boat at 14 miles, 60 miles from the convoy. No evasive action by sub until PBY one mile away, when it began a left turn. When 600 yards away gunfire came from the boat and four men could be seen in the conning tower. Despite this gunfire, they attacked from 100 feet, releasing 3 x 325 lb D/Cs, but all undershot. Return fire from the PBY had begun at about the time the U-boat had commenced firing. The aircraft turned and made a second attack as the boat was diving, the Mk 24 mine was released, falling on the swirl, but nothing further was immediately seen. Later bubbles and oil seen to break the surface and then two-thirds of the sub broke surface but began to settle at once until only about 30 feet of the stern was still visible. On close observation the stern could be seen split open with about 10–15 feet of the after compartments visible. There was no propeller or rudder seen. As the boat went down, debris and bubbles were left on the surface.

U-388, on her first patrol, went straight to the bottom in position 5736/3120, south-east of Cape Farewell. She had sailed from Kristiansund on 8 June.

Lieutenant Wood later received the British DFC.

24 June, 1943

U-194, a type IXC/40 submarine, commanded by Kapitänleutnant Hermann Hesse, sunk.

Liberator 'H' AM929, 120 Squadron, on patrol 1336–1951 hrs.

F/L A.W. Fraser, DFC	Pilot
Sgt H.J. Oliver	2nd pilot
F/Sgt L.C. Heiser	Nav
Sgt A.W. Parsons	Eng
F/Sgt K. Johnson	1 WOP/AG
F/Sgt E.A. Mincham	2 WOP/AG
F/Sgt E. Stott	3 WOP/AG

Flying out from Reykjavik for convoy ONS 11, sighted a U-boat on the surface in position 5815/2525 at 1628 hrs. As the aircraft dived, the boat opened fire and the aircraft replied, but it was hit in the port wing and front port fuselage, damaging the hydraulics and accumulator, as well as starting a petrol leak in a wing tank. Two D/Cs were dropped from 50 feet, the other two failing owing to the bomb door creep because of the damage by the sub's guns. The D/Cs straddled and in a second run a 600 lb D/C failed to release, again because of the damage. However, oil and bubbles were coming to the surface, then about 15 survivors and some wreckage was seen. The convoy was informed, but because of the damage, and also because the Flight Engineer having been slightly wounded, Fraser decided to return to base. When he reached base, the nose wheels were lowered by emergency systems, and as the nose wheel appeared damaged Fraser got all the crew to move to the back of the Lib. With all the weight there, he managed a tail-down landing with only superficial damage to the rear fuselage.

U-194 had been on her first patrol, having left Kristiansund on 12 June.

Flight Lieutenant Fraser, an Australian, was awarded a bar to his DFC. He was killed in a flying accident on 4 July, 1944.

24 June, 1943

U-200, a type IXD/42 submarine, commanded by Kapitänleutnant Heinrich Schonder, sunk.

PBY-5A Catalina 'G', VP 84 Squadron, US Navy.

Lt J.W. Beach	Pilot
Lt E.T. Allen	2nd pilot/Nav
ARM1/c J.C. McMahan	Radio
ARM2/c W.P. Merck	Gnr
AMM1/c L.C. Greenfield	Mech
ACMM S.H. Morris	
AOM2/c J.E. Tarver	
AOM2/c G.B. Fotsch	Gnr

At 1607 hrs, south of Iceland, sighted a U-boat on the surface and attempted to attack, but D/Cs failed to release. The Catalina circled, and in a second attack two 325 lb D/Cs were dropped manually. One dropped short, the other about 50 feet astern. Gunfire was exchanged and then the boat submerged.

U-200 was sunk in position 5900/2618 and credited to this attack by the Catalina of Patrol Squadron 84. She was on her first patrol, having sailed from Kiel on 12th June for a sortie into the North Atlantic.

Lieutenant E.T. Allen was awarded the British DFC. This was his fourth attack on a U-boat, and although usually a first pilot, he was acting as Navigator on this occasion. Lieutenant Beach had also flown as second pilot and navigator and had also made four U-boat attacks. He was later killed. Crewmen Fotsch, Morris and Tarver had been involved in the sinking of U-657 a month earlier.

3 August, 1943

U-489, a type XIV supply submarine, commanded by Oberleutnant Adalbert Schmandt, damaged.

Hudson 'J' V9053, 269 Squadron, on patrol 0439–1048 hrs.

F/Sgt E.L.J. Brame	Sgt Y.T. Borland
F/Sgt W. Styring	Sgt E. Beaudry

While engaged on a 'Moorings' patrol, sighted a fully surfaced U-boat in position 6203/1252 at 0732 hrs. Aircraft closed to 2 miles and U-boat began to circle and so did the Hudson, but then attacked with D/Cs but had to turn away because of the intense flak barrage. At 0800 hrs, the aircraft tried again from 3500 feet with one 100 lb bomb, which overshot. The sub had remained on the surface and continued firing. Five minutes later the Hudson dropped another A/S bomb, which fell 30 yards on the boat's beam. Another attack, this time with machine guns, led the aircraft to pull up into cloud and when it came down the boat had submerged.

On her first sortie from Kristiansund, having sailed on 22 July, this tanker submarine was damaged and had begun a trip home. However, it was found the next day and sunk by 423 Squadron. Schmandt was taken prisoner along with his crew.

19 September, 1943

U-341, a type VIIC submarine, commanded by Oberleutnant Dietrich Epp, sunk.

Liberator 'A' 586, 10 RCAF Squadron.

F/L R.F. Fisher	Pilot
FO P. Dale	2nd pilot
FO B. Murray	Nav
FO J. Johnson	WOP
WO J. Barabanoff	WOP
WO J. Lamont	WOP
Sgt E. Flinn	WEM/AG
Cpl C. Holder	Mech

This all-Canadian crew had been part of the escort to Winston Churchill, returning in HMS *Renown* from the Quebec Conference, and was returning to Gander from Iceland. On their way home, they made a sweep around convoy ONS 18 at 3000 feet, and over a rough sea sighted a fully surfaced U-boat at 1½ miles at 0859 hrs. It was in position 5840/

2530, 165 miles from the convoy. The Lib dived to attack, making a hard turn to starboard, then to port, but it was unable to lose enough height to make an attack and flew over the target at 500 feet. Curving down and round the aircraft came in again and dropped six Mk XI D/Cs. The U-boat had begun firing during the Lib's first run and continued on this second attack. The first D/C appeared to explode right alongside the boat, the others straddling along the boat's length. The bows lifted and about 20 seconds later an explosion occurred at the bow from which much debris flew into the air. The sub came to a halt, settled and then disappeared. An oil slick appeared and as the aircraft turned to make another attack, the boat was just about under, but four D/Cs splashed into the swirl and oil and later some objects were seen floating on the water. The aircraft had sustained some slight flak damage to the starboard wing tip, and left to continue its sweep 25 minutes later. It was assessed as probably destroyed.

However, U-341, which had left La Pallice on 31 August for its second patrol, went down in this position, south-west of Iceland.

Corporal Carl Holder, an engine mechanic, was making his first flight in an aircraft, having been taken along in case the aircraft was diverted, while on its original duty away from base. Robert Frank 'Tony' Fisher, in his youth, lived just five doors away from Harry Sheardown, who sank U-620 in February 1943. Tony Fisher had joined 10 RCAF Squadron in October 1942. He was Mentioned in Despatches. Receiving news that his brother Bill had been killed in a Liberator crash in India, on 7 October, 1943, Fisher and some of his crew were granted leave. They flew as passengers in another Liberator, but it crashed near Quebec on 19 October, and all aboard were killed, including Johnnie Johnson, Joe Barabanoff, Eric Flinn and Jim Lamont.

No. 10 RCAF Squadron was not normally under the control of Coastal Command, but this Liberator had been, while on the duty of escorting HMS *Renown*. This same airfcraft, JK-A (586), sank U-420 on 26 October, 1943, while under the command of Flight Lieutenant R.M. Aldwinkle, RCAF.

20 September, 1943

U-338, a type VIIC submarine, commanded by Kapitänleutnant Manfred Kinzel, sunk.

Liberator 'F' AM917, 120 Squadron, on patrol 0425–2024 hrs.

F/L J.K. Moffatt, DFC	Pilot
F/Sgt L.W. Lenz	2nd pilot
FO A.T. Good	Spare pilot
F/Sgt V.C.S. Wilson	Nav
F/Sgt R.W. Barrett	Eng
F/Sgt F.H. Fitzjohn	1 WOP/AG
Sgt J.P. Hanton	2 WOP/AG
Sgt J.A. Earp	3 WOP/AG

From Reykjavik, met convoy ONS 18 at 0850 hrs and ordered to fly a 'Reptile' patrol. Two hours later they spotted a surfaced U-boat at 5 miles and dived to attack with cannon to which the U-boat replied. Four D/Cs went down, but they undershot. Aircraft circled, firing with the front .5 in. gun. At 1112 hrs the boat submerged and it was immediately attacked with a 600 lb D/C – in reality a 'Fido' homing torpedo. A destroyer was homed in and the aircraft flew back to the convoy. At 1514 hrs another boat was seen, but it quickly went down.

U-338 went down in position 5740/2948 and all 51 crewmen perished. She was on her third patrol having left St Nazaire on 25 August, and was approaching the convoy when sunk south-east of Cape Farewell. She had sunk five ships.

This was John Moffatt's second kill and third successful attack. It was the first recorded success of Fido – usually identified as the Mk 24 mine for security reasons.

4 October, 1943

U-336, a type VIIC submarine commanded by Kapitänleutnant Hans Hunger, sunk.

U-305, a type VIIC submarine commanded by Kapitänleutnant Rudolf Bahr, damaged.

Ventura 'B', VP 128 Squadron, US Navy.

Cdr C.L. Westhofen and crew	Pilot

Sighted and attacked U-boat which submerged in

position 6040/2630, then left the area and began baiting tactics, before returning. They then sighted a surfaced U-boat dead ahead at 10 miles in position 6100/2653, which was 12 miles from the first attack. The Ventura dived into the attack, meeting flak, as the boat turned to present its stern to the aircraft. As it came in the aircraft too opened fire, then three Mk 44 D/Cs went down from 50 feet. The first appeared to explode under the stern, the second under the conning tower and the third under the bows. As the aircraft circled to make a machine-gun attack, bluish-white smoke came pouring from the tower as the boat stopped dead and began to settle. A large oil patch appeared and then the crew could be seen abandoning ship. Aircraft opened fire from bow guns. Small rafts were now being launched then the sub went down, leaving oil and debris and survivors in the four or five rafts, with others in the water.

U-336 had been on her fourth patrol, leaving Brest on 14 September. She had sunk one ship. U-305 had been on her third patrol when damaged. She was later sunk by HMS *Wanderer* on 17 January, 1944, on her fourth sortie.

(There is a possibility that Westhofen actually sank U-279 – see next entry.)

4 October, 1943

U-279, a type VIIC submarine, commanded by Kapitänleutnant Otto Finke, sunk.

Liberator 'X' FK236, 120 Squadron, on patrol 0933–2149 hrs.

F/L W.J.F. McEwen	Pilot
FO R.D. Ker	2nd pilot
FO H.J. Bates	Nav
F/Sgt R. Fallon	Eng
PO N.D. Hartnell, RCAF	WOP/AG
Sgt A. Allwood	WOP/AG
Sgt H. Dixon	WOP/AG
Lt Leonard, USN	Passenger

Bob 'Paddy' Fallon, the Flight Engineer on this crew, remembers: 'We took off to give cover to convoy ONS 19. Wing Commander Longmore, our CO, took off just behind us to do likewise to another convoy some 10–20 miles apart. During the day we saw them in 'V' on the horizon. His signal to Group that they had sighted and were about to attack a U-boat was picked up by our WOP/AG on duty. Nothing further was heard and Group ordered us to go and investigate. We arrived over the area a short

time later, but saw nothing – no survivors, no debris and no U-boat.

'We resumed our patrol and later picked up a signal from a Lockheed Hudson on transit to the UK saying that he had sighted a fully surfaced U-boat and gave its position. Somewhat out of our way as we were about to set course for Reykjavik, Group suggested we had a look and after a fuel state check we set off. The Skipper decided to do a square search and as the setting sun was low down on the horizon, between us and the sun was our U-boat, still fully surfaced. McEwen had his crew trained so that all that was required was his call "U-Boat!"

'My position during an attack was on the catwalk, to open and keep open the bomb doors, also to prepare and drop two marine markers as the D/Cs went down. U-279 was split open like a pea pod. The Skipper asked the crew to count the survivors and our average was nine to eleven. Our American Naval friend counted sixty!

'The Skipper ordered me to drop two emergency food, first aid, etc, containers and also three "K"-type one-man dinghies. This I did, opening the CO_2 cock on each bottle so that the things would be inflated when they reached the survivors. One blond swimmer was seen to shake his fist at us. Fuel state was getting low and so we set course for base. We had been airborne for 12 hours 20 minutes.

'There was a purge on the squadron when it was discovered that Wing Commander Longmore's crew were tour expired. As I had had 18 months and one thousand hours of flying (a tour was 800 hours or 12 months, whichever came first), I was returned to the UK for resting.'

U-279 had gone down in position 6051/2826 at 1912 hrs. She had been on her first patrol, leaving Kristiansund on 4 September. At the start of her war cruise she had landed an agent in Iceland.

Flight Lieutenant McEwen received an immediate DFC. Paddy Fallon later got on to 547 Squadron and was involved in another sinking in May 1945. Wing Commander R.M. Longmore had found U-539, commanded by Oberleutnant Lauterbach-Emden, in position 6357/2850. After circling and exchanging gunfire Longmore had attacked but was hit on the run in. With both starboard engines on fire he released six D/Cs, which fell ahead of the port bow. The aircraft then went into the sea, exploding on impact (FL923). One of U-539's crew was slightly wounded and what damage there had been was slight.

(There is a possibility that McEwen actually sunk U-336, see previous entry.)

4 October, 1943

U-731, a type VIIC submarine, commanded by Oberleutnant Alexander Graf Keller, damaged.

Hudson 'S' V9047, 269 Squadron, on patrol 0730-1232 hrs.

PO H.B. Smith Pilot	F/Sgt W.A. Allan
Sgt J. Carrington	F/Sgt G.E. Cartwright

Flying from Reykjavik to escort convoys ONS 19 and ON 204, at 0910 hrs sighted a U-boat on the surface at 6 miles in position 6202/2827. The Hudson attacked with front guns and D/Cs, although only one of the latter was seen to explode close to the stern. The boat zigzagged and returned the fire with cannon. The aircraft made two further runs, firing front and turret guns before the U-boat finally submerged at 0940 hrs and was not seen again.

U-731 was on her second patrol, having left Brest on 29 August. It was damaged and some casualties had been inflicted, so it turned for home. It was attacked again by aircraft from an American escort carrier before reaching base on 1 November. It was sunk on its fourth cruise when it attempted to get into the Mediterranean, being sunk on 15 May, 1944, by two Catalinas of VP 63, USN.

5 October, 1943

U-389, a type VIIC submarine, commanded by Kapitänleutnant Siegfried 'Udo' Heilmann, sunk.

Hudson 'F' FK764, 269 Squadron, on patrol 0753-1512 hrs.

F/Sgt G.C. Allsop (Aust)	WO D.G. Pilon
PO E.B. Shields	WO E.T. Bromley

On a sweep near convoy ONS 19, sighted a surfaced U-boat at one mile in positon 6243/2717. Aircraft turned and dived as U-boat opened fire with a concentrated flak barrage. Eight rockets fired – first pair at 800 feet at a range of 800 yards, 2nd pair 600 feet at 600 yards and then four in salvo at 400 feet, 400 yards. When the first pair went off the U-boat stopped firing. One of this pair hit the boat's deck forward of the conning tower and the other hit just above the water line forward of this position. The second pair hit just aft of the tower on the water line

while one of the salvo also hit forward of the conning tower. With so many hits the boat's fate was sealed. Blue smoke came from the conning tower and the boat came to a stop. Then the stern rose out of the water at a very steep angle before sliding back under the water. Before it disappeared the boat opened fire once more and the rear gunner replied with 900 rounds. An oil patch was left along with about 15 survivors, all covered in the oil, and appeared to be motionless. When the aircraft flew over a few minutes later the men and the debris had gone, leaving just the oil patch. The attack was timed at 0900 hrs.

U-389 was on her first cruise from Trondheim, leaving there on 18 September. Heilmann had earlier been the commander of U-97. U-389 was lost with all hands south-west of Iceland.

Flight Sergeant Gordon Campbell Allsop, RAAF, was awarded the DFM. Later commissioned, he flew with 23 and 25 Squadrons, SAAF.

8 October, 1943

U-762, a type VIIC submarine, commanded by Oberleutnant Walter Pietschmann, damaged.

Liberator 'G' FK225, 120 Squadron, on patrol 0828-0124 hrs.

WO B.W. Turnbull (NZ)	Pilot
F/Sgt H.J. Oliver	2nd pilot
F/Sgt D.A. Harborne	Nav
F/Sgt A.E. Storey	Eng
F/Sgt N.R. Tingey (NZ)	1 WOP/AG
F/Sgt R. Copperthwaite	2 WOP/AG
WO G.S. McDonald	3 WOP/AG

From Reykjavik on passage to convoy SC 143, a U-boat was sighted 80 miles from the convoy and attacked in position 5743/2538 with a 600 lb D/C, and then three D/Cs after the boat had dived. Bryan Turnbull: 'This was my 35th operational sortie with 120 Squadron and my longest so far, at 11 hours 15 minutes day and 6 hours night – total 17 hours 15 minutes. We met flak and our front gun hit one German. We straddled after submergence, but no results were observed and we landed back at Ballykelly. This was four days after our CO, Wing Commander Longmore, had gone missing and I didn't relish having to attack a U-boat which may have taken them prisoner and worried about it long afterwards until, years later, I discovered the full details.'

The official assessment recorded 'improbable

that U-boat sustained any damage'. However, U-762 had been damaged and had suffered casualties. Having sailed from Bergen on 28 September, she made her way to Brest, where she arrived on 15 November. She did not sail again until after Christmas and was sunk on 8 February, 1944, by the sloops of the 2nd Escort Group.

This was Bryan Turnbull's second damaging attack – U-135 and now U-762.

16 October, 1943

U-844, a type IXC/40 submarine, commanded by Oberleutnant Gunther Moeller, sunk.

Liberator 'S' FL984, 59 Squadron, on patrol 0453-1454 hrs.

PO W.J. Thomas	Sgt G.W. Gerring
Sgt J.F.E. Seaver	Sgt J.J. Primeau
WO R.N. Pike	Sgt W.C. Wallace
Sgt E. Ormerod	

Flying from Meeks Field, Iceland, as escort for ONS 206, they found a fully surfaced U-boat in position 5830/2716, 15 miles from the convoy and made two attacks. They had been homed in by another Liberator which was circling nearby. After straddling with the first four D/Cs, a deep red flash was seen about 30 seconds afterwards and the boat started to submerge. Half a minute later four more D/Cs went down in front of the swirl. Return fire from the U-boat shot up the starboard inner engine, but none of the Lib's crew was injured. On the return flight another U-boat was seen and attacked with machine-gun fire despite more flak. This was U-540, which was sunk next day.

The Liberator seen circling was L/86 Squadron (FL952) flown by Flight Lieutenant E.A. Bland. He had made an attack, but had been severely hit by return fire. His two port engines were hit and damage inflicted to the port side of the fuselage. The D/Cs failed to release. The SNO had been informed and then S/59 was homed in. Bland had attempted another attack after Thomas's first drop, but again his D/Cs would not release. They were then jettisoned as his damaged aircraft was now in trouble. He attempted to ditch alongside the convoy, coming down near HMS *Pink*. He ditched into wind, hit tail first and nosed into a 10-foot-high wave, at 117 mph. The Lib broke up and the survivors were rescued by *Pink*, although the second pilot and one of the NCOs were killed, Bland and his

navigator being injured.

U-844 had sailed from Bergen on 6 October for its first patrol.

Eric Bland received the DSO.

17 October, 1943

U-540, a type IXC/40 submarine, commanded by Kapitänleutnant Lorenz Kasch, sunk.

Liberator 'D' BZ712, 59 Squadron, on patrol 0549-2222 hrs.

F/L E. Knowles, DFM	Sgt H. Robinson
FO E.J.A. Stephenson	Sgt J. Branagan
Sgt P.C. Moore	Sgt A.E. King
Sgt C.A. Honey	

Liberator 'H' AM929, 120 Squadron, on patrol 0558-2223 hrs.

WO B.W. Turnbull (NZ)	Pilot
F/Sgt H.J. Oliver	2nd pilot
F/Sgt D.A. Harborne	Nav
F/Sgt A.G. Storey	Eng
F/Sgt N.R. Tingey	1 WOP/AG
F/Sgt R. Copperthwaite	2 WOP/AG
WO G.S. McDonald	3 WOP/AG

Both Liberators found this U-boat on the surface at around 1820 hrs in position 5838/3156. Knowles made two attacks despite being on his homeward flight to Meeks Field. In his first attack four D/Cs overshot, and in the second run, two were seen to straddle. Bryan Turnbull had met convoy ON 206 at 0939 hrs that morning, and was also on his way back to Reykjavik when the U-boat was sighted. As he came in he opened up with his front cannons. Bryan recalls: 'The success against U-540 can very largely be credited to our engineer, Gerry Storey, because after the initial cannon attack, I sent Gerry down to check the setting of the Mickey Mouse (bomb release switchboard) and by the time I was ready two minutes later to attack with D/Cs, he had had time to make sure that a stick of four would drop. In my cannon attack, to which we were more or less committed, because the other Liberator was obviously beginning his run-in and probably hadn't seen us, we flew over the U-boat at 150 feet to avoid the possibility of a collision, and also to confuse the German gunners and do some damage if possible. We could see the Lib's D/Cs overshooting, and the U-boat turning to port, but remaining on the surface. When we attacked, our first four D/Cs splashed across the bows and our second stick too straddled. Mac McDonald, in the rear turret taking photos of the action, called back on the intercom that he could see the bow and the stern both pointing upwards. Then the other Lib called up on the R/T, "You got him - good show!"'

As the two aircraft circled, about 30 survivors could be seen in the water. The boat had been blown in two by Bryan Turnbull's second straddle.

Noel Tingey remembers: 'I shall never forget the attack on U-540 until my dying day. I picked it up on radar, which was most unsophisticated compared with today's radar, and was able to home Bryan on to it. Imagine our delight when it turned out to be a surfaced U-boat, no doubt charging its batteries.'

U-540 did not complete her first war sortie into the North Atlantic. She had left Bergen on 4 October, and went down in the U-boat graveyard south-east of Cape Farewell, with all hands. Her radio man managed to get off a signal that she was under attack, the time and position coinciding with the later RAF pilot reports. The previous day, U-540 reported driving off a Liberator which failed to make an attack. This was S/59 Squadron, which an hour earlier had been involved with L/86 in the sinking of U-844.

Bryan Turnbull received the DFC for his successful attack, his third with 120 Squadron (1 kill, 2 damaged), and was later commissioned. It was also another kill for Liberator H-How (AM929). Pop Oliver later became a crew captain and was credited with a U-boat in April 1945 (see 15 Group).

6 March, 1944

U-737, a type VIIC submarine, commanded by Oberleutnant Paul Brassack, damaged.

Liberator 'B' BZ764, 120 Squadron, on patrol 1214-0138 hrs.

F/L H.F. Kerrigan, RCAF	Pilot
FO A.M. McLennan	2nd pilot
FO P.R. Rackham, RCAF	Nav
FO W.J. Hartrick	2 Nav
Sgt P. Cole	Eng
WO J.P. Foy	1 WOP/AG
F/Sgt S.T. Levinsky	2 WOP/AG
F/Sgt J.J. Grassam	3 WOP/AG
F/Sgt T.W. Chapman	WOM

Took off from Meeks Field and at 1748 hrs made two radar contacts. The first disappeared, but the second turned out to be a surfaced U-boat in position 6857/0316. It was attacked with six D/Cs,

running through intense flak. The Lib's guns fired back, hitting the conning tower, but the aircraft's No. 4 engine was also hit and set on fire, plus other damage. After the attack a second boat was sighted and again an attack was made in the face of severe AA fire. The nose of the Lib was hit, wrecking the bomb sight and wounding both navigators. The aircraft began to lose height, so the rest of the D/Cs were jettisoned, the burning engine feathered and the fire put out. Flying Officer Hartrick was seriously wounded, but Flying Officer Rackham, despite wounds to his head, legs and body, remained in his position and navigated home, assisted by the co-pilot. They were diverted to Skitten, landing there on two engines.

U-737 was on her fifth cruise, sailing from Hammerfest on 28 February, and forced to return damaged on 12 March. She was eventually sunk on her 10th patrol on 19 December, 1944, under the command of Oberleutnant Friedrich August Greus, west of Tromso after an accidental collision with a German minesweeper.

Flight Lieutenant Harold Fleming Kerrigan received the DSO and Flying Officer Paul Remby Rackham received the DFC for their actions. Kerrigan, with Foy, Grassam and Chapman, had helped to sink U-470 in October 1943 (see 15 Group).

17 April, 1944

U-342, a type VIIC submarine, commanded by Oberleutnant Albert Hossenfelder, sunk.

Canso 'S' 9767, 162 RCAF Squadron.

FO T.C. Cooke Pilot	F/Sgt E.N.C. Tilander
F/L E.W. Wiskin	Sgt E.S. Hall
FO B.F. Hunter	Sgt T.E. Hooson
FO P.P. Ficek	WO G.R. McMacken
F/Sgt E.A. Johnson, RAF (Met Obs)	

On a patrol combined with a met. flight, the co-pilot sighted a wake at 6 miles at 1017 hrs. Flying to investigate, a U-boat was identified through the binoculars at 4 miles in position 6023/2920. The aircraft began a run-in from out of the sun, meeting flak at 3000 yards, and so began evasive action, and at 1200 yards the Canso opened up with its nose gun. At 300 yards the flak ceased and an attack was made from 50 feet with three D/Cs. The first fell close to the boat's starboard side, the other two on the port – and three men were seen in the conning tower. After the plumes subsided the boat made a tight turn to starboard and after one circle it turned to port and seemed lower in the water. Meanwhile the Canso circled, the port blister gunner firing into the boat. Some minutes later there was a violent explosion 15 feet forward of the conning tower and the boat immediately sank. Wreckage appeared – pieces of wood and large cylindrical objects. Three hours later a large patch of oil could be seen up-wind of the wreckage.

The boat was assessed as destroyed and so it was. U-342 on her first patrol, sailing from Bergen on 3 April, went down south-west of Iceland.

Flying Officer Thomas Charles Cooke and Flight Lieutenant Eric Walter Wiskin both received an immediate DFC.

4 August, 1944

U-300, a type VIIC/41 deep diving submarine, commanded by Oberleutnant Fritz Hein, damaged.

Canso 'F' 9759, 162 RCAF Squadron.

FO W.O. Marshall	F/Sgt J. Newa
PO A.J. Beck	F/Sgt G.D. Thomas
WO K.B. Klager	F/Sgt R. Waldbauer
PO J.V. Raymond	Sgt G.F. Schmidt

Just before 1025 hrs sighted a wake at 3 miles and on closing saw it was a U-boat, 65 miles from convoy UR 130. The existing weather conditions made it imperative to make an immediate attack, as contact would have been lost if time had been taken to gain a more favourable position. Marshall made a steep diving turn as the boat began to dive, and released three D/Cs from 50 feet which fell across the bows. The aircraft then made a steep bank to port and turned to drop a 600 lb D/C, but nothing further was seen. The attack was assessed as a severe shake-up.

U-300 was on her first patrol, having left Horten on 18 July, and had to return to Trondheim with damage, on 17 August. She was sunk on her third sortie, sailing to the Gibraltar area, by HM ships, survivors being rescued.

AHQ Gibraltar

25 October, 1941

***Ferraris*, an Italian submarine of the Archimede class, commanded by Tenenti di vascello Filippo Flores, sunk.**

Catalina 'A' AH538, 202 Squadron, on patrol 0400-0035 hrs.

SL N.F. Eagleton   Pilot
and crew

On a creeping line-ahead search in front of convoy HG 75 at 1041 hrs, sighted a submarine on the surface and attacked with two D/Cs which did not explode. The submarine remained on the surface and the aircraft did not drop remaining D/Cs, but continued circling and called up HMS *Lamerton*. Submarine made off at speed on the surface but HMS *Lamerton* gave chase, firing her guns at 6 miles. Closing in, *Lamerton* continued firing and the Italian crew then scuttled their boat and were rescued by the British ship.

The *Ferraris*, which began service in 1934, was officially credited as shared between 202 Squadron and HMS *Lamerton*, whose joint actions resulted in its loss. It had sailed from Bordeaux on 14 October.

Squadron Leader Norman Eagleton later received the DFC.

6 December, 1941

U-322, a type VIIC submarine, commanded by Oberleutnant Eberhard Huttleman, damaged.

Catalina 'B' AH562, 202 Squadron, on patrol 0601-0320 hrs.

F/L H. Garnell   Pilot
and crew

At 1545 hrs Garnell sighted a U-boat 6 miles on the port bow in position 3645/0925. It appeared to be stationary, but crash-dived as soon as the Catalina was seen. When 1½ miles away, the boat had disappeared, but an attack was carried out and three D/Cs were dropped in a stick, 80 feet apart. One failed to explode and the fourth hung up, but the other two exploded 100 yards ahead of the swirl, 45 seconds after the boat had submerged. No wreckage was seen, but an oil patch and bubbles were later seen.

U-332 was on its first patrol, having sailed from Kiel on 30 October, and was making for La Pallice when attacked and damaged. It managed to reach the port on the 16th. On her sixth cruise she was damaged by T/172 Squadron in 1943 and lost on her seventh trip when sunk by M/461 Squadron on 2 May, 1943.

Flight Lieutenant Hugh Garnell later went to 205 Squadron and in early 1942 was with this unit in Western Australia after the war with Japan began. On 3 March he and three of his crew were killed when six Japanese Zero fighters strafed the flying boat base at Broome, destroying a number of the aircraft.

1 May, 1942

U-573, a type VIIC submarine, commanded by Kapitänleutnant Heinrich Heinsohn, damaged and lost to the German navy.

Hudson 'M' AM735, 233 Squadron, on patrol 1159-1745 hrs.

Sgt Brent
Sgt Vernon
and crew

East of Gibraltar, this crew spotted the submarine on the surface in position 3700/0100 at 1456 hrs. Brent attacked from 1700 feet in a dive across the U-boat, dropping 3 x 250 lb D/Cs from 30 feet. The boat was still on the surface with decks awash and two of the D/Cs exploded against the starboard side of the conning tower. The boat submerged and a patch of oil developed, 100 yards in diameter. One minute later, 10 feet of bows appeared perpendicularly out of the water and then slid back. Then the U-boat was seen at a steep angle, bows first, before settling back on an even keel. The crew appeared on deck with hands raised, but the aircraft had to leave at 1520 hrs without being able to exploit the capture.

U-573 had been badly damaged in the attack, which took place north-west of Tenes, off Algeria. After the Hudson left, the crew got the vessel under way and managed to limp into Cartagena, Spain, where she was paid off and subsequently sold to the Spanish Government. She had left St Nazaire for the Mediterranean on 11 December, 1941, entering on the night of 18/19 December.

2 May, 1942

U-74, a type VIIB submarine commanded by Leutnant Karl Friedrich, sunk.

Catalina 'C' AJ162, 202 Squadron, on patrol 0236-2014 hrs.

F/L R.Y. Powell   Pilot
FO Ramsay
and crew

At 1306 hrs, sighted a U-boat 7 miles away on the surface. The Catalina was at 3000 feet and approached for an attack, losing height. The boat began to dive and Powell released 7 x 250 lb Mk 8 D/Cs from 50 feet which fell beyond the swirl, 10 seconds after the boat had gone under. No oil or bubbles were seen although the aircraft remained in the vicinity until 1745 hrs. Two destroyers arrived 90 minutes after the attack and made contact with the sub, which was later sunk.

U-74 was based at La Spezia, having entered the Mediterranean from St Nazaire on the night of 16/17 December, 1941. She had already carried out five patrols before December 1941, and she had sunk six ships. She went down in position 3716/0100, south of Cartagena, shared by 202 Squadron and the destroyers *Wishart* and *Wrestler*.

Flight Lieutenant Powell received the DFC in July, and in August 1944 was awarded a bar. By that date he was a squadron leader and had made attacks on seven submarines.

7 June, 1942

Veniero, an Italian submarine of the Marcello Class, commanded by Tenente di vascello Elio Zappetta, sunk.

Catalina 'M', 202 Squadron, on patrol 0702-1830 hrs.

FO R.M. Corrie, RAAF   Sgt Lowe
PO C.A. Rimmington, RAAF   Sgt Lee
Sgt Lower
and crew

At 1128 hrs began a creeping line-ahead patrol down-sun. Thirteen minutes later an ASV contact was made 16 miles to port. The Cat was at 1500 feet and Corrie turned to investigate and sighted a surfaced U-boat at 1144 hrs. Corrie lost height and made a diving attack from astern, but on nearing the target the bomb racks failed to roll out. The aircraft made a turn, its gunners firing into the boat, and made a second attack, but only the four D/Cs on the port side released, but they exploded on target. The U-boat was firing too and Sergeant Lee was hit above the heart as the aircraft circled to begin a gun duel. Then the boat began to submerge and another attack was made with four D/Cs, which landed slightly ahead of the swirl. At 1156 hrs, an oil patch began to spread on the surface with air bubbles, but then ceased. The aircraft left the scene and landed at Ansiola to get attention for Lee and to inspect other damage. It then flew back to the area, where a considerable oil patch was now in evidence, but nothing else was seen.

The *Veniero* had entered service with the Italian Navy on 6 June, 1938.

Flying Officer Colin Rimmington was killed on 22 August, 1942. Flying Officer Corrie received the DFC.

9 June, 1942

Zaffiro **an Italian submarine of the Sirena Class, commanded by Tenente di vascello Carlo Mottura, sunk.**

Catalina 'J' Z2143, 240 Squadron, on patrol 0100-1850 hrs.

F/L D. Hawkins, DFC Pilot	Sgt Hill
PO Parry	Sgt Aston
Sgt Greenhaugh	Sgt Faulkes
Sgt Beverley	Sgt Robertson
Sgt Dawkins	

Flying in a cloudless sky at 2000 feet, a U-boat was sighted near the Balearic Islands at 1130 hrs on the surface 10 miles away, in position 3821/3021. The Catalina dived to attack, the sub opening fire when at 200 feet, at 1,000 yards range. After taking avoiding action, Hawkins flew over the boat, and 4 x 450 lb TNT D/Cs fell away from 100 feet while the boat was still on the surface. A gun duel then commenced as the aircraft circled, but then the boat dived, leaving much oil on the the surface. Five minutes later it resurfaced, but was clearly settling by the stern. The crew began to appear on deck, some diving overboard while others fell when the aircraft again opened fire. This ceased after a white flag was waved, and then the boat went down, leaving oil and survivors in the sea. Hawkins attempted to make a landing in order to take prisoners and leave life-saving apparatus but the heavy swell prevented this, and the hull of the flying boat was slightly damaged in the attempt. They finally had to leave the scene at

1315 hrs, by which time several of the U-boat's crew were clearly dead in the water.

Flight Lieutenant Hawkins had been with 240 Squadron since September 1941 and had received the DFC for a 'special' flight in April 1942, Aston, Faulkes and Beverley being part of his crew on that occasion. In February 1942 he was acting CO of the squadron.

The *Zaffiro* had entered service with the Italian navy on 4 June, 1934.

14 September, 1942

Alabastro **an Italian submarine of the Accaiao Class, commanded by Tenente di vascello Giovanni Bonadies, sunk.**

Sunderland 'R' W6002, 202 Squadron.

FO E.P. Walshe, RAAF
PO D.C. McLeod
and crew

One hour after sighting a Ju 88, at 1430 hrs, a U-boat was sighted visually on the surface, 5 miles away, off Algiers. Walshe made an approach, but the boat stayed on the surface and opened fire with a heavy gun. The Sunderland made its attack at 1434 hrs with six D/Cs, but one failed to release while another fell with the fusing wire still attached. Four explosions were seen, two against the boat's port bow and two within 5 feet of the conning tower on the starboard side, while the U-boat still fired. The aircraft then circled out of range, but the crew saw the boat lifted slightly and for almost half an hour the Sunderland circled while a front gun was continually trained on it by the sub crew. Then the boat was seen to be down by the bows and about 20 men appeared on deck. At 1507 hrs the U-boat began to submerge with the crew still on the deck. This was thought to be a ruse by the Sunderland crew and they made an approach as if to bomb, but then some of the sub crew were seen to be launching dinghies while others jumped into the water. Later the boat sank bow first with the stern sticking up vertically. Thirty-six men were counted, 20 of them in a dinghy, in position 3728/0435.

The *Alabastro* had only entered service on 9 May, 1942.

Walshe was later awarded the DFC, and also became a flight lieutenant. He was the first RAAF man to achieve, unaided, the sinking of an enemy submarine. He had previously flown with 209 Squadron.

13 November, 1942

U-411, a type VIIC submarine, commanded by Kapitänleutnant Johann Spindlegger, sunk.

Hudson 'D', 500 Squadron, on patrol from Gibraltar 1150 hrs.

SL J.B. Ensor	PO R.F. Mason
PO G.P. Ward	F/Sgt R. Pearce

A U-boat was observed 5 miles off and the aircraft dived and attacked it from stern to bows. Four D/Cs were released from 50 feet which fell across the sub, 150 yards ahead of the diving boat's swirl, 40 seconds after it had gone under. No results were observed.

U-411 had sunk eight ships. After her initial cruise from Kiel in August 1942, she had sailed from St Nazaire on 7 November to patrol west of Gibraltar. She was believed to have been lost on or about 28 November, 1942, but it is now understood to have been lost earlier, to this crew and aircraft, in the area of her patrol, in position 3600/0935.

John Ensor received the DFC for this attack. Strangely, there were two pilots named Ensor on 500 Squadron at this time, John and Mick.

13 November, 1942

U-458, a type VIIC submarine, commanded by Kapitänleutnant Kurt Diggins, damaged.

Hudson 'S', 500 Squadron, on patrol from Tafaraouri 0927 hrs.

FO M.A. Ensor	Pilot
PO N. Atkinson	Nav
Sgt H.J. Roe	WOP/AG
Sgt C. Prior	WOP/AG

Early in the patrol this Hudson crew sighted two Caproni 135 aircraft, but no combat took place. Then at 1402 hrs, a U-boat was sighted and attacked from 30 feet, four D/Cs straddling its bows. One minute later the boat came back to the surface, but was down at the bows. One A/S bomb was then dropped from 500 feet, which fell 20 yards off the sub's starboard bow. The U-boat then began to circle very slowly and opened fire with light machine guns. 'S' also fired back and at least six men were seen to fall into the sea. When PLE was reached, the sub was still circling and aparently sinking. Mick Ensor recorded in his flying log-book: 'Attacked U-boat with four D/Cs just after it submerged. Damaged U-boat surfaced and manned machine-guns on conning tower. We shot them up with our guns until out of ammo, leaving several of gun crew dead and wounded. U-boat last seen down at the bows and making little headway.' This was Ensor's 63rd operational flight.

U-458 was severely damaged in this attack and Kurt Diggins had to limp back to Spezia. Her first cruise had been to the American seaboard between June and August, 1942. She left Brest on 1 October for the Mediterranean, entering on the night of 10/11 October. She was eventually sunk on 22 August, 1943, by a RN and a Greek destroyer, by D/Cs, gunfire and finally by ramming. Mick Ensor was to have a major encounter with a U-boat two days later.

14 November, 1942

U-595, a type VIIC submarine, commanded by Kapitänleutnant Jurgen Quaet-Faslam, sunk.

Hudsons of 608 Squadron, on patrol 0730-1310 hrs.

FO G. Williams	– in a/c 'C'
PO J.J. Kennedy-Finlayson	
Sgt K. Daniels(?)	
F/Sgt H.E. Marshall(?)	
PO C.A. Livingstone	– in a/c 'D'
F/Sgt D. Roxburgh	
F/Sgt J.C. Burns(?)	
F/L E.S. Dawson(?)	

Hudsons of 500 Squadron, from Tafaraouri, Oran, patrols began 0900 hrs.

WC D. Spotswood, DFC	– in a/c 'X'
F/L J.R. Paine, DFM	
PO W.D. Rooney	
PO G.P. Ward	
FL H.G. Holmes	– in a/c 'J'
PO Mackinley	
PO Sutherland	
Sgt Thomas	
FO H.M.S. Green	– in a/c 'F'
F/Sgt R. Wakelin	
Sgt Cobb	
Sgt A.A. Odell	
FO G.A.B. Lord	– in a/c 'K'
FO I.R. Mitchell (NZ)	

F/Sgt K. Elvidge
Sgt Davies

PO J.H. Simpson   – in a/c 'W'
F/Sgt R.N. Bassett
Sgt A.S. Kempster
Sgt Brown

The two 608 Squadron Hudsons operating from Oran found a U-boat and Williams attacked with four D/Cs from 30/50 feet and explosions were seen on either side of the sub, which then appeared to sink on an even keel. A few minutes later the boat resurfaced and Williams engaged it with gunfire until Livingstone attacked with four D/Cs which straddled it. The sub rose out of the water then turned slowly in a tight left-hand circle and was seen to be down by the stern, its bows out of the water. Both aircraft then circled and fired with their side guns. They then climbed and made diving attacks with their front guns, the sub replying with cannon fire. One of the Hudsons was slightly damaged in the wing. At 1031 hrs a Ju 88 dived out of the clouds, and as it passed, the rear gunner of Williams's machine fired a short burst which caused the 88 to make for cloud cover without firing.

Six Hudsons of 500 Squadron, also operating from Oran, flew anti-submarine patrols and located the U-boat attacked by 608 Squadron. Because of the damage, the U-boat was unable to submerge and therefore it became a sitting duck for 500 Squadron. WC Spotswood, the squadron's CO, attacked first, although his aircraft was hit by flak. Green then attacked, but his D/Cs hung up and he too was hit as he flew over. 'K' was also hit in his attack and his D/Cs fell short, while 'F', making a second run, was again hit, but his D/Cs fell ahead of the U-boat. It was now apparent that the U-boat had had enough and was heading for the beach. 'W' made two attacks with D/Cs then an A/S bomb, just as the sub beached itself, flak coming up all the time. Despite the damage to the aircraft, all landed safely, although FO Lord had to come in on one engine. A sixth Hudson did not take part in the attack. Jim Paine records: 'The U-boat was firing away merrily and must have upset the aircraft's aim somewhat. The CO asked, "How do I attack this thing?" and I said, "Aim in front of the conning tower and go across it 30 degrees so as to straddle it." I, meantime, armed myself with an F.4 camera ready to take the U-boat picture of the year – if my hands would keep steady. The gunner manning the U-boat's aft gun was a blond, and his gunnery was very accurate. Streams of tracer came whistling at us and I yelled, "Use your front guns." "Not close enough," said the CO. Just then the rear gunner said, "There's an awful smell of petrol about." I checked the fuel gauges and found one which read zero. We had been hit in a tank! Then there was a clunk and the port undercarriage looked a bit of a mess. We flew damned near up the muzzle of the gun and broke off to see the D/Cs explode near the stern. I got my photograph – it is now framed on my wall.'

U-595 was on its third cruise, sailing from Brest for the Mediterranean on 31 October, entering through the Straits of Gibraltar on the night of 6/7 November. She beached west of Tenes, on the coast of Algeria, and later sank. The crew were taken off by the French. In correspondence after the war, the U-boat's first officer confirmed that it had been 608 Squadron's attack which had caused the major damage, the sub being unable to dive.

Flight Lieutenant Holmes later received the DFC & bar, Pilot Officer Simpson the DFC, Flying Officer Mitchell the DFC and Wing Commander Spotswood the DSO (later Marshal of the RAF, Sir Denis). Flight Lieutenant Paine had won his DFM during the Battle of France, flying with the CO of 139 Blenheim Squadron against the bridges at Maastricht when all but two of the unit's aircraft were shot down by flak and fighters.

14 November, 1942

U-605, a type VIIC submarine, commanded by Kapitänleutnant Herbert Victor Schutze, sunk.

Hudson 'B' FH332, 233 Squadron, on patrol 1120-1820 hrs.

PO J.W. Barling	Pilot
FO H.W. Thomson, RNZAF	Nav
F/Sgt W.G. Staten	WOP/AG
Sgt J.T. Forbes	WOP/AG

At 1620 hrs, sighted a surfaced U-boat in position 3620/0101 and attacked, releasing three D/Cs, all of which scored direct hits on the hull, which lifted from the water, then slid back leaving no swirl. An oil patch appeared immediately and numerous objects were observed on the water.

Hugh Thomson remembers: 'I remember John Barling pointing out this wake some miles ahead of us. It was a beautiful clear day and we could see for miles. Initially I was of the opinion that it must be a MTB or a High Speed Launch as the vessel appeared very small when first sighted. However, John, with the aid of binoculars, soon ascertained that it was in fact a submarine. We had none of our own subs in the area so were free to attack. We were on the last leg of our patrol and about an hour from base. I have yet to understand why the U-boat was caught unawares. In such conditions we should have been sighted miles away. I can only presume that the lookouts were looking westward, towards Gibraltar, into the lowering sun and into the direction from which they would expect an attack.

'A definite identification being made, it was nose down, bomb doors open and D/Cs activated, followed by a low-level attack by John from about 40–50 feet. All credit must go to him for a successful attack – his was the judgement and expertise we all relied upon. I, being down in the navigator's compartment, had a bird's-eye view of the U-boat as we attacked. The conning tower was fully surfaced, but decks were awash as it commenced its dive. Our WOP/AG in the turret had another bird's-eye view as we pulled away and as the D/Cs exploded. We circled for 10–15 minutes, took a few photographs and, as fuel was getting low, headed for home. We could see in the attack area quite a lot of what appeared to be brown wooden slats and there was also quite a patch of oil.

'John Barling and we his crew had quite a few experiences within a month. On 13 October we had a night ditching (in fog) in Gibraltar Bay, but were picked up by a naval vessel. On 8 November we were engaged by a Ju 88 heading towards Gib. The enemy jettisoned its bomb load, as we did, and fled after one attack. On 14 November, the attack as mentioned above.'

U-605's first war cruise had been into the Altantic between July and September 1942, then she had been ordered into the Med, entering on the night of 10/11 October, 1942. She was last heard of on 9 November, 40 miles west of Algiers and was ordered to patrol off Oran. She was then lost and was presumed sunk by a RN corvette, but it is now understood she was sunk by 233 Squadron.

This was John Barling's first success and he received the DFC. It was only after the war that the naval authorities credited U-605 to a Navy corvette, despite the strong evidence of a kill. But Barling and his crew had scored a success and Barling went on to add another U-boat to his tally, flying with 224 Squadron in England. Hugh Thomson returned to New Zealand after his tour with 233, flying with a transport squadron in the Pacific.

15 November, 1942

U-259, a type VIIC submarine, commanded by Kapitänleutnant Klaus Kopke, sunk

Hudson 'S', 500 Squadron, on patrol 0850 hrs.

FO M.A. Ensor, DFC, RNZAF Pilot
PO N. Atkinson   Nav
Sgt H.J. Roe   WOP/AG
Sgt C. Prior   WOP/AG

Mike Ensor recalls: 'We were flying north of Algiers when the crew reported a surfaced U-boat to the north of us some distance away. We were flying under a clear blue sky and over a calm sea. I was fairly confident that we could not be seen by it thanks to our white undersurface and high altitude (7000 feet). I immediately swung the Hudson around and down, whereupon the boat came into my line of vision, fully surfaced and making a great white wake. I dived to sea level, made my approach and pressed the button, but a second later something went badly wrong. There was a great "Woomph" and I instinctively pulled up only to find the control wheel come back uselessly into my lap, and the trim lever too I found useless.

'By now I could see the sparkling blue sea streaking under the nose so I rammed the throttles fully open and with very little aileron control held the wings level. Slowly the Hudson's nose came up and I felt we were starting to climb. I stabilized any stall problem and using the crew as ballast conveyed my idea to them. The side windows had gone so it was very noisy on the flight deck.

'I called Horace in the rear gun position, who told me the sub had blown up, but that the elevators and one rudder had gone while the other rudder was just hanging on. He also had a great hole under his feet. I told him to come forward, watch my hand signals and organize the other two accordingly. At least we were flying, but in the wrong direction – away from land. Looking at the wings I could see about 6 feet of each wing tip was bent upwards, bending the outer portions of each aileron with them. I tried a slow climbing turn to the south, my human elevator working well. The splendid discipline of those men was beyond all praise – their situation must have been terrifying.

'Although we had gained about 3000 feet we were now slowly losing height and as obviously I was not going to be able to land the Hudson in its state, the only way down was by parachute. We all had our 'chutes on by this time, although Cyril Prior's had come partly opened in the explosion, but they thought it would be OK. We were now about 20 miles from the coast and I had my eyes on a naval vessel ahead and to the left. Then the port engine lost power, and having to reduce power to the other to keep us from diving down to the left, it was time to leave. I could not tell the others to abandon, but when they saw me begin to leave my seat, it was enough and out they went.

'The weight was now all in the rear cabin and the Hudson seemed to be nose up and banking to the left, making the escape door face upwards! I helped Neville Atkinson out, but the order of the other two is unclear. I had difficulty in levering myself over the ledge, but then I pulled the ripcord and it worked. Looking down I saw the Hudson crash into the sea with a great splash.'

Mike Ensor and Horace Roe were picked up by HMS *Erne* and HMS *Leath*, but unhappily Neville Atkinson and Cyril Prior were dead. Atkinson's parachute had failed to open and Prior was knocked out when he left the aircraft and was drowned.

U-259 went down in position 3720/0305, north of Algiers, and the Hudson crashed at approx 1250 hrs. The U-boat had entered the Med on 8/9 November, having sailed from La Pallice on the 5th – her second cruise.

Mike Ensor received the DSO and Roe the DFM. Later that month Ensor returned to England, going to HQ Coastal Command. He had joined 500 Squadron in July 1941, and had flown 65 sorties by the time he returned to England.

In August 1943 he went to 224 Squadron and was appointed CO in January 1944, later receiving bars to his DSO and DFC, and sinking U-579 in May 1945 (see 18 Group).

17 November, 1942

U-331, a type VIIC submarine, commanded by Kapitänleutnant Freiherr Hans-Dietrich von Tiesenhausen, sunk.

Hudsons of 500 Squadron from Tafarauri, Oran, on patrol 0800-1445 hrs.

SL I.C. Patterson	– in a/c 'Z' AM714
FO E.A. DeVuyst	
PO Barrell	
F/Sgt Merry	
F/L A.W. Barwood	– in a/c 'L'
Sgt Broomfield	
F/Sgt McKinnon	
F/Sgt McCourt	
Sgt Young	– in a/c 'C'
Sgt McSwiney	
Sgt Austin	
Sgt Stupart	

Patterson first sighted the U-boat on the surface and straddled it with three D/Cs, lifting the bows out of the water, and some crewmen were seen coming from the conning tower. An A/S bomb was then dropped from 600 feet and fell into the sea amongst some of the crew who were in the water. Sergeant Young then attacked and dropped D/Cs and machine-gunned the boat, and more men fell into the sea. Then Barwood attacked and dropped four D/Cs, following which more men jumped overboard. The latter two aircraft then left, leaving Patterson to circle, and a white flag was waved from the sub. He then had to leave and flew back to Maison Blanche, where he informed the Navy of the situation and it was promised that a destroyer would be sent, and a Hurricane took off to fly with Patterson's Hudson as he returned to the sub. They found the crew sitting on deck, awaiting rescue. At 1600 hrs a RN Martlet fighter, escorting a Swordfish and an Albacore, arrived. Despite frantic signals by Patterson and two more Hudsons, the Martlet strafed the boat and then the Albacore dropped its torpedo at the U-boat, completely destroying it. A few survivors were later picked up by a Walrus and Patterson returned to Maison Blanche at 1635 hrs, bitterly disappointed that their prize was lost and fiercely angry at the Navy's cold-blooded action.

U-331 had left Lorient on 24 September, 1941, went through into the Med on 29/30th and entered Salamis on 11 October. On 25 November, 1941, it sunk the battleship HMS *Barham*, which blew up so spectacularly while being filmed as it turned over to sink. U-331 went down in position 3705/0224, north-west of Algiers, shared by 500 Squadron and the Albacore of 820 Squadron FAA from the carrier HMS *Formidable*. A total of 17 survivors, including the CO, were picked up and landed at Gibraltar. Von Tiesenhausen had previously served on U-93 and U-99 before being given command of U-331 in late 1940. He received the Knight's Cross for sinking *Barham*.

Squadron Leader Ian Patterson received the DSO and Flight Lieutenant Andrew Barwood received the DFC.

17 November, 1942

U-566, a type VIIC submarine, commanded by Kapitänleutnant Hans Hornkohl, damaged.

Hudson III 'U' FH240, 233 Squadron, on patrol 0657-1345 hrs.

Sgt E.H. Smith	Pilot
WO T.A.N. Watt	Nav
Sgt D.H. Beniston	WOP/AG
Sgt H. Pike	WOP/AG

Over a rough sea a wake was sighted at 10 miles in position 3540/1118, which on closer inspection was a conning tower and aft portion of the hull of a U-boat. At 2 miles it became obvious that the aircraft had been spotted as the boat began a turn, then it dived. Smith released four D/Cs from 100 feet 11 seconds after the target had gone down, and three explosions seen just ahead of the swirl. Oil and air bubbles came to the surface, which continued for about 5 minutes, and 15 minutes later the patch had spread some 200 yards across. Smith circled for half an hour, but nothing further was seen. Time of attack – 0856 hrs.

The official assessment was that the attack would seem to have caused serious damage – and it had. U-566, on her fifth patrol, beginning from Brest on 28 October, had to put back, arriving home on 1 December. She was damaged again on her seventh patrol and sunk on her ninth, by A/179 Squadron, on 24 October, 1943.

For Sergeant Smith, this was the first of several successful attacks against German U-boats.

18 November, 1942

U-613, a type VIIC submarine, commanded by Korvettenkapitän Helmut Koppe, damaged.

Hudson 'V', 608 Squadron, on patrol 0922-1645 hrs.

FO J.B.R. Petrie	Pilot
Sgt E.J. Shepherd	Nav
and possibly:	
PO W.H. Chapman	WOP/AG and
Sgt C.J. Collins	WOP/AG

This crew sighted a U-boat on the surface at 1517 hrs west of Gibraltar, and dived with front guns firing. One sailor seen to be trying to man cannon aft of the conning tower, then was seen scrambling into the tower hatch. Released D/Cs, turned and machine-gunned the boat. Ten minutes after it had gone down it reappeared suddenly and began steering a circular course to the right, its decks just above the water. The Hudson again attacked with front guns and turret, the U-boat replying with cannon – one shell going through the aircraft's elevator without exploding. The aircraft used all its front gun ammo and later the boat submerged.

U-613 was on its way to La Pallice, having sailed from Kiel on 22 October. It arrived, damaged, on 27 November. This had been its first patrol and it was lost on its fourth – a sortie to lay mines off Jacksonville. It was sunk south of the Azores by US ships and aircraft giving cover to convoy UGS 12 on 27 July, 1943.

19 November, 1942

U-413, a type VIIC submarine, commanded by Oberleutnant Poel, damaged.

Hudson 'C', 608 Squadron, on patrol 0955-1647 hrs.

FO A.F. Wilcox	Pilot
Sgt N.H. McNaught	Nav
and possibly:	
Sgt A.E.F. Swadkin	WOP/AG
Sgt H.P. Russell	WOP/AG

Patrolling at 2200 feet over a moderate sea – visibility 20 miles sighted a U-boat on the surface 9 miles off in position 3538/1148. Wilcox went into cloud at 2500 feet and turned to make his approach. A second sighting through cloud at 4 miles confirmed their position and at 1½ miles he broke cloud and dived to attack. Four Mk XII D/Cs went down, 15–20 seconds after the boat had submerged, straddling the line of advance, 70 yards ahead of the swirl. One minute later, a circular patch of oil came to the surface, which continued until the aircraft left 8 minutes later, when PLE was reached.

The official assessment was not conclusive, although the pilot was praised for an excellent approach and attack. CCHQ noted that it had been a pity there was not sufficient evidence to say what had happened to the U-boat.

U-413 had been extensively damaged and forced to return to base. This was her first war patrol, having left Kiel on 22 October for the west of Gibraltar. She reached Brest on 25 November. She did not sail again until 3 February, 1944, and on that patrol she sank HMS *Warwick*. Her third patrol began on 6 June, but she was then damaged by F/502 Squadron two days later. She was finally sunk by destroyers on 20 August, 1944, on her eighth patrol.

After the war it was assessed that Flying Officer Wilcox had sunk U-98, but it is now known that U-98 was sunk by HMS *Wrestler* on 15 November, 1942 (in position 5021/0001), and that his attack had been upon U-413.

24 November, 1942

U-263, a type VIIC submarine, commanded by Kapitänleutnant Kurt Noelke, damaged.

Hudson 'Q' FH260, 233 Squadron, on patrol 0916-1555 hrs.

Sgt E.H. Smith	Pilot
WO T.A.N. Watt	Nav
Sgt D.H. Beniston	WOP/AG
Sgt H. Pike	WOP/AG

The U-boat was sighted on the surface, 6 miles off, in position 3640/1158. Smith dived head-on, but the boat turned to starboard at the last minute, but four D/Cs were released from 50 feet while the boat was still partly surfaced. The D/Cs appeared to explode all together around the U-boat, and oil and bubbles followed. The oil continued to come to the surface for several minutes. Nothing further seen and aircraft continued its air cover to convoy MK 73.

This was U-263's first patrol, having sailed from Kiel on 27 October. It limped into La Pallice on 29 November. It did not sail again until 19 January, 1944, only to hit an RAF-laid mine the following day and sink outside the harbour.

Smith and the other two sergeants in the crew were all promoted to Flight Sergeant before completing their tour on 9 January, 1943.

10 February, 1943

U-108, a type IXB submarine, commanded by Korvettenkapitän Klaus Scholtz, damaged.

Catalina 'N', 202 Squadron, on patrol 0406-0040 hrs.

SL W.E. Ogle-Skan Pilot	Sgt W. Durkin
PO J.H. Kerr	Sgt L.S. Hibbert

FO F.W. Kilgour	Sgt S. Griffiths
F/Sgt A. Ferris	Sgt G. Envis
Sgt R. Judkins	

At 1015 hrs in position 3234/1608, U-boat sighted on the surface at 10 miles. The U-boat saw the aircraft as it came down to attack and began to dive at 4 miles, but four D/Cs were dropped 90 seconds after it had gone. Two explosions were seen close to the outline of the boat, which was clearly visible below the water. However, nothing further was seen.

Nevertheless, U-108 was damaged in the attack, cutting short its 10th patrol, which had begun from Lorient on 20 January, for the Canaries. It returned on 24 February. In April it returned to Kiel to become a training boat and her captain was given command of the 12th U-boat Flotilla. U-108 had sunk 23 ships. On 11 April, 1944, she was damaged in an American air raid, in Stettin harbour.

Squadron Leader William Ogle-Skan (AFC) later commanded 209 Squadron.

12 February, 1943

U-442, a type VIIC submarine, commanded by Korvettenkapitän Hans Joachim Hesse, sunk.

Hudson 'F', 48 Squadron, on patrol 1134–1734 hrs.

FO G.R. Mayhew	Sgt D.L.M. Matheson
FO D.F. Stewart	Sgt W.L. Sargent

At 1402 hrs sighted a fully surfaced U-boat in position 3732/1156 while flying at 3500 feet. Mayhew dived to attack coming in from dead astern to release D/Cs from 40 feet. The second D/C exploded right alongside the U-boat, level with the conning tower on its port side, while two more exploded in line ahead of the boat. During the attack, the pilot fired his front guns and the rear gunner fired 400 rounds as they flew over. The aircraft then circled and photographed oil and debris 200 yards in diameter before leaving 40 minutes later.

U-442, which had been in action against convoy PQ 14 on its first cruise in September 1942, had then sailed to St Nazaire. This second cruise had begun on 20 December and she was returning from the Azores when sunk west of Cape St Vincent. She had seven ships to her credit.

Geoffrey Richard Mayhew received the DFC.

14 February, 1943

U-620, a type VIIC submarine, commanded by Oberleutnant Heinz Stein, sunk.

U-381, a type VIIC submarine, commanded by Kapitänleutnant Wilhelm Heinrich Graf von Puckler und Limburg, damaged.

Catalina FP223 'J', 202 Squadron, on patrol 0958-0700 hrs.

F/L H.R. Sheardown, RCAF	Pilot
F/Sgt J.E.A. Cox, RNZAF	2nd pilot
F/Sgt J.W. McIntyre, RCAF	Nav
Sgt D.G. Watkins, RAF	Eng
Sgt R.C. Sprague, RAAF	WOP/AG
Sgt J.C. Fletcher, RAAF	WOP/AG
Sgt H. Upson, RAF	Eng
Sgt G.A. Chew, RAAF	WOP/AG
Sgt A.L. King, RAF	WOP/AG

Their first contact at 16 miles at 1420 hrs did not develop and they met up with convoy KMS 9 at 1718 hrs. At 2240 hrs they sighted a surfaced U-boat in position 3911/1107 but it submerged before an attack could be made. Nearly an hour later another boat (or the same one) was seen after making radar contact, and this they attacked. Five D/Cs went down, but they overshot the submerged boat. At 0105 hrs, another boat was found on the surface 3½ miles off in position 3727/1134. An attack was made with the remaining D/Cs while boat was going down, and explosions were seen near its stern. No results observed so aircraft returned to the convoy.

Harry Sheardown remembers: 'We reached the convoy, which was about 180 miles north-west of Cape St Vincent, Portugal. An Aldis message from an escort vessel stated that a U-boat had been sighted to starboard and another 5 miles off the port quarter. Investigation revealed no contacts. I was carrying a passenger on this trip who was a trained ASV/radar operator. At last light we went into our normal left-handed circuit of the convoy, keeping about 5 miles away, and keeping station by radar. While aft of the convoy and at 2000 feet I spotted a fully surfaced U-boat in the moonlight, which we failed to see again or contact when getting into an attack position.

'Within an hour the ASV operator aboard had us homing in on a contact. At ¼ mile I switched on the landing lights of the Catalina, the U-boat became visible, our front gunner opened fire, six D/Cs were dropped, a flame float was thrown out and a high-speed low-level turn was made. The target was again visible, temporarily, in the moonlight during the turn.

'Less than an hour later another contact was made in the dark and we immediately homed in down-moon again. This time the U-boat was not visible, as we had missed contact by flying too far to port. I made a steep turn to starboard, and it became visible, and the lights showed it crash-diving with both props out of the water. The remaining two D/Cs were dropped without visible effect as all was darkness behind the aircraft. We made no further contact and returned to Gib having been in the air 22 hours 20 minutes.'

It was not known at the time, but the first attack, at 2330 hrs in position 3918/1117, had damaged U-381, forcing the boat to return to base. The boat sustained damage to the aft area and lost the use of her port electric motor. This boat was on her second patrol, having left St Nazaire on 19 December for the Azores. She was lost on her third cruise.

The second attack had been upon U-620, on her second cruise, which sank north-west of Cape St Vincent in position 3927/1134. She had left La Pallice on 19 December for the Azores and was hunting around this convoy on her way home. Like U-442, her first patrol from Kiel had been against PQ 14 and she had sunk two ships.

Harry Sheardown, who ended the war as a Squadron Leader, was posted with his crew and squadron to the east coast of Canada shortly after this sortie. He completed two tours of ops, flying both Catalina and Sunderland flying boats. He had earlier been flying Catalina FP114 and in some accounts this aircraft is shown as being that flown against U-620. However, although Harry Sheardown flew this machine on 25 ops, he had taken over FP223 in January 1943. In late 1944 he saw FP223 again at Koggala, Ceylon, when he was flying with 230 Squadron in the Far East. As a boy he had lived just five doors from his friend Frank Fisher, who sank U-341 in September 1943, which must be quite a unique fact.

4 March, 1943

U-83, a type VIIB submarine, commanded by Kapitänleutnant Ulrich Woriszhoffer, sunk.

Hudson 'V', 500 Squadron, on patrol from Blida, 0641-1245 hrs.

PO W.H.E. Slade	Sgt J.C. Joy
SGt V.S. Salmons	Sgt C.W. Sherriffs

This crew were 80 miles off Oran at 1002 hrs, flying at 3500 feet, when at 5 miles they sighted a fully surfaced U-boat in poor visibility. The U-boat began to take avoiding action as the aircraft prepared to attack. Three 100 lb A/S bombs were dropped from 1500 feet, but no results were observed. The boat had fired during the attack, but no hits were scored, and 'V' had replied. Then an attack was made with three D/Cs from 35 feet which exploded around the sub, and white smoke/fumes were seen to come from aft of the conning tower. The boat then began to sink on an even keel and then about 15 men were seen swimming in the water, amid an oil patch. After the boat had gone down, more men were seen, totalling 25. Two K-type dinghies were dropped, but these appeared to sink.

U-83, which had sunk two ships, went down in position 3710/0005. Under a previous CO, she had completed two war cruises in 1941, and then under the command of Worishzofer had sailed for the Med from Brest on 11 December, entering via the Straits on the night of 18/19th.

28 March, 1943

U-77, a type VIIC submarine, commanded by Kapitänleutnant Otto Hartmann, sunk.

Hudson VI 'L', 48 Squadron, on patrol 0757–1405 hrs.

FO J.B. Harrop	PO D.R. Parsons
Sgt J.P. Touhey	Sgt R.G. Heywood

Hudson 'L' T9430 233 Squadron on patrol 1456–2109 hrs.

FO E.F. Castell	FO M.E.S. Bathurst
F/Sgt J. Hare	F/Sgt T.H. Bailey

Flying Officer Harrop first spotted the U-boat at 1125 hrs by its wash at 2 miles, then a conning tower was identified through binoculars. He was flying at 1700 feet and turned to starboard and attacked in a diving turn. Seeing the danger the U-boat began to dive, but the periscope wake was still visible when the D/Cs went down to straddle the track. Oil appeared and then a long streak of oil and bubbles, which rose for several minutes.

Later that day, at 1745 hrs, Castell and his crew intercepted a message to base from another aircraft that they had spotted a damaged U-boat on the surface. Castell flew to the given position and attacked with four D/Cs and in several runs fired off 3000 rounds of ammo, then dropped an A/S bomb,

which fell 15 yards astern of the boat.

Badly damaged, U-77 finally went down in position 3742/0010, east of Cape de Palos, Spain. She had been on her fourth patrol when she entered the Med in December 1941 and had made other patrols since. She had accounted for at least four ships. In January 1942 she had sunk the destroyer *Kimberley* off Tobruk and on 12 June had sunk the destroyer HMS *Grove*.

Flying Officer Edgar Frederick Castell received the DFC.

5 April, 1943

U-167, a type IXC/40 submarine, commanded by Korvettenkapitän Kurt Sturm, sunk.

Hudson 'W' AM931, 233 Squadron, on patrol 0659–131 hrs.

F/Sgt K.R. Dalton	F/Sgt E.R. Fennessy
Sgt J. Eason	Sgt G.M. Suley

Hudson 'L' V9169, 233 Squadron, on patrol 1329–1938 hrs.

F/L W.E. Willets	FO D.D. Lipman
Sgt W. Thomas	Sgt F. Poole

At 0927 hrs, in position 2748/1458, Dalton and his crew sighted a U-boat 3 miles away which opened fire as the aircraft circled. It then began to submerge and the aircraft attacked with four D/Cs from 50 feet while the stern was still visible. Two or three minutes later oil and bubbles came to the surface making several patches.

At 1656 hrs, Willets saw the U-boat in position 2734/1518, 6 miles off. He attacked from astern with four D/Cs from 50 feet while it was still on the surface, and then with one A/S bomb after the boat had gone down. As the aircraft circled an oil streak over 400 yards long and 50 yards wide was seen and air bubbles came to the surface.

U-167, on her second cruise, left St Nazaire on 27 February for the Canary Islands. Attacked by these two Hudsons, she was so badly damaged that it was decided to scuttle her the next day, east of Grand Canary Island, where her crew went ashore with her injured commander.

Both Hudsons were on detachment to Agadir, and William Edward Willets received the DFC. In 1944, Flight Lieutenant Donald Drummond Lipman also received the DFC.

23 April, 1943

U-602, a type VIIC submarine, commanded by Kapitänleutnant Philipp Schuler, sunk.

Hudson 'N', 500 Squadron, on patrol from Tafaraouri.

WO R. Obee	Pilot
Sgt A.F. Blackwell	Nav
F/Sgt K. Weatheritt	WOP/AG
F/Sgt C.R. Carruthers	
F/Sgt A.S. Kempster	WOP/AG

Having already flown twice over the patrol area, an SE contact was made at 2309 hrs, at 12 miles. Homing in and reducing height, a fully surfaced U-boat was spotted as the aircraft was down to 200 feet. Closing in the boat began to fire, its first burst passing over the aircraft's starboard wing, but then a cannon shell exploded in the cockpit. The pilot was hit in the abdomen and his clothing set on fire. The controls were taken over by Alfred Kempster, while Obee was removed from the seat and Sergeant Arthur Blackwell closed the bomb doors after dropping the D/Cs. First aid was attempted, but Ronald Obee was dead. Meantime, the front gunner, Carruthers, had fired at the boat, scoring hits on the conning tower. Blackwell then took over control of the Hudson and flew back to base. Informing those on the ground of their position, and with the Hudson damaged, he ordered the rest of the crew to bale out over base, then set the Hudson on a westerly course and baled out himself. They all landed safely, while the Hudson crashed a few miles further on.

Apparently the D/Cs did their work, for U-602 later sank. Her first patrol had been to the North Atlantic from Kiel between September and November 1942. On 1 December she sailed from Lorient for the Med, entering on the night of the 7/8th. She had sunk the destroyer HMS *Porcupine* on 9 December, 1942.

For his skill and courage, Blackwell received the Conspicuous Gallantry Medal, while Kempster received the DFM.

7 May, 1943

U-447, a type VIIC submarine, commanded by Oberleutnant Friedrich-Wilhelm Bothe, sunk.

Hudson 'X' FH373, 233 Squadron, on patrol from Gib 1555–2210 hrs.

Sgt J.V. Holland	Sgt J.T. Smith
Sgt T. Kilcourse	Sgt J. Simpson

Hudson 'I' T9453 233 Squadron, on patrol 1612–2215 hrs.

Sgt J.W. McQueen	Sgt W. Dewhurst
Sgt J. Hickey	Sgt J.L. Dods

At 1845 hrs in position 3530/1155, both aircraft sighted a surfaced U-boat. 'X' attacked with four D/Cs, three of which fell to starboard and one to port. The U-boat appeared to be lifted by the explosions and an object was thrown into the air.

'I' also attacked with four D/Cs which fell 50–70 yards to the port side of the boat and then both aircraft made three machine-gun attacks while U-boat fired back. Then, however, the boat was seen to settle stern first, resurface slightly, then go down by the stern.

On her first patrol in February 1943, U-447 had been damaged by U/201 Squadron on her way to Brest. On 27 April, she left port to head for the Mediterranean, but was sunk *en route*.

28 May, 1943

U-755, a type VIIC submarine, commanded by Kapitänleutnant Walter Going, sunk.

Hudson 'M' AM725, 608 Squadron, on patrol 1115–1537 hrs.

FO G.A.K. Ogilvie,	FO J.L.J. Tester
FO E.J.C. Hammill	Sgt J.V. Morrow

Flying out from Blida on anti-submarine patrol, they sighted and attacked a U-boat which they found in position 3958/0141. Firing rocket projectiles into it, it sank in 9 minutes, leaving 40 men in the water. This occurred north-east of Valencia and survivors were later rescued by the Spanish Navy.

U-755's first war cruise began from Kiel on 4 August, 1942, to the North Atlantic, reaching Brest on 5 October. On 1 November she was sent to the

Mediterranean, passing through the Straits of Gibraltar on the night of 9/10 November.

4 June, 1943

U-594, a type VIIC submarine, commanded by Kapitänleutnant Friedrich Mumm, sunk.

Hudson 'F', 48 Squadron, on patrol 1055–1725 hrs.

FO H.C. Bailey, DFM	Sgt H. Cover
F/Sgt D.D. Tod	FO S.G. Watson

'F' was flying at 4000 feet when at 1503 hrs a wake was seen and Bailey made his attack from out of the sun. The boat, which began to dive, was in position 3555/0925 when the Hudson was about a mile off. Bailey fired eight No. 1 Mk II rockets. The first four undershot but a later RP entered the water close to the boat's hull about 10 feet aft of the conning tower. Ten to 15 seconds later the U-boat resurfaced, but then lost way and went down on an even keel. A few seconds later a vivid pale blue-green patch appeared, but nothing else was seen.

U-594 had sunk two ships in its career of six patrols. Its first war cruise had been in March 1942, but she had been damaged by 120 Squadron in April 1943 during her fifth cruise. Her final sortie had begun from St Nazaire on 23 May in order to proceed to the Mediterranean, but she was sunk south of Cape St Vincent.

'Ginger' Bailey had previously been with 233 Squadron. He later received the DFC and became a Squadron Leader.

8 July, 1943

U-603, a type VIIC submarine, commanded by Oberleutnant Rudolf Baltz, damaged.

Catalina 'G', 202 Squadron, on patrol 0653–0048 hrs.

F/L G. Powell	F/Sgt M.J. Airlie
Sgt R.A. Holloway	Sgt L. Weisberg
PO R.J. Ward	Sgt J. Allen
PO J.P. Britton	F/L S.A. Warren
Sgt S. Mason	Sgt N. Jackson

This U-boat was sighted at 1728 hrs in position 4205/1340, on the surface. During the approach, the front gunner fired 100 rounds, and the port blister gunner, 70 rounds. The D/Cs straddled the boat, which was still on the surface, and it appeared to be lifted by the bows and disappeared one minute later. Air bubbles and oil came to the surface, but nothing further.

U-603, on its third patrol, was severely damaged. It was on its way back to Brest. having sailed on 5 May for the North Atlantic and the Azores. It was out of commission for some time and finally sunk on its fifth patrol, which began on 5 February, 1944. She sank in position 4855/2610 after the attentions of the US destroyer *Bronstein*, while under the command of KvtLt Hans Bertelsmann, who had previously commanded the boat during 1942-43.

9 July, 1943

U-435, a type VIIC submarine, commanded by Kapitänleutnant Siegfried Strelow, sunk.

Wellington 'R', 179 Squadron, on patrol 1202–2247 hrs.

FO E.J. Fisher	Sgt P.G. Vine
F/Sgt J. Allman	Sgt F. Jenkinson
FO W.F. Barker	Sgt G.T. Greaves

An early contact turned out to be a Portuguese yacht, but then at 1715 hrs a message was received reporting a U-boat in position 3959/1523. The aircraft reached this position half an hour later, but found nothing. At 1811 hrs in position 3948/1422 a wake was seen by the pilot and then a fully surfaced U-boat at 4 miles. Fisher was at 1300 feet and he continued on for 2 miles before diving. Men could be seen in the conning tower, but no fire came from the target despite gunfire from the Wellington's front turret. Four D/Cs went down from 50 feet, which straddled. The U-boat lost way and stopped, then settled by the bows. The stern rose out of the water then, as it too settled, two violent explosions occurred which threw up debris. The boat began to turn over as it went down, leaving frothing water and debris on the water.

U-435 had been part of the Arctic Flotilla until November 1942. It began its third and last Atlantic patrol on 20 May, from Brest, for the Azores and went down south-west of Oporto. She had sunk six ships, including the Fleet minesweeper HMS *Cromer* on 20 September, 1942, and Strelow had received the Knight's Cross.

24 August, 1943

U-134, a type VIIC submarine, commanded by Kapitänleutnant Hans-Gunther Brosin, sunk.

Wellington XIV 'J', 179 Squadron, on patrol 1900–0348 hrs.

FO D.F. McRae (Can)	Pilot
F/Sgt G.V. Cormack	
F/Sgt J. Stead	
FO R.K. Senior (Aust)	WOP/AG
FO R.W. Hegan	
F/Sgt D.E. McKenzie	

At 10 minutes past midnight an SE contact at 5 miles was homed in to. When 1½ miles away the Leigh Light was switched on, which illuminated a stationary U-boat which made no attempt to evade. Switching off the light a turn was made and McRae came in again, the light again picking up the boat, which now opened fire. The Wellington was at 300 feet and reduced height still further to drop six D/Cs, making a straddle across the conning tower. Fire from the U-boat became erratic and then stopped. The aircraft circled, but visibility was poor and no sign of the boat or debris was seen.

U-134 had been with the Arctic Flotilla until early 1942. This fifth patrol had been eventful prior to 24 August. Sailing from La Pallice on 5 June, she had travelled to Florida and the Caribbean. On 19 July she had been sighted by the US Navy Blimp K-74 when north of Cuba, but when attacked the U-boat's fire had shot down the airship. Three days before its fateful meeting with the Wellington, U-134 had been lucky to escape from the escort to convoy UGS 14, consisting of the carrier *Croatan* and the destroyers *Belknap*, *Paul Jones* and *Parrot*. Although McRae and his crew did not see her end, U-134 went down in position 4707/0930 with no survivors. She had sunk two Allied ships, and one German ship – in error!

McRae received the DFC in September and U-134 was only one of his victims.

His Australian WOP/AG, Flying Officer Senior, also received the DFC.

6 September, 1943

U-760, a type VIIC submarine, commanded by Kapitänleutnant Otto Ulrich Blum, damaged, but lost to the German Navy.

Wellington 'C', 179 Squadron, on patrol 1811–0520 hrs.

FO D.F. McRae, DFC	
F/Sgt G.V. Cormack	
F/Sgt J. Stead	
FO R.K. Senior, DFC	WOP/AG
FO R.W. Hegan	
F/Sgt D.E. McKenzie	

They made an SE contact at 2318 hrs in position 4318/0922 at 2 miles, but McRae decided he was too close to make an attack, so made a wide turn, lowered the Leigh Light and lost height to 400 feet. Picking up the contact at 3 miles he homed in and then illuminated a fully surfaced U-boat at ½ mile. With his front gunner firing, six D/Cs went down with a flame float at each end of the stick, from 100 feet, straddling the boat just aft of the conning tower. Turning back, nothing could be seen.

At 0505 hrs the port engine of the Wellington cut and almost immediately afterwards the starboard engine failed. McRae made a forced landing in a field – wheels down, but the ground was very uneven and the sudden appearance of a low road forced McRae the retract the wheels to avoid crashing down on to it. The Wellington was badly damaged. They had come down 70 miles south-west of Raselma and managed to get transport to Raselma airfield, where they were picked up by the squadron CO, WC Greswell, on the 9th.

U-760 was so badly damaged that her captain was forced to put into the Spanish port of Vigo on the 8th, where she was interned. This was her second cruise, having left La Pallice on 24 July for the US coast, but she had been damaged by an American Liberator of 103 Squadron on 12 August and forced to return, only to meet Donald McRae and his crew.

This was McRae's second success.

11 September, 1943

U-617, a type VIIC submarine, commanded by Kapitänleutnant Albrecht Brandi, sunk.

Wellington 'J', 179 Squadron.

PO W.H. Brunini	Pilot
Sgt A. Jones	
FO V.H. Johnson	
Sgt F.M. Crowdis	WOP/AG
F/Sgt H.W. Barnfield	
F/Sgt W. Jones (Aust)	WOP/AG

Wellington 'P' 179 Squadron, on patrol 2039-0445 hrs

SL D.B. Hodgkinson (Can)	Pilot
Sgt J.N. Wilson	
FO A.H. Price	
F/L J. Birnie	
PO E.W. Murphy	WOP/AG
Sgt L. Mitchell	WOP/AG

Squadron Leader Hodgkinson picked up a radar contact at 0050 hrs and lost height and then a silhouette of a U-boat was seen in the moonlight, dead ahead. At ½ mile the Leigh Light went on, and despite heavy flak they dropped six D/Cs, which straddled across the conning tower. Circling some way off they watched as oil appeared and the boat began an erratic course which seemed to indicate it was unable to steer properly. They kept the U-boat in sight and informed base and at 0315 hrs Wellington 'J' arrived. The boat seemed to be making for neutral waters, but 'J' found and illuminated the vessel, attacking with six D/Cs in the face of intense flak, which hit and mortally wounded rear gunner Flight Sergeant Jones. Flames were seen to come from the conning tower and the rear gunner continued to fire, the crew being unaware that he had been wounded. Shortly before 0400 hrs another member of the crew found him dead in his turret. When they left, the U-boat was down by the stern about ½ mile from the Spanish coast, in position 3513/0321.

At 0615 hrs a Hudson – 'W' – of 233 Squadron (FO Henderson) arrived near the scene and saw an explosion and flames at the position of the U-boat. When there was sufficient daylight the U-boat was seen lying on its port side, down by the stern with its conning tower awash, on the coast. Some of the German crew had obviously got ashore, as dinghies were seen pulled up on the beach and later men were seen drying clothes. Later Hudsons of 48 and 233

Squadron attacked the sub with bombs and rockets, while two Swordfish of 833 and 886 FAA Squadrons also scored rocket hits on the wreck. It was finally shelled by the Navy and seen to be on fire.

U-617 made its first patrol in the summer of 1942, then in November she sailed into the Mediterranean and made patrols there. She was badly damaged by air attacks on 11 September, south-west of Alboran Island and beached herself in Spanish Morocco. Her crew got ashore and were rounded up by Spanish troops. U-617 was officially shared between 179 Squadron and HM corvette *Hyacinth*, the trawler *Haarlem* and the Australian minesweeper *Woolongong*. She had sunk five Allied ships, including the destroyer HMS *Puckeridge* on 6 September, 1943, and the minelayer HMS *Welshman* on 1 February, 1943. Freg.Kpt Brandi received the Knight's Cross with Oak Leaves, and later commanded U-380 and U-967. In 1944 he was on the staff at Kiel.

Squadron Leader Hodgkinson received the DFC, and Sergent Mitchell the DFM.

24 September, 1943

U-667, a type VIIC submarine, commanded by Oberleutnant Werner Lange, damaged.

Wellington XIV 'D', 179 Squadron, on patrol 1621–0100 hrs.

FO A. Chiltern	PO K.G. Nichols
PO G.H. Macolmson	PO R.P. Pepperdine
Sgt T. O'Brien	Sgt G.H. Hammond

Wellington 'R', 179 Squadron, on patrol 2239-0400 hrs.

F/Sgt D.J. McMahon	Sgt J. Gregg
F/Sgt N. Atkinson	Sgt M. Crisp
Sgt G.E. Ferrero	Sgt W.J. Thomas

At 2045 hrs, 'D' picked up an ASV contact at 12 miles and lost height and when it had closed to ½ mile the Leigh Light illuminated a fully surfaced U-boat in position 3652/0908. Both the aircraft and the U-boat opened fire, then six D/Cs were falling from 80 feet, but when 'D' turned to fly back nothing could be seen. For U-667, this was just the start of her troubles.

Wellington 'R' picked up the sighting report and later obtained a radar contact. Just minutes past midnight (the 25th), flying through rain, the light was put on at ½ mile, which picked out the sub. Both parties opened fire, but because of the rain no attack was made. The aircraft circled and came in again to drop six D/Cs, which were thought to have overshot, but again the sea was empty when the aircraft returned.

The U-boat may well have been the one attacked earlier on the 24th by Flight Sergeant A.W. Ellis in Wellington P/179 Squadron, and there were more attacks to come.

On the 26th a Wellington of 179 and two Hudsons of 233 and 48 Squadrons found U-667 again, already damaged by the attacks of the previous 24 hours.

Wellington 'X' 179 Squadron.

FO S.H. Nicholson	Pilot
F/Sgt Keenan	
Sgt J. D'Alpuget	
Sgt V. Fournier	WOP/AG
Sgt G. Gibson	
Sgt D.G. Davies	WOP/AG

Hudson 'T' AE505, 233 Squadron, on patrol 0640–1342 hrs.

FO A.G. Frandson	Pilot
FO A.M. Lipman	
Sgt J. Graham (Can)	
Sgt R. Dexter	

Hudson 'N' EW924, 48 Squadron, on patrol 0852–1508 hrs.

FO E.L. Ashbury	FO T. Davidson
FO L. Honderich	F/Sgt H.P. Roode

X/179 and T/233 were flying an ASR search for Squadron Leader Riddell, who had failed to return to base. At 0805 hrs 'X' circled off Cape St Vincent to await 'T', and then F/48 Squadron. ' X' and 'T' made a creeping line-ahead search, but then they saw a ship ahead and thought it was the destroyer known to be in the area. However, it turned out to be a U-boat, and 'X' attacked with six D/Cs from 50 feet, which straddled ahead of the conning tower, despite last-minute fire from the sub. One D/C was thought to have exploded on contact. Circling, the aircraft called up 'T', which came in and attacked the U-boat with rockets at around 1123 hrs. Two pairs went down and then the final four in salvo, some appearing to hit the boat. Return fire hit the Hudson in the tail, severing several strands of the elevator cable. The Hudson then circled and homed in 'N' of 48 Squadron.

'N' had already received the sighting report and was on its way, and just before midday the crew spotted the U-boat – still on the surface – and attacked with eight RPs, also firing two pairs and then a salvo of four, but some over or undershot and it could not be determined if any hits had been made. The Hudson was also hit by flak and had to break off and return to base.

U-667 had left St Nazaire on 18 September, her second patrol, for the Mediterranean. She was extremely lucky not to have been sunk by the combined efforts of five or possibly six aircraft using both D/Cs and rockets over this three-day period. However, she was badly damaged and had to abort her mission and return to St Nazaire, where she arrived in a sorry state on 11 October. On 22 July, 1944, she began her fifth patrol to the north coast of Cornwall, but upon her return she hit an RAF-laid mine and sank off La Pallice on 25 August.

21 October, 1943

U-431, a type VIIC submarine, commanded by Oberleutnant Dietrich Schoneboom, sunk.

Wellington XIV 'Z', 179 Squadron, on patrol 1900–0645 hrs.

Sgt D.M. Cornish (Can)	Sgt L.M. Neale
Sgt F. Clayton	Sgt L.H. Gould
Sgt C.R. Ford	Sgt C.P. Willats

At 0145 hrs, flying at 800 feet, an ASV contact was picked up at 11 miles to port. The aircraft at once turned, losing height, and at just under a mile a wake was seen in the moonlight. At ½ mile the Leigh Light went on, picking out a fully surfaced U-boat. The front gunner fired in reply to the sub's gunfire, and then six D/Cs were going down from 50 feet. The light was switched off, but the sub continued to fire and the rear gunner replied with 300 rounds. As the D/Cs exploded, so the flak ceased, although the aircraft had been hit in wing and fuselage. As the aircraft circled, the boat could be seen stationary between two flame floats. The Wellington turned steeply to port, down-moon, but the boat was not seen again. Returned to the spot 2 hours later, but still nothing could be seen.

U-431 was sunk in position 3720/0043, although 179 Squadron did not know it. After the war, this U-boat was credited to the Navy, as U-431 was deemed to have been sunk on 30 October. This was merely because the boat had not made any radio calls since the 21st, and a sub had been attacked on the 30th, but evidence now shows that the latter attack had been on U-73, which had successfully escaped destruction. U-431 had completed three patrols in 1941 before going into the Med. She had sunk at least one ship.

Sergeant Don Cornish did not know of his success, and had to be content with the knowledge that his attack on U-566 three nights later was a kill, when survivors were picked up. Nevertheless, two kills in three days was good going (see next entry).

24 October, 1943

U-566, a type VIIC submarine, commanded by Kapitänleutnant Hans Hornkohl, sunk.

Wellington 'A' HF132, 179 Squadron, on patrol 2133–0753 hrs.

Sgt D.M. Cornish (Can)	Pilot	Sgt L.M. Neale
Sgt F. Clayton		Sgt L.H. Gould
Sgt C.R. Ford		Sgt C.P. Willats

At 0106 hrs a radar contact was picked up at 6 miles in position 4112/0920 and the aircraft homed in. At one mile the navigator thought he could see bluish lights, so the pilot tracked over the object and on looking down the crew saw it was a U-boat. Turning, Cornish headed back and at ½ mile and from 100 feet the Leigh Light was switched on to bathe the U-boat in light. The boat immediately opened fire, causing slight damage to the Wellington's tail, but six D/Cs went down from 50 feet, falling on either side of the target, the plumes obliterating the vessel. Flak ceased, and coming back to the flame floats the U-boat was seen to be stationary, and remained so until the aircraft had to leave at 0410 hrs. Ten minutes after it flew off the radar contact ceased. The boat later sank and survivors were rescued by the Navy.

U-566 had sunk three ships during its nine war patrols and had already been attacked by 19 Group aircraft twice in the previous year.

Sergeant Cornish received an immediate DFM, was promoted to Warrant Officer and became tour expired in January 1944.

1 November, 1943

U-340, a type VIIC submarine, commanded by Oberleutnant Hans Klaus, sunk.

Wellington 'R', 179 Squadron, on patrol 2059–0506 hrs.

FO A.H. Ellis	Pilot
FO F.E. Knight	2nd pilot
F/Sgt W. Smith	Nav
F/Sgt Smithson	WOP/AG
Sgt O.F. Hyndman	WOP/AG
Sgt P. Pennefather	WOP/AG

Just over an hour into the morning of the 1st, an ASV contact was obtained at 2½ miles, and when passing over the target it was confirmed as a U-boat. The captain flew on and turned, picking up the contact again at 6 miles and homed in from 100 feet to drop six D/Cs across the sub, which was in position 3500/0600. The U-boat remained on the surface for about 45 seconds after the attack, when all contact was lost. The area was swept with the Leigh Light, but nothing was found. The aircraft circled to home in help, but a bad engine vibration developed and the captain had to return to base.

U-340 had been damaged and was later located and hounded by the destroyers *Active* and *Witherington* plus the sloop *Fleetwood*. She had managed to reach the approaches to Gib, having left St Nazaire for the Mediterranean on 2 October, but the damage sustained made it impossible for her to continue. On the 2nd, her captain decided to skuttle and the crew were picked up by a Spanish fishing vessel. However, they were seen on deck by HMS *Fleetwood*, who stopped the Spaniard and transhipped the men into captivity.

Arthur Hubert Ellis was promoted to Warrant Officer and later received the DFC. He and Hyndman, who was also promoted to Warrant Officer, were both part of a crew reported missing on 21 February, 1944.

8 January, 1944

U-343, a type VIIC submarine, commanded by Oberleutnant Wolfgang Rahn, damaged.

Wellington 'R', 179 Squadron, on patrol at 1722 hrs.

FO W.F.M. Davidson	Pilot

FO L.J. Frost   2nd pilot
Sgt C. Parker   Nav
Sgt A.G. Fuller   WOP/AG
Sgt R. Eminsang   WOP/AG
Sgt J.V. Dadson   WOP/AG

Catalina 'J', 202 Squadron, on patrol 1003–0053 hrs.

F/L J. Finch   FO R.K. Bell
FO B.J. Goodhew   F/Sgt V. Sheridan
Sgt E. Wass   PO A.F.H. Barber
F/Sgt A.D.S. Sugden   F/Sgt A.P. Newman
F/Sgt L. Radcliffe

At 2240 hrs, in position 3654/0145, a fully surfaced U-boat was seen by R/179. The moon was full and the Leigh Light was not required as they attacked, guided also by the flak fire. Despite the heavy gunfire, Davidson continued in and released six D/Cs from about 80 feet which fell just to the rear of the boat, but the Wellington was severely hit in the port wing by the U-boat's fire. It caught fire and made control impossible. Despite his efforts the captain was unable to regain control as the Wellington went down to port and crashed into the sea. Davidson was thrown clear, sustaining facial injuries, but the rest of the crew went down with the aeroplane. On finding himself in the water he saw the aircraft's dinghy about 15 yards away, which he boarded. He then saw the U-boat approaching, so feigned unconsciousness. The boat actually rammed the dinghy, but six members of the crew seen on the conning tower presumably assumed he was dead – his face was covered in blood – and headed away to the west.

Meanwhile, Flight Lieutanant Finch had spotted the flak 5-6 miles away and had turned his aircraft and lost height, but then the flak ceased and nothing could be seen. John Finch, flying over a moonlit sea, spotted the U-boat's wake at ½ mile. The boat's gunners opened fire and the Cat's front gunner replied, which eventually silenced the enemy. However, the aircraft had been hit in the port mainplane and fuselage, injuring the engineer in the shoulder with shrapnel. Both petrol tanks were also holed. The aircraft released six D/Cs from 30–40 feet as the boat was turning to starboard. U-boat flak, which had started again, stopped as the D/Cs exploded about the vessel and the starboard blister gunner fired as they flew by. With the aircraft damaged, the pilot had to leave the scene for base.

U-343 was damaged. It had sailed from La Pallice on Boxing Day 1943 and had only entered the Mediterranean on the night of 5/6 January. It was later sunk by the trawler *Mull*, north-west of Bizerta,

on 10 March.

Davidson later received the DFC. John Finch and most of his crew were to have further success the following month.

24 February, 1944

U-761, a type VIIC submarine, commanded by Oberleutnant Horst Geider, sunk.

Catalina 'G', 202 Squadron, on patrol from Gib 0657–1740 hrs.

F/L J. Finch Pilot   FO R.K. Bell
FO B.J. Goodhew   F/Sgt A. Lowe
F/Sgt L. Radcliffe   Sgt E. Wass
F/Sgt A.D.S. Sugden   WO A.W. Martin
F/Sgt A.P. Newman

PBY-5A Catalina, No. '15', VP63, US Navy, on patrol 1158 hrs.

Lt T.R. Woolley   Pilot
Lt E.W. Kellogg   2nd pilot
Ens R.D.J. McCarty   Nav
ARM2/c B.G. Henderson   MAD Op
ARM2/c J.A. Cunningham   Radio
AMM2/c B.F. Martin   Mech
Ens K.C. Peterson
Ens M.B. Cummins   Mech
AMM3/c K.E. Green   Gnr
AOM2/c L.M. Coker

PBY-5A Catalina (08437), No. '14', VP63, US Navy, on patrol 1200 hrs.

Lt H.J. Baker   Pilot
Ens W.F. McSharry   2nd pilot
Lt R.M. Brush   Nav
ARM2/c M. Crider   MAD Op
ARM2/c C.L. Gravel   Radio
AMM2/c F.R. Pearson   Mech
AMM2/c W.N. Franklin   Gnr
AMM1/c E.H. Tanneberg   Gnr
AOMB2/c J.C. Jellison

While on patrol, the RAF Catalina crew intercepted the message at 1615 hrs: 'Have obtained ASV contact, probable U-boat, at 3551/0645.' Nearing this position, they saw D/Cs plumes and then two destroyers. Two US Navy Catalinas from Port Lyautey, French Morocco (Fleet Air Wing Fifteen) and a USN Ventura (No. 46) were also circling nearby. The two US PBYs had picked up contact with the U-boat at 1559 hrs, carrying 24 x Mk VI retro-bombs. At 1712 hrs a U-boat surfaced and the destroyers, turning, commenced firing. One US Catalina then attacked, firing a salvo of retro-bombs on contact, which appeared to overshoot. 'G' attacked from the boat's starboard beam, following the US aircraft, several of the sub's crew being seen in the water behind the boat. At 1717 hrs the submarine blew up. Finding a petrol leak, Finch turned for home. During the attack a Spanish Ju 52 aircraft was seen, flying south past the scene of action.

Lieutenant T. Russell Woolley, captain of PBY No. 15, remembers: '24 February was an action day for two planes of our squadron on station in the Straits of Gibraltar. Lieutenant Baker's crew and mine. We were out of Port Lyautey, under US Fleet Air Wing 15 and VP63. Flying an oval track across the straits and back, my plane observed a magnetic signal of a submerged metal object. We tracked it and on each contact placed a smoke flare on the surface. Both planes marked the track and both bombed what was apparently a Nazi U-boat. In a while the prow of the boat surfaced. Crew members abandoned the craft. Some other explosives were thrown by a land plane and by HMS *Wishart*. A few Germans were killed, but most of them were taken from the water and taken to Gib for interrogation. We took aerial photos to confirm all this, one of my ordnance men dangled outside the plane in the slipstream beneath, taking the pictures, while other men held on to him.' One man almost dangling below the aircraft was Melvin Boyd Cummins: 'At the time I was an enlisted man. My position was the senior aircrewman, and I was the Plane Captain – First Flight Mechanic. (The other services refer to this position as the Flight Engineer.) During the attack I was taking pictures in the aft blister area whilst directing the picture taking. It is also possible to open a hatch in the after section of a PBY and look straight down. Leaning out of the blister I almost fell out of the aircraft, although I did have on a safety belt. I do remember that several other aircraft tried to get in on the kill, also a ship, and tried to claim part of the kill. However, VP63 found and sunk the sub without any problem and did not need any help.'

Lieutenant Howard Jefferson 'Jeff' Baker, noted from the flight log:
'1559 – Planes gained contact on submerged U-boat; tracked with retro flight lights.

1610 – HMS *Anthony* entered pattern, contact lost.
1615 – Set up expanding spiral (2 planes); two British frigates cleared area.
1645 – Contact regained – tracking with lights.
1656 to 1658 – aircraft 15 and 14 attacked with 24

bombs each.
1702 – U-761 surfaced out of control (bow only).
1704 – U-761 submerged out of control.
1707 – HMS *Anthony* and HMS *Wishart* dropped depth charges.
1710 to 1720 – U-761 resurfaced stern down; commenced abandoning ship and set off scuttling charges.
1717 – PV from VB127 arrived from patrol some 20 miles to the west and dropped depth charges.
1718 – British PBY circled scene.
1720 – U-761 sank; 48 survivors inc CO, picked up by frigates and taken to Gib.'

Jeff Baker also recorded: 'We were ordered to remain on patrol until relieved, hence we arrived back at Port Lyautey some time after VB127 and then were on buoys for some time during a rainstorm and boating delay. In the meantime, the 127 crew and "brass" were the guests of the Commodore in his mess and they were claiming full credit for the sub sinking. Only after Russell Woolley (who had earlier been my co-pilot for three years prior to his promotion to command his own crew) and I were debriefed did the full story come out – and as I recall, the 127 chaps were ushered out and replaced by the VP63 skippers and crews. The VB127 crew were awarded DFCs and AMs within two weeks, whereas we waited over a year (3 April 1945) for our awards at Dunkeswell, England.'

U-761, on its second patrol, had left Brest 12 days earlier for the Med but only got as far as the straits, north-east of Tangier. She went down in position 3555/0545, and was shared between two MAD Cats of the 63rd US Navy Squadron, a Ventura of 127 USN Squadron, G/202 and the destroyers *Wishart* and *Anthony*, although doubtless VP63 gained the lion's share. A total of 48 survivors, including the CO, were picked up by the frigates and taken to Gibraltar.

All the officers of the two PBYs eventually received DFCs while the enlisted men received Air Medals. Russell Woolley rose to full Commander. USNR and Boyd Cummins later became a Lieutenant Commander, serving his country in the Korean and Vietnam wars, the latter as a Wing Commander on an aircraft carrier off north Vietnam. Jeff Baker, who had joined the US Navy in 1937, rose to the rank of Captain and received a Gold Star to his DFC as well as the Air Medal. In 1973 he received the Legion of Merit. He also saw service in the Korean war in destroyers and later was Naval Attaché in the Lebanon. He retired from the Navy in 1973. John Finch later became a Group Captain CBE DFC AFC. This was the first of three U-boats sunk in which US Navy Catalina aircraft of VP63, based at

Port Lyautey, French Morocco, were to be involved, while under Coastal Command control.

16 March 1944

U-392, a type VIIC submarine, commanded by Kapitänleutnant Henning Schumann, sunk.

Three PBY-5 Catalinas, of VP63 Squadron, US Navy, on patrol 0730 hrs.

Aircraft No. '8' (08154)

Lt R.C. Spears	Pilot
Lt G.L. Knight	2nd pilot
CAP F.B. Bowen	
Ens J.R. MacDougall	Nav
ARM2/c A.J. Chaisson	MAD Op
ARM2/c C.H. Haupt Jr	Radio
AMM1/c P.F. Ware	Mech
AOM2/c T.A. Comstock	Gnr
ACMM C.E. Stewart	Gnr
AOM2/c H.M. Bolsinger	

Aircraft No. '1'

Lt V.A.T. Lingle	Pilot
Ens E.W. Zinger	2nd pilot
ARM2/c J.V. Mauch	MAD Op
ARM2/c E.J. Willenborg	Radio
AMM3/c A.K. Williamson	Mech
AP1/c W.W. Heath	Gnr
AMM2/c W H Murren	Gnr
AP1/c R.H. Whalen	Gnr
AOM3/c W.W. Taylor	
AMM2/c D.I. Mayhew	

Aircraft No. '7'

Lt M.J. Vopacek	Pilot
Lt W.S. Andrus	2nd pilot
ACM1/c J.P. Chiapulis	
Ens H.O. Gillespie	Nav
ARM3/c P.A. Bonanne	MAD Op
ACRM L.P. Harris	Radio
AMM3/c M.F. Socha	Mech
Lt M.J. Firey	
AMM2/c W.R. Berge	Gnr
ACMM E.F. Clausen	

All three patrolling PBYs picked up MAD contact, but Plane '8' made the first one, at 0753 hrs. The aircraft was patrolling in the Straits of Gibraltar, the other two further west. With the presence of a submerged U-boat confirmed, the first PBY called the other two, who then made contact. Then MAD contact was lost, but a French submarine and a French sloop approached from the west and this probably caused the U-boat to take evasive action. A further search was commenced and at 0935 hrs contact was regained by Plane '8' in position 3554/0542. At 0942 hrs Plane '8' fired its 24 contact retro-bombs followed by Plane '1', while the British destroyer *Vanoc* stood by. Lieutenant Spears then asked the destroyer to attack on their strong MAD contact, which it did, firing a hedgehog pattern at 1028 hrs. Contact was again lost, but a thin trail of oil was seen. Plane '7' then made contact, but then lost it. All three PBYs then commenced a trapping circle as three British frigates arrived, which began a search pattern. The U-boat was located on sonar by the ships and an attack made at 1212 hrs. Plane '7' thought it saw part of a U-boat's hull after the attack but later the *Affleck* launched a boat and this collected debris which was identified as German. The aircraft continued to search, but no further contact could be found.

Ralph Spears remembers: 'I picked up the sub with the MAD gear at 0755 hrs that morning and started a clover leaf pattern, dropping float lights on every contact. I had about seven lights burning on the water in a straight line, maybe a little curve to the left. Anyway, I lost contact and immediately went into a spiral pattern and picked up the sub after about three spirals. I tracked him for about 10 more float lights. I had a nice straight line, so I made a bombing run. My plane carried 24 retro-bombs. They all left the plane on the 8-8-8 pattern. One hung up on the last 8 and I carried it back to base. Then I notified Lieutenant Lingle to make his bombing run. All of his bombs left his aircraft.

'A ship was on the scene – HMS *Vanoc* – and I told them that we had a contact and requested them to keep clear so that it would not interfere with the MAD, which he did. Shortly after our two attacks, Lieutenant Vopacek arrived on the scene, but could not make radio contact, so requested *Vanoc* to follow up the attack. I continued to track the sub after our bomb runs, but the signals got weaker and weaker on the MAD gear. In fact, on my last pass I dropped a float light to indicate to the ship the location of the sub. I never doubted the sub was sinking.

'The next day it was reported to me at base that the ship said after each bomb drop, my plane and Lingle's, that they heard three and two distinct explosions some 8 seconds after the bombs hit the water and heard loud explosions some 30 seconds later. This confirmed that Lingle and I had gotten three and two hits apiece and the loud explosions were the rest of the bombs striking the bottom – as the retro bombs had contact fuses.'

Also aboard Ralph's PBY was his dog 'Sniffer' –

perhaps the only dog ever to be present in an aircraft during the sinking of a U-boat in WW2. 'Sniffer' in fact flew on several flights and operational patrols during 1943-45. On his return from this 16 March flight, he received an ice cream cone and a chocolate Hersey bar for helping to 'sniff' out the U-boat!

Van Lingle relates: 'Two aircraft were scheduled to take off from Port Lyautey (now Kinitra) during the late afternoon of the 15th for Gibraltar, in order to arrive on station in the straits early on 16th March. I assume our CO, Commander Hutchings, had intelligence that a sub could possibly attempt a transit on this date and therefore wanted us on early patrol.

'On the morning of the 16th, our two PBYs took off from Gib at approx 0800 hrs and were on patrol 10 minutes later, flying an oval-shaped barrier across the Straits at an altitude of 100 feet. I do not recall which aircraft received the first signal from its magnetometer at approx 0850 hrs, indicating that the aircraft had flown through the magnetic anomaly created by a submerged submarine. In any event, both aircraft immediately began tracking the sub by dropping a smoke light each time we alternately passed along and across its course. When the sub's course was established accurately by at least 15 smoke lights, sonobuoys were dropped in the water prior to the bombing.

'On my bombing run all 30 bombs were fired in a pattern of three sticks with 10 bombs in each stick. The intervolometer spaced each stick 100 feet apart with about 13 feet between each bomb. The crew member monitoring the sonobuoy receiver heard three distinct explosions 10 seconds after the bombs entered the water, indicating that they had struck a hard object 220 feet below the surface. The water was approx 1800 feet at this location.

'We continued tracking the submarine after the attack and noted that it was altering course to the south, towards the African coast. At this stage, British destroyers were called in to finish the job. Later it was learned that oil and bubbles came to the surface along with pieces of wood, identified as locker tops. Lieutenant Vopacek and crew were on the scene for the purpose of setting up a second barrier east of our regular barrier in case the sub slipped through undetected.'

U-392 was on its second patrol, leaving Brest on 29 February bound for the Med. It was caught in the Straits of Gibralter north-east of Tangier by three MAD Catalina aircraft of VP63 and HM frigate *Affleck* (K462) and the destroyer HMS *Vanoc* (H33). She sank in position 3555/0541. The attack had been carefully planned following the sighting of a periscope two days earlier by Aircraft No. 91 of US Bombing Squadron VPB112 (Lt D. Hill). On the

15th a Leigh Light Wellington from Gib also obtained an ASV contact on the same U-boat. Thus the PBY squadron were waiting for the U-boat to enter the straits and were fully ready for it, supported by the Royal Navy.

Ralph Spears had been an Ensign in December 1941, stationed at Kaneohe, Hawaii, with VP14, and was actually in the air when the Japanese attacked Pearl Harbor. The following year he became a founder member of VP63. He received two DFCs for his war service and retired from the US Navy as a Commander in 1962. 'Sniffer' retired from the Navy in 1945 and died ten years later.

Van Lingle received the DFC and later a Gold Star in lieu of a second DFC. He retired from the US Navy as a Commander in 1963 after 22 years of active duty.

15 May, 1944

U-731, a type VIIC submarine, commanded by Oberleutnant Alexander Graf Keller, sunk.

PBY-5 (08437), No. 14, VP63 Squadron.

Lt M.J. Vopacek   Pilot
and probably the same crew as on 16 March.

PBY-5, No. 1, VP63, US Navy

Lt H.L. Worrell Pilot	Lt J.S. Elliott
Ens J.C. Logue	ACRM W.T. Ramsey
ARM H.N. Beam	AMM B.F. Pfannsteil
AMM D.W. Rusbuldt	AMM P.J. Turner
AOM J.A. Willey	

At 0320 hrs a magnetic contact was made by Lieutenant Vopacek when flying at 130 feet and a clover leaf tracking pattern was flown while surface vessels were called up. The contact was attacked by both aircraft with their retro bombs at 1530 and 1552 hrs. Some pieces of wood were seen on the sea and the sonobuoy picked up undersea noises. With the contact still held, HMS *Kilmarnock* was then homed into the position of the sub and she fired a pattern of hedgehogs at the spot marked by the PBYs. Oil and bubbles were later seen by the warship.

U-731 was on its fourth war cruise, travelling from Lorient, which it had left on 18 April, for the Mediterranean. It was attacked and sunk in the straits, in position 3554/0545, north-west of Tangier, by two MAD Catalinas and HM anti-sub vessel *Kilmarnock* and the trawler *Blackfly*. On its second patrol in the autumn of 1943 it had been damaged by S/269 Squadron and again by aircraft from a US escort carrier.

On board one of the PBYs was a non-flying Personnel Officer, Lieutenant M.J. Firey, who had repeatedly asked to be allowed to fly on a patrol, having stated that if he was, a submarine would be caught!

On 20 May, 1944, the German High Command issued orders that no further U-boats were to be sent into the Med due to the number of losses sustained while passing through the straits.

Azores – 247 Group

9 November, 1943

U-707, a type VIIC submarine, commanded by Oberleutnant Günther Gretschel, sunk.

Fortress 'J' FL459, 220 Squadron, on patrol 0500–1653 hrs.

F/L R.P. Drummond	Pilot
FO R.D. Thompson (Can)	2nd pilot
FL G.A. Grundy	Nav
PO J.B. Brodie	Mid-upper
F/Sgt F.L. Fitzgibbon	WOP/AG
F/Sgt J. Fitzpatrick	Eng
Sgt L.S.G. Parker	ASV Op
Sgt F.D. Galloway	Rear Gunner

En route to convoy MKS 29A, and when 40 miles from it, at 0725 hrs, Flight Sergeant Fitzpatrick sighted a surfaced U-boat from his front lookout position. It was still almost dark and the boat was right below them before it was spotted, in position 4031/2017. The sub immediately opened fire which was heavy and accurate, and the tail gunner fired back as they flew past. The Fortress circled as the mid-upper gunner also fired. Coming in low, four D/Cs were dropped from 40 feet, after which the boat was seen to be down by the stern and stopped. The bows came clear of the water with a list to port. A second attack sent three more D/Cs down from 30 feet and several of the crew saw a mild glow underwater, amidships, as if from an underwater explosion. Then the boat went down stern first.

Some of the RAF men thought they saw a dozen or so men in the water; a large oil patch and wreckage were certainly seen. Half an hour later in better light a man was seen swimming amongst the wreckage and a 'K'-type dinghy was dropped to him, which he was seen to climb into. A parachute pack with rations was also dropped. Nearly two hours later the aircraft reported to the convoy and received a 'Well done' from the SNO.

U-707 was making its third patrol. It had left St Nazaire on 2 October for the Azores and had sunk two ships. Oblt Gretschel had previously been an officer aboard U-93.

Flight Lieutenant Roderick Patrick Drummond received an immediate DFC.

19 November, 1943

U-211, a type VIIC submarine, commanded by Kapitänleutnant Karl Hause, sunk.

Wellington XIV 'F', 179 Squadron, on patrol 2243–0925 hrs.

FO D.M. McRae, DFC (Can)	
FO R.K. Senior, DFC	WOP/AG
PO S. Brookes	
FO R.W. Hegan	
F/Sgt J. Stead	
F/Sgt D.E. McKenzie (NZ)	WOP/AG

At 0202 hrs a convoy, assumed to be SL 139 and MKS 30, was sighted 5 miles to starboard but it was too dark to check. Flew a creeping line-ahead search, with 15 miles between each track. At 0340 hrs an ASV contact was made 3 miles to port and the aircraft turned to investigate. In the moonlight a U-boat was seen and an attack was made without the Leigh Light, hoping to take the German by surprise. Four D/Cs were released, two falling either side of the boat. Flak came from the sub and a very brief burst was fired by the front gunner. As they flew over the rear gunner saw two bright blue flashes amidships. Nothing further was seen of the boat.

However, U-211 had been sunk in position 4015/1918, south-west of Cape Finisterre. She was on her fifth patrol, having sailed from Brest on 14 October for the Azores. She had been converted into a flak boat, but this had not helped her on this night. She had previously been damaged in February, 1943 by a USAAF aircraft. During her war patrols she had sunk three ships, including the destroyer HMS *Firedrake* on 16 December, 1942.

This was McRae's third success, although he

didn't know it then. He had already sunk U-134 in August and forced U-760 to be interned in Portugal in September, while flying from Gibraltar.

28 November, 1943

U-542, a type IXC/40 submarine, commanded by Oberleutnant Christian Brandt Coester, sunk.

Wellington XIV 'L' HF168,★ 179 Squadron, on patrol 1952–0657 hrs.

SL R.G. Knott	Pilot
FO E.C. Allison	2nd pilot
FO C.S. Downes (Aust)	Nav
Sgt G. Greene	WOP/AG
Sgt W.D. Moon	WOP/AG
F/Sgt E.E. Hughes (Aust)	WOP/AG

Flying in support of convoys SL 140 and MKS 31, which had been reached at 2345 hrs, an ASV contact was made at 0100 hrs, 4 miles to port. The aircraft descended to 400 feet, homed in and the crew sighted the wake of a U-boat, but too late to attack. Flying on, Squadron Leader Knott regained contact at 4 miles and returned, switching on the Leigh Light at ½ mile when down to 300 feet. A fully surfaced U-boat was illuminated, but as he felt he was at 600 feet (they had no radio altimeter) he again flew on and returned, rapidly losing height and the light again found the boat which this time had six D/Cs released across it. One of these was believed to have exploded on contact. While this had been happening, the boat and the front gunner had been exchanging fire. After the attack the boat seemed to be stationary and the gunfire ceased. The Wellington was now approaching PLE and Knott had to break off. He informed the SNO of the boat's position, and when they left it was still sitting on the surface, in position 3904/1625. Ronnie Knott knew nothing of U-542's fate and relates: 'Your letter came as a complete surprise. None of the information about the U-boat was within my knowledge. This might be explained by the fact that I left the RAF immediately post-war, rejoining only in 1949.

'Ted Allison was the second pilot, Clive Downes the navigator. The WOP/AGs took turns at radar/radio/rear turret, but Hughes was certainly on the radar, as he was for two subsequent attacks on U-boats. He had a real flair for it. We were on distant escort for the convoy and had no subsequent information from it. Just possibly this was because we had been on detachment in the Azores and information was not passed back to Gibraltar (where we were diverted on this night); but a successful attack was generally red-hot news and it seems strange. The attack was assessed as "Probably severely damaged, may have sunk." by the joint RN/RAF assessment authority at Northwood. I personally thought that optimistic on the very scanty information we had – just the circumstances and technique of attack with Leigh Light, an ill-seen target, a flash – usual as depth-charges exploded – and that's all.'

Nevertheless, U-542 went down in that position. thus failing to return from its first war patrol, which began from Kiel on 2 October.

Ronald Knott later became an Air Vice Marshal, CB, DSO, DFC, AFC.

★ a 172 Squadron aircraft, flown with a 179 Squadron crew.

6 January, 1944

U-270, a type VIIC submarine, commanded by Oberleutnant Heinrich Schreiber, damaged.

Fortress 'U' FA705, 206 Squadron, on patrol 1447 hrs.

F/L A.J. Pinhorn, DFC	Pilot
FO J.H. Duncan	2nd pilot
F/Sgt T. Eckersley	Nav
FO F.D. Roberts	
WO R.N. Stares	
WO D.L. Heard, RCAF	
WO O.A. Keddy, RCAF	
Sgt R. Fabian	WOP/AG
F/L R. Brown	Passenger (Sqn Navigation Officer)

A sighting report was received from this crew at 1812 hrs and 6 minutes later the position 4353/2332 was received. After that – silence. They failed to return.

U-270, on her fourth patrol, had encountered the Fortress, which her gunners had shot down as it attacked. However, the boat received damage in the encounter and was forced to return to St Nazaire, from where she had sailed on 8 December. She was sunk on a passage trip by 461 RAAF Squadron (see 19 Group) on 12 August, 1944.

Flight Lieutenant Pinhorn and his crew were lost, and Pinhorn's DFC had been announced the day before his last sortie.

13 January, 1944

U-231, a type VIIC submarine commanded by Kapitänleutnant Wolfgang Wenzel, sunk.

Wellington 'L' HF168, 172 Squadron, on patrol 1822–0156 hrs.

PO W.N. Armstrong (Can)	Pilot
FO R.D. Haryett (Can)	
PO N. Ellis (Can)	
FO B.W. Heard	WOP/AG
WO Corbett	
F/Sgt R.R. Kersey (NZ)	

On escort to the 6th Escort Group, commenced a creeping line-ahead patrol at 2225 hrs. Half an hour later, in position 4415/2038, they found a fully surfaced U-boat and attacked despite flak from the sub. They dropped three D/Cs, but the rear gunner, Flying Officer Heard, was badly wounded in the leg and his turret was put out of action. The Wellington made other runs, but then had to return to base to get help for the wounded crewman.

This had been U-231's third patrol, which had begun on 26 December. On her second patrol in late 1943, she had rescued survivors from U-964, sunk by 86 Squadron. They had been attacked and damaged by Fleet Air Arm aircraft on 12 May, 1943, during the first cruise from Kiel to La Pallice. After Armstrong's attack, the CO gave orders to abandon ship and the crew were rescued by US warships some hours later. Under interrogation, the crew said they had been at sea for a total of 121 days and had only fired one torpedo, which had missed! After he gave the order to abandon, Wenzel had attempted suicide by shooting himself in the mouth, but was unsuccessful and the bullet lodged harmlessly in the back of the neck.

Pilot Officer Armstrong was awarded an immediate DFC, and so too was Flying Officer Beard, who had to have his badly injured leg amputated. Their Wellington had been that same one used in the sinking of U-542 in November 1943.

13 March, 1944

U-575, a type VIIC submarine, commanded by Oberleutnant Wolfgang Boehmer, sunk.

Wellington XIV 'B' HF183, 172 Squadron, on patrol 2216–0838 hrs.

FO J.P. Finnessey	Pilot

F/Sgt J.A. Secord	2nd pilot
F/Sgt G.M. Smith	
FO J.H. Hart	
Sgt W.E. Burrows	
Sgt J. King	

Fortress 'R' FA700, 206 Squadron, on patrol 0327–1653 hrs.

F/L A.D. Beaty	Pilot
F/Sgt J.J.V. Glazebrook	2nd pilot
F/Sgt J.L. Johnston	Nav
Sgt L. Meaker, RAAF	WOP/AG
Sgt N.S. Draper	WOP/AG
Sgt J. Cunningham	Eng
Sgt F.R. McManus	WOM/AG(MU)
Sgt P. Laird	WOP/AG

Fortress 'J', 220 Squadron, on patrol 0816–2017 hrs.

FO W.R. Travell	Pilot
F/Sgt E.A. Eadon	2nd pilot
F/L D.O. Andrews	Nav
Sgt B.J.P. Robinson	F/Gnr
F/Sgt R.D. Glass (NZ)	WOP/AG
WO W.A. Ellis	Rear Gnr
WO W.W. Bittle (Can)	M/Upper
F/Sgt F.D. Galloway	AG

Finnessey and his crew picked up a radar contact and in position 4613/2728 found and attacked a surfaced U-boat with D/Cs, at 0151 hrs. The attack left the boat still on the surface, so the aircraft commenced homing. They remained in the area until 0330 hrs, when the contact disappeared, so dropped marine markers.

Then a 206 Squadron Fortress arrived at the scene, spotting the markers, but cloud covered the moon and visual sighting was difficult. They remained in the area until dawn, when they saw a U-boat surfacing 2 miles north of the markers in position 4620/2720. This was 75 miles from convoy ON 227. As the aircraft got off a sighting report the U-boat opened fire, and as obviously the boat was going to remain on the surface, Beaty circled out of range. David Beaty remembers: 'We couldn't get through on our W/T so I was faced with the dilemma, do I attack without reporting my position or do I wait till I do get through before going in? The suspense of risking U-575 diving was too much, so in the end we did attack. Our mid-upper and front gunner fired as we went in. The flak was heavy, but we weren't hit. I made a diving turn to port, attacking 30 degrees to port of line astern. The oil slick was considerable afterwards, on the near calm sea.'

Jim Glazebrook, the second pilot, also recalls:

'Our crew was called immediately on receipt of the Wellington's signal, and briefed for a sortie timed to reach the area about dawn. An important factor was the accuracy of the navigation. It was all dead reckoning in those days. We regularly flew 12½-hour patrols in the middle of the Atlantic – and had to find our way back to an island 10 miles long, with no alternative airfield within 1000 miles!

'We had been flying for about three hours and the navigator was in the act of saying "I think we should be about there now, Skipper," when I saw the Wellington's flame floats. It was not quite light and David had turned the controls over to me, to circle, while he crawled forward to the nose to work out a search pattern with the navigator. It was getting light and there were great patches of water that were absolutely glass-like – as still as an inland pond. I actually had my eye on one patch, and was marvelling at such a sight in the middle of the ocean when, right in the spot I was gazing at, the bow of the U-boat broke surface! I sounded the alarm bell and commenced a steep diving turn, while David scrambled back to his seat, but we were too high and too close to get into an attacking position before the U-boat was fully surfaced and manning her guns. Having lost the element of surprise, David decided we should try to get a signal to base before we attacked, but we were too far and too low to make contact, and we dared not climb for fear the U-boat would dive.

'Eventually David asked if we were game to have a go without the security of radio contact and we all agreed. So we dived to the attacking height of 50 feet, but David corkscrewed on the approach to put off the gunners, and our navigator got on to the nose gun, using it effectively, and our mid-upper also fired. The four D/Cs, slung externally (which was all we could carry on the Fortress so our range could be increased), fell one on one side of the U-boat and three on the other. After the explosions the submarine appeared stationary on the surface and then submerged stern first, with the bows at a steep angle, with two large oil patches beginning to spread on the surface.

'We then climbed, radioed our position, and circled for 5 hours, homing in Fortress J/220 Squadron and the Naval Task Group 21.11. We later saw one Avenger aircraft, which made off again after having a look at us.'

The pilot of J/220 was Wilfred 'Pip' Travell, who recollects: 'The previous day our CO had asked me if I would go up and try out a new American low-level gyroscopic bomb sight. Andy Andrews, our Bombing Leader, came along, and we found it very good under practice conditions. Next morning, the 13th, I was called out in a hurry to render assistance

to a convoy which was threatened by a U-boat which had been attacked by a Wellington in the night. The new bomb sight was hurriedly transferred to FL459, and Andy again came along. Upon arrival at the estimated position of the U-boat we had to make a search until we found an oil slick from the boat, which had obviously been damaged in the previous attacks by B/172 and R/206.

'The oil slick formed an arrowhead, which to us indicated that the U-boat was moving slowly under water, so to verify this a smoke float was dropped at the point of the arrow and as the arrowhead continued beyond this point we knew that it was moving slowly under water. It was decided that as we were going to use the new bomb sight we would drop only two D/Cs out of the four we carried under the wings of the Fortress, in case the sight went wrong. We attacked forward of the arrowhead at an angle of 30° degrees to the sub's heading, but about 5 seconds before we dropped, Andy shouted that the gyro had toppled and for me to drop visually. This I did and the D/Cs entered the water one on each side of the arrowhead. Photos later showed the aim was pretty accurate.

'After this attack, more oil came to the surface and formed a "roundel", and after observing for several minutes, we noticed that no other arrowhead had formed so that we had done more damage to the fuel tanks and stopped forward movement of the U-boat. The circle of oil increased quite considerably as time went on and whilst circling we received a radio message from base that a frigate and a destroyer were on course and would I home them in. They later appeared and I dropped smoke floats to mark the exact spot. We were about to watch things, but one of the ships signalled to us to leave as we were interfering with their Asdic signals, so reluctantly we left.'

HMCS *Prince Rupert*, the US destroyers *Haverfield* and *Hobson* continued the action and were able later to confirm the sinking and the rescue of survivors, including the captain. The U-boat had been forced to the surface where she was shelled by the ships and also attacked by three aircraft from the US escort carrier *Brogue*. It was officially credited to the three RAF aircraft, aircraft of VC95 USN, the two US destroyers and the Canadian frigate.

U-575 was on her 10th patrol, sailing from St Nazaire on 29 February, fitted with schnorkel. She had 11 ships to her credit, including the Corvette HMS *Asphodel*.

Flying Officer Pip Travell was awarded the DFC in October 1944 and promoted to Flight Lieutenant. David Beaty later became a well known author and novelist. He received the DFC, to which he added a bar before the end of the war. Jim Glazebrook was commissioned and also received the DFC, while John Patrick Finnessey, who had first located the U-boat, was also awarded the DFC. For Sergeant Galloway, this was his second sinking, having been with Roddy Drummond on 9 November when U-707 was sunk.

As for the Fortress, J-Johnny – FL459 – this was her fourth success, having been the aircraft involved in the sinking of U-624 (7 Feb. 43), U-633 (7 Mar. 43), U-707 (9 Nov. 43) and now U-575.

26 September, 1944

U-871, a type IXD/42 supply submarine, commanded by Kapitänleutnant Erwin Ganzer, sunk.

Fortress 'P' FK191, 220 Squadron, on patrol 1103–2023 hrs.

F/L A.F. Wallace	Captain
FO E.C.W. Fields	Pilot
FO A. Paruk (Can)	2nd pilot
PO R.W. Knight (Can)	Nav
F/Sgt N.V. Ryan (Aust)	Front Gnr
Sgt D.D. Fraser (Can)	M/Upper
Sgt R.J. Carter	WOP/AG
Sgt F. Brunt	Rear Gnr
Sgt G.E. Squire	WOP/AG

Flying escort cover to convoy CU 40, north-west of the Azores. At 1300 hrs flew over the *Irish Rose*, which had apparently broken down, and base was informed. An hour later a flash report was intercepted from H/220 Squadron (F/L M.L.H. Carter) of a U-boat sighting in position 4255/3605. Arrived at this position at 1453 hrs and circled a marker with aircraft 'H' and also aircraft 'F' of 220 (F/L A.R. Chisholm). At 1535 hrs ordered to drop a smoke float with 6-hour delay and at 1544 hrs Flying Officer Paruk sighted visually a periscope wake in position 4318/3629. The Fortress attacked with three D/Cs from 50 feet, straddling the conning tower, which was just breaking the surface. After the explosions, oil began forming a patch, which 50 minutes later covered an area 700 x 1600 yards, followed by debris and bodies.

U-871, a supply transporter boat, was on its maiden cruise, having sailed from Trondheim on 31 August, bound for the Indian Ocean, and equipped with schnorkel.

Flight Lieutenant Arthur Francis Wallace later received the DFC and left the squadron in November 1944. He was the Squadron Navigation Leader and while not the pilot was the 'captain' of the crew.

Index of U-boats

	Day	Mo	Yr	Code
Alabastro	14	09	42	GIB
Enrico Tazzoli	16	05	43	19G
Ferraris	25	10	41	GIB
Luigi Torelli	04	06	42	19G
Luigi Torelli	07	06	42	19G
Marcello	06	01	41	15G
Reginaldo Guiliano	01	09	42	19G
Reginaldo Guiliano	02	09	42	19G
Veniero	07	06	42	GIB
Zaffiro	09	06	42	GIB
U26	01	07	40	15G
U46	25	10	40	18G
U51	16	08	40	15G
U55	30	01	40	15G
U66	10	11	42	19G
U68	14	06	43	19G
U71	05	05	42	19G
U74	02	05	42	GIB
U77	28	03	43	GIB
U81	04	03	43	GIB
U89	16	08	42	15G
U89	05	11	42	ICE
U93	10	02	41	15G
U105	11	06	42	19G
U106	27	07	42	19G
U106	02	08	43	19G
U107	18	08	44	19G
U108	10	02	43	GIB
U109	04	05	43	15G
U123	07	11	43	19G
U126	03	07	43	19G
U129	01	04	42	19G
U132	05	11	42	ICE
U134	24	08	43	GIB
U135	08	02	43	ICE
U155	14	06	43	19G
U155	23	06	44	19G
U159	12	07	42	19G
U167	05	04	43	GIB
U169	27	03	34	15G
U189	23	04	43	ICE
U193	28	04	44	19G
U194	24	06	43	ICE
U200	24	06	43	ICE
U206	30	11	41	19G
U211	20	02	43	19G
U211	19	11	43	AZO
U212	07	06	44	19G
U214	06	05	43	19G
U216	20	10	42	19G
U218	02	08	43	19G
U221	27	09	43	19G
U225	15	02	43	ICE
U227	30	04	43	18G
U229	17	05	43	18G
U231	13	01	44	AZO
U236	04	05	45	16G
U240	16	05	44	18G
U241	18	05	44	18G
U243	08	07	44	19G
U244	25	07	44	18G
U251	19	04	45	18G
U253	23	09	42	18G
U254	08	12	42	ICE
U256	31	08	42	19G
U256	07	06	44	19G
U258	20	05	43	ICE
U259	15	11	42	GIB
U261	15	09	42	15G
U262	26	09	42	18G
U263	24	11	42	GIB
U263	27	11	42	19G
U265	03	02	43	15G
U266	14	05	43	15G
U267	07	07	43	19G
U268	19	02	43	19G
U270	10	01	44	AZO
U270	13	06	44	19G
U270	12	08	44	19G
U271	28	01	44	19G
U273	19	05	43	ICE
U274	23	10	43	15G
U279	04	10	43	ICE
U280	16	11	43	15G
U283	11	02	44	15G
U290	14	06	44	18G
U292	26	05	44	15G
U296	22	03	45	15G
U300	04	08	44	ICE
U304	28	04	43	ICE
U305	04	10	43	ICE
U317	26	06	44	18G
U319	15	07	44	18G
U320	07	05	45	18G
U321	02	04	45	19G
U325	30	04	45	15G
U327	27	02	45	19G
U331	17	11	42	GIB
U332	06	12	41	GIB
U332	21	03	43	19G
U332	02	05	43	19G
U333	11	06	44	19G
U336	01	10	43	ICE
U337	15	01	43	15G
U338	17	06	43	15G
U338	20	09	43	ICE
U339	26	03	43	18G
U340	01	11	43	GIB
U341	19	09	43	ICE
U342	17	04	44	ICE
U343	08	01	44	GIB
U347	17	07	44	18G
U361	17	07	44	18G
U364	30	01	44	19G
U368	03	07	43	19G
U373	03	01	44	19G
U373	08	06	44	19G
U376	10	04	43	19G
U381	14	02	43	GIB
U383	01	08	43	19G
U384	19	03	43	15G
U385	11	08	44	19G
U387	19	07	44	18G
U388	20	06	43	ICE
U389	05	10	43	ICE
U391	13	12	43	19G
U392	16	03	44	GIB
U393	04	05	45	16G
U396	28	06	44	18G
U396	23	04	45	18G
U404	28	07	43	19G
U408	05	11	42	ICE
U411	13	11	42	GIB
U412	22	10	42	18G
U413	08	06	44	19G
U415	01	05	43	19G
U415	05	01	44	19G
U415	07	06	44	19G
U417	11	06	43	15G
U418	01	06	43	19G
U419	08	10	43	15G
U423	17	06	44	18G
U426	08	01	44	19G
U431	21	10	43	GIB
U435	09	07	43	GIB
U437	29	04	43	19G
U440	31	05	43	15G
U441	13	11	42	GIB
U441	24	05	43	19G
U441	12	07	43	19G
U441	12	06	44	19G
U441	18	06	44	19G
U442	12	02	43	GIB
U445	02	01	44	19G
U447	07	05	43	GIB
U449	15	06	43	ICE
U450	06	06	43	15G
U452	25	08	41	ICE
U454	01	08	43	19G
U456	12	05	43	15G
U456	13	05	43	15G
U458	13	11	42	GIB
U459	24	07	43	19G
U461	30	07	43	19G
U462	21	06	43	19G
U462	02	07	43	19G
U462	30	07	43	19G
U463	15	05	43	19G

U-Boat	Date			Area	U-Boat	Date			Area	U-Boat	Date			Area
U464	20	08	42	ICE	U610	08	10	43	15G	U763	24	09	44	18G
U465	06	02	43	ICE	U611	10	12	42	ICE	U772	30	12	44	19G
U465	10	04	43	19G	U613	18	11	42	GIB	U804	16	06	44	18G
U465	07	05	43	19G	U614	09	02	43	15G	U804	09	04	45	18G
U467	25	05	43	ICE	U6145	29	07	43	19G	U821	10	06	44	19G
U469	25	03	43	15G	U617	11	09	43	GIB	U843	09	04	45	18G
U470	16	10	43	15G	U619	05	10	42	ICE	U844	16	10	43	ICE
U476	24	05	44	18G	U619	05	10	43	ICE	U846	04	05	44	19G
U477	03	06	44	18G	U620	14	02	43	GIB	U863	20	07	44	18G
U478	30	06	44	18G	U621	31	05	43	19G	U865	27	07	44	18G
U489	03	08	43	ICE	U621	13	01	44	15G	U867	19	09	44	18G
U489	04	08	43	15G	U623	21	02	43	15G	U871	26	09	44	AZO
U502	06	07	42	19G	U624	07	02	43	15G	U905	20	03	45	18G
U508	26	02	43	19G	U625	10	03	44	15G	U921	24	05	44	18G
U508	12	11	43	19G	U627	27	10	42	15G	U927	24	02	45	19G
U514	08	07	43	19G	U628	03	07	43	19G	U954	19	05	43	ICE
U518	27	06	43	15G	U629	04	01	44	19G	U955	07	06	44	19G
U519	10	02	43	19G	U629	12	03	44	19G	U958	26	05	44	18G
U523	24	05	43	19G	U629	08	06	44	19G	U960	27	03	44	19G
U525	03	03	43	19G	U632	06	04	43	15G	U963	07	06	44	19G
U528	28	04	43	ICE	U633	07	03	43	15G	U964	16	10	43	15G
U528	11	05	43	19G	U635	05	04	43	ICE	U966	10	11	43	19G
U534	05	05	45	18G	U640	14	05	43	ICE	U968	19	07	44	18G
U535	08	06	43	ICE	U643	08	10	43	15G	U970	07	06	44	19G
U535	05	07	43	19G	U646	17	05	43	ICE	U971	20	06	44	19G
U540	17	10	43	ICE	U650	23	06	43	15G	U971	24	06	44	19G
U542	28	11	43	AZO	U653	18	08	42	15G	U976	25	03	44	19G
U545	10	02	44	15G	U663	05	05	43	19G	U980	11	06	44	18G
U552	29	05	43	15G	U664	01	11	42	ICE	U981	12	08	44	19G
U558	20	07	43	19G	U665	22	03	43	19G	U988	29	06	44	19G
U563	01	12	41	19G	U666	19	03	43	15G	U989	07	06	44	19G
U563	31	05	43	19G	U667	24	09	43	GIB	U990	25	05	44	15G
U564	13	06	43	19G	U667	26	09	43	GIB	U995	21	05	44	18G
U564	14	06	43	19G	U668	17	05	44	18G	U998	16	06	44	18G
U566	17	11	42	GIB	U669	07	09	43	19G	U1008	06	05	43	18G
U566	26	04	43	19G	U672	24	04	44	18G	U1017	29	04	45	15G
U566	24	10	43	GIB	U675	24	05	44	18G	U1055	30	04	45	19G
U570	27	08	41	ICE	U681	14	08	44	19G	U1060	29	10	44	18G
U571	28	01	44	19G	U681	11	03	45	19G	U1061	30	10	44	18G
U573	01	05	42	GIB	U705	03	09	42	19G	U1062	22	12	43	18G
U575	13	03	44	AZO	U706	02	08	43	19G	U1065	09	04	45	18G
U578	10	08	42	19G	U707	09	11	43	AZO	U1106	29	03	45	18G
U579	05	05	45	18G	U710	24	04	43	15G	U1107	25	04	45	19G
U582	05	10	42	ICE	U715	13	06	44	18G	U1168	05	05	45	18G
U590	14	04	42	19G	U716	19	07	44	18G	U1222	11	07	44	19G
U591	15	05	43	19G	U731	15	05	44	GIB	U1225	24	06	44	18G
U592	29	01	44	19G	U731	04	10	43	ICE	U1228	19	09	44	18G
U594	06	04	43	ICE	U737	06	03	44	ICE	U2335	19	04	45	18G
U594	04	06	43	GIB	U740	09	06	44	15G	U2338	04	05	45	16G
U595	14	11	42	GIB	U742	18	07	44	18G	U2359	02	05	45	18G
U597	12	10	42	ICE	U743	20	06	44	18G	U2365	05	05	45	18G
U599	24	10	42	19G	U751	17	07	42	19G	U2534	06	05	45	18G
U601	25	02	44	18G	U753	23	06	42	19G	U2502	19	04	45	18G
U602	23	04	43	GIB	U755	28	05	43	GIB	U2503	04	05	45	16G
U603	08	07	43	GIB	U756	02	09	42	ICE	U2521	05	05	45	18G
U605	14	11	42	GIB	U760	06	09	43	GIB	U2524	03	05	45	16G
U607	13	07	43	19G	U761	24	02	44	GIB	U3503	05	05	45	18G
U608	09	08	44	19G	U762	08	10	43	ICE	U3523	05	05	45	18G